Lecture Notes in Computer Science 2956

Edited by G. Goos, J. Hartmanis, and J. van Leeuwen

Springer
Berlin
Heidelberg
New York
Hong Kong
London
Milan
Paris
Tokyo

Andreas Dengel   Markus Junker
Anette Weisbecker (Eds.)

Reading
and Learning

Adaptive Content Recognition

 Springer

Series Editors

Gerhard Goos, Karlsruhe University, Germany
Juris Hartmanis, Cornell University, NY, USA
Jan van Leeuwen, Utrecht University, The Netherlands

Volume Editors

Andreas Dengel
Markus Junker
German Research Center for Artificial Intelligence
(DFKI GmbH)
P.O. Box 2080, 67608 Kaiserslautern, Germany
E-mail: {andreas.dengel,markus.junker}@dfki.de

Anette Weisbecker
University of Stuttgart
Institute for Human Factors and Technology Management
Fraunhofer Institute for Industrial Engineering
Nobelstr. 12, 70569 Stuttgart, Germany
E-mail: Anette.Weisbecker@iao.fhg.de

Library of Congress Control Number: 2004104165

CR Subject Classification (1998): I.5, I.4, H.3, H.4, I.2, I.7

ISSN 0302-9743
ISBN 3-540-21904-8 Springer-Verlag Berlin Heidelberg New York

Springer-Verlag is a part of Springer Science+Business Media

springeronline.com

© Springer-Verlag Berlin Heidelberg 2004
Printed in Germany

Typesetting: Camera-ready by author, data conversion by PTP-Berlin, Protago-TeX-Production GmbH
Printed on acid-free paper   SPIN: 10997871   06/3142   5 4 3 2 1 0

Foreword

The amounts of information that are flooding people both at the workplace and in private life have increased dramatically in the past ten years. The number of paper documents doubles every four years, and the amount of information stored on all data carriers every six years. New knowledge, however, increases at a considerably lower rate. Possibilities for automatic content recognition in various media and for the processing of documents are therefore becoming more important every day.

Especially in economic terms, the efficient handling of information, i.e., finding the right information at the right time, is an invaluable resource for any enterprise, but it is particularly important for small- and medium-sized enterprises. The market for document management systems, which in Europe had a volume of approximately 5 billion euros in 2000, will increase considerably over the next few years.

The BMBF recognized this development at an early stage. As early as in 1995, it pooled national capabilities in this field in order to support research on the automatic processing of information within the framework of a large collaborative project (READ) involving both industrial companies and research centres. Evaluation of the results led to the conclusion that research work had been successful, and, in a second phase, funding was provided for the collaborative follow-up project Adaptive READ from 1999 to 2003. The completion of these two important long-term research projects has contributed substantially to improving the possibilities of content recognition and processing of handwritten, printed and electronic documents.

Under the direction of the German Research Centre for Artificial Intelligence (DFKI) in Kaiserslautern, a total number of 15 partners, including 7 research centres and 4 SMEs, cooperated in the projects. The overall financial volume of both projects was 32 million euros, of which about 16 million euros were made available by the German Federal Ministry of Education and Research.

In an exemplary manner, the researchers successfully addressed both basic research and application-oriented development, and achieved major breakthroughs, which can be expected to promote the creation of high-tech jobs in the participating companies and to enhance Germany's attractiveness as a place for research and production. The projects have so far resulted in 110 scientific publications and in as many as 20 applications for patents or intellectual property rights. Owing to a considerable number of spin-off jobs, along with 20 spin-off products, including new reading devices for forms and business letters, the German companies participating in the project have become world leaders in this field.

The results of relevant research activities are of great importance in government provision for future needs (applications in the Federal Agency for Employment and in health insurance schemes), and moreover they offer new possibilities for applications in industrial enterprises. More than half of all private health insurance companies that rely on electronic document processing are already using Adaptive READ systems. The research activities will also inspire and influence the development of new, intelligent technologies for Internet searching.

This report on the results of the research project is addressed to the scientific community with the aim of passing on the findings, and to business enterprises that intend to create high-tech jobs in Germany in this field.

December 2003   Dr. Bernd Reuse
Head of Software Systems Division
Federal Ministry of Education and Research

Preface

The information flood to be tackled every day by enterprises continues to increase. Every year about 200 million pages of paper worldwide are filed and more than 250 km of new folders are produced. The improvement of information management is considered as a relevant competitive factor by a growing number of enterprises. Enterprises demand a distribution of information in line with their needs and look for really relevant targeted statements and content. It is difficult to acquire relevant expertise, whether in intra-company networks, Internet use or traditional documentation, without efficient support systems that selectively cover information needs.

Existing interests, tasks and roles require that relevant information from multimedia documents of very different forms and structures has to be processed in such a way that it complies with individual requirements in the context of persons or enterprises. Furthermore, globalisation requires that information is available, independent of language, for very different missions and applications.

Under the heading "Reading and Learning – from Document to Knowledge", the research project Adaptive READ united German efforts from research and industry with the objective of elaborating comprehensive concepts for document opening systems that provide fitness for learning processes and putting them into practice in terms of prototypes. The improvements in identification techniques and component-based software development constitute additional focal points. Eleven partners, including four research organizations, worked together for three and a half years in Adaptive READ on this challenging task. This book provides a description of the trendsetting results of the Adaptive READ research project.

While in previous research projects the improvement and completion of reading abilities were the most important parts of the research, the goal in Adaptive READ had a much larger dimension. It was not the incremental improvement of existing algorithms for recording documents that was most important, but rather the formulation and prototype style of the implementation of concepts to make document analysis systems adaptive in practical scenarios. The motivation for such systems is obvious: Unlike previous systems, they are not subject to the "law of progressive mismatching" on the one hand, and on the other hand they need much less engineering capacity to sustain them. The goal of the project was to create and specify the basis for architectures, which, contrary to current document analysis systems with their predefined and frozen parameters and knowledge bases, are able to automatically adjust to the slowly changing characteristics of document layout, fonts, and writing habits. In systems in which automatic learning is not possible at all or only with difficulty, people have to take on this adaptation task. Adequate and intuitive user-friendly parameters, as well as significant analysis and diagnostics, should be provided to do this.

Unfortunately, however, a fully automated learning procedure was not feasible for a series of recognition tasks. In many cases (e.g., the need for random sampling and its management) it was too costly. In these cases it was necessary to adjust the user-controlled instructions of the system so that they could be executed by a system administrator or end-user. Administration tools were needed for this, which make the recognition system cycle transparent. Also recognition methods were demanded, which, in the case of errors, make possible clear classifications according to the adaptation elements to which they belong (e.g., the parameters of a method). Moreover recognition systems must be easily tailored to the respective application areas.

Overview

After scanning, in order to be able to analyze documents electronically, they have to be aligned according to the orientation of the writing. In the first paper, "Error Tolerant Paper Deskew," Woitha and Janich present a solution to a particularly difficult case in document alignment – i.e., when the edges of the documents are mostly ruined. A further problem at a very early stage of document analysis is the differentiation between foreground and background information. In the second paper, "Adaptive Threshold," Woitha and Janich describe a promising technique that works with a dynamically defined threshold to distinguish between fore- and background information. Distinguishing between foreground and background in color documents is a special challenge. In "Neighborhood Related Color Segmentation Based on a Fuzzy Color Classification Tool" Frei, Hund and Schnitzlein describe the exploitation of specific background knowledge concerning the colored composition of documents and the document-specific color design for this task.

The contribution "Improving Image Processing Systems Using Artificial Neural Networks" by Rebmann, Michaelis, Krell, Seiffert and Püschel is concerned with two further problems involving the scanning of documents. A special type of hardware is introduced which, with the help of neural networks, shows ways of compensating for the effects of non-flat originals (e.g., books that are not fully opened). Furthermore, in this contribution they show, based on the techniques of neural networks, how to reduce picture artifacts as they emerge through the JPEG compression process.

When analyzing map material, the normal way of dividing fore- and background into two classes does not work. In "Adaptive Segmentation of Multicolored Documents Without a Marked Background" Eberhardt, Römer and Saedler show how information from color documents can be dissected into as many classes as required.

New techniques for handwriting recognition were also issues in the Adaptive READ project. In the paper "Recognition of Short Handwritten Texts," Boldt and Asp describe a new generation of handwriting readers that couple the old way of strict successive analysis steps, image processing, character recognition and syntactic alignment with feedback. The contribution "Handwritten Address Recognition Using Hidden Markov Models" by Brakensiek and Rigoll is devoted to the problem of regionally different styles of writing for address recognition, and proposes various solutions using hidden Markov models.

Different systems for optical character recognition (OCR) usually have different strong points and weaknesses. The contribution "Adaptive Combination of Commercial OCR Systems" by Wilczok and Lellmann describes a flexible framework for the combination of recognition results of various OCR systems on the lexical level. It stands out particularly because words can be synchronized with the help of geometric criteria, which means that incorrect character segmentation can be avoided.

In the area of software engineering it appears that component-based approaches show promise in developing new application systems quickly and cheaply. In "Component-Based Software Engineering Methods for Systems in Document Recognition, Analysis and Understanding," Höß, Strauß and Weisbecker describe the bases of application of component-based approaches in document recognition systems. The design and implementation of a concrete and real component-based system for document recognition is described by Middendorf, Peust and Schacht in the contribution "A Component-Based Framework for Recognition Systems." The contribution "*smartFIX*: An Adaptive System for Document Analysis and Understanding" by Klein, Dengel and Fordan describes the smartFix system for extracting information from paper documents. It includes results on medical bills and prescriptions.

In "How Postal Address Readers Are Made Adaptive," Kreuzer, Miletzki, Schäfer, Schambach and Schulte-Austum deal with adaptive postal address readers. The ultimate goal in this area is to address readers, which, on the basis of reading the daily post, can adapt continuously to places, address structures, and handwriting. The paper also puts forward, with the support of Adaptive READ, solutions for cost reduction with the new services "forwarding" and "renumeration security."

The analysis of already existing electronic documents, such as e-mails or Web sites using learning methods was also of special interest in Adaptive READ. The contribution "A Tool for Semi-automatic Document Reengineering" by Drawehn, Altenhofen, Stanišić-Petrović and Weisbecker covers techniques for the semi-automatic structuring of full text documents. In "Inspecting Document Collections" Bohnacker, Franke, Mogg-Schneider and Renz describe further methods which help to analyze large document collections quickly, whereby documents that belong together are clustered and user-adaptive document-spanning combinations are generated. A model for so-called Collaborative Information Retrieval (CIR) was developed and resulted in a set of new search algorithms. The idea in CIR is to monitor search processes of a search engine in order to optimize future search processes – i.e., to find the desired information faster. Two different methods to find a solution to this problem are shown in the contributions "Introducing Query Expansion Methods for Collaborative Information Retrieval" by Hust and "Improving Document Transformation Techniques with Collaborative Learned Term-Based Concepts" by Klink. Whereas in these approaches the goal is to find relevant documents, the contribution "Passage Retrieval Based on Density Distributions of Terms and Its Applications to Document Retrieval and Question Answering" by Kise, Junker, Dengel and Matsumoto focusses on finding relevant passages within documents.

Finally, in the framework of Adaptive READ two representative surveys were conducted in companies on tool application in the document management environment. Apart from other factors, the results described in "Results of a Survey About the Use of Tools in the Area of Document Management" by Altenhofen, Hofman, Kieninger and Stanišić-Petrović provide a profound insight into the infrastructural prerequisites in German companies, the current degree of utilization of various technologies, and the degree of user satisfaction.

December 2003   Prof. Dr. Andreas R. Dengel
                                                      Dr. Markus Junker
                              Priv.-Doz. Dr.-Ing. habil. Anette Weisbecker

Table of Contents

Error Tolerant Color Deskew

Dirk Woitha and Dietmar Janich

Janich & Klass Computertechnik GmbH
www.janichklass.com

Abstract. The problem of angled feeds happens mainly with fast production scanners. This is a mechanical problem of most feeders when feeding pages in high speed. To improve the image quality, it is necessary to have a high speed deskew algorithm that eliminates the skew in an electronic way. First the skew of the document must be found. After this, the skew can be corrected. This chapter shows how to find the skew, even if the document is damaged. It also shows several methods to deskew the document.

1 How to Find Out the Skew Angle

Before a skew can be corrected, first the skew angle must be found out. There are two methods:

Method 1: Searching the image contents for horizontal or vertical structures

- *Advantages:* No brightness difference is required between document and background. Also documents without any scanned background can be processed.

- *Disadvantages:* A very complicated algorithm is required in order to securely find horizontal or vertical structures on different originals; but eventually still wrong angles remain. The algorithm returns just an angle, but not the outer borders of the scanned document.

Method 2: Searching for the borders of the scanned document.

- *Advantages:* Finding the borders of a document is far easier, faster and more reliable than finding structures in the document. In addition to the angle, also the outer borders of the scanned document are recognized.
- *Disadvantages:* The document must be scanned in "oversize". It makes sense to scan an additional rim of about 2cm. There must be a difference in brightness or colour between scanner background and document.

When scanning with production scanners, the method to find the borders suggests itself as its advantages predominate. The alleged disadvantage of scanning in oversize is often seen as advantage.

On one hand, a slightly larger image format must be captured if tilted documents must be expected and no information shall get lost at the rim. If for example A4 documents are scanned exactly with A4, their corners will be cut if the document had a skew.

A. Dengel et al. (Eds.): Adaptive READ Research Project, LNCS 2956, pp. 1–13, 2004.
© Springer-Verlag Berlin Heidelberg 2004

On the other hand, a larger image format may be set, and all smaller image formats can be scanned without changing the parameters. Finding the borders and subsequent deskew will then deliver what in principle is wanted: *"A straight document without any additional rim"*.

The necessary difference between background and document can usually be realized without problems. A black background mostly gives enough contrast to the original. If search for borders is started from a bitonal document, problems may arise if dark elements exist at the rim of the image. In this case, precautions have to be taken when searching for borders.

2   The Practice of Border Finding

The sample image below serves for illustrating the border finding; it shows the detected border pixels and the rectangle resulting from it.

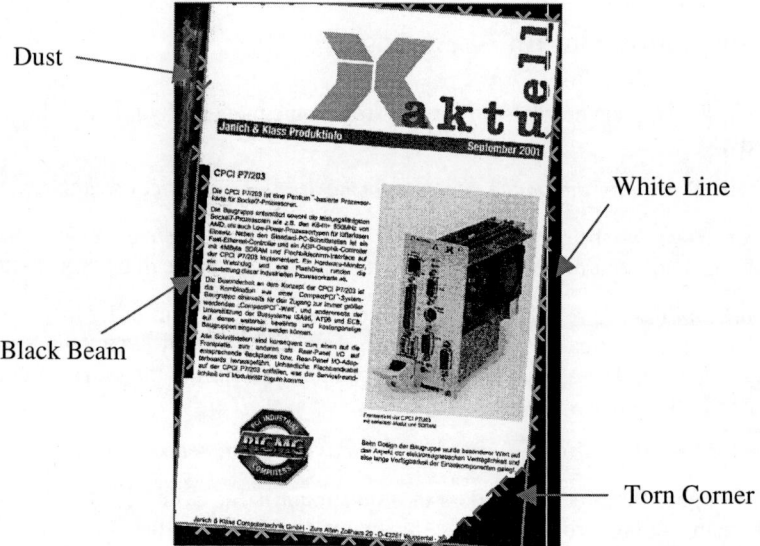

Fig. 1. Skewed Document

Below follows a closer description of the realized algorithm for border finding. This algorithm bases on a light document on a black background as this is the case most often occurring in practice.

The document has some typical problem areas; their processing will be detailed later:

- Non-clean background (dust, for example)
- Black beam at the document border
- Torn corner
- Non-interrupted white line (dust or CCD error, for example)

To find the borders of the document shown in Fig. 1 several working steps are required.

2.1 Finding Pixels on the Document Border

The image is searched for a document border, in regular intervals, starting from the image border. The document is supposed to be where a dot is lighter than an adjustable threshold.

This would however deliver also all void pixels on the background, as document border. For that reason, there are some further conditions:

- At least n subsequent pixels must underpass the threshold. Proven values lie between 4 and 16, depending on the quality of the scanned background. The example in Fig. 1 uses the default value 4. This is sufficient to ignore the dust and the white line. If this value is set too high, difficulties may appear if the document itself contains darker areas close to its borders.
- Recognized border pixels are interpreted as non-valid if they are too close to the border. The experience with many different scanners has shown that many ignorable void pixels exist at the border of the scanned area. Also, the document itself may reach to the scan border so that no usable border exists here.

If it is a colour scan, you can additionally use the colour information. The brightness of a colour pixel (RGB) is determined by means of the following formula:

$$Y = \frac{Red \times R + Green \times G + Blue \times B}{Red + Green + Blue} \tag{1}$$

With the factors *Red*, *Green* and *Blue*, certain colours can be stressed so that a colour-sensitive border finding is possible.

In Fig. 1 all pixels found by this method are marked in green or violet. The form of the arrow shows the search direction.

2.2 Removing Void Pixels

All pixels lying on a document border should ideally result in a straight line. So it is the next step to determine, for each pixel, its gradient towards its neighbor. The most often occurring gradient is taken as mean gradient.

Next is to investigate whether the gradient of a pixel towards its neighbor pixel deviates too far from this mean gradient. If this is so, this pixel is declared as void. These are the violet pixels in Fig. 1.

As you can see, this will remove all pixels that touch the "wrong" border and other void pixels (dust, torn corner). Only the false pixels in the black beam at the document border will remain.

2.3 Determination of the Document Border

From the remaining pixels, the document border is determined by means of the Linear Regression. The Linear Regression minimizes the error square of the distance of every pixel from the determined straight line. The formulas to determine the straight equation from n pixels x_i, y_i are as follows:

$$y = a + bx \tag{2}$$

$$d = n\sum_{i=1}^{n} x_i^2 - \left(\sum_{i=1}^{n} x_i\right)^2 \tag{3}$$

$$a = \frac{\sum_{i=1}^{n} y_i - b\sum_{i=1}^{n} x_i}{n} \qquad b = \frac{n\sum_{i=1}^{n} x_i y_i - \sum_{i=1}^{n} x_i \sum_{i=1}^{n} y_i}{d} \tag{4}$$

Because there may be still void pixels that entered in the calculation, once more every pixel is investigated for its distance to the calculated straight line. If this distance lies outside an error tolerance, the pixel becomes void. The size of this error tolerance depends on the scan quality (eventual distortions), the originals, and the size of the originals. A distance of 3 pixels is the proven default value for the error tolerance. If all distances are below this tolerance, the straight line is interpreted as document border.

Otherwise, the "worst" pixel is removed, still considering that pixels which are supposed to lie inside a document are to be deleted preferably, because of the high probability that void pixels were already eliminated from outside the document (due to their wrong gradient).

In our example, preferably the pixels in the black beam must be eliminated. For this reason, there is a settable factor which enlarges the error of pixels lying on the document-side of the calculated straight line. Now the worst pixel is eliminated as long as either the straight line is determined, or less than 3 pixels remain. In this case, the straight line is supposed to be not found.

2.4 Determination of the Document Rectangle

Now you have 0 to 4 document borders from which the rectangle must be determined to describe the document itself.

With 0 detected borders, border finding has failed. In all other cases, there follows an investigation whether the recognized borders are plausible, i.e. they have the same gradient. For it, the gradients of the upper and lower borders are transformed so that all gradients are the same.

If a straight line deviates too far from the mean gradient, it will be declared as invalid. This might happen, for example, if a sheet is folded at one of its borders (big dog-ear).

The now remaining borders serve for the final determination of the required rectangle. You may decide, parameter-wise, how many borders must be found to declare the rectangle as valid. If you are sure that positively every scan should deliver four proper borders, you can deliver an error message at fewer borders, in order to, for example, get the just mentioned dog-eared sheet.

Images scanned on fast production scanners sometimes hinder finding the upper border as the scanner starts scanning only when the sheet begins. In such cases, one should be content with 3 borders or go down to 2 or even one border if damaged originals are expected.

The deskew algorithm following next requires a mathematically exact rectangle; therefore the remaining straights are now corrected to the mean gradient.

2.5 Handling Missing Borders

If not all four borders could be found, we assume that the document is partly outside of the scanned area.

In Fig. 2, for example, the right-hand border could not be found as it lies outside the scanned area. In this case, the missing fourth border is supposed as shown above; so it is supposed where it is just outside the scanned area.

The grey areas lie outside the scanned area, but within the skewed image, and must therefore be filled-up later.

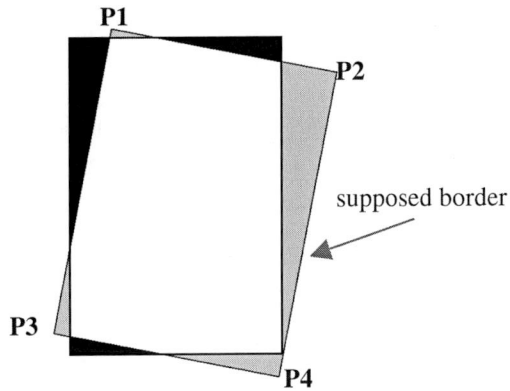

Fig. 2. Missing Borders

2.6 Result of Border Finding

The result of border finding, if it does not fail, are the points P1 to P4 (Fig. 2). These points may lie inside or outside the scanned area.

The realized algorithm of border finding also returns the angle and the border lengths of the found rectangle. These values can easily be calculated from the points P1 – P4.

Before the image is deskewed using these values, tests can be included to check the found values for their plausibility. Which tests make sense here, strongly depends on the originals and the scan parameters.

Examples for useful tests might be:

- Does the size of the found rectangle meet your expectations? If you scan only originals in A4 format, for example, the found rectangle must also have this size.
- At double-sided scans, you might check whether the results for front page and back page do match.

Now all information exists which is required to deskew the image.

2.7 Speed of Border Finding

The realized algorithm for border finding requires the following times, on a 2.53 GHz P4 computer, for an A4 document with 200 DPI:

Table 1. Speed of border finding

24 Bit Colour	1-5 ms
8 Bit Grey	1-3 ms
1 Bit Bitonal	< 1 ms

3 Methods for Deskewing

There are two different methods to deskew a document using the corner points found out by border finding.

3.1 Alignment

Smaller angles allow the alignment method. This will correct the skew practically in two steps.

The first step realizes an alignment in parallel to the x-axle:

$$x' = x + my \qquad\qquad Ss = \begin{pmatrix} 1 & m \\ 0 & 1 \end{pmatrix} \qquad\qquad (5)$$
$$y' = y$$

In the second step, then the alignment is executed in parallel to the y-axle:

$$x'' = x' \qquad\qquad Ss = \begin{pmatrix} 1 & 0 \\ n & 1 \end{pmatrix} \qquad\qquad (6)$$
$$y'' = y' + nx'$$

Ss is the transformation matrix, that transforms the Point P to P'.

$$P' = P \times Ss \qquad P = (x, y),\ P' = (x', y') \qquad\qquad (7)$$

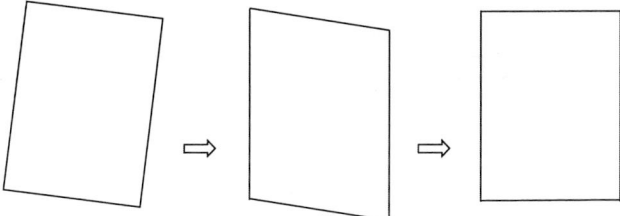

Fig. 3. Alignment

As shown in Fig. 3 the alignment method will not really rotate the image, but will correct first the vertical skew and then the horizontal skew of the document by moving its individual pixels.

By expert programming, these two steps can be effected in one operation. Then, the algorithm is extremely fast.

The algorithm for deskew by alignment requires less then 10 ms (P4 2.53GHz) for a bitonal A4 document. This is ten times faster than the deskew with real rotation requires.

But the alignment has two disadvantages: It can be used only for small angles. Alignment can be programmed optimized if the skew is not more than one pixel per Byte (8 pixels). This restricts the deskew to a maximum of about 7 degree. As skewed feeds mostly have a smaller angle, this restriction rarely ever happens .

The more important disadvantage of alignment is its bad image quality: As simply every pixel is moved to another position, lines and characters look slightly deformed. This effect becomes worse with increasing angles.

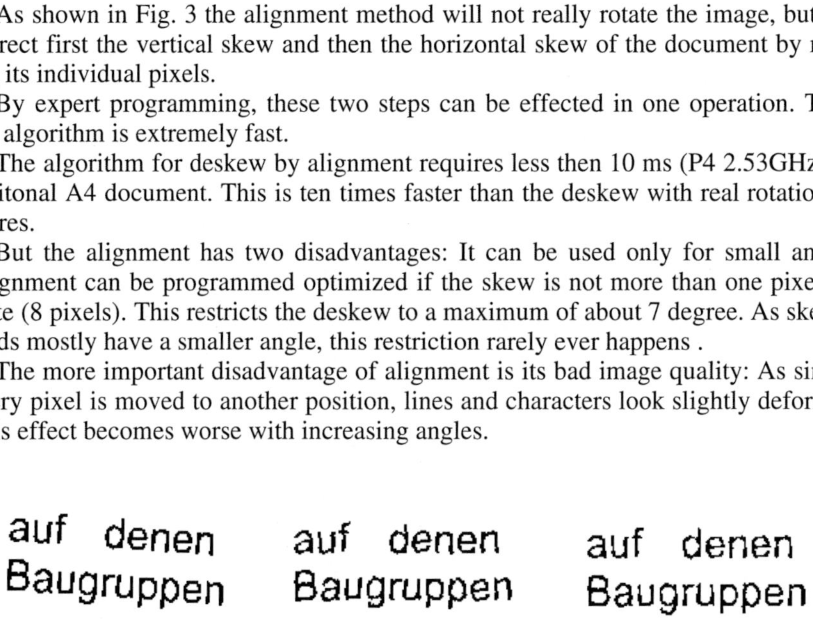

auf denen   auf denen   auf denen
Baugruppen   Baugruppen   Baugruppen

Fig. 4. Bitonal Deskew

Fig. 4 shows this effect. The left part shows the still skewed original image. The center shows the image after the alignment. Although the text now is straight, it looks slightly deformed. At right, the same text is shown after the extensive 4-Points-Deskew which will be described later. This returns a far better image quality.

You still can see that deskew on bitonal images has its limits. Grey images and colour images allow for better results. The next chapter about real rotation tells you why.

3.2   Rotation

The ideal deskew would move every pixel of the original image mathematically correct to its new position in the now straight image. This is impossible, unfortunately, as the individual pixels lie in a fixed grid.

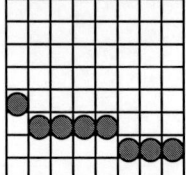 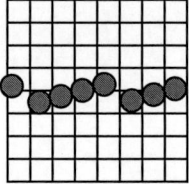

Fig. 5. Ideal Rotation

Fig. 5 shows how an ideal rotation would create pixels that are not inside the grid. In practice, this is impossible. Another problem comes on top: As the pixels are distributed to this fixed grid already during scanning, an originally horizontal line becomes steps, caused by the skewed feed. As one can see, the ideally rotated line would still be as stepped as in the original scan. For these reasons, the rotation must work somewhat different.

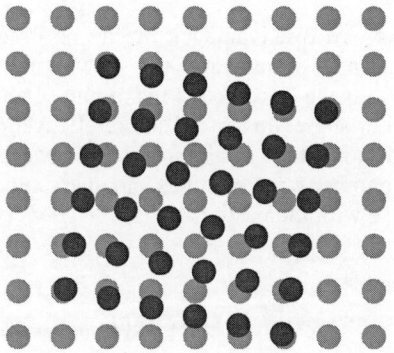

Fig. 6. Real Rotation

Fig. 6 shows how pixels are arranged in the original image and in the rotated image. The green pixels correspond to the pixels in the scanned image. The red pixels show the pixels of the rotated image, how they would be placed in the original image. You can clearly see that a pixel may be placed anywhere among the pixels of the original image.

If you inspect a single pixel of the deskewed image, it is placed somewhere between 4 pixels of the original image.

The target pixel X to be determined in Fig. 7 can now be calculated by different methods from the four surrounding pixels A-D and their distances a-d from the pixel X.

We will explain three methods which are distinguished by the number of pixels they use in the original image:

- The 1-Point-method (here Pixel A)
- The 2-Points-method (Pixel A and D)
- The 4-Points-method (Pixel A,B,C and D)

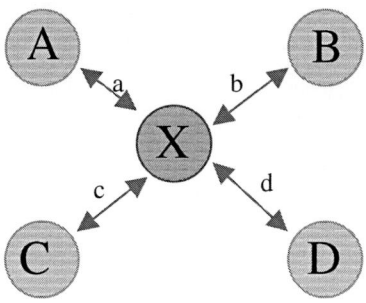

Fig. 7. Calculating one Pixel

The following will explain how the brightness of pixel A results from the brightness of its surrounding pixels A-D.

At bitonal images, we assume for the brightness of white pixels the value of 255, and the value of 0 for black pixels. If the result is below 128 (50%), the pixel X turns black, otherwise it will be white.

At 8-Bit grey images, the brightness of dot X is calculated by means of a complex mathematic formula.

At 24-Bit colour images in RGB format, the calculation is executed analogously to a grey image individually for each colour component.

3.2.1 The 1-Point-Method

This is the easiest and fastest method, but it also returns the worst image quality. At this method, pixel X is simply the most proximate pixel of the original image. In our example in Fig. 7 this would be pixel A.

The achieved image quality is quite similar to the alignment method, but the restriction to small angles is void.

$$auf\ denen \qquad\qquad auf\ denen$$
$$Baugruppen \qquad\qquad Baugruppen$$

Fig. 8. 1-Point Deskew

3.2.2 The 2-Points-Method

This method uses twi pixels, A and D, for determination of pixel X. Here, Pixel X is calculated by using the following mathematic formula:

$$n = \max(a, d) \tag{8}$$

$$a_n = \frac{n}{a} \qquad d_n = \frac{n}{d} \tag{9}$$

$$X = A\frac{a_n}{a_n + d_n} + D\frac{d_n}{a_n + d_n} \tag{10}$$

The closer pixel X lies to one of the pixels A or D, the stronger this pixel will be stressed in the calculation.

auf denen   auf denen
Baugruppen   Baugruppen

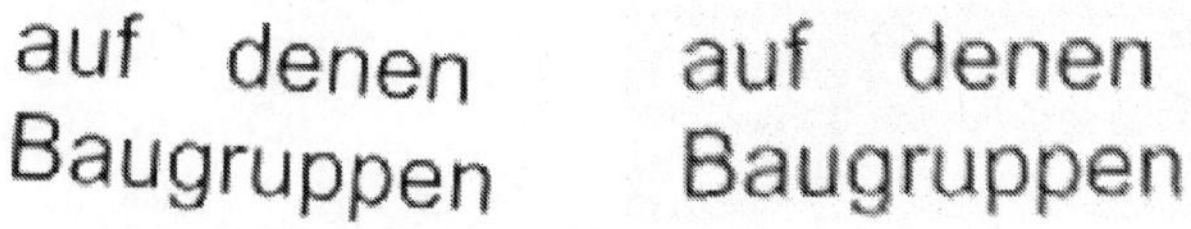

Fig. 9. 2-Point Deskew

The 2-Points method returns a considerably better result than the 1-Point-method. But it requires more calculation time.

3.2.3 The 4-Points-Method

This method utilizes the pixels A-D to determine pixel X.

$$n = \max(a,b,c,d) \tag{11}$$

$$a_n = \frac{n}{a} \qquad b_n = \frac{n}{b} \tag{12}$$

$$c_n = \frac{n}{c} \qquad d_n = \frac{n}{d}$$

$$S_n = a_n + b_n + c_n + d_n \tag{13}$$

$$X = A\frac{a_n}{S_n} + B\frac{b_n}{S_n} + C\frac{c_n}{S_n} + D\frac{d_n}{S_n} \tag{14}$$

The closer pixel X lies to one of the pixels A-D, the stronger this pixel will be stressed in the calculation.

This method will return the best results as the scanned document is re-calculated to a so-to-say gritless document which is then newly scanned. Certainly, this requires the longest calculation time.

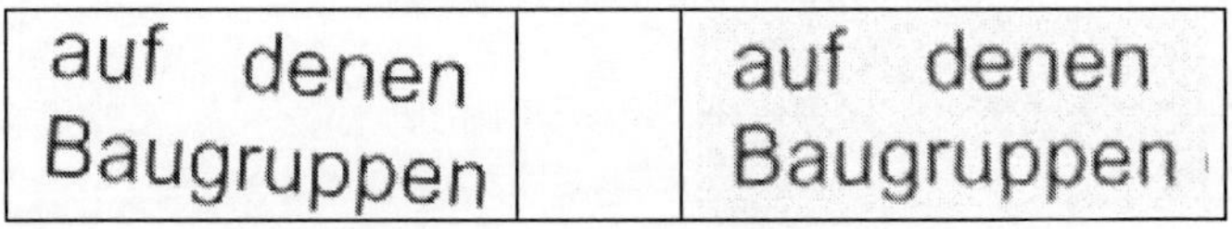

auf denen | auf denen
Baugruppen | Baugruppen

Fig. 10. 4-Point Deskew

3.2.4 Improvement of the Bitonal Deskew

The rotation methods listed above can be used for bitonal images in a restricted manner only, as only 2 brightness values (black and white) are available. If ever possible, a deskew should therefore be executed on the grey image before thresholding.

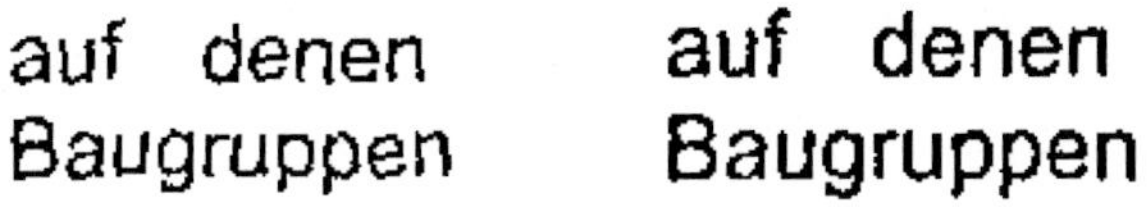

auf denen   **auf denen**

Baugruppen   **Baugruppen**

Fig. 11. Improved Bitonal Deskew

Fig. 11 shows the far better image quality of a bitonal deskew made on the grey image (at right), compared to the direct deskew on the bitonal image (at left).

3.2.5 Side Effects of the Rotation

Further to the better image quality, the rotation has the advantage that the algorithm allows to process some other image processing functions simultaneously without requiring extra calculation time:

- Additional rotation of the image by 90°, 180° or 270°
- Mirroring of the image in horizontal or vertical direction

For both these operations, the original image is just scanned in a different way (from right to left instead left to right, for example).

- Modify the image resolution

The original image is simply scanned with a higher or lower resolution.

Fig. 12. Changing Resolution

Fig. 12. shows an example with halved resolution. Useful values for changed resolutions are in the range of 0.5 to 2. Reducing the resolution by more than 50% will mean losing too much information as no longer all original pixels will be evaluated. A virtual increase in resolution by more than 2 returns nothing but larger files, but no additional information.

On the other hand, it will make sense to scan an image with 200DPI in colour, to calculate it up to 300DPI and finally transform it to a bitonal image, using a good thresholder. This will utilize the high amount of information included in a colour image to create a bitonal image with a higher resolution.

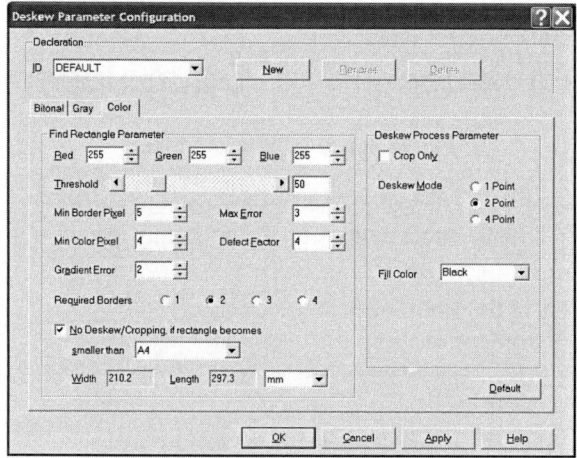

Fig. 13. Deskew Parameter Configuration

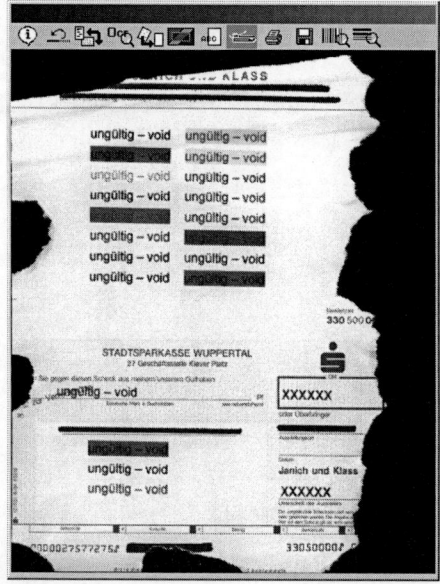

Fig. 14. Deskew of an Extremely Damaged Original

3.3 Other Methods

There are also other methods available to calculate a point in the deskewed image. These methods are, for example, the bi-cubic interpolation or the spline interpolation. The formulas for this transformations, however, are too complicated to use them for a high speed production scanner. This may be possible in the future, when the available computer performance increases.

3.4 Deskew Speed

The realized deskew algorithm requires the following times, on a 2.53 GHz P4 computer, for an A4 document with 200 DPI:

Table 2. Speed of Deskew

	Alignment	1-Point	2-Points	4-Points
24 Bit Colour		60 ms	140 ms	160 ms
8 Bit Grey		30 ms	45 ms	75 ms
1 Bit Bitonal	< 10 ms	45 ms	94 ms	125 ms

3.5 Setting Dialog for Deskew

Using the dialog as per Fig. 13, the parameters for border finding and deskew method can be set as described. If the required borders are set at two borders, even an extremely damaged form as shown in Fig. 14 can be deskewed trouble free.

References

1. Bartsch, Taschenbuch Mathematische Formeln, ISBN 3 87144 239 9
2. Bronstein, Semendjajew, Taschenbuch der Mathematik, ISBN 3 87144 492 8
3. CCITT, Red Book, Volume II, Fascicle VII.3, Terminal Equipment and Protocols for Telematic Services, ISBN 92-61-02291-X
4. Rafael C. Gonzalez, Richard E. Woods, Digital Image Processing, ISBN 0201180758
5. Bernd Jähne, Digitale Bildverarbeitung, ISBN 3540412603
6. Michael Seul, Michael J. Sammon, Lawrence O'Gorman, Practical Algorithms for Image Analysis: Descriptions, Examples, and Code, ISBN 0521660653
7. Yann Le Cun, Léon Bottou, Patrick Haffner, Paul Howard, DjVu: a compression method for distributing scanned documents in color over the internet, *Color 6*, IST, 1998
8. Specification of DjVu Image Compression Format Version of 1999-04-29 15:46 EDT Copyright (c) 1999 by AT&T, http://www.djvuzone.org/techpapers/index.html#specs

Adaptive Threshold

Dirk Woitha and Dietmar Janich

Janich & Klass Computertechnik GmbH
www.janichklass.com

Abstract. Still today, bitonal images (black & white images without any shades in between – just black and white) of high quality are the precondition for trouble-free automatic text recognition (OCR). The challenge is to distinguish between relevant information and background information – at the same time, however, image processing may not create damage to character structures. Due to the high calculation amount and the necessity to use uncompressed images as source image for processing, mainly hardware-oriented image processing methods were used in the past, and they are widely in use still today. Due to the risen PC calculation power and by optimizing calculation steps, a method could be developed for dynamic thresholding of greyscale images that returns optimal results even from extremely difficult images; in the spring of 2003, it delivered about 600 images per minute (A4, 200dpi).

1 The Optimal Bitonal Image

In order to judge the quality of a thresholder, there certainly is the question how the optimal result shall look like. As an example, we use the below grey image and the bitonal images resulting from it.

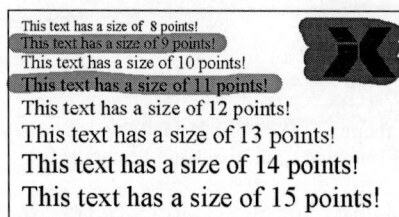

Fig. 1. Comparison of different Threshold Results

A. Dengel et al. (Eds.): Adaptive READ Research Project, LNCS 2956, pp. 14-25, 2004.

Bitonal Images 1, 2 and 3 were created from the same grey image with different thresholder parameters. We will later find details about these parameters and about their effects. First we want to investigate the different results.

Bitonal-Image 1:
Certainly, this image contains the highest amount of information. One can recognize that two lines in the grey image were highlighted by a text marker, and also the JK logo that was highlighted, or "crossed out" by a pen in the grey image. So, if you want to save most every information of the grey image into the bitonal image, *Bitonal Image 1* will be the correct choice.

Bitonal Image 2:
In this image one can no longer see that some text had been highlighted in the grey image. If the text is to be recognized by OCR, this is not even wanted. The frames for the markings as shown in *Bitonal Image 1* would hinder only. In such a case, *Bitonal Image 2* should be selected.

Bitonal Image 3:
The text marker lacks also in this image. The crossed-out logo that probably should be defaced is completely black. So, if certain areas shall be defaced on the original document and they should not be visible on the bitonal image, *Bitonal Image 3* may be the right one.

As you can easily see, the optimal bitonal image does not exist. Always, information will get lost by the transformation. It depends on the actual application which part of the information must be kept. A good thresholder must therefore grant setting possibilities to yield different results.

2   The Static Thresholder

The easiest method to transform a grey image into a bitonal image is a static thresholder. It will decide, using a fixed threshold, which pixels turn to black or white.

2.1   Simple Static Thresholder

For a pixel in the grey image with the brightness h the pixel p in the bitonal image will be black if the following condition is true: [1]

$$p = 1 \quad if \quad h < s \qquad (1)$$

s is the static threshold. If it is under-passed, the pixel will be black. As default, the value of 128 is recommended. The images in Fig. 2 were processed with the static thresholder.

---

[1]   The following is based on 8-Bit grey images where the brightness h of a pixel lies between 0 (black) and 255 (white). A pixel in the bitonal image is represented by a bit where 0 is white and 1 is black. Certainly, these arrangements may, in practice, also be vice-versa.

As one can see, the result is not satisfactory in both cases, with the static thresholder and the default threshold of 128. At the first image, the text disappears on dark background, at the second image the light text disappears. You might get the complete text at both images by modifying the threshold, but there is no threshold that will work for the left and for the right image simultaneously.

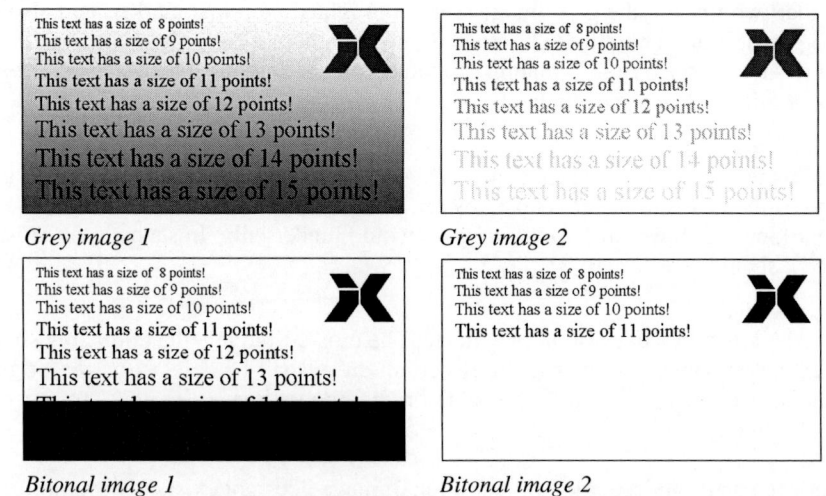

Grey image 1   Grey image 2

Bitonal image 1   Bitonal image 2

Fig. 2. Static Thresholder

2.2   Static Thresholder with Backtracker

In order to improve the results of the static thresholder and to get an adoption to different kinds of originals, you can add a so-called backtracker. It will determine the mean brightness of the lines around the pixel that is to be transformed. The mean brightness of background be b, the corrected threshold s_b. Then it is:

$$s_b = \frac{\max(b,32) \times s}{256} \qquad (2)$$

Pixel p is accordingly blackened, if:

$$p = 1 \quad if \quad h < s_b \qquad (3)$$

The threshold s is thus adapted to the average image brightness. The image brightness is calculated across several lines. This value is adjustable. Practice has proven that a range of 1-2 mm (corresponding to 8 to 16 lines at 200 DPI) delivers good results.

Practice also shows that there is no use in shrinking the threshold to very low values. The average image brightness is therefore limited to 32.

The following, once more, shows the image with the background that is getting darker; this time it was transformed with the backtracker turned on and again with the threshold 128.

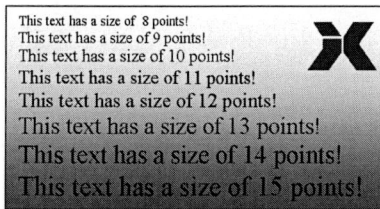

Grey image   Bitonal image

Fig. 3. Static Thresholder with Backtracker

Now an undisputable result is achieved. The second image with the text getting lighter, however, would not be improved by the backtracker, as the average image brightness is nearly constant on the whole sheet.

So, the backtracker helps to process originals with differently light background without the need to modify the static threshold.

3   The Dynamic Thresholder

In order to get round the limits of the static thresholder, you require a second method that not simply evaluates the brightness of a pixel, but also the brightness fluctuations of the pixel to its next neighborhood.

3.1   Simple Dynamic Thresholder

The dynamic thresholder uses a small window (1-2mm) around the target pixel. In this window, the mean brightness h_d is determined. The pixel p is set (to black) if the following condition is true.

$$s_{dx} = \frac{255 - s_d}{8} \; if \; s_d \neq 0 \qquad\qquad s_{dx} = 255 \; if \; s_d = 0 \tag{4}$$

$$p = 1 \quad if \quad h < h_d - s_{dx} \tag{5}$$

First, the dynamic threshold is converted. Again, it reaches from 0 to 255, and it shall create a darker image with higher values (analogous to the static threshold).

As the dynamic thresholder shall react to low local deviations in brightness, the value area is restricted by dividing the value through eight. Furthermore, the dynamic thresholder shall be disabled with the value zero.

A pixel is now set if the brightness h of the pixel is the mean brightness of the pixel in the window minus the corrected dynamic threshold.

This time, good results are yielded at both images with identical parameters. As the differences in brightness are achieved, it makes no difference whether there is dark text on dark background, or light text on a light background.

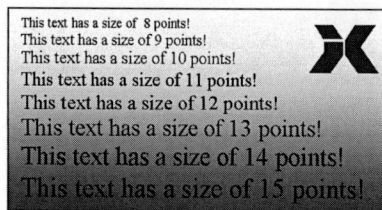

Grey Image 1

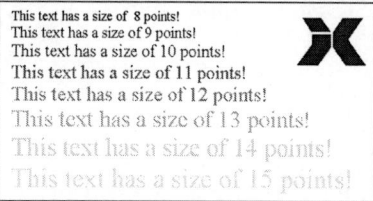

Grey Image 2

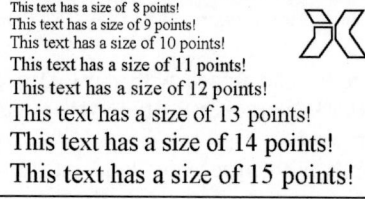

Bitonal Image 1

Bitonal Image 2

Fig. 4. Dynamic Thresholder

But also the disadvantage of the dynamic thresholder becomes obvious. Characters consisting of lines that are large, compared to the selected window, are displayed just as framed, because the thresholder reacts only to brightness deviations at their borders. You can see this so-called *outline effect* at the hollowed JK logo in Fig. 4.

Sometimes, however, this effect is very useful in order to, for example, make text visible that is highlighted by a text marker.

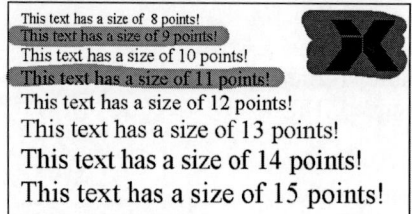

Grey Image

Bitonal Image

Fig. 5. Outline Effect of the Dynamic Thresholder

3.2 Static and Dynamic Thresholder

You will also see in Fig. 5 that the JK logo is shown completely black. This was possible as we used a combination of static and dynamic thresholder.

In order to prevent the outline effect at large and very dark areas, it makes sense to blacken everything that is below a certain threshold. You will, however, not use the default of 128 for the static thresholder, but a somewhat lower value, like 40. Everything that is darker than 40 will become a black area, while the dynamic thresholder will react to all brightness deviations in the lighter areas.

$$p = 1 \quad if \quad h < h_d - s_{dx} \; or \; h < s \tag{6}$$

3.3 Recognizing Dark Areas

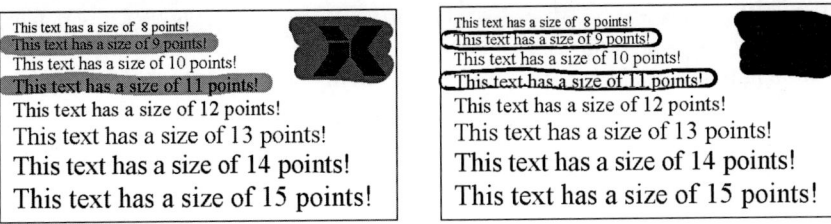

Fig. 6. Threshold without Dark-Area-Detection

The combination of both thresholders bears, however, also risks. So, all pixels lying below the threshold of the static thresholder are blackened, even if the dynamic thresholder has still recognized brightness deviations in this area. A slightly modified static threshold delivers, for example, the result in Fig. 6.

The JK logo is no longer recognizable. If you will not do without the information that lies in such dark areas, you can add the so-called dark area detector.

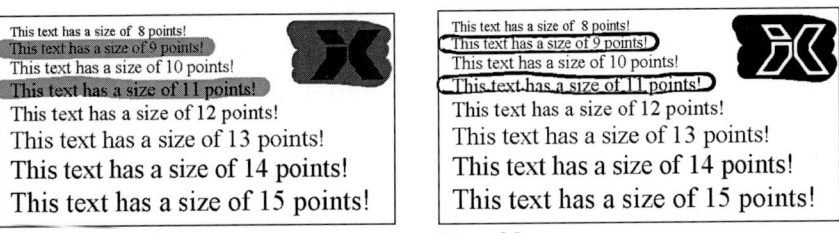

Fig. 7. Threshold with Dark-Area-Detection

The JK logo is now visible again; it appears as reversed frame in the black area. A pixel p is now calculated to this :

$$S = 1 \quad if \quad h < s \tag{7}$$

$$D = 1 \quad if \quad h < h_d - s_{dx} \tag{8}$$

$$I = 1 \quad if \quad h_d < s \tag{9}$$

$$p = 1 \quad if \quad (\bar{I} \ and \ (S \ or \ D)) \ or \ (S \ and \ \bar{D}) \tag{10}$$

The first two lines describe the already known static thresholder S and the dynamic thresholder D. The value I in the third line describes whether the pixel is inside a dark area. For it, the mean brightness of the window from the dynamic threshold is compared with the static threshold value. If the mean brightness is below the static threshold, a dark area is assumed.

A pixel is now set as per the fourth line. In the *normal* areas (I=0) a pixel is still blackened as usual, if one of the two thresholders sets it. In the dark areas, however, the static thresholder may set a pixel only if the dynamic thresholder has not found something at the same time.

This combination allows to fill dark areas completely with the static thresholder without the risk that eventually information gets lost in the dark areas.

3.4   Removing Noise

As the dynamic thresholder reacts to deviations in brightness, it certainly also captures deviations that in principle are just noise.

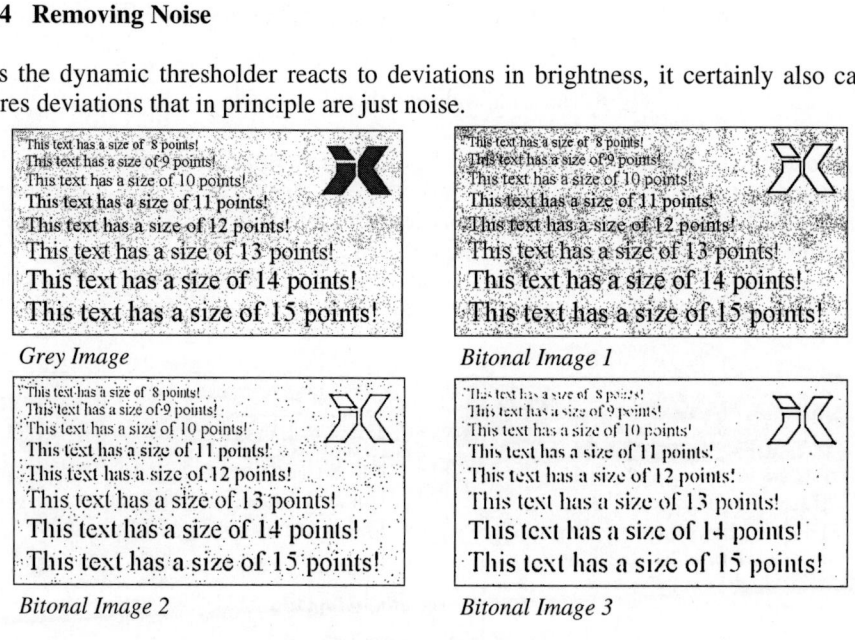

Grey Image

Bitonal Image 1

Bitonal Image 2

Bitonal Image 3

Fig. 8. Noise Removal

The grey image shown in Fig. 8 has many noise as it may happen during scanning. Such noise can be captured by the dynamic thresholder. It will even get worse, as the grey noise now certainly is black (Bitonal Image 1).

On one hand, you can try to erase this noise from the created bitonal image by searching for isolated pixels or for small groups of pixels, and removing them. Here, we will show how such noise can be prevented or even removed during thresholding.

A second, smaller window is defined in the window for the dynamic threshold.

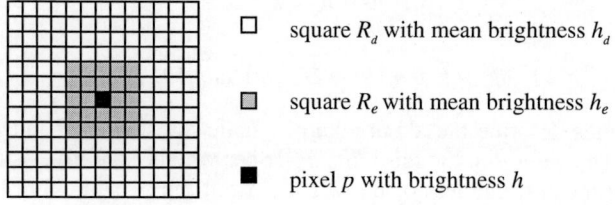

□   square R_d with mean brightness h_d

▨   square R_e with mean brightness h_e

■   pixel p with brightness h

Fig. 9. Pixel with *Dynamic Window* and *Noise Window*

Further to the brightness of pixel h and of window h_d we now have the mean brightness h_e of the smaller square. The noise removal bases on the following idea:

Noise consists of individual pixels or small amounts of pixels. If pixel p is a noise pixel, it is most likely that only few noise pixels are in the square R_e. The mean brightness h_e thus is high. If however it is a pixel that, for example, belongs to a character, there probably are some neighboring pixels that also are dark. So, the mean brightness h_e is lower.

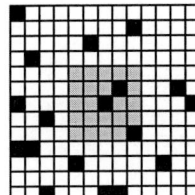 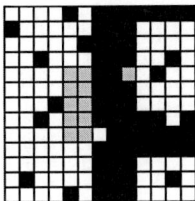

Fig. 10. Noise Pixels and Useful Pixels in the Threshold Window

This is illustrated in Fig. 10 where, for reasons of simplification, the pixels are shown as black and white only. In reality, there certainly are darker and lighter grey shades. But you can clearly see that the mean brightness h_e is considerably higher in the left window than in the right window where a character is captured.

The decision whether the pixel p is set in the bitonal image is made to the following formula. Further to the already known dynamic threshold s_d, there is the new parameter s_e that determines the power of noise removal. Thus, it is again converted, analogously to the dynamic threshold S_d to the value s_{ex}.

$$s_{ex} = \frac{255 - s_e}{8} \; if \; s_e \neq 0 \qquad\qquad s_{ex} = 255 \; if \; s_e = 0 \tag{11}$$

Pixel p now is:

$$p = 1 \quad if \quad (h < h_d - s_{dx}) \; and \; (h_e < h_d - s_{ex}) \tag{12}$$

The left-most term describes, as usual, the dynamic thresholder. But in addition, the mean brightness h_e is compared, using the same method, to the threshold s_{ex} and the brightness h_d. Only if both conditions are fulfilled, the pixel is set.

The *Bitonal Image 2* in Fig. 8 was processed using a noise-removal square R_e with the size 3x3. Most noise is removed, some larger ones however are still there. The Bitonal Image 3 in Fig. 8 has nearly no noise any more. Here, the square R_e was enlarged to 5x5. Now, however, the smaller characters are already affected. Therefore, caution is advised at originals with very fine text. Practice has proven that only the sizes 3x3 (fine noise removal), 5x5 (medium noise removal) and 7x7 (rough removal) make sense.

4 Programming the Thresholder

The operations required for the threshold are quite easy, in principle. Caused by the high amount of such operations, however, some programming tricks are necessary in order to process an image in an acceptable time.

4.1 Determination of the Mean Brightness

One of the essential calculations required for the threshold algorithm is to determine the mean brightness of a square. This brightness in principle corresponds to the sum of the brightness h of all pixels in the square[2]. If we assume a DIN A4 page with 200 DPI (1664 x 2368) and a window of 13x13 pixels, 169 additions are reached per window, and 665.919.488 additions for the whole page. This must be simplified.

You can take advantage of the fact that the image is converted pixel by pixel from left to right and line by line from top to bottom. So, the squares required subsequently differ only slightly.

Therefore, at the start of the conversion, first the Column Sum S_x is formed over the height of the required window (13) for every column across the total image width (n). The brightness of a pixels is denominated h_{xy} (Column x, line y).

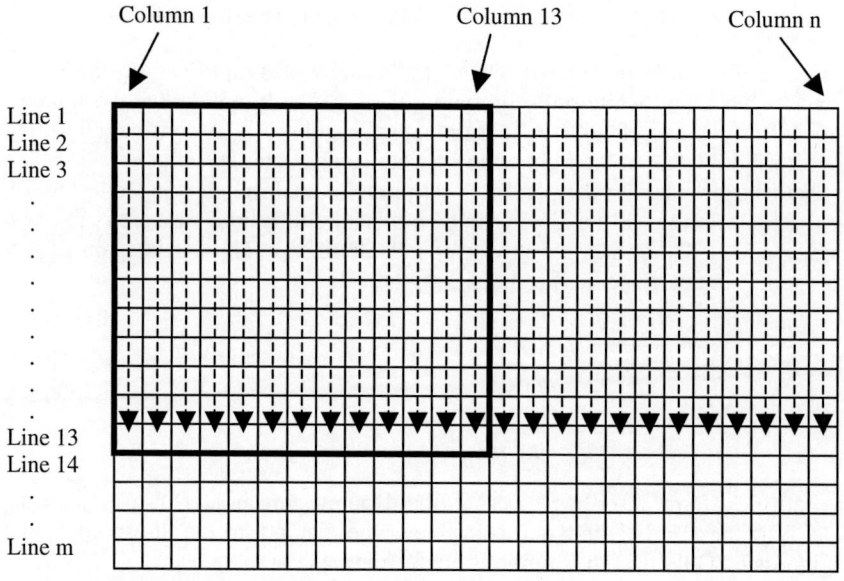

Fig. 11. Column Sum

$$\textit{Valid for all columns x is}: \quad S_x = \sum_{y=1}^{13} h_{xy} \qquad (13)$$

---

[2] Normally, one would divide this sum by the number of pixels in order to return to a value in the range between 0 and 255. In practice, however, it makes more sense to multiply the constant comparison values with the pixels and to do without the division.

The brightness h_{d1} of the first square results simply from the addition of the first 13 column sums.

$$h_{d1} = \sum_{x=1}^{13} S_x \qquad (14)$$

Now, the brightness of the next square h_{d2} can simply be calculated by adding the next column sum and subtracting the former column sum. Generally:

$$h_{dn} = h_{d(n-1)} + S_{(n+6)} - S_{(n-7)} \qquad (15)$$

Instead of 169 additions, now just two operations are required.

When changing to the next line, each column sum can also be corrected by two operations (subtraction of the void brightness / addition of the new brightness).

This results, for the above example, in the following number of operations:

Table 1. Number of Operations for the Brightness Determination

Calculation Step	Calculation	Operations
Calculation of the Column Sums	1664 x 13	21.632
Adaptation of the Column Sums for the next Line	1664 x 2	3.328
Calculation of the First Squares in a Line	2368 x 13	30.784
Calculation of the Following Squares	2368 x 1663 x 2	7.875.968
Sum		7.931.712

Compared to the initially required 665.919.488 operations, now only 7.931.712 are left. This is no more than 1,2% of the originally required additions!

4.2 Handling Points near a Border

We did not consider so far how to handle points where the square around this point lies partially outside the document area.

We handle this by virtually enlarging the document by half square size to all directions. Points outside the image area get the grey shade of the next point inside the image.

This makes calculation a little bit more complicated. However, calculating the border points does not really slow down the algorithm, because these are only a few points compared to the whole image.

4.3 Speed of the Thresholder

For a DIN A4 document with 200 DPI, the Thresholder requires the following times on a 2,53 GHz P4 computer.

Table 2. Speed of the Thresholder

Operation	Time
Static Thresholder	15 ms
Static and dynamic Thresholder	60 ms
Static and dynamic Thresholder with Backtracker	75 ms
Same and additional Noise Removal	100 ms

4.4   Parameter Configuration and Preview

The speed of the thresholder allows scanning with the fastest production scanners, while processing the images in real time. However the speed has another advantage too. It is possible to immediately see the effects when changing parameters.

Fig. 12 shows the parameter dialog. In combination with the preview window Fig. 13 it is simple to find the best threshold parameters.

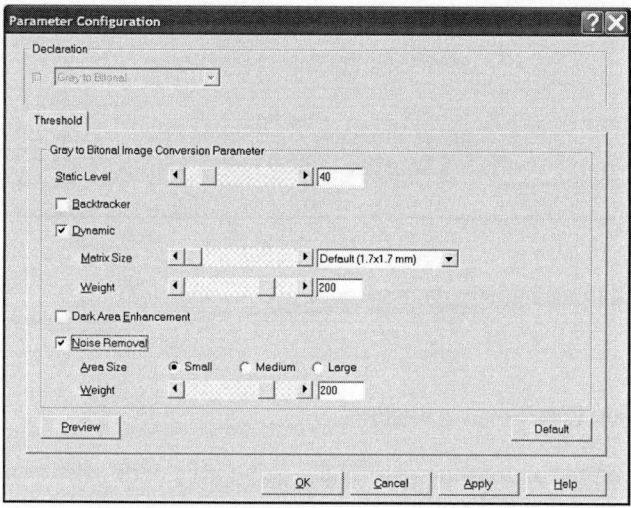

Fig. 12. Threshold Parameter Configuration

Fig. 13. Threshold Preview Window

References

1. Bartsch, Taschenbuch Mathematische Formeln, ISBN 3 87144 239 9
2. Bronstein, Semendjajew, Taschenbuch der Mathematik, ISBN 3 87144 492 8
3. CCITT, Red Book, Volume II, Fascicle VII.3, Terminal Equipment and Protocols for Telematic Services, ISBN 92-61-02291-X
4. Rafael C. Gonzalez, Richard E. Woods, Digital Image Processing, ISBN 0201180758
5. Bernd Jähne, Digitale Bildverarbeitung, ISBN 3540412603
6. Michael Seul, Michael J. Sammon, Lawrence O'Gorman, Practical Algorithms for Image Analysis: Descriptions, Examples, and Code, ISBN 0521660653
7. Yann Le Cun, Léon Bottou, Patrick Haffner, Paul Howard, DjVu: a compression method for distributing scanned documents in color over the internet, Color 6, IST, 1998.
8. Specification of DjVu Image Compression Format Version of 1999-04-29 15:46 EDT Copyright (c) 1999 by AT&T, http://www.djvuzone.org/techpapers/index.html#specs

Neighbourhood Related Color Segmentation Based on a Fuzzy Color Classification TooL

Bernhard Frei, Marin Hund, and Markus Schnitzlein

Océ Document Technologies GmbH, Department DE
Scan Technology and Image Processing,
Max-Stromeyerstr. 116, 78467 Konstanz
Markus.Schnitzlein@odt-oce.com
www.odt-oce.com

Abstract. The starting point for an automatic character recognition system (OCR, ICR) as well as for an automatic document analysis system is an optimized image processing system which performs an image separation into useful and useless information. A two-dimensional colour segmentation method is presented, which is based on a colour and structure based analysis of the pixels to provide a separation of the useful and useless image information with the aim to extract only the useful information. The specific background knowledge concerning the coloured composition of documents and the document specific colour design can be combined with the help of a fuzzy based training tool. This colour classification is the basis for a colour segmentation algorithm, which is able to adapt to the colour variations within documents. The colour segmentation itself operates on a (m x n) matrix.

1 Introduction

1.1 Problems with the Document Composition

Documents are the base for most business processes of administration departments within both industrial enterprises and public authorities. Today about 70%-80% of all documents are sent and archived in paper. The digital content extraction and further processing enforce the use of image processing, image analysis and ICR (Intelligent Character Recognition) methods.

Especially forms and semi-structured documents - like invoices and bill of deliveries – show various colour compositions. The separation of useful information on papers with a not clearly defined colour composition of the background is difficult, but is fundamental for a reliable character recognition system.

A. Dengel et al. (Eds.): Adaptive READ Research Project, LNCS 2956, pp. 26–36, 2004.

Due to the large spectrum of document compositions and significant variances within the results of the printing process at forms, it is necessary that even on well defined structured forms, intelligent and adaptive image processing methods have to be applied in order to receive acceptable recognition results for subsequent processing. The adaptive segmentation, which is described later, based on problematic and poorly defined forms, shows an image processing algorithm that performs a reliable colour separation even with a substantial similarity between the colours of useful and useless image information. Moreover, it shows a robust behaviour regarding image artefacts and noise.

1.2 Variances in Printing Technology and Artefacts of the Scan Process

The colour based analysis of documents necessitates the consideration of typical artefacts which result from the production of pre-printed forms as well as from the digitization process (scanning).
In particular:

- Variations of colour saturation across document width
- Use of different printing colours due to not clearly defined colour definitions
- Missing colour blending when scanning halftone prints at high resolutions. The scanner detects every single halftone pixel instead of the resulting mixture of halftone dots.
- Registration errors at colour sensors
- "Coloured" noise mainly because of shot noise.
- Use of scanners without ICC colour profiling
- Compression artefacts

2 Neighbourhood Related Color Segmentation

Before automatic character recognition is performed, usually a separation between useful and useless image information is necessary. A very simple method is separating darker text from brighter background using a thresholding algorithm. This is a standard procedure for normal black-on-white documents. With coloured background this separation can be a complex task. Many forms have a pre-printed coloured text and coloured frames which guide the user in filling the forms with appropriate information. In many cases the colour of this guiding information is not clearly defined and moreover for a better readability it is designed with dark colours. In many cases the conventional methods of colour segmentation are not able to decide based on the colour information of a pixel only, whether a pixel should be assigned to foreground information (text) or to the background, because the colour artefacts (see above) lead to similar and sometimes identical colour values of single pixels for foreground and background information.

The neighbourhood based colour segmentation defines a method which assigns pixels to foreground or background by analyzing the colour information of neighbour pixels. That way the neighbourhood based colour segmentation allows for a precise separation between foreground (useful information) and background (useless information) even when partially the same combination colours occur in script regions and background print.

For the primary determination between useful and useless information (foreground vs. background), colours are defined, which definitely belong to e.g. background colours. These colours are used as seed points for the neighbourhood based (2-dimensional) colour segmentation algorithm.

The specification for the colours of these seed pixels is performed using a definition for hue, saturation and intensity.

To simplify the training process, areas within a document can be selected, which are concerning their colour information subsequently analyzed: The results are visualized as histograms and can be used to select the relevant seed colours.

2.1   Color Training Methods

It is exceedingly difficult to select the right colour references for the training of the colour types "foreground" and/or "background" based on a selection out of predefined colour reference charts. And a selection of the right colours based on a training document is not much easier and additionally quite inefficient.

Neither comparing the ideal selected colour with reference charts nor the selection of single pixels within an image is a reasonable task for any user (even it is a well trained user). And moreover there are many sources of errors.

For the definition of document colours (foreground / background) a method is presented, which operates – derived from the visual human perception – in the colour space "CIE-LCH". This colour space offers an intuitive colour characterization for hue, saturation and intensity in combination with a device independent reference.

The training of the background (foreground) colours is performed based on a global histogram analysis referring to a reference (training) document. Supported by this histogram a simple and stable colour description can be achieved. This colour definition uses hue, saturation and intensity as variables. This training method will be used to define colours that certainly can be assigned to the background (foreground). These colours will be the seed colours (pixels) of the neighbourhood based 2-dimensional colour segmentation process.

For the three variables hue, saturation and intensity a histogram is calculated from a selected document region. The slanted border lines, which isolate trapezoidal areas, describe the strength of the membership of the hue, saturation or intensity values concerning the colour classes. With an interactive drag and drop technique the edges of the trapezoids can be positioned along the axes for maximum and minimum membership.

Fig. 1. Color histogram (hue, saturation or intensity) of ROI

The same procedure is applied for all three description fields. Within the coloured appendix there are figures of all three fields.

Based on this inexact description of hue, saturation and intensity a fuzzy based approach is used to calculate the membership function concerning the colour classes (e.g. background).

A special colour class is used for "colourless" colours. Especially near the grey axis of the colour space there is no relevance of the variables hue and saturation. The range for "colourless" is also defined by a fuzzy description.

Implicit rules define that colours of the class "colourless" will be assigned to foreground or background using only the intensity value. It depends on the scanner and its quality of grey level reproduction which extent this range has.

For the algorithm the following requirements have been established:

1. The training procedure must be performed using random samples. At best there is a reference document with a colour composition, which allows for a definite assignment of a colour to the subsequent processing steps. In the simplest case this is an assignment of colours to the two elements of a bitonal image (black / white).

2. It should be possible to define typical variances of the scanning process and the used print materials.

3. The relation between colour and meaning should be freely definable. For example: It depends on the application if all red elements should be suppressed or interpreted. But this definition of all red elements is not sufficient. Sometimes only the specific red of a stamp should be read and the frame in different red should be suppressed.

4. The system should be able to work with colours defined in an absolute colour metric. This requirement implies the usage of device independent colour spaces like XYZ or CIE-Lab.

5. Also printing colour systems widely used in the printing industries like Pantone or HKS should be supported.

6. An additional requirement is that the different ways of defining colours can be mixed in order to make it possible to define the backgrounds in the Pantone system whereas the used inks are defined with the variables intensity, hue and saturation.

For the realization of these requirements a Graphical User Interface is developed. For the free definition of a colour a fuzzy method is used which works with the variables intensity, hue and saturation. This is the best adaptation on the human perception with colours. But the usually used colour spaces HSI, HSL and HSV are not device independent and this is a strict requirement in point 3 and 4.

The optimal solution is to use a colour space which is derived from a CIE standardised space: LCH.

The LCH model is a derivative of L*a*b*. The L represents luminance, just as in L*a*b*, with a range of 0-100, black to white. The C stands for chroma and is representative of saturation or purity of colour. The H stands for hue and is measured as hue angle.

The L and C components are readily understandable. The hue angle is a new description element. It works on the principle of the colour wheel. The origin is 0° and represents red. As we move around the circle, the hue angle changes as the colour changes. Some of the prominent colour positions are yellow 90°, green 180°, blue 270°, and red 0°/360°. The interesting thing about this model is that it is highly intuitive. It is very easy to visualize where a colour is in relation to another colour. Perfect complementary colours are always 180° apart. This is similar to the red/ green, yellow/blue axes of the L*a*b* model.

For using the variables with fuzzy methods the normally used range of values is projected on a range from 0 to 1.

We can now directly interpret the resulting member value as a grey level and use it as an input for a thresholding mechanism or we use it as start colours for the adaptive structure related colour segmentation.

2.2 Adaptive Structure Related Color Segmentation

The conventional single pixel based colour segmentation is frequently not able to perform a valid assignment to foreground or background information. Figure 3 clarifies this situation.

The paper has a slightly green colouring. The green colour of the print has to be filtered out and assigned to the background (useless information). In terms of an automatic character recognition system only the grey print is the useful information. To suppress the green print as useless information, the green pixels of the pre-printed form have to be defined as background colours. Since the process of filtering out and suppression of the green background information should also work with varying qualities of the pre-printed form, an additional tolerance region in colour space has to be calculated around the actually existing green colours of the document with regard to changing print quality and paper colour. The number of colours that have to be filtered out will be increased by this tolerance region. Partially the combination of the grey print over greenish paper leads to exactly the same colours that are previously defined in the tolerance region. Therefore, a 1-dimensional filter out process will inevitably assign pixels to the background information, although these pixels belong to useful text.

Figure 6 shows this problem. Even though the conventional 1-dimensional segmentation suppressed not all green regions, the grey characters are already damaged. This prevents the reasonable use of an automatic character recognition system.

With the neighbourhood based segmentation now a method is defined, that assigns the pixels to foreground or background information based on an colour analysis of neighbouring pixels. It allows for a precise separation between foreground and background information even when, as described above, the same combination colours between text and pre-printed form colours occur.

For the subsequent description it is presumed that the pixels of an image have to be identified, that belong to the background and consequently should be suppressed. A pixel that should be suppressed will e.g. receive the colour value that is typical for the paper. The described algorithm can analogously be defined, that pixels have to be identified, that belong to the text characters (foreground) and consequently should not be suppressed.

Definitions:
Every colour within an arbitrary colour space (e.g. RGB, HLS, YCrCb, Lab, YIQ, CMYK, ...) will be assigned to one of the following regions:

Region 1 / Certain background

All colours that certainly can be assigned to the background will be assigned to this region. Colours that result from a combination of text and background colour will not be assigned to this region.

Region 2 / Possible background

All colours that have a specific likelihood to be also a background colour will be assigned to this region. This region includes the combination colours. A definition for this region could be: All colours that are located within a predefined tolerance distance within colour space (e.g. saturation ± 10%, intensity ± 5%) around colours of region 1.

Region 0 / Unknown.

All colours of a given colour space, that do not belong to region 1 or region 2 will be assigned to this region.

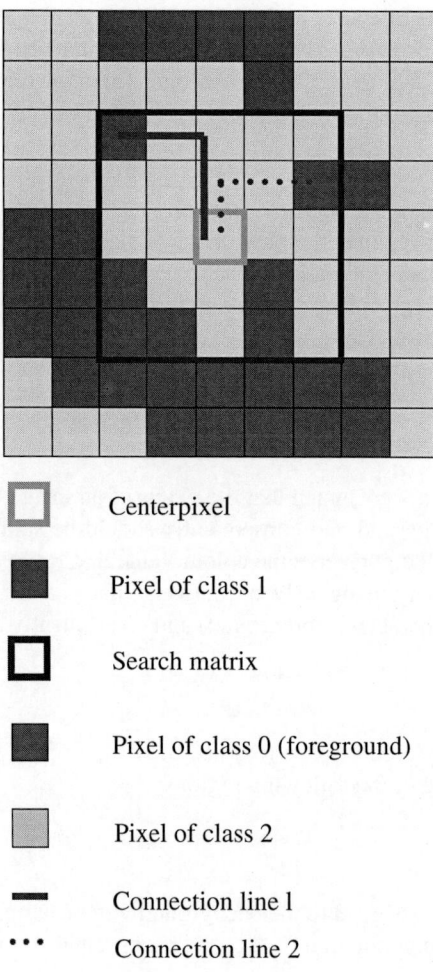

▢   Centerpixel

■   Pixel of class 1

□   Search matrix

▦   Pixel of class 0 (foreground)

▨   Pixel of class 2

—   Connection line 1

•••   Connection line 2

Fig. 2. Definition of the matrix

For the segmentation process an access matrix is defined which slides step-by-step across an image which consists of in lines and columns arranged pixels. During the segmentation process every pixel out of the image will be one time the centre of the matrix. The size of the access matrix is small compared to the image size.

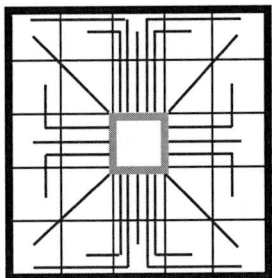

Fig. 3. The illustration shows an example of a 5x5 matrix and some possibke lines of connection.

Subsequently a decision will be made whether the centre pixel will be assigned to the background or shall be treated as foreground pixel (e.g. script information). The following four rules shall be applied:

1. If the centre pixel is a member of region 1, then the centre pixel is definitely part of the background and will be suppressed in the resulting image by an appropriate method.
2. If the centre pixel is a member of region 2 and at least one of the direct neighbours (there are in principle 8 direct neighbour pixels) is member of region 1, then the centre pixel will be interpreted as part of the background and will be suppressed in the resulting image.
3. If the centre pixel is a member of region 2 and at least one of the pixels (=destination pixel) within the access matrix is member of region 1 then the centre pixel will be interpreted as part of the background and will be suppressed in the resulting image, if all pixels that lie under a connecting line from centre pixel to destination pixel are members of region 2 or 1. It is sufficient, if one connecting line within the access matrix fulfils the requirements.
4. If the centre pixels cannot be assigned according to the rules 1 – 3, the colour of the pixel will not be changed and the pixel will be interpreted as foreground information.

The maximum length of the connecting lines, the form of the permissible connecting lines as well as the size of the access matrix provide many means for the adaptation to a given application.

The algorithm can be a pre-processing step in front of a thresholding algorithm. The classification mechanism (foreground vs. background) of the algorithm is also capable of performing - based on colour images - a direct conversion to a bitonal image, which is typically the input for an ICR system.

3 Summary

The studies of several approaches concerning an adaptive colour segmentation show that a system which is adapted to the human perception permits a reliable handling of the colour training. The benefits of this method, which are complemented by the 2-dimensional colour segmentation, are proven on critical test documents. Compared to conventional algorithms, a significant improvement could be reached.

An implementation in hardware is proposed, since often a synchronous processing of the documents is required to keep up with the fast scan process.

4 Appendix / Illustration

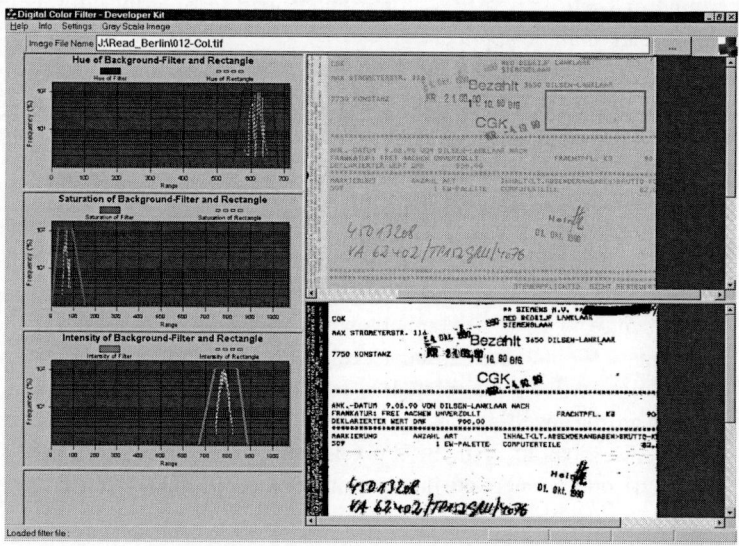

Fig. 4. GUI for the training of document colors: Example of suppressing the background colors by the neighbourhood related color segmentation

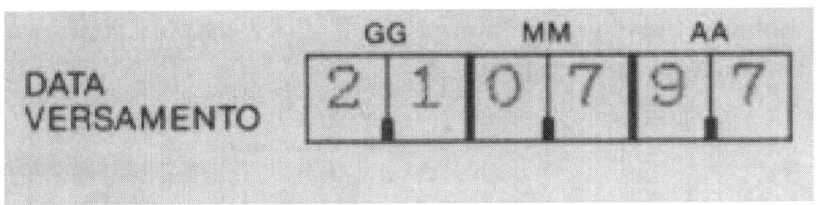

Fig. 5. Original document

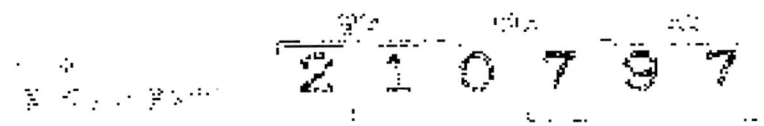

Fig. 6. Result of a standard binarization

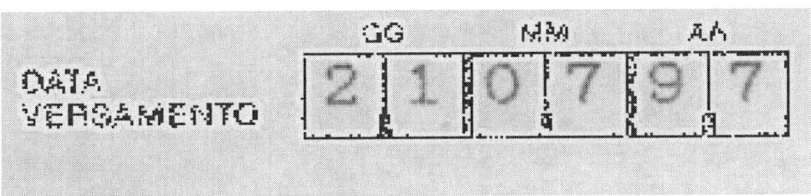

Fig. 7. Marking of search areas for the neighbourhood related color segmentation (Red = Area 1, Yellow = Pixels, which are located by the neighborhood-related color segmentation in area 2)

Fig. 8. Subpression of background colors by the neighbourhood related color segmentation

Fig. 9. Result of the neighbourhood related color segmentation after binarization

Example for the Segmentation of Hand Writing by Neighbourhood-Related Color Segmentation

geb. am   24.06.1963

Postleitzahl, **Wohnort**/Firmensitz, Straße und Haus-Nr.

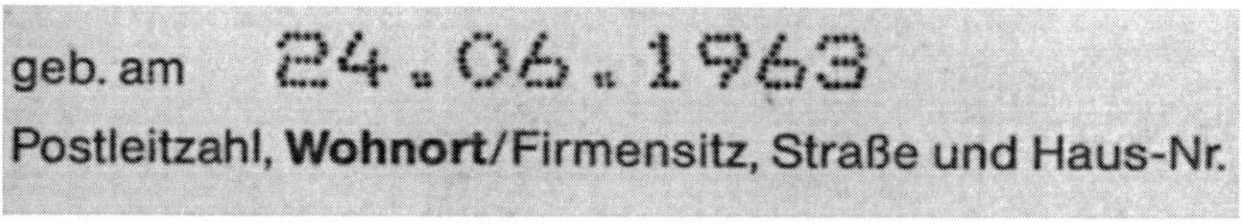

Fig. 10. Original document

24.06.1963

Fig. 11. Result of a standard binarization

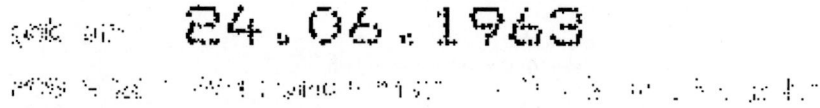

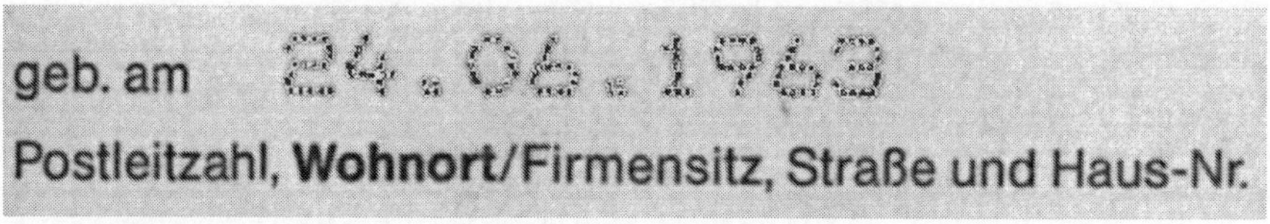

geb. am   24.06.1963

Postleitzahl, **Wohnort**/Firmensitz, Straße und Haus-Nr.

Fig. 12. Marking of search areas for the neighbourhood related color segmentation (Red = Area 1, Yellow = Pixels, which are located by the neighbourhood related color segmentation in area 2)

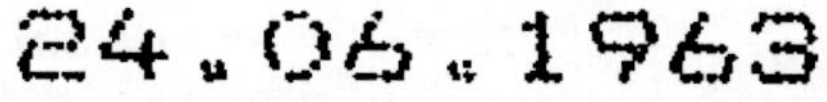

24.06.1963

Fig. 13. Result of the neighbourhood related color segmentation after binarization

Improving Image Processing Systems
by Artificial Neural Networks

R. Rebmann, B. Michaelis, G. Krell, U. Seiffert, and F. Püschel

Institute for Electronics, Signal Processing and Communications (IESK)
Otto-von-Guericke-University Magdeburg, P.O. Box 4120
D-39016 Magdeburg, Germany
{krell, michaelis}@iesk.et.uni-magdeburg.de
iesk.et.uni-magdeburg.de

Abstract. Document analysis systems require documents in electronic format. An image acquisition and display system for scanning and saving documents is presented, whereby the recognition capability (for example, series-connected OCR systems) is improved by correction components. Components for improving image acquisition, archiving documents and for reducing compression errors during archiving are integrated in the overall solution. The deployed components are suitably trained artificial neural networks. The projected improvements are assessed.

1 Introduction

The objective of the "Adaptive READ" project is the development of a new generation of document analysis systems. These are information systems that cater for the requirements of an enterprise or an individual user.

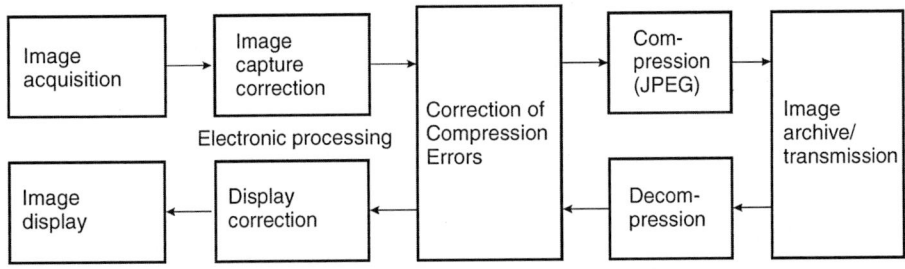

Fig. 1. Image acquisition, archive and display system with correction feature

The documents may be in electronically readable or electronically not directly readable format (for example, paper). To enable further electronic processing all documents that are not readable electronically have to be converted accordingly. A typical conversion solution is given in Fig. 1. An OCR system is introduced in order to extract electronics-based texts from the input images.

A. Dengel et al. (Eds.): Adaptive READ Research Project, LNCS 2956, pp. 37-64, 2004.

The captured image data must be archived in order to meet requirements such as implementing image acquisition and text recognition as separate modules, running the text recognition system offline, and processing the captured image documents in accordance with requirements yet to be defined.

Systematic errors encountered in individual processing steps can be minimized by means of artificial neural networks. Research carried out at Magdeburg University as part of "Adaptive READ" [15,17] is based on the signal flow illustrated in Fig. 1. The main focus of investigations is on reducing the compression artifacts. Also, the recognition capability of the following OCR system is improved.

If a standard A4 sheet (210 mm x 297 mm) with a resolution of 300 dpi is scanned with an image capture system with real colors (8 bits/color), then the size of the file in the image archive will be 24.8 Mbytes. It is clear that enormous amounts of memory capacity would be needed to archive a document consisting of numerous pages. Memory requirements can be reduced, however, by compressing the image data before archiving. If a further reduction in memory is required, then lossy compression techniques must be used (the decompressed images contain data, that is, compression artifacts). Due to the compression artifacts it becomes more difficult to automatically process the captured documents and the observer is presented with poor picture quality.

The image acquisition and display system (Fig. 1) employs the JPEG compression procedure. This procedure features [4]:

- high data compression factors
- different screen formats and different brightness resolutions (PCM quantizer levels) are supported
- progressive transmission (reconstruction quality improves as transmission progresses)

The JPEG compression procedure is used in a host of commercial image processing systems, for example, digital fixed image cameras and planetary scanners with integrated compression. To all extents and purposes the concepts being investigated can be adapted to the JPEG 2000 standard, featuring the new wavelet-based compression algorithms.

The procedure causes unsharpness and distortions in both image acquisition and image display. In line with previous research [9,13,10,2] corrections are made with artificial neural networks. Larger distortions may also be corrected with special graphics processors. Methods and experimental results are described in section 2. The main focus of this project is the correction during image acquisition. Generally, the reconstructed image/text information is electronically processed at a later stage (Fig. 1).

The methodology outlined in section 2 leads on to the description in section 3 of artificial neural networks as another means of reducing compression errors. In this solution compression errors are corrected with associative memories for particular image classes that are automatically determined with the help of a self-organizing map (SOM). Attainable improvements are demonstrated with experimental data.

2   Correcting Image Acquisition/Display Errors

2.1   Underlying Principles

Distorted color images are corrected by artificial neural networks based on the compensation of the transfer function of the image acquisition by a trained filter with "inverse" characteristics (Fig. 2). Typically, additional constraints for a realistic solution are introduced [3,9]. In the proposed method constraints are introduced during the learning phase.

In the learning phase an image of a known template is captured that contains the disturbances. A filter for use on any images can then be trained using the a-priori known learning template and the image. The filter can be tuned by comparing the acquired and corrected image with the ideal learning template by minimizing the difference between template and corrected image. Should the difference be negligible, then the filter is said to be trained and is ready for use to correct any images.

During the recall, that is, the actual correction of color images, corrected image and template are not compared.

The image correction procedure should cover the following image errors caused mainly by the optical characteristics and the electronic modules:

- out of focus blur caused by defective lens and incorrect lens adjustment
- geometrical distortions
- non-uniform illumination
- noise (TFT screen, CCD chip, AD/DA converter)
- space variance of parameters
- color errors (due to incorrect adjustment of color channels)
- color errors at transitions (incorrect convergence or different point spread functions in color channels)

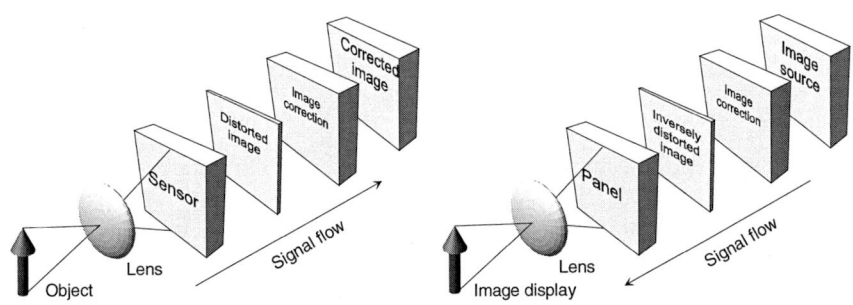

Fig. 2. Image correction of image acquisition (left) and image display (right)

A similar method was employed (Fig. 2) for correcting systems for image display as well as image acquisition. Image correction is downstream for input image correction. For image display, image correction is applied to the (ideal) image data for display on the screen. The image is inversely "distorted" with respect to the characteristics of the image display, so that the effects are practically neutralized and, ideally, a perfect image is reproduced on the screen.

In the case of image acquisition, the ideal image data is represented by the captured object, whereas in the case of image display, this data is given by the displayed image source. Section 2.2 contains a detailed explanation. Due to the structural scope of practical architectures artificial neural networks can only compensate for image deformations and distortions to a limited extent. In these cases additional procedures are available for deformation correction (see section 2.3).

2.2   Artificial Neural Networks for Correcting Image Acquisition/Display

Generally speaking, classical procedures for image restoration, such as Wiener or Inverse Filtering, can be applied. However, measurement of the system point spread function and assessment of the statistical parameters regarding disturbances are prerequisites for these solutions. Furthermore, geometrical distortions, space-variant parameters and unknown errors with the known solutions are very difficult to handle.

Models and algorithms in artificial neural networks offer a number of benefits for processing image signals. Important considerations are extensive investigations on biological models, where visual information is preprocessed by neural layers directly after the photoreceptors in the eye [9]. A critical advantage of this "softcomputing" solution is that the model of the system to be corrected does not have to be described explicitly, rather the parameters are adapted in a learning phase.

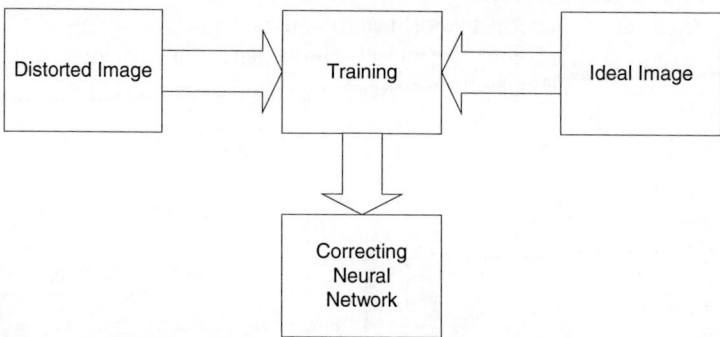

Fig. 3. Training the correction of image data with an artificial neural network (ANN)

The imaging system is calibrated by a training procedure in the correcting neural network (Fig. 3). Test patterns are input to the image acquisition or display system and compared with the "ideal" data (training pattern). When an image display is corrected the displayed test pattern must be rescanned.

A suitable error criterion is required for calibration. When the image source is restored, the mean quadratic deviation between target pattern and current output of the correcting network can be minimized. Superimposed noise thus impacts automatically on the adjustment criterion. Geometrical distortions are taken into consideration in the quality criterion, as no geometrical errors occur in the target pattern. Other quality criteria can be useful: for example - when a particular contrast enhancement or increase in image sharpness with respect to the image source is desired.

The scheme depicted in Fig. 4 uses three color channels. Each of the color channels is connected to the inputs of the correcting neurons. Training data is generated as described above. Colored training templates are recorded, and target patterns are generated. The color balance is obtained and corrected as required by carefully selecting the calibration templates together with suitable constraints in the quality function.

The network is trained using a gradient technique, or - assuming linear behavior of the lighting or sensor elements - with the help of the calculus of observations. The system must be recalibrated if the behavior of the image producing system changes.

The filter comprises a set of coefficients, that calculates one pixel of a color separation in the reconstructed image from all three color separations of the input image in a restricted area around the target pixel.

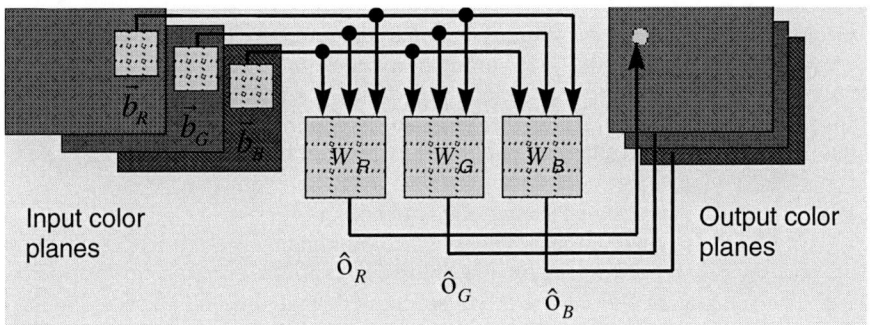

Fig. 4. Processing color channels: generating the corrected color pixel by neural coupling of the environment around all color separations in the input image

When the color channels are coupled together, interactions between the channels are taken into consideration when the image is corrected. The contributions of the coefficients used for calculating the same color separations are naturally much greater than those between different separations.

The reconstruction of a color pixel from image vector and filter matrix is described in Eq. (1) and Fig. 4. The indices represent the color channels (R : red, and so forth).

$$\begin{bmatrix} \hat{o}_R \\ \hat{o}_G \\ \hat{o}_B \end{bmatrix} = \begin{bmatrix} W_{R,R} & W_{G,R} & W_{B,R} \\ W_{R,G} & W_{G,G} & W_{B,G} \\ W_{R,B} & W_{G,B} & W_{B,B} \end{bmatrix} \begin{bmatrix} \vec{b}_R \\ \vec{b}_G \\ \vec{b}_B \end{bmatrix} \tag{1}$$

and in summation notation:

$$\hat{o}_{K\,x,y} = \sum_{i=1}^{2\mu+1}\sum_{j=1}^{2v+1} w_{R,K_{i,j}} b_{R_{i+x-\mu-1,j+y-v-1}} + \sum_{i=1}^{2\mu+1}\sum_{j=1}^{2v+1} w_{G,K_{i,j}} b_{G_{i+x-\mu-1,j+y-v-1}}$$

$$+ \sum_{i=1}^{2\mu+1}\sum_{j=1}^{2v+1} w_{B,K_{i,j}} b_{B_{i+x-\mu-1,j+y-v-1}}$$

μ, v are the size of the filter input area and K the actual color channel of the output pixel.

This filter for coupling the color channels is nine times larger than the filter needed for correcting gray value images.

Generating the Training Pattern

The learning template is an important aid in training the correction filter. The geometry and color of objects in this learning template have to meet certain specifications.

Geometrical objects on the learning template that are easy to describe have proven to be practical with the gray level correction procedure. Rectangles arranged as a chessboard on the learning template are well suited for generating the ideal learning template from the input image of the template. Assuming linear activation functions of the neurons, the approaches for parameter estimation by test functions known from systems theory yield.

Black rectangles used thus far are not good enough for color image correction. The colors cannot be assigned uniquely because the color channels are fully coupled in the filter, and the filter does not learn the color designations correctly in the learning phase. The rectangles should therefore be colored, and the color space should be covered as much as possible. When training templates are printed on color printers, color fringes occur with many color combinations due to incorrect superimposing of printing inks, which have a negative effect on the correction results. Furthermore, colors should be used for the learning template, that are not constituted from the superimposition of primary colors during printing, as incorrect colors can also occur in the print process and the homogeneity in the color field is not assured. The subtractive color model with the primary colors cyan, magenta and yellow are used in conventional printing technology. These colors are therefore the colors from which the learning template has to be created.

In order to preclude side effects from a color superimposition, the chessboard pattern cannot be used as a template. With the chessboard pattern individual rectangles touch at the corners, so that mixed colors can occur on the printouts due to incorrect positioning of the colors. There should be gaps between individual rectangles. A pattern consisting of two colored squares with edges 2.1 mm long, 0.7 mm gaps between them, and offset from one another by two-thirds their length, has proven to be a suitable template.

In determining the size of the squares a tradeoff was made between sufficient surface area for each colored square and as large a number of squares per unit surface as possible. This compromise was necessary, on the one hand, due to the limited resolution of the acquisition system (when the edge of a square is 2.1 mm long and the system resolution capacity is 400 ppi, the length of the edge is 33 pixels) and, on the other hand, due to the need to restrict the number of pixels for the filter computation.

Fig. 5. Section of learning template for training the fully coupled filter from the printer primary colors cyan, magenta and yellow

The ideal template $\hat{o}_{ideal}$ is obtained from the input image of the learning template during the learning phase. This procedure is executed using knowledge of the geometry and topology of the colored squares in the template. To avoid color distortion in the filter computation the color of every square in the idealized template is obtained from the mean values of the pixel colors of the associated square in the input learning template.

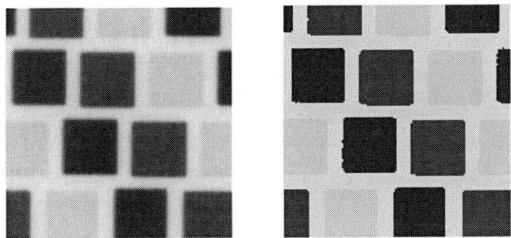

Fig. 6. Image of learning template and idealized learning template (target pattern)

Learning Procedure for Calculating the Compensation Parameters

The product of the filter coefficients and image section in the input learning template to be filtered is calculated to train the compensation parameters. The result $\hat{o}$, the value of a pixel for a color selection, is compared with the ideal learning template $\hat{o}_{ideal}$, and the filter coefficients are adapted according to the size and value of the difference. The object function $\hat{o}$ of the learning template replaces the object function o of any object in the learning procedure.

This procedure is performed for every pixel in the learning template to ensure stable filter operation. Upon completion of the training procedure the filter coefficients are set so that the difference between the chosen image section and the target pixel is minimized. Therefore, the quality function for the learning template is

$$Q(\hat{o}) = \left\| \hat{o}_{ideal} - \hat{o} \right\|^2 \Rightarrow Min \tag{2}$$

The elements of vector $\hat{o}$ are described by Eq. (1).

Space-Invariant Correction

During the training process the filter is produced from subareas in the learning template. When generating a space-invariant filter a cut-out in the middle of the template is used in the learning process.

The space-variant filter is applied across the entire image during recall. This procedure is only suited for images containing no significant space-variant disturbances. Space-variant parameters in the image are not taken into consideration when the image is corrected. This is particularly true of out of focus blur at the margin.

Fig. 7. Learning template with designated area for calculating space-invariant filter

Fig. 8. Uncorrected (left) and space-invariant corrected image (right) of a document. The much improved focus clearly improves the higher spatial resolution in the image.

Space-Variant Correction

Space-variant disturbances usually render errors at the boundaries of images more distinctive. In order to be better able to take such effects into account during correction, space-variant filters must be calculated. During the training process subfilters are generated for defined areas of the learning template The number of space-variant subfilters trained is a measure of the space variance of the disturbances (see Fig. 9). These subfilters can be calculated for each pixel as well as for large sections of the image. A disadvantage of space-variant filtering is the very laborious learning phase and the large filter matrix comprising submatrices for spatial filters.

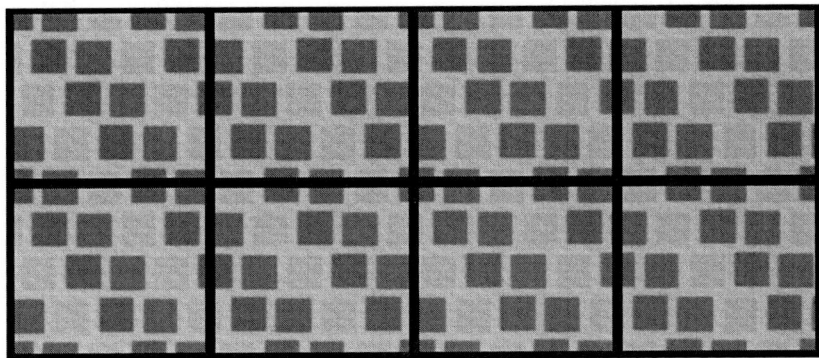

Fig. 9. Learning template split into eight space-variant filter areas

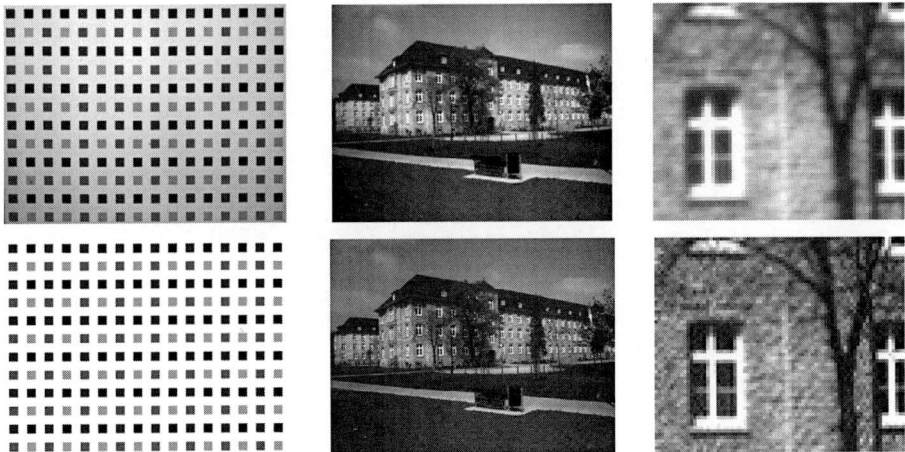

Fig. 10. Training pattern (left), recall pattern (center), section of recall pattern (right), top without, below with space-variant correction

Fig. 10 shows the results of this type of correction: quantitative quality features, such as brightness distribution, distortion parameters and spatial resolution; also, subjective improvement in quality can be clearly seen.

2.3   Correction of Geometrical Image Distortions

Image deformations can arise for different reasons. Real lens systems exhibit varying degrees of geometrical distortions that must be taken into consideration when the images are used in measuring applications. Large distortions cause visible deformation of images, that often interfere with visual evaluation. Distortion-free lenses are expensive and almost impossible to build with wide-angle focus length.

Classical algorithms for image correction generally address geometrical errors separately from other error classes. But, with the technique proposed in section 2.2 very small deformations are corrected along with other errors. However only deformations in the framework of the coupling range of the correcting neurons can be taken into consideration. Nonetheless, in the interests of efficiency one should eliminate any larger distortions before applies this technique.

The "Adaptive Read" project deals mainly with the processing of documents. One idea is that library stock should be made available in future in electronic format. Book scanning is an important area of document scanning, and image deformations are an important consideration here.

When a book is scanned with a planetary scanner, imaging errors occur and the page image is blurred. This is caused by the curvature of the pages in the book and the resulting difference in height of the sampling points on the book surface. These imaging errors can be avoided by smoothing the opened book with a glass plate. However, there is a danger that the book or the edges of the book could be damaged. To avoid this, the resulting imaging errors can be alternatively corrected by subsequently processing the scanned images.

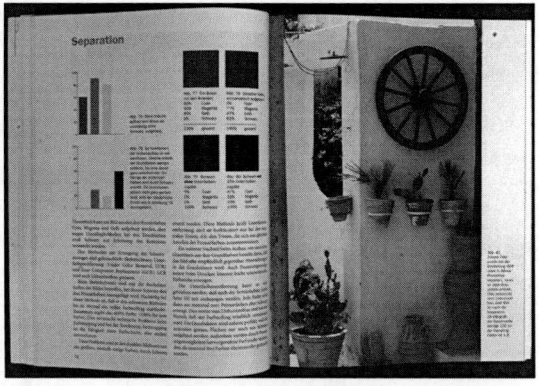

Fig. 11. Scanned book

Fig.11 shows a book scanned with a matrix camera. The imaging behavior of the matrix camera is the same as the behavior of a moving linear-array camera, as used by the Océ company with planetary scanners because only the linear-array camera is moved with planetary scanners and not together with the optics as in other scanners.

The deformation at the edges of the book can be clearly seen in Fig. 12.

Fig. 12 illustrates how points (x1, x2, x3), sampled by the image sensor and to which color values are assigned, must be moved to locations (x1', x2', x3') to eliminate distortion in the image coordinates. The error along the elevation section can be corrected by extending the sampling points.

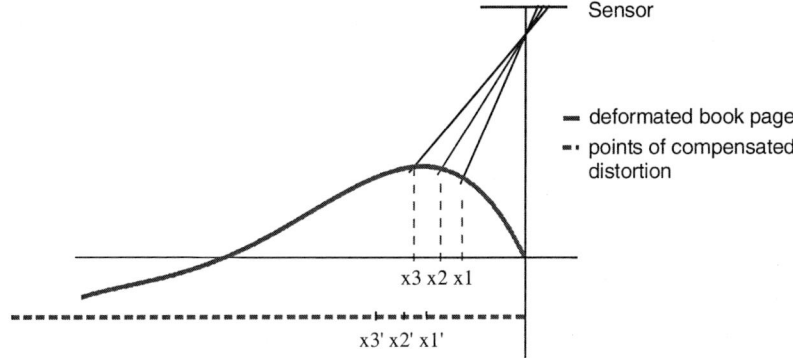

Fig. 12. Side view (elevation section) of a book being scanned

It follows with

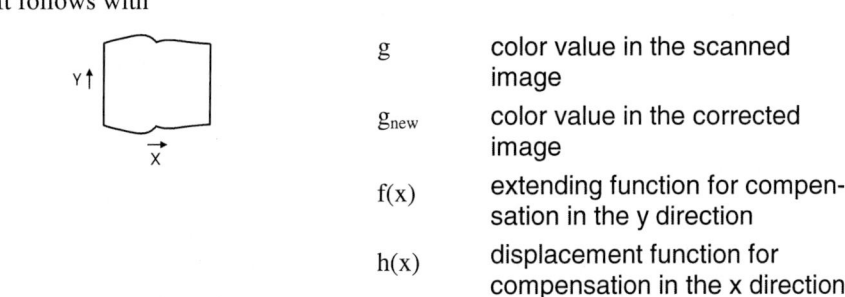

g	color value in the scanned image
g_{new}	color value in the corrected image
f(x)	extending function for compensation in the y direction
h(x)	displacement function for compensation in the x direction

for the transformation of every color value

$$g_{new}(x, y) = g(x + h(x), y * f(x)) \qquad (3)$$

Equation (3) describes how the scanned image must be transformed in order to correct deformations occurring during scanning.

To determine f(x) and h(x) the surface of the scanned object (for example, the book) must be measured. Trials were run with different procedures to establish their practicality and ease of use. The principle differences between the procedures is the acquisition of the geometrical data from the scanned surface. Distortion parameters were extracted from the geometrical data by each procedure in the same manner. The procedures examined are listed in Fig.13.

The 3D measurement with Gray code and 3D measurement with matching procedures are known in the literature [12,21,25]. With the 3D measurement with edge detection, the edge of the scanned surface is segmented to determine the 3D data. The shape of the surface can be approximated from the shape of the edges. If the edge cannot be distinguished from the background due to its color values or if there are irregularities in the curvature on the surface between the edges, then measuring errors can occur.

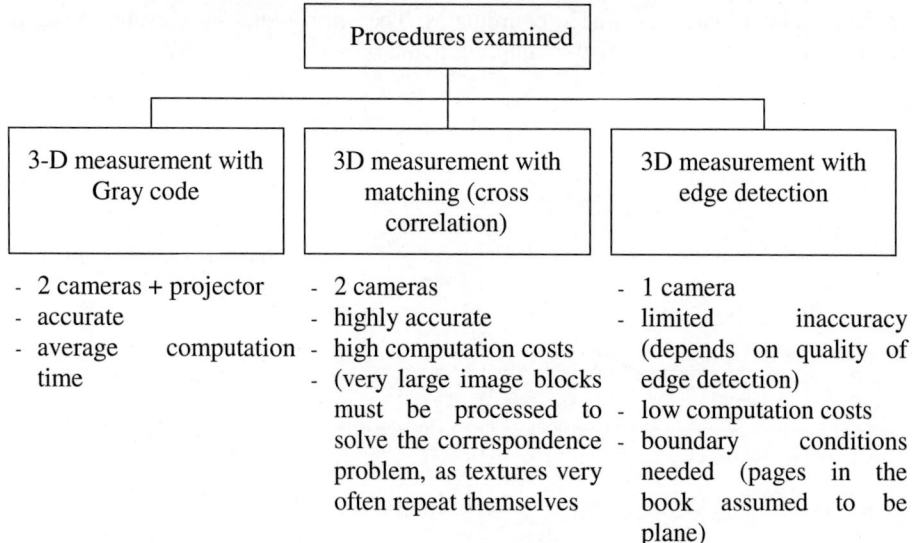

Fig. 13. Comparison of procedures for surface measurement

The suitability of a particular procedure depends mainly on the desired accuracy and the time available for compensation. The solution with edge detection delivers marked benefits, as no additional sensor needs to be integrated in the scanner.

3   Reducing Compression Errors with the Help of Artificial Neural Networks

Different concepts for the reduction of compression artifacts in JPEG compression were examined. The sum of error squares served as a quantitative measure of error.

Image falsifications are difficult to define. The deviation between scanned and error-free image as a sum of the error squares is often used as a quantitative measure (also its root, RMS or others). Also, the signal-to-noise ratio is a frequently applied criterion. The subjective assessment of an image often deviates from such simple integral criteria and often depends on the subjective opinions of the group of viewers [23,24].

To avoid extremely time-consuming interviews and to be compatible with other investigations, the mean quadratic error was used in the sections below and was supplemented as well by qualitative analyses.

JPEG compression mainly comprises transformation, quantization and coding components [4,18,22]. When these components are converted to algorithms   very slight computation errors are encountered, that have almost no effect on the compression artifacts occurring at high levels of compression. The specifications for the accuracy of the algorithms are set out in the JPEG standard [5].

Quantization and subsampling of color images are known sources of error. Undesirable effects are caused by processing pixels block-by-block with a high degree of quantization.

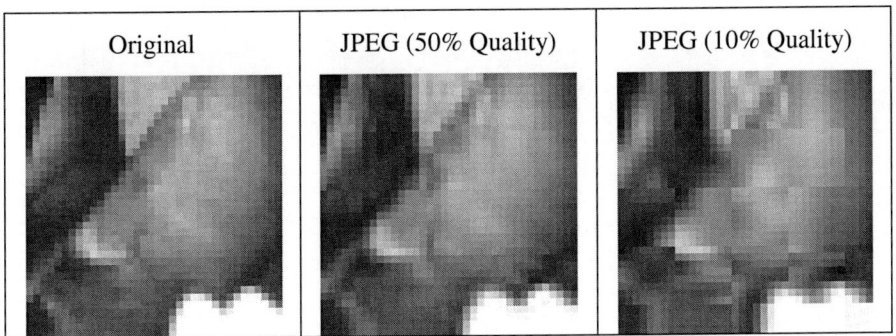

| Original | JPEG (50% Quality) | JPEG (10% Quality) |

Fig. 14. Errors caused by increasing compression as demonstrated by an example

Errors become at the block boundaries (see Fig. 14) very obvious. If the AC coefficients of the JPEG standard were to be quantified to a maximum, only homogeneous blocks that differ in brightness would be seen.

It is also worth noting that the edges are smoothed due to greater quantization of the higher spatial frequencies (using the standard quantization table) - thus giving the impression of a blurred image. Due to the quantization of spatial frequencies and related "incomplete" IDCT in areas with a very distinctive gray-value gradient, new gray-value gradients occur near this gray-value gradient.

The discussions in sections 3.1, 3.2 and 3.3 relate to the correction of monochrome images. The compensation of the compression artifacts in colored images is examined in section 3.4. This is an extension pretty much the same as that outlined in section 2. The correction for colored images is an "extended monochrome correction" as individual color components are processed separately in the JPEG compression.

3.1   Reducing Compression Errors with an Associative Memory

The images are divided into 8x8 pixel blocks for the correcting procedure. Thus the same image blocks are passed to the correcting procedure as with the JPEG compression and the computation costs are acceptable. The 8x8=64pixel are numbered though and give the first index in the matrix elements. The second index is the block number. The following relationships apply to the k -th block of an image

$$O_k = \begin{bmatrix} b_{IN_{1,k}} & b_{IN_{9,k}} & \cdots & b_{IN_{57,k}} \\ b_{IN_{2,k}} & & & \\ \vdots & & \ddots & \\ b_{IN_{8,k}} & & & b_{IN_{64,k}} \end{bmatrix}; \quad R_k = \begin{bmatrix} b_{JPG_{1,k}} & b_{JPG_{9,k}} & \cdots & b_{JPG_{57,k}} \\ b_{JPG_{2,k}} & & & \\ \vdots & & \ddots & \\ b_{JPG_{8,k}} & & & b_{JPG_{64,k}} \end{bmatrix} \qquad (4)$$

whereby original images are split in blocks O_K and decompressed images in blocks R_K. Gray-scale values for the respective images are $b_{JPG_{i,j}}$ and $b_{IN_{i,j}}$ (the column k presents the grey values of block k). The resulting number K of blocks k are vectorized in the matrices B_{IN} and B_{JPG}.

$$
B_{JPG} = \begin{bmatrix} b_{JPG_{1,1}} & \cdots & b_{JPG_{1,k}} & \cdots & b_{JPG_{1,K}} \\ \vdots & & & & \\ b_{JPG_{i*j,1}} & & \ddots & & \\ \vdots & & & & \\ b_{JPG_{64,1}} & & & & b_{JPG_{64,K}} \end{bmatrix} ; \qquad B_{IN} = \begin{bmatrix} b_{IN_{1,1}} & \cdots & b_{IN_{1,k}} & \cdots & b_{IN_{1,K}} \\ \vdots & & & & \\ b_{IN_{i*j,1}} & & \ddots & & \\ \vdots & & & & \\ b_{IN_{64,1}} & & & & b_{IN_{64,K}} \end{bmatrix} \qquad (5)
$$

The use of the procedure assumes that real images are subdivided into image classes. The full potential for variety in the image is not fully exploited in many cases, for example: checks, road traffic scenarios, and the like. There are internal relationships in the images (often unknown) that can serve to reduce redundancy. Thus the compression technique can be optimized within image classes while at the same time exhibit inferior characteristics for other (different) image classes.

Indeed, a better approach seems to be to adapt a correction procedure that is related to the image classes, and that practically compensates for the information loss during image compression. Missing information on the relationship within an image class after decompression is called up from an associative memory or a neural network with the aim of reducing compression artifacts. This idea is elaborated on below. B_{IN} thus acquires K blocks from an image class, so as to characterize the image contents. B_{JPG} makes a similar statement on the compressed images generated by the compression, saving and subsequent decompression processes.

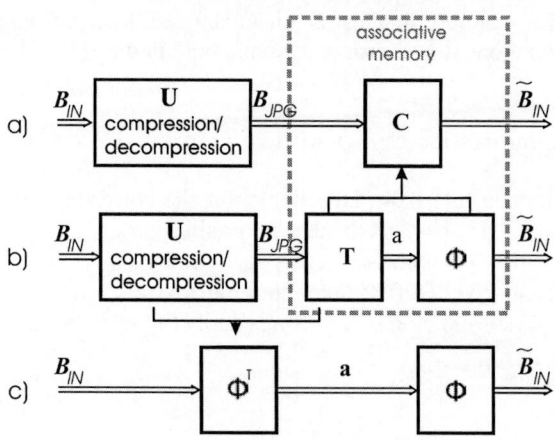

Fig. 15. Associative memory for correcting compression errors

The solution with the associative memory is explained according to Fig. 15. Experimental trials have shown that the relationship between original image and decompressed image can be described approximately by a linear set of equations. According to the systems theory for weakly non-linear systems the describing function method [19] can be applied. Therefore in order to simplify the mathematical model, compression/decompression can be replaced approximately at this point by the system matrix U (see Fig. 15a).

$$B_{JPG} = U \, B_{IN} \qquad (6)$$

The overdetermined set of equations (Eq. (6), K>>1) is then solved by the method of least squares. The values of the elements in U are determined by reducing the error squares.

$$U = B_{JPG} B_{IN}^{T} \left(B_{IN} B_{IN}^{T} \right)^{-1} \qquad (7)$$

Upon examination it was found that a number of eigenvalues in the system matrix U were zero or almost zero (see Fig. 16).

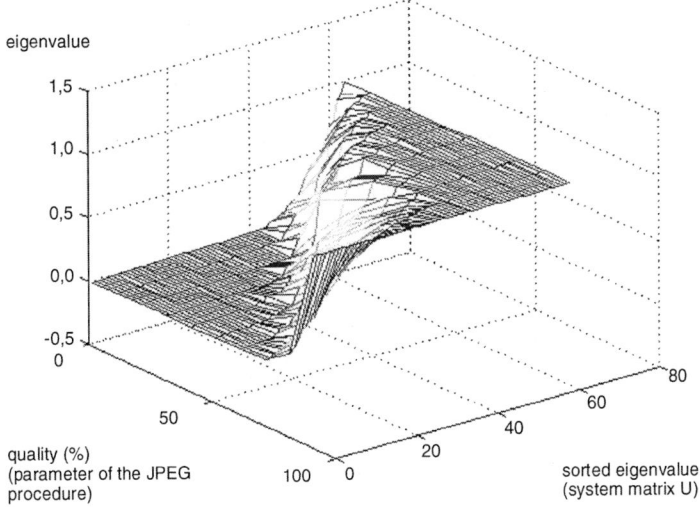

Fig. 16. Relationship between eigenvalues in the system matrix U and the compression rate

As the compression rate increases (poorer quality) the number of eigenvalues in U, whose value approaches zero, also increases. The increase in zero values with respect to the compression rate is almost linear. This observed behavior forms the basis of the procedure described below, where the compression errors are reduced by saving a-priori knowledge in the associative memory.

An auto-associative memory is used. This memory can be split into two subsystems with the help of the Karhunen-Loéve transformation [1] (see Fig. 15c).

The object of training is the reproduction of B_{IN} with $\tilde{B}_{IN}$ (auto-association). The corrected image $\tilde{B}_{IN}$ is called up from the actual associative memory Φ by the vector a.

From Fig. 15c we get

$$\tilde{B}_{IN} = \sum_{v} a_v \varphi_v = \Phi a,$$ (8)

whereby φ_v is the v th row and a_v is the v th input signal in Φ.

The following applies for the auto-associative system:

$$\tilde{B}_{IN} = \Phi \Phi^T B_{IN} \rightarrow B_{IN}$$ (9)

Consideration of the image data for an image class results in (an interpolation between the stored patterns is performed for K >> 1) the eigenvalue problem.

$$B_{IN} B_{IN}^T \Phi = \Lambda \Phi$$ (10)

The transformation matrix Φ is calculated by solving the eigenvalue problem Eq. (10) [6,11]. The primary diagonal in matrix Λ contains the eigenvalues of $B_{IN} B^T{}_{IN}$.

The eigenvalues λ_v are a measure for the mean size of the input signals a_v. Input signals λ_v may be ignored for λ_v approaching zero, without considerably influencing the characteristics of the overall system for the particular image class. Only redundant information would be transmitted (or no information or noise). If a_v for ignored $\lambda_v > 0$ smoothing and noise reduction is carried out. If one now assumes that the rank of matrix U is limited - a measure for the compression rate - then the assigned number of signals a_v should be used for image reconstruction with the help of the a-priori knowledge stored in the associative memory. To adapt the systems in figures 15a and 15c a matrix T must be introduced and it follows

$$\Phi^T = UT$$ (11)

This results in

$$T = U^{-1} \Phi^T$$ (12)

and the resulting correction matrix in Fig. 15a:

$$C = T \Phi = U^{-1} \Phi^T \Phi.$$ (13)

The Moore-Penrose Inverse must be calculated for U^{-1}. The matrices Φ, Φ^T depend on the length of vector a.

Results for reducing the compression errors in two typical images are plotted in Fig. 17 and 18. The compression error can be reduced by up to 20% approximately depending on image contents and quality factor. Similarly, an up to 25% higher compression rate can be used with the same compression error.

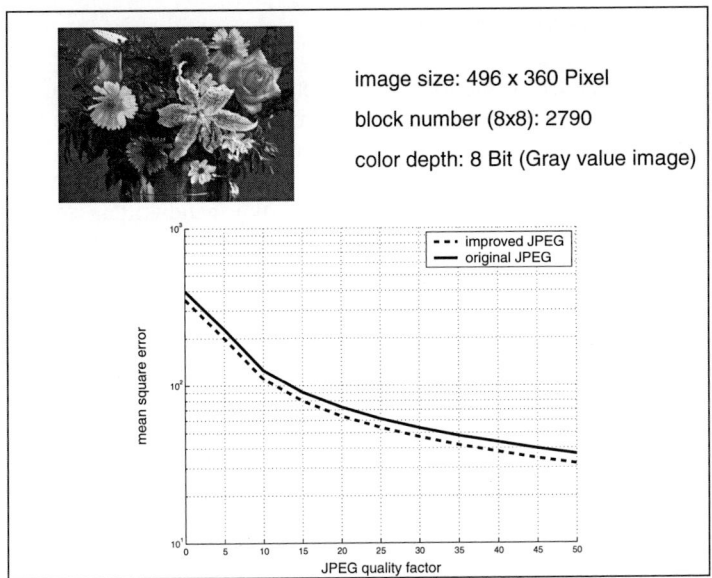

Fig. 17. Reducing the compression error for a typical image (image 2)

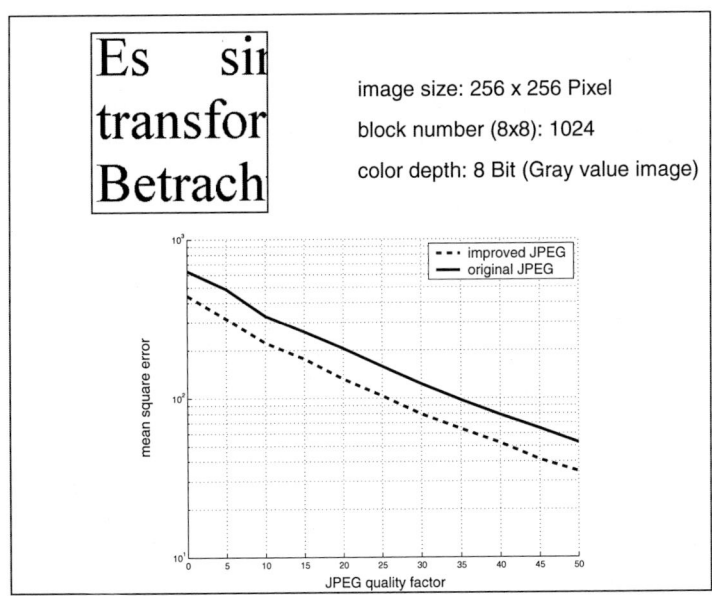

Fig. 18. Reducing the compression error for a typical image (image 3)

3.2 Space-Variant Correction

The procedure explained in section 3.1 is a space-invariant correction. All blocks in the entire image are corrected with an associative memory. In practice large numbers of documents with similar content are processed. A typical example is the processing of forms. The blank form remains constant from image to image; it contains a significant part of the information and only the handwritten sections change. Assuming that the form is located approximately at the same position when scanned, it is recommended that the location of the image blocks are taken into account during correction and, thus, that a space-variant correction is performed.

As with the space-invariant correction, images in the space-variant correction are divided into 8x8 pixel blocks (in this case the blocks are arranged according to their location).

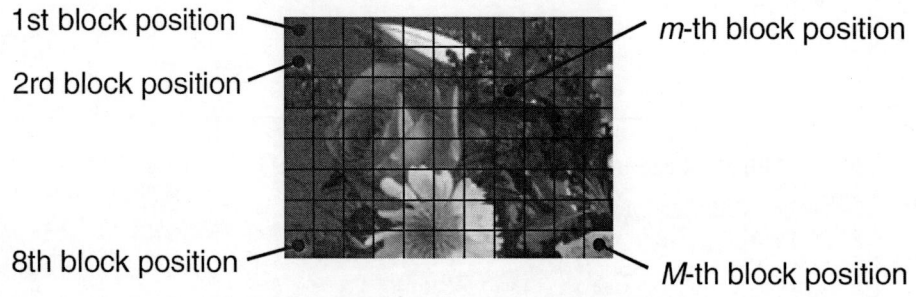

Fig. 19. Dividing the images into blocks

A number of training images are required (image n=1,...N; N>>1) for the training data set in the associative memories (a separate associative memory is trained per block position m, s. Fig. 19). A total of M associative memories are trained.

The original images are divided into blocks $O_{n,m}$ and the decompressed images are divided in blocks $R_{n,m}$ The gray-scale values in the original images are $b_{IN_{*,n,m}}$ and $b_{JPG_{*,n,m}}$ in the decompressed images. The 8x8 pixel of a block are numbered column wise by each element and give the first index * of the matrix elements. This produces:

$$O_{n,m} = \begin{bmatrix} b_{IN_{1,n,m}} & b_{IN_{9,n,m}} & \cdots & b_{IN_{57,n,m}} \\ b_{IN_{2,n,m}} & & & \\ \vdots & & \ddots & \\ b_{IN_{8,n,m}} & & & b_{IN_{64,n,m}} \end{bmatrix} ; R_{n,m} = \begin{bmatrix} b_{JPG_{1,n,m}} & b_{JPG_{9,n,m}} & \cdots & b_{JPG_{57,n,m}} \\ b_{JPG_{2,n,m}} & & & \\ \vdots & & \ddots & \\ b_{JPG_{8,n,m}} & & & b_{JPG_{64,n,m}} \end{bmatrix} \quad (14)$$

Blocks $O_{n,m}$ are vectorized in matrices $B_{IN_1} \ldots B_{IN_M}$ whereby matrix B_{IN_m} contains in its column the N blocks for all original images at position m, (s. Fig. 19).

$$
B_{IN_m} = \begin{bmatrix} b_{IN_{1,1,m}} & \cdots & b_{IN_{1,n,m}} & \cdots & b_{IN_{1,N,m}} \\ \vdots & & \ddots & & \\ b_{IN_{64,1,m}} & & & & b_{IN_{64,N,m}} \end{bmatrix} \tag{15}
$$

The same applies to blocks $R_{n,m}$ and matrices $B_{JPG_1} \cdots B_{JPG_M}$.

$$
B_{JPG_m} = \begin{bmatrix} b_{JPG_{1,1,m}} & \cdots & b_{JPG_{1,n,m}} & \cdots & b_{JPG_{1,N,m}} \\ \vdots & & \ddots & & \\ b_{JPG_{64,1,m}} & & & & b_{JPG_{64,N,m}} \end{bmatrix} \tag{16}
$$

Each associative memory m can be calculated by using the algorithm described in section 3.1 (equations (4) to (13)). Thus a separate correction matrix is produced for every block position.

$$
C_m = T_m \Phi_m = (U_m^{-1} \Phi_m^T) \Phi_m . \tag{17}
$$

Space-invariant and space-variant corrections are compared using an example to illustrate the results for forms. In the chosen example, 136 Eurochecks were created and scanned. The position of the checks (size = 864x392 pixels) does not change, except for slight displacements of up to ± 4 pixels.

Fig. 20. A blank check filled in by hand writing

The checks were filled in by hand writing by different persons to avoid repetitions. Fig. 20 shows a check from the data set in the example.

Fig. 21 gives a comparison between the space-invariant and space-variant correction using the mean quadratic error for the selected data set in the example. Much better results for reducing the compression errors can be achieved with the space-variant correction.

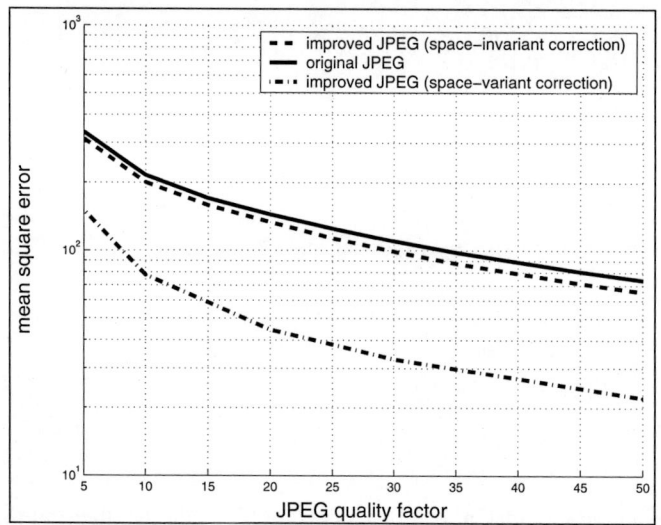

Fig. 21. Comparison between space-invariant and space-variant corrections

A disadvantage of the space-variant correction is that each block m must have its own correction matrix. This means that large data volumes generated for large images must be stored. If the space-variant correction is realized in hardware, then the parameters in the hardware must be changed for every new block (this is a laborious task). And. The images must be accurately positioned.

3.3   Reducing the Compression Errors with an Associative Memory by Automatically Generating Block Classes

The correcting procedure explained in the previous sections are subject to the limitation that they can only efficiently correct images in a trained image class. Should a number of image classes be trained, then the correcting capability of the system is impaired. Best results are obtained with an associative memory, when it only has to correct as narrow an image class as possible. This insight leads to the idea of block-class formation before correction. If the images, that can originate from a number of image classes, are distributed among a number of associative memories, good results can be expected even with a high degree of variance in image contents.

Fig. 22 shows a correction system with a block-class formation and memory selection by a self-organizing map (SOM). The SOM divides the blocks according to their content into the maximum number of classes determined by the size of the SOM, and selects for every block the associative memory that can be assigned for the correction (see Fig. 22).

The blocks should be subdivided automatically and unattended when the associative memories are being trained and during correction. Artificial neural networks are ideally suited for this type of classification task. The SOM, proposed and developed by Kohonen in the early '80s [7,8], was chosen for this correction system because of its characteristics [16,20].

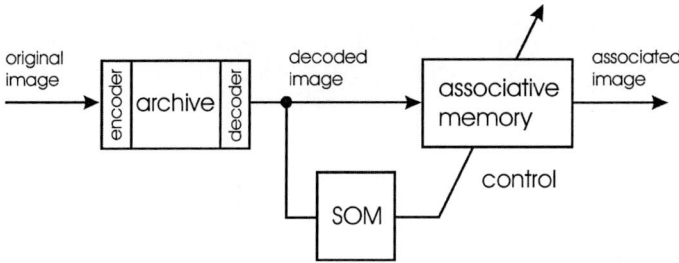

Fig. 22. SOM controlled associative memories

The data set for training the system described in Fig. 23 consists of image pairs (original images, decompressed image) needed to deal as far as possible with the image spectrum to be corrected later. The blocks of the decompressed images are separated into S classes by the SOM (see Fig. 14). The blocks in the original images are also divided into classes as per the dividing scheme for the decompressed blocks. In other words, the class s of original blocks contains the corresponding blocks for class s of decompressed images.

Each correction matrix C_s is calculated its assignable block class s of original images and decompressed images using the algorithm. explained in section 3.1

Using a number of typical images, the results of reducing the compression errors with an associative memory are illustrated with the help of the automatic block-class formation.

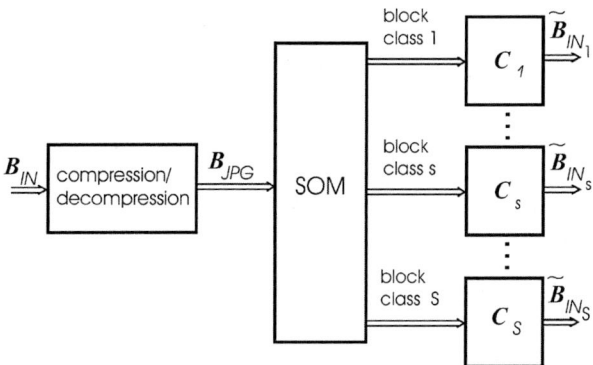

Fig. 23. Correcting the compression errors with the help of a block-class formation using a SOM

Fig. 24 shows the images used for training. The contents of the images differ greatly. The left-hand image contains recurring structures (leaves, and the like). The right-hand image contains a text, where the letters (black) are very sharp-edged structures on a white background.

Fig. 25 shows the distribution of the image blocks for typical images among the block classes after training with a SOM with dimensions 4x4 neurons. The distribution is almost uniform and all available classes are occupied. This ensures that all associative memories and thus, the total capacity of the correction system, is utilized.

Fig. 24. Typical images (left to right: image 1, image 2, image 3)

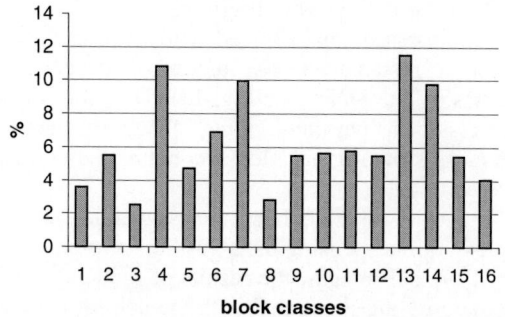

Fig. 25. Distribution of image blocks after training among block classes with a 4x4 SOM

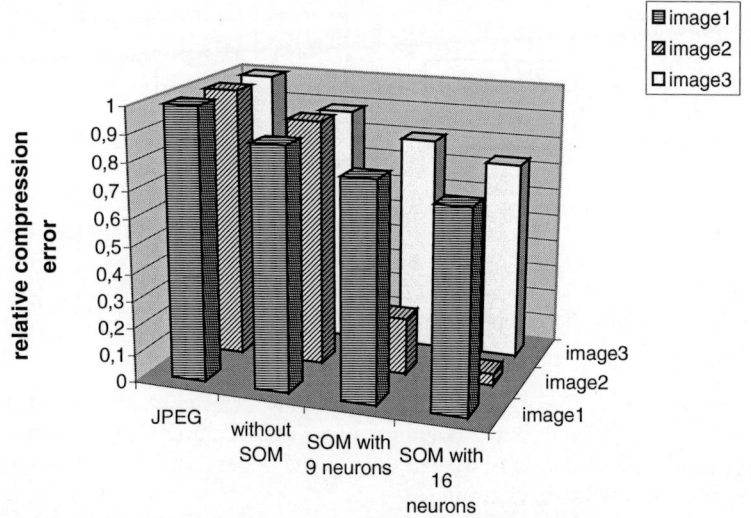

Fig. 26. Comparison of compression errors with and without SOM (for image allocation see Fig. 24)

Fig. 26 shows the comparison between the correction without SOM (see section 3.1) and the correction with differently dimensioned SOMs for the images introduced in Fig. 24. The system with SOM is able to correct all three images, although their content varies greatly. Further improvements are observed with an increasing number of neurons in the SOM. However, it should also be noted that with increasing number of neurons = increasing maximum number of classes, more associative memories are needed and thus the size of the total system increases. The requirements on the scope of the training data increase accordingly.

3.4   Correcting Colored Images

Compression artifacts in color images arise for practically the same reasons as artifacts in monochrome images. When compressing color images, individual color channels (here: R, G, B) are processed in the same way as the brightness channel in monochrome images. Differences are only encountered with quantization tables for the compression of color channels and typically the chrominances before the DCT are subsampled, thus causing additional errors.

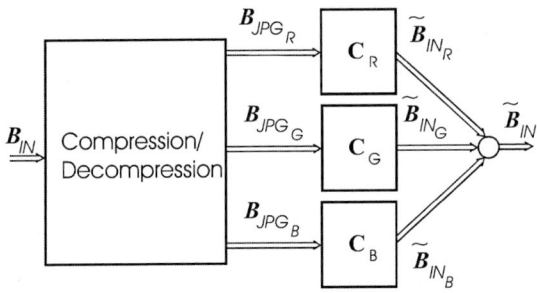

Fig. 27. Separate correction of individual color channels

Reducing the compression artifacts with an isolated correction of individual color channels was examined first. An associative memory for every color channel was used for correction (see Fig. 27). The correction matrices C_R, C_G, C_B were calculated in the same way as with monochrome images.

Three associative memories for each color channel were used for the correction with coupling between the color channels (see Fig. 28). Thus errors, arising out of the coupling between the color channels, are more easily corrected. The three associative memories per color channel are calculated in the same manner as the uncoupled channels. The difference here is that the matrix for the color channel in question comprises

- the data from one color channel with the procedure with uncoupled channels

- and the data from all color channels with the procedure with linked channels.

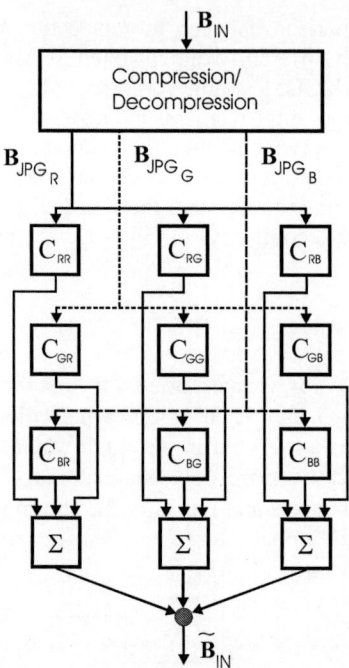

Fig. 28. Correction with coupling between the color channels

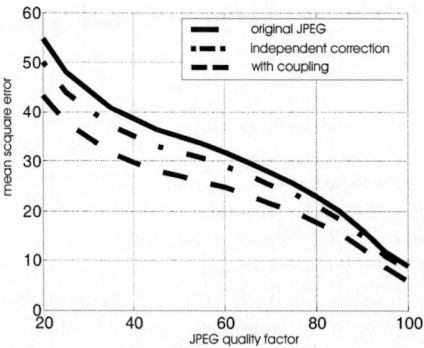

Fig. 29. Comparison of correction with and without coupling of color channels

Fig. 29 shows the comparison between the correction with and without coupling of color channels using the typical image for the red-channel. Investigations showed that different errors arose for the color components red, green and blue.

The luminance Y and chrominances U and V are obtained from the following relationships [22].

$$Y = 0.3R + 0.59G + 0.11B$$
$$U = 0.4937(B - Y)$$
$$V = 0.877(R - Y)$$

(18)

The luminance is not subsampled with the JPEG compression and is normally quantified with smaller quotients than the chrominances. Because green is the largest component in the luminance, the most insignificant error occurs in the green channel. The error for red and blue is also proportional to the respective component of the luminance. This weighting does not apply in special cases (images where R, G or B are completely missing).

Fig. 29 shows that the correction with coupling between the color channels can give better results than the system without coupling. More effort is required for better results (nine associative memories instead of three).

3.5   Influence of Reduction of Compression Errors on Text Recognition

Text documents are mainly processed today by computer-based systems. For printed forms or other documents (in the postal services for example) to be processed in such a manner, they must be converted to electronic format. This conversion generally occurs in two steps. Firstly, a scanner or similar imaging device generates an electronic image of the paper document. A compression technique is needed to handle the ensuing data volumes. After scanning, a character recognition procedure (OCR) generates a text from the image. Should a second-rate compression technique be used, the text recognition process will be adversely affected by the resulting compression artifacts.

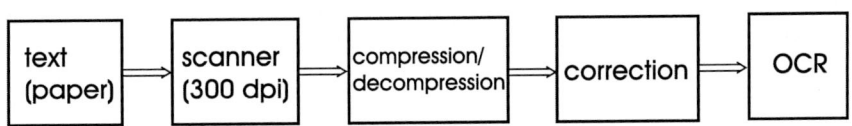

Fig. 30. OCR systems with error correction by a neural network

A system is given in Fig. 30 that examines the influences of compression errors on the text recognition. System configurations with enabled/disabled error correction were compared to determine the impact the Adaptive READ procedure for reducing the compression artifacts has on the text recognition process. A conventional middle-of-the-range OCR software package with no special adaptation features was used for text recognition.

Experimental results outlined below were obtained with a printed text (A4 sheet). The text was scanned and saved with different compression rates. Stored images were then converted to text files (Software Recognita Standard OCR 3.2). The detected texts were compared with the original text and the error count was recorded.

Errors encountered during text recognition are given in Fig. 31 depending on the compression quality for systems with and without correction of compression errors. It is clear that the compression artifacts with low compression quality (corresponds to a high compression rate) have a negative impact on the text recognition. With increasing error count, the correction technique used here (a series-connected artificial neural network, section 3.1) was able to reduce considerably these errors in comparison with the system without correction.

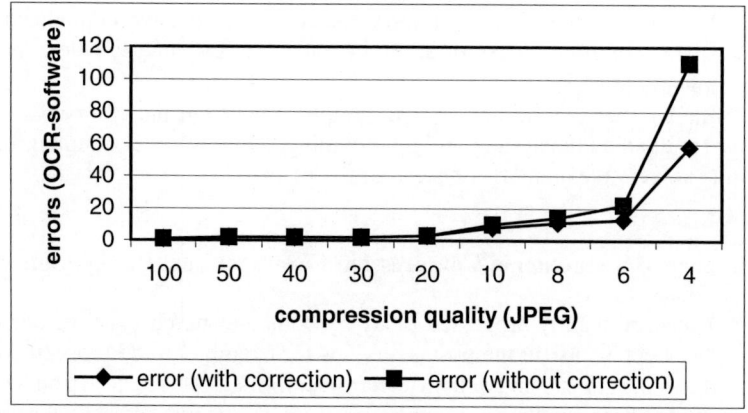

Fig. 31. Recognition errors with and without correction of compression errors

4   Conclusion

A coherent concept for image correction with the aid of artificial neural networks is proposed.

This concept lends itself for use for correction of image acquisition and image display. Out of focus blur and distortions can be compensated to a large degree with approximating "inverse filtering". Correction quality is improved by a-priori knowledge on image contents stored in the neural network.

The procedure can also be applied for image compression/decompression. In this case, a-priori-technical knowledge of image contents serve for restoration.

Self-organizing maps (Kohonen maps) have proven their ability to adapt to different image classes. Custom image classes should be introduced for special space-variable systems (for example, checks). A significant improvement can thus be achieved.

The concept is suited for use with color images when extended to the three primary colors *RGB* and modified for *YUV* space. This, of course, is a more laborious task.

The development of modern hardware renders the transfer of the proposed technology to the compression standard JPEG 2000 possible. A detailed description of such a configuration is beyond the scope of this paper and will have to be dealt with in a later publication.

The proposed concept has proven its suitability for image and text information, that can be divided into narrow image classes.

Space-dependent correction filters were trained for image acquisition, image display and image compression with the help of artificial neural networks. These filters enable an efficient image improvement by using a-priori knowledge of the image classes. The parametric filters satisfy approximately the same quality criterion as the Wiener filter.

Acknowledgement. The investigations took place in the context of the project "Adaptive Read". The project is sponsored by the Federal Ministry for Education and Research of the Federal Republic of Germany (01IN 902 J) and by the federal state Sachsen-Anhalt (0032KB099).

References

1. Abbas, H.M., Fahmy, M.M.: A Neural Model for Adaptive Karhunen Loéve Transformation (KLT). Proceedings International Joint Conference on Neural Networks, vol. 2, Baltimore, Maryland (1992) 975-980
2. Daniel, F., Krell, G., Schnelting, O., Schünemann, S.: Elektronische Bildkorrektur für Rückprojektionsdisplays zur Qualitätsverbesserung und Kostenoptimierung. Accepted for Electronic Displays, Wiesbaden September 24/25 (2003)
3. Gonzalez, R. C., Wintz, P.: Digital Image Processing. Addison-Wesley, (1987)
4. Hung, A.C.: PVRG-JPEG CODEC 1.1. Portable Video Research Group, Stanford University (1994)
5. ISO/IEC JTC1 10918-1, ITU-T Rec. T.81: Information technology - Digital compression and coding of continuous-tone still images. Requirements and guidelines (1994)
6. Kielbasinski, A., Schwetlick, H.: Numerische Lineare Algebra. Deutscher Verlag der Wissenschaften, Berlin (1988)
7. Kohonen, T.: Self-Organizing Formation of Topologically Correct Feature Maps. Biol. Cybern. 43 (1982) 59-69
8. Kohonen, T.: Self-Organizing Maps. 3rd ed., Springer-Verlag, London (2001)
9. Krell, G.: Bildkorrektur unter Einsatz künstlicher neuronaler Netze, Anwendungs-orientierter Beitrag zur Vorverarbeitung visueller Daten. Dissertation, Otto-von-Guericke-Universität Magdeburg (1995)
10. Krell, G., Rebmann, R., Seiffert, U. Michaelis, B.: Improving Still Image Coding by an SOM-controlled Associative Memory. Accepted for 8th Iberoamerican Congress on Pattern Recognition, 26-29 November, Havana (2003)
11. Lilienblum, T., Albrecht, P., Calow R., Michaelis, B.: Dent Detection in Car Bodies. 15th International Conference on Pattern Recognition (ICPR), vol. 4, Barcelona (2000) 775-778
12. Luhmann, T.: Nahbereichsphotogrammetrie: Grundlagen, Methoden, Anwendung. Wichmann-Verlag, Heidelberg (2000)
13. Michaelis, B., Krell, G.: Artificial Neural Networks for Image Improvement. In: Lecture Notes in Computer Science 719, Springer Verlag, (1993) 838 - 845
14. Ohm, J.-R.: Digitale Bildcodierung. Springer-Verlag, Berlin Heidelberg (1995)
15. Rebmann, R., Daniel, F., Krell, G., Michaelis, B.: Laboraufbau zur Untersuchung von Möglichkeiten der Leistungsverbesserung von Bildkompressionsverfahren durch Anwendung künstlicher neuronaler Netze. Deliverable D3.5 Adaptive READ (2000)
16. Rebmann, R., Krell, Seiffert, U., G.,Michelis, B.: Associative Correction of Compression Artefacts with a Self-Organizing Map Classifying the Image Content. DCC2003, IEEE Computer Society (2003) 446
17. Rebmann, R., Michelis, B., Krell, G., Meißner, K.: Neuronale Netze zum Abgleich des Bildaufnahme und –reproduktionszyklus. Deliverable D3.8 Adaptive READ (2001)
18. Salomon, D.: Data Compression the Complete Reference. Springer-Verlag (2000)

64   R. Rebmann et al.

19. Schlitt, H.: Stochastische Vorgänge in linearen und nichtlinearen Regelkreisen, Verl. Technik, Berlin (1968)
20. Seiffert, U.: Wachsende mehrdimensionale Selbstorganisierende Karten zur Analyse bewegter Szenen. Dissertation, Magdeburg (1998)
21. Strutz, T.: Ein genaues aktives optisches Traingulationsverfahren zur Oberflächenvermessung. Dissertation, Magdeburg (1993)
22. Strutz, T.: Bilddatenkompression. Friedr. Vieweg & Sohn Verlagsgesellschaft mbH, Braunschweig/Wiesbaden (2000)
23. Tizhoosh, H.R.: Bildverbesserung mit Rücksicht auf das subjektive Expertenwissen unter besonderer Verwendung von Fuzzy-Ansätzen. Dissertation, Magdeburg (2000)
24. Tizhoosh, H.R., Krell, G., Michaelis, B.: Enhancement of Megavoltage Images in Radiation Therapy Using Fuzzy and Neural Image Processing Techniques, FUZZY SYSTEMS IN MEDICINE, Physica-Verlag, (1999) 314-335
25. Wahl, M.: A Coded Light Approach for 3-Dimensional (3D) Vision. IBM Research Report RZ 1452 (1984)

Adaptive Segmentation of Multicoloured Documents without a Marked Background*

G. Eberhardt, S. Römer, and J. Saedler

Graphikon GmbH, Berlin (Germany)

Abstract. This is a description of procedures which allows us to decompose automatically technical documents of a field of application without previous knowledge about the colours, topology and geometry which are to be expected. These procedures have been developed for the adaptive segmentation of coloured texts and graphic structures as a premise for a later interpretation (text recognition, vectorizing) or for the decomposition of printed coloured documents in representation classes, such as texts, photo-realistic areas, graphs and background areas regarding the printing structure for a later representation of each class in a high quality standard.

1 Introduction

In spite of the rapid increase of electronic documents, there is still an important market for the interpreting (reading) of documents on paperwork as well as for the editing of these documents. The process for the first steps of the process sequence, the pre-processing of images (segmentation of colours and recognition of objects) need to be developed.

The quality of the segmentation, i.e. the separation of the objects which are to be interpreted and the treatment of the transition between those objects and the background is the decisive prerequisite for the recognition result. Whereas with grey valued documents, the image is being ensued one-dimensionally by a relatively little number of intensity values (generally up to 256), the colours in the three-dimensional space (intensity, hue, saturation) are to be segmented with a high number of values (generally up to about 16.7 millions). Aggraving to the segmentation, there is the fact that for the human eye with its limited resolution, the impression is given that homogeneous areas are being generated when printing by the stochastic arrangement of dots in different sizes with a few primary colours and different colour mixtures appear in the documents. Whereas for decades specific procedures of segmentation for grey valued images were being developed, the colour segmentation is currently presenting a scientific challenge. This is especially the case when there is no distinctive background in the document or in predefined parts and the decomposing shall not only be performed in two colour classes.

By the means of the segmentation procedures, which have been developed, it is possible to decompose adaptively coloured documents into a higher number of objects or image classes. They are to be treated equally without previous knowledge of the

---

* This research was supported by BMBF under 01IN902F/2

A. Dengel et al. (Eds.): Adaptive READ Research Project, LNCS 2956, pp. 65–90, 2004.

structure of the documents which need to be interpreted. We could use existing procedures for pre-processing and classification, especially of listing-oriented region analysis [1], [5], [6]. Apart from multicoloured text blocks and areas as well line graphics are considered in decomposition and in the building of objects. Photorealistic scenes are being recognized as such, but they are not further decomposed.

2   General Approaches to Procedures and Special Requirements to the Segmentation

Analysing systems generally do not directly work with the image of the scanned document, but they are using the results of segmentation procedures. In this case, the segmentation of an image means its decomposition into regions. The result of recombining these regions is again the total document.

The decomposition (binarisation) of a printed page into non-printed clear („white" parts of the paper (background) and the dark („black") texts (the objects which are to be analysed and recognized) is a simple, but typical example for the segmentation. If the intensity values between the background and the objects only varies in a way that they do not (or only insignificantly) overlap for an exact segmentation a single, simple threshold value i.e. is being derived from the histogram of grey values for the image.

In complex and/or faulty images (of closely neighbouring lines upon elder yellowed drawings up to coloured images of natural scenes) the recognition result does decisively depend on the quality of the segmentation. Generally valid procedures, which guarantee that the derived regions exactly correspond to the object model of the documents does not exist. The result and the procedure, which are to be selected, is determined by printing procedure, textures, noise, superposition and closely neighbouring and therewith influencing structures.

The regions fulfil homogenity criteria, such as identical or similar grey values or colours, textures or other defined modifications. They are limited by discontinuities (transitions, edges). The evaluation of these properties constitute the basis of all segmentation procedures. When segmentation according to scenes, texts and graphs, the non-existing homogenity can be used as a further criteria. In this case, you can incorporate the knowledge of the expected properties and influences as well as about dimensions, forms and neighbouring.

Already with the traditional procedures of segmentation of images by means of grey values [2], [3], there are no procedures which are generally suitable. The most essential approaches to procedures are as follows:

1. to classify by pixels according to their matching to grey value areas (determination of threshold values from local or global histograms);
2. to detect edges, i.e. to search for discontinuities as boundaries of „homogeneous" areas (regions) or in a special case to search for centres of lines when there are thin lines or wavy profiles;
3. region based procedures where the matching is determined by homogenity criteria or growth respectively disassembling processes;
4. the combination of the procedures.

The possible approaches to procedures for the processing of colours are the same, but distinctly different solutions are being required. The features do not image in a one-dimensional, but in a multidimensional space. On one hand, the multidimensionality increases the distinction of regions, but on the other hand, it requires a distinctly more complex and time-consuming procedure. The classification by pixels enlarges to a cluster analysis in a three-dimensional colour space or a separate analysis of histograms in each colour channel with a subsequent suitable evaluation.

In the colour treatment, additional difficulties are resulting from the fact that transition between regions or interferences may lead to mixed colours and that instead of the usual 256 grey values, about 16.7 million colours may appear, i.e. as well that the interferences image in the multidimensional space which needs to be analysed. At the same time, generally, distinctions of the background and objects are no longer possible, as the regions may build backgrounds as well as neighbouring objects by different colours, such as it is typical for coloured maps. The most commonly used procedure group in the grey value proceeding, which contributes the research of boundaries in the regions (edges), can practically not be used with colours, i.e. in this case it is only possible (but not as a general matter of fact) to use the differences in intensity. Furthermore, there is a need to consider the colour structures based on the printing process in a suitable way. A basic, still actual overview of procedures for colour treatment is described under point [4].

A direct segmentation with traditional procedure for instance by classifying according to similarities of their images in a colour space would not be sufficient as then, only classes of printing colours can be imaged in different intensity. Mixing considerably complicates to determine expected colours and the segmentation, so that in the development of procedures, a compromise is to be found, but especially for thin lines, which most of the texts are composed of.

As a further detail, it needs to be pointed out that during the printing process points of different sizes may be arranged stochastically in tones of yellow, cyan and magenta, so that the viewer sees certain tones as homogeneous areas. This may for instance mean that the impression of a homogeneous "white" area can result from an arrangement of points with tones of yellow, cyan and magenta. When scanning, the colour values are being mixed in accordance with the resolution with their surrounding. Modern procedures apply up to 6 more colours.

It must also be considered that the printed image which is to be segmented, is influenced and changed depending on the resolutions of the scanning functions and of the colour characters of the scanner, i.e. the colour values are averagely recorded with their surrounding. Figure 1 shows three enlarged details of the document which is selected for the demonstration with a typical background and the corresponding text or line elements. As a rule, it is to be assumed that there are no information about the arrangement of the coloured dots as well as their size and the colours used, and that only the parameters of the scanner are being known.

An analysis of the patterns would generally be possible, but it is too time-consuming for the target setting and it would only allow to determine the masks for filters or histograms in an optimum way.

The procedures had been developed for three classes of tasks, i.e.,

- to segment large-format maps in regions and the overlaying texts and graphic structure for later vectorizing [12] and text recognition to edit with CAD programs;

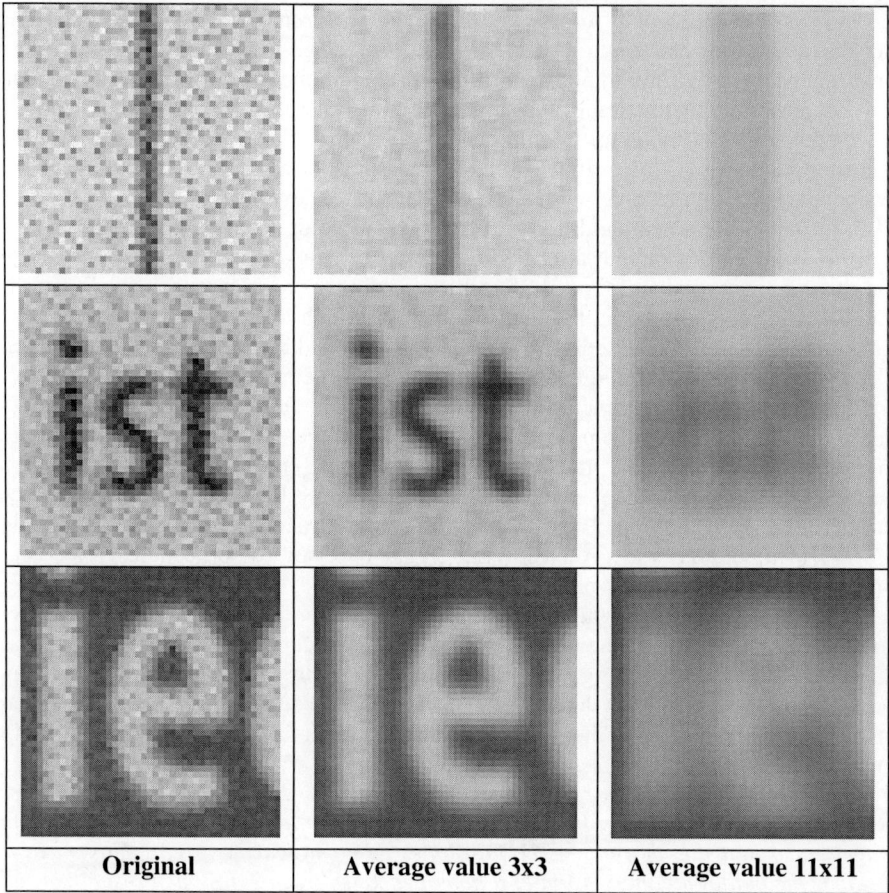

| Original | Average value 3x3 | Average value 11x11 |

Fig. 1. Details of a coloured original document which clearly show the printing matter and the smoothing by filtering (enlarged by 1:10.5)

- to segment in a suitable way into coloured printed documents with predominant text portions, texts for later recognition processes or
- to decompose them for a high-grade reproduction (reprography) in areas with mostly texts, graphic structures or photo-realistic scenes.

Due to the tremendous amount of data in coloured maps and the need to keep pace with the scanning process in text interpretation and reprographic edition in printed documents, the shortest treatment durations were an essential criteria. This requires to reduce the data quantity in earlier treatment steps and to omit a pixel-oriented treatment, both without loss of relevant information. Descriptions of the documents by region referred models and features and rule-based procedures are the used methods. Therefore, adaptive procedures had been developed, where their knowledge of regions from global segmentation steps for later fine analysis or object building are being used.

Due to the manifold of graphic structures and regions, you cannot fall back on a large number of spot samples for teaching, but you have to establish a collection of rules about the features of structures and their boundary regions and to extend them by learning during the evaluation. This includes as well back leaps into the image of the original with the knowledge gained with the interpretation (suppositions), especially in the area of mixed colours with structures or with colour changes.

Due to the different structures of the documents and objectives, different process details and –steps are required in the three classes of tasks. The procedures, which are developed to recognize the mixed pixels on the region boundaries and with thin lines, can be used in all classes of tasks. During the handling of a high-grade reproduction, it is especially essential to recognize exactly not only the line, but as well the assigned colour value.

Coloured **maps** are being formed by regions with any contours reproduced in detail. They are overlaid by texts (or other symbols) and geographical structures and often contain changings of colours and textures. For the rough segmentation, the derived or preset colour pallete on the colour images and their modifications by rule collections are used according to the specific structures of the maps.

The **printed documents** are frequently divided into blocks. Images and graphical presentations are then divided in a rectangular manner, partially by an additional frame. They often show printing columns which pass vertically over the whole document. For a reprographic reproduction, exact and smooth boundary lines of these areas are to be deducted. Another speciality is that text blocks are dominating and that relevant features are to be determined, which nearly point to the font size. Therefore it turned out to be practical to start with the analysis of text blocks, then to search for photo-realistic scenes and only in the last step to edit and to summarize the background areas.

To separate text blocks, graphs and photo-realistic scenes quickly and efficiently into binary images and to transmit the relevant features of the individual text blocks to the text recogniser. This is an assignment which is being solved for years [10]. The possibility of different treatments of the varied structures is nowadays typical for modern reprography systems for grey valued documents, without any description of procedures being found in literature. For distinctly more complex assignments of segmentation of coloured printed documents which fulfil these assignments, no procedures are known.

For the segmentation of coloured documents in image classes and for conclusions on the approximate font size, clear features are to be derived. In this way, the texts show a large amount of regularly arranged edges per each area unit. In photo-realistic areas, they are distinctly less, their gradients are less, the number of colours is distinctly higher, colours in the neighbouring text regions are similar and partial regions have irregularly formed contours. Areas produced synthetically, which image the graphical structures, show distinctly less colours, larger homogeneous areas and sharp separations (edges) between the areas. The edge pairs or centres of thin lines are characteristics for graphic structures, which continue over large areas, which can maintain as well single text characters and small photo-realistic scenes even artificially generated ones.

Generally, the background and the texts show a distinct difference in contrast. In the majority of the documents, the intensity is sufficient for the pre-segmentation. The text and the background may as well have approximately the same intensity, i.e. they can only be distinguished by their colours. Generally, the background and the characters which belong to a text block show each the same intensities and colours when the printing process is being neglected. Only beginnings of text blocks or words which are being set off are an exception. If the background for text blocks itself represents an approximately photo-realistic scene, this is being considered for the segmentation of texts and it is being identified as such. If all the image classes appear overlaid or if they are not clearly recognized, the regions are as well marked photo-realistically.

In order to reach the necessary speed and robustness, in the rough segmentation, it falls back on areas after an averaging without gliding windows (not overlapping tiles 1 x 1 mm²). Even then, the speed requirements can only be fulfilled when local histograms and/or filters with optimally separable masks (for instance gliding average value filters) are used in connection with table techniques. The fine segmentation and the verification then take place for each image class with specific procedures.

For later printing processes, the colour values are optimally transmitted for the different areas of the documents, an RIP (Raster-Image-Program) for the print editing.

3   Segmentation of Large-Scale Coloured Maps and Building of Objects

3.1   Pre-processing of Images

For the sequence of the required procedures to the pre-processing, the developed procedures are being modified [1], [5], [6] and summarized to the following course:

1. The RGB image is transformed into the **HSV space** (Hue-Saturation-Intensity), i.e. "intensity and "colour" are being united and imaged separately in a colour pyramid. This is a system which is similar to the human colour sensitivity differentiation which on one hand offers good segmentation results and on the other hand distinguishes by special clarity and easy calculability. The coloured classification can be explained by the size comparison with boundary values in the three dimensions. Different procedures are available (for colour metrical formulas, look-up tables and hash tables) according to the specific assignment.
2. The **rough segmentation** takes place in a pixel-oriented colour classification, whereas the data are being reduced to a maximum of 256 different classes. The learning of the colour classes can be performed by clicking into the digital image or by entering the boundary values and by defining the colour areas in the palette. In the result, all colour values are described by the rotation ellipsoids in the HSV space.
   The supervised and unsupervised classification as well as the combinations are implemented. Then, an rough segmentation does take place automatically by assigning each colour value which appears in a document to a single colour value (place in the colour space). If it is not part of any of the colour classes, they can be enlarged or the colour value can be assigned to a rejection class.
3. Reducing of the regions which are especially in the marginal areas of unavoidable, but interfering mixed pixels by **modal filters**. In this case, the most frequent label value is assigned to each central pixel of a gliding window, after the evaluation of a local histogram. (see figure 2)

4. Derivating of **regions** as well as the relations between them and the features. These procedures are described first under point [7] and in detail under point [1], [5]. This offers as well a hierarchy of regions as the essential features of the regions.

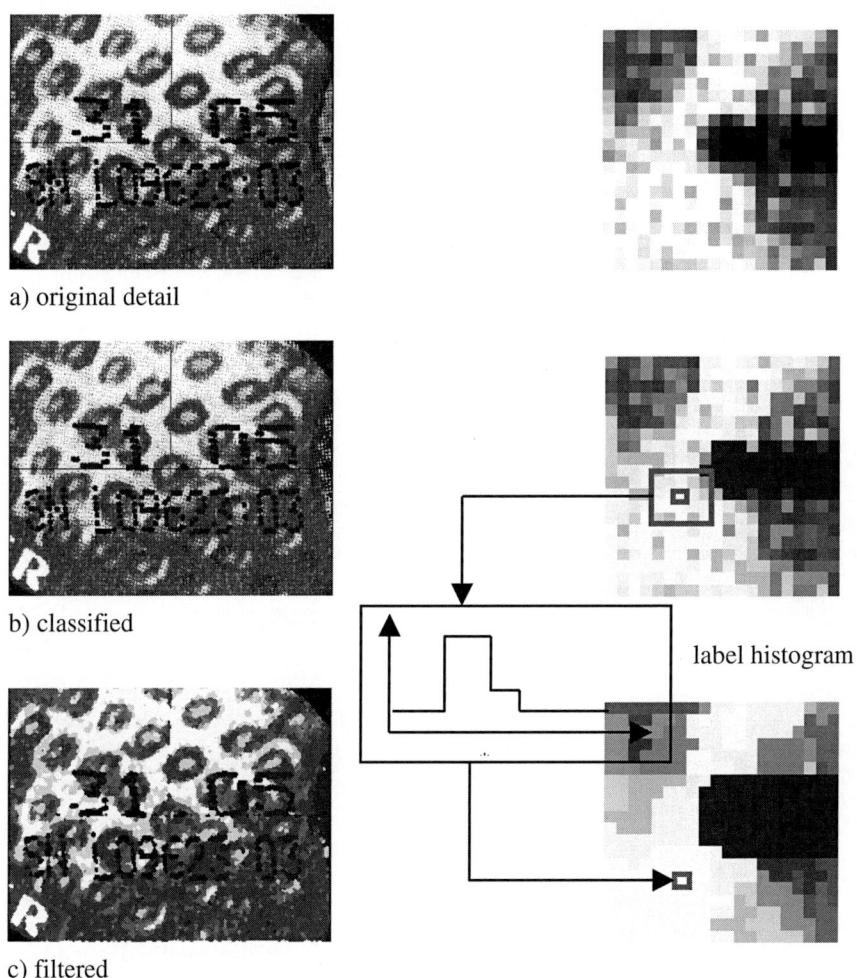

a) original detail

b) classified

label histogram

c) filtered

Fig. 2. Modal filter

The following items are at disposal for the automatic fine analysis in the result of the pre-processing:

1. Listings of all regions with the attributes (colour values) and the geometric and topological features;
2. The original image and the segmented filtered copy;
3. Statistical details of the regions such as the locations and dimensions of the rotation ellipsoids in the colour space, the distribution of the values, histograms (R, G, B) and/or (H, S, V).

The target of the fine analysis is to reduce the number of the regions and to eventually split them as accordingly, for instance, if several distinctly similar colours and mixed pixels in the region boundaries and with thin lines (text and graph) are being assigned.

3.2 Adaptation of Colour Palletes

In the procedures, it is assumed that colour palletes (figure 3) are built and saved in order to reduce colour values and to show homogeneous regions. In this case, colour palletes are understood as matrix images of look-up-tables for colour transformation. These original palletes can be derived interactively from typical documents so that they exactly correspond to the visual ideas of the viewer or are being built by an automatic classification [1]. They can be derived from a typical part, from the whole document or from sequences of them.

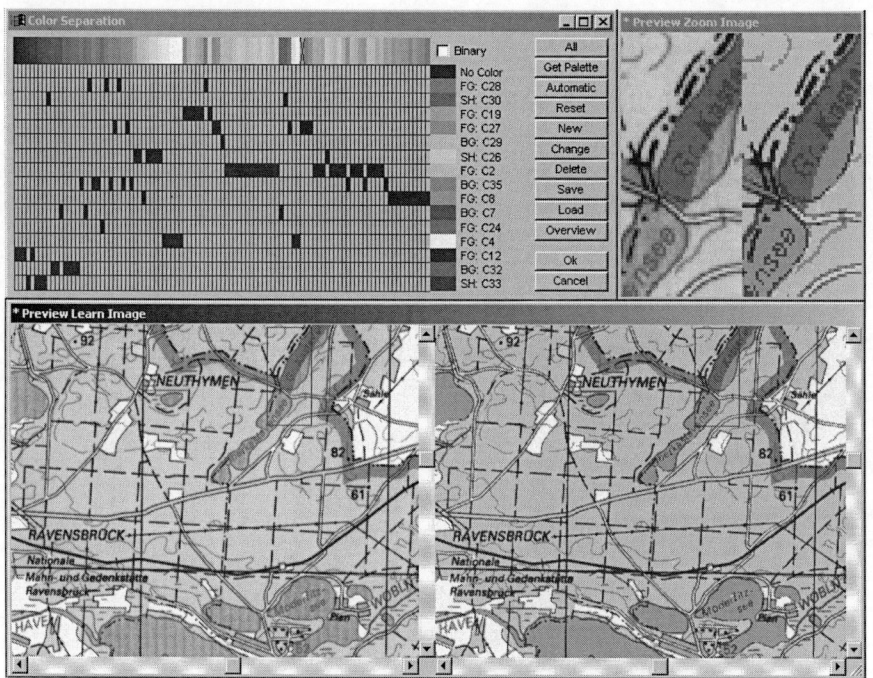

Fig. 3. Segmentation of a map detail with learned standard pallete

With the adaptive procedure, based on the existing imaging of colour values in the feature space are adapted to the specification of the document which needs to be classified, respectively to one or more relevant parts in a way that a optimum segmentation is being realized. It is realized without an essential increase in the number of classes compared to the original pallete. It should be mentioned that global statistic procedures as those which are often generally used cannot consider local distribution. This means that, for instance, a small area even with a single distinct colour value is being imaged in the feature space in the same way as the same number of single pixels spread over the document (as well as those created by colour mixtures).

The frequency of the colour values and their range of variety in the colour space differ considerably from one another in maps or different parts of those maps, i.e. mainly in the mountain areas, vegetation, developments or bodies of water. According to that, brown / white, green, red / yellow or blue colours are predominant. There might be a necessity to summarize similar values or to show as well changes of the colour values by new regions. This can be explained by using water. Small lakes or rivers can appear in a little portion of the total amount of blue pixels and must be recognized as such. Bigger bodies of water will show a higher number of different colour values (according to the depth and/or printed texts in blue colour as well as lines for the same depth).

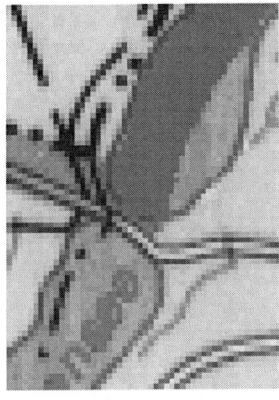
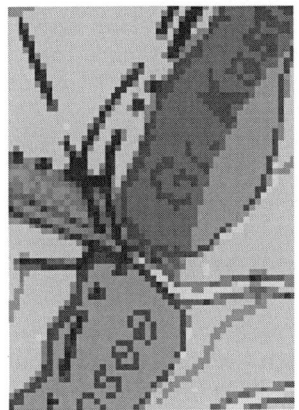

a) without adaptation (the text fades in   b) with adaptation (in the lower lake
   the upper lake due to mixture with the   there is also a better separation of the
   overlaid boundary of the district)   text)

Fig. 4. Segmentation with a pallete which is automatically adapted to an image part

The procedure which had been developed contains the following steps for the analysis and adaptation of the feature space for the document which currently needs to be segmented:

1. All pixels where the colour values belong to a rotation ellipsoid in the feature space are assigned to its central value and therewith to an existing colour class. For all further pixels, a single rejection class is built.
2. The probabilities of the distribution of colour values are inferred from the number of each class (including the rejection class) of assigned pixels.
3. Clusters, which show a minimum number of pixels being maintained and later analysed, whether they show a distinct accumulation and/or if marginal spaces are only covered to a minimum. As a result, the cluster can be decomposed to new parts, rotation ellipsoids can be minimized and/or new main axis can be determined. The pixels, which then do no longer belong to the clusters, are assigned to the rejection class.
4. The rejection class is being analysed with the described classification algorithm [1] concerning the building of new clusters and the possibility to enlarge the existing

clusters without touching the existing ones or without passing the boundary values of the number of pixels.

5. The residual quantity remains in the rejection class.

When the segmentation criteria are being fulfilled, the adaptation can be terminated after any step in the procedure. Figure 4b describes the improvement of the result of the segmentation by a pallete which is automatically adapted to the distribution and accumulation according to the result reached by the standard pallete.

3.3   Adaptation of Regions According to Specific Features

The analysis starts in the regions which are in the upper level of the hierarchy [1], [5] and where it is possible to derive a „homogeneous" area from the number of pixels and the factors of forms. The analysis is being performed by means of a one-dimensional histogram of H, S and V in the selected region (figure 5a) of the filtered original image.

The following different cases may occur:

1. All colour values of the region spread into a preset range, i.e. the region is homo-geneous, no further adaptation is necessary;
2. In one of the histograms of a region are two or more maxima, such as:
   - Textures with similar colour and intensity values,
   - Texts or lines with similar colour and intensity values,
   - Areas with different colour or intensity values,
   the region is being maintained, but it is as well decomposed to partial regions for further analysis;
3. In the histogram, the colour and intensity values are being spread approximately uniform, such as:
   - Continuous colour and intensity modifications which depend on locations
   - Unstable as well as periodical variations of colour or intensity values.

Areas with assumed textures or variations in colour or intensity are being verified roughly parting from the centre of the region by line profiles into the 4 main direc-tions and assigned by an additional attribute. The procedure is being performed in all regions where a „homogeneous" area is derived from the number of pixels and the form factors.

In the next step, the remaining regions are being analysed. They are composed by a number of small regions, often of single pixels which were built by colour mixtures. Therefore, the residual quantity is being summarized to such regions, independent from their colour value, so that they are only limited by the regions which have been already analysed. (figure 6a).

In the first partial step, all created regions are analysed which are located in a re-gion which had already been processed. Here the following cases are treated:

1. Single irregularly appearing „regions" where the area is below a boundary value are being considered as interferences and their colour value is being replaced by a value of the surrounding region;

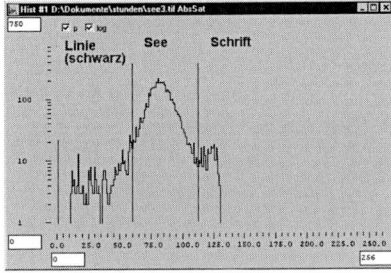

a) Region „lake"

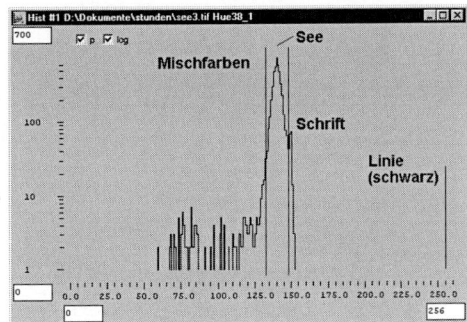

b) Histogram of colour values (H)

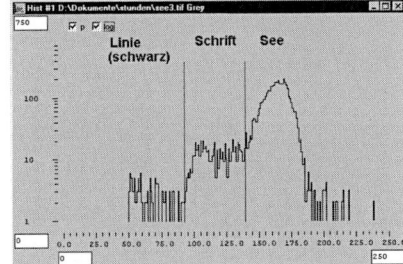

c) Histogram of saturation (S)

d) Histogram of intensity values (V)

Fig. 5. Analysis of regions

2. Single partial regions or partial regions which appear several times, where the number of pixels or the features of the form and/or which show similar distances as a pattern, to which also texts may belong, are being determined as „regions" of pattern (figure 6c) and a uniform colour value is assigned to the region where they are located;
3. Areas where the form factors describe thin long structures (for instance altitude lines) are shown as coloured thin lines or parts of those lines. A further process is performed according to paragraph 3.4.

Then the assigned regions, which are located between the summarized „areas" of pixels with different colour values, are analysed. Summarized areas where the size and form factor imply regions are shown as "coloured scenes", but with previous knowledge they can also be shown as homogeneous areas (boundary of a district with overlaid writing in figure 6b). There are mainly overlaying areas between the regions. The mixed colours are derived from the colours of the surrounding regions and can show further colours, for instance to highlight contours (figure 6c). Those areas are building thin lines, which are further processed according to paragraph 3.4.

As a result, there is a segmentation into regions with additional attributes (such as texture, scene, pattern, local colour modification) as well as into „regions" where the form factor is shown as thin lines and as well as transition areas of regions. The figure 6d shows the result of the segmentation of figure 4b with the derived overlaid colour areas, where the non-processed classes (streets, ways, black boundary lines) are shown in white.

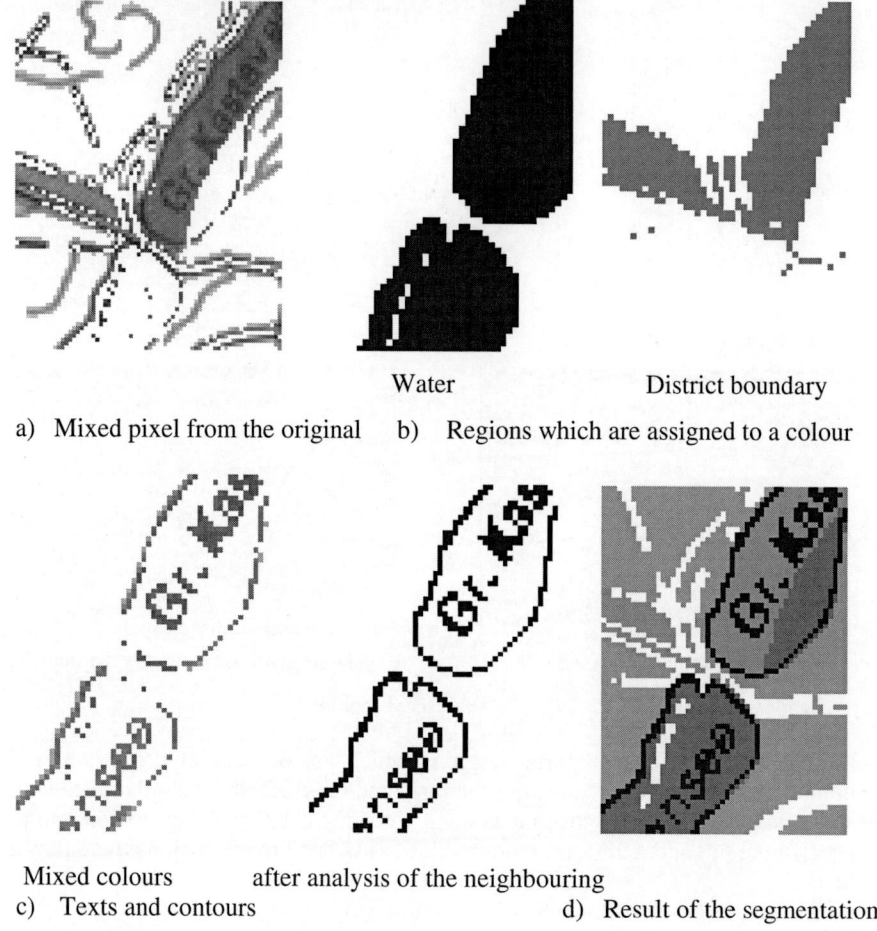

a) Mixed pixel from the original   b)   Regions which are assigned to a colour

Mixed colours   after analysis of the neighbouring
c)   Texts and contours   d)   Result of the segmentation

Fig. 6. Fine analysis of mixed colours

3.4   Derivation of Thin Lines

A procedure is used as a basis for the fine analysis which had been successfully developed for the derivation of highly disturbed holographic interference fringes in grey value images [8], [9]. In this case, the local characteristics of the lines of the intensity profile G(i,j) is used analogous to the visual analysis. The lines are interpreted similar to the viewing of mountain areas as a systematic sequence of ridges, slopes and valleys, whereas the peaks or hollows (interferences) or plateaus (homogeneous regions) may appear. The ridges and valleys characterize the course of the lines, the slopes characterize their width.

For the extraction of the features, the difference between each pixel (i,j) in a region and its 8 neighbouring pixels which are symmetrically located around (i,j) in a digital distance R, is being calculated. The differences are compared to the predefined threshold value T.

If $| G(i,j) - G(i+R, j+R)| \geq T$, a bit is placed into a byte, so that with the neighbouring relation can be shown with its 8 bits. Otherwise, the "0" is maintained in position of the bit. In this case, the entry is performed in a 1st byte when the difference is positive (mountain, ridge, and slope) and in a 2nd byte when the difference is negative (hollow, valley).

The code in byte for the neighbouring relations is described in figure 7. The 256 possible codes can be reduced to 36 rotationinvariant patterns. Depending on the line width which is expected, the radius R may be selected differently. You may as well work with several radiuses in order to verify or to adapt automatically to different widths. In order to get correct results at the same time are useful to perform the segmentation of the 8 neighbouring regions by two orientation angles (0° and 22.5°) and then to combine the results according to figure 7b. The evaluations is quickly and simply performed by look-up-tables.

Whereas the variations of the grey values on images in the grey value area are one-dimensional, those of the colour values in the feature space are three-dimensional. In this case, there is basically the possibility to derive the difference of the colour values of the pixels which need to be compared from the difference of the feature vectors. There remains a difficulty in the evaluation of the differences in the multidimensionality. This means among others that different colours may for instance show the same intensity.

Experiments have shown that separate building of the differences for H,S, and V and then the derivation of the assumption for the assignment of a pixel to the ridge, valley, mountain / hollow or slope leads to the best results. You can then infer the classification from the assumption of any central point. In the analysis, you can take the following as a standing point that:

1. By the form of the region you can derive with high possibility that there are lines and where to expect the centre of the lines;
2. It is useful to enlarge the area which is to be analysed by some pixels which are presented by parameters;
3. The assigned colour values of the surrounding regions are known as expected values, which allows,
   - To consider the matching of colour values when building the differences to the regions;
   - To conclude from the colour profiles which are to be expected to the transition areas;
   - To consider modifications of colours and intensity in the course of lines over different regions (for the verification, it is essential to incorporate a second larger radius, where the pixels are located in the surrounding region).

From the known values of the surrounding regions you can derive with no doubt if there are lines with their own colour values or transition areas between regions and then to which region the analysed pixel is being assigned. It is facilitated by the added possibility, to preset expectance values for all lines and then to assign the detected colour values to the most similar preset value. If this is not the case, an average colour and intensity value is assigned to all pixels shown as ridge or valley in the region which is been analysed. Therewith, controlled by parameters (expected line width, enlargement of the preset number of pixels or building of an average width), a part of the pixels of the line which belong to the slopes and of the surrounding area are being assigned. With this new developed procedure of special „thin" coloured lines, an important improvement of the segmentation has been reached compared to traditional procedures. (figure 6c).

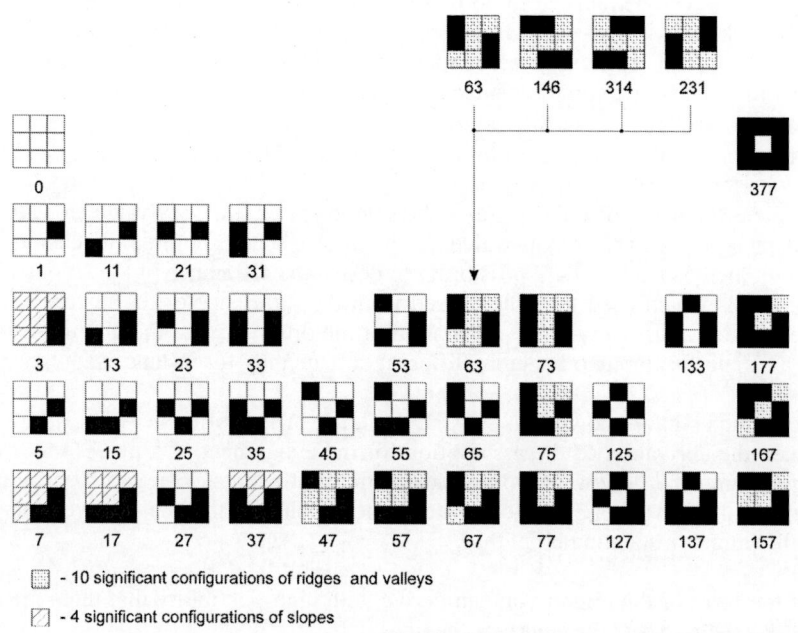

a) 36 rotationinvariant octale pattern candidates

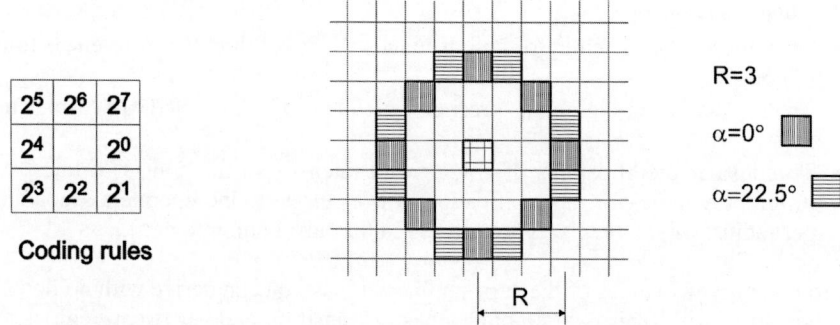

b)   Distribution of the 8 neighbouring pixel for the orientation of the angles α=0°and α=22,5° and a distance R=3

Fig. 7. Code pattern

Fig. 8. Printed and scanned coloured document (original, scaled down)

4 Segmentation of Coloured Documents in Image Classes

4.1 Derivation of Relevant Features for the Segmentation in Image Classes

After the scanning, a digital copy of the document is being created with about 8 to 23 million pixels in the format DIN A4 and 300 to 500 dpi with 24 bits (RGB) each. Figure 8 shows a typical printed document.

For this assignment it is not necessary to perform transformation for a rough segmentation. You can directly work in the RGB colour space. In order to minimize the influence of the colour spots created in the printing process, you can guide a small average value filter (3 x 3 or 5 x 5) over the whole document (figure 1). The average value is being built by separate addition in the three colour channels and an assignment in the colour space by look-up tables.

The number of edges per area or length unit (figure 9) are the relevant features to distinguish the segments of the document. For the majority of the text areas, a reliable derivation of edges from the intensity values (grey values) is sufficient [9], [11]. In some cases it is only possible to distinguish the colour areas by the edges. Therefore, general edge filters are used in the colour area.

In order to quickly detect the edges in the original of a scanned document, filters with a size 3 x 3 pixels are used which are optimised for vertical and horizontal edges. For the description of the filter function, the following nomenclature is used:

$$\begin{pmatrix} R_{00} \\ G_{00} \\ B_{00} \end{pmatrix} \begin{pmatrix} R_{01} \\ G_{01} \\ B_{01} \end{pmatrix} \begin{pmatrix} R_{02} \\ G_{02} \\ B_{02} \end{pmatrix}$$

$$\begin{pmatrix} R_{10} \\ G_{10} \\ B_{10} \end{pmatrix} \begin{pmatrix} R_{11} \\ G_{11} \\ B_{11} \end{pmatrix} \begin{pmatrix} R_{12} \\ G_{12} \\ B_{12} \end{pmatrix}$$

$$\begin{pmatrix} R_{20} \\ G_{20} \\ B_{20} \end{pmatrix} \begin{pmatrix} R_{21} \\ G_{21} \\ B_{21} \end{pmatrix} \begin{pmatrix} R_{22} \\ G_{22} \\ B_{22} \end{pmatrix}$$

The use of the simple combination of the operator for average value and differences has proved that advantages compared to the Sobel operator as the higher impact effect of low pass has slightly reduced the interfering dithering. The enlargement of the operators in the calculation of the vertical edges (gradient in x-direction) in the RGB colour space and of the horizontal edges (gradient in y-direction) are shown in the following equation.

$$DX_{11,R} = (R_{02} + R_{12} + R_{22}) - (R_{00} + R_{10} + R_{20})$$
$$DX_{11,G} = (G_{02} + G_{12} + G_{22}) - (G_{00} + G_{10} + G_{20})$$
$$DX_{11,B} = (B_{02} + B_{12} + B_{22}) - (B_{00} + B_{10} + B_{20})$$

$$DX_{11} = \max \left\{ DX_{11,R}, DX_{11,G}, DX_{11,B} \right\}$$

$$DY_{11,R} = (R_{20} + R_{21} + R_{22}) - (R_{00} + R_{01} + R_{02})$$
$$DY_{11,G} = (G_{20} + G_{21} + G_{22}) - (G_{00} + G_{01} + G_{02})$$
$$DY_{11,B} = (B_{20} + B_{21} + B_{22}) - (B_{00} + B_{01} + B_{02})$$

$$DY_{11} = \max \left\{ DY_{11,R}, DY_{11,G}, DY_{11,B} \right\}$$

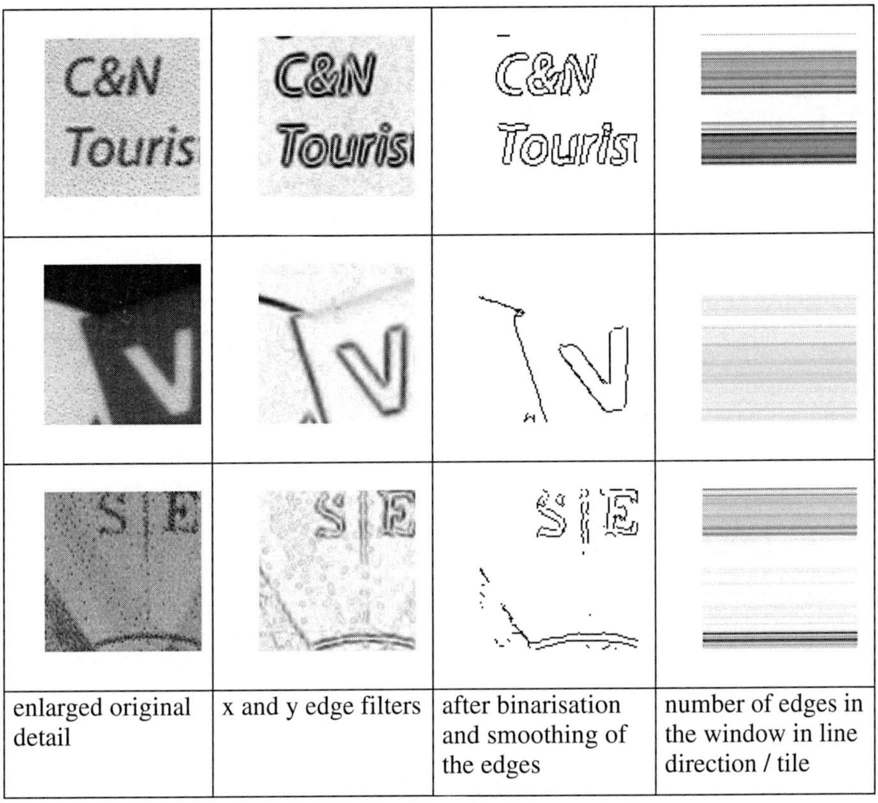

enlarged original detail	x and y edge filters	after binarisation and smoothing of the edges	number of edges in the window in line direction / tile

a) Derivation of edges in details (enlarged)

b) Number of edges per window (scaled down) in x- and y-direction

c) Number of edges in x-direction with 10x10 mm gliding average value filter over 11x11 tiles (scaled down)

Fig. 9. Edges as features for image classes

A second feature results from a comparison of average colours between small, not overlapping image areas (tiles) of the document. Independent from the resolution in scanning, the absolute values between 1 x 1 and 2 x 2 mm² (from 12 x 12 to 40 x 40 pixels) have proved to be an optimum size for these tiles. It is not necessary to determine each colour value in a time consuming manner by averaging the colours of its surrounding, but it is sufficient to calculate the average value of each tile. Therewith, in the rough segmentation, the factor 144 to 1.600 is reached by reducing the number of pixels which are to be evaluated.

To verify the photo-realistic scenes, the gradients are entered as the third feature. The majority of the gradients in continuous transition is smaller that in areas with text or graphs. It is useful to derive a fourth feature by line filters (see 3.4) as well by using the colour values as thin lines and graphs, which are mainly composed by them, and they can only be located in this way. As these filters locate the central line pixels (skeletons), they additionally allow to reflect the colour values as well in text areas which are mixed to a minimum scale with the colour values of the background. Edge pairs (edges with increasing and decreasing slopes in the line profile) are used to recognize broad lines as a fifth feature.

4.2   Rough Segmentation in Different Image Classes

The segmentation is performed by the features assigned to each central pixel of each tile in windows with sufficient size. The summarized original values are significantly more robust towards local interferences and characteristics in great increases in speed than the processing by pixels. In result, each of the segments of the document is described by a rectangular area or by a polygon where the basic attributes such as text as well as further derived features which may be useful for the fine analysis for the printing process or the text interpretation are being assigned. Please note that a certain inclination of the documents is unavoidable and it is determined in the recognition process. The steps which are to be performed, are:

(1) Recognition of Text Blocks

First, it is started with text blocks, as they form the largest part of the printed area and they are most easy to recognize. By a text block, we understand a sequence of alphanumeric characters which show at least 2 text lines or it is valued as one text line (headline, caption). It is assumed that the line is almost horizontal.

The segmentation is performed by statistic procedures of the distribution of edges. In this case, the size of the windows is limited by the expected dimension of the text blocks. The following dimensions resulted to be useful: 30 x 30 mm² (i.e. also 30 x 30 tiles) for general and 30 x 10 mm² as well as 10 x 10 mm² for further analysis. Due to the relatively low number of tiles, a gliding window is used, i.e. in the window, the sum of the edge pixels of the surrounding is assigned to each central tile.

First, the window 30 x 30 mm² which contains the highest number of edges is evaluated. By building a gliding window, it is assumed that it is located within a text block. If the window is completely located within a text block, it will overlap 5 to 12 text lines, which contain 10 to 20 characters per line. The number of edges within each line and within each column, which are created by the tiles, are being calculated within the overlapped area.

By the following general rules, a periodical is derived from the number of edges per line:

1. Upper line (capitals, points on the i and mutated vowels as well as d, f, h, k, l, t) with a few edges;
2. First lines of lowercase letters with a local maximum of horizontal and with a few vertical edges;
3. Lines within the lowercase letters with a high almost constant number of vertical edges;
4. Lowest line of the majority of letters with vertical and additionally horizontal edges (but the latter being considerably less than under point (2));
5. Lower lines with no or only a few edges (g, p, q).

The number of edges will be almost equal in all columns which are not overlapped by the window as the spaces between the words for all lines will not be located in one column. Except for the columns which do not contain any edges and are considered as block boundaries.

Features for the text blocks are derived from the evaluated data:

1. The number of edges in the lines / length unit;
2. The number of edges in all lines, which are limited by the two background lines / length unit (i.e. the edges in a paragraph of the text line);
3. The periodicy, i.e. the space between the background lines respectively to verify between the lines which contain most of the edges.

If there are columns in an area which is overlapped by the window, which show no or considerably more edges than the average of the other columns (possible edges of photo-realistic images), these columns and all columns which are further away from the centre are not included in the calculation. The empty columns are shown as boundary lines of the text block.

Each line which does not contain any edges can limit the text block at the top and at the bottom, but it cannot be assumed as boundary of the text block without any further analysis. As such lines also separate the text lines, a new calculation of the edge numbers in the lines above the line without edges is being performed. If more than the double number of lines without edges and/or a line with values which are deviating distinctly from the calculated statistics (image edge, other text structure) are being located, the horizontal boundary of the text bock is assigned to the first upper or bottom line without edges. If the upper and bottom boundary lines are found, the boundaries are prolonged in a way that they build a closed contour. All tiles evaluated in the result of the rough segmentation are marked to be part of a first text region.

If the area which is overlapped by the window is evaluated, the procedure described is repeated in the neighbouring windows. Then, the procedure is repeated step by step in the adjacent windows above and below the evaluated area, until the text block is completely marked. The same procedure is performed for all regions where the number of edges is above a boundary value. Areas which do not show clear characteristics of text structures are rejected as non-processed areas. Then, the procedure is performed with slightly modified rules in the smaller windows in order to find headlines and captions.

(2) Photo-Realistic Image

The remaining areas which contain edges are photo-realistic images, graphical structures or transitions between homogeneous areas. Photo-realistic images are often clearly limited from the background so that there is a clear accumulation of edges in their boundary areas. Within some of these images, modifications in colour and intensity occur in such a continuous way that only a little quantity of edges is found with the procedures which we described up to now. Only the boundaries of partial regions with similar colours offer a firm sufficient quantity of edges. They are easily derived within the images by using threshold values (as well as equidensities). As in this case, content-based thresholds are not necessary for instance for the research of objects, but which are only needed for the derivation of statistic values in order to prove photorealistic images, the threshold values can be derived arbitrarily from the histograms.

When verifying the photo-realistic images, the amounts of the gradients of the edges which were already derived in former steps and the threshold values of additionally built edges are incorporated. The latter edges are treated as edges with small gradients without being exactly determined.

As a basis for the first possible photo-realistic segment, the window 30 x 30 mm² is selected from the areas which are not yet marked in the document that contain the highest number of edges derived by the 3x3 filter. Here, columns and lines with the maximum number of edges are researched. In order to prevent it from displacement of edge pixels, caused by possible effects by slants of the documents and of mixed colours, the values are evaluated from each 3 summarized lines and each 3 columns of tiles.

If such a sequence of edges has been found, this could also be a line segment of a graphical structure or a boundary of homogeneous regions. If edge pairs are found which are located in the area that is overlapped by the window, it is marked as an assumed segment with graphical structure. If this is not the case, and if the neighbouring areas do not show any characteristics of inhomogeneous areas (other edges), the segment is being marked as boundary between homogeneous areas. In order to control this, the window is selected where a segment boundary is located at the centre. In both areas of the window, which is separated by the segment boundary, an analysis is then realized. Therefore, the number of different colours of the gradients as well as of the edges and edge pairs are determined. If a boundary of a photo-realistic area is being derived, within them, an evaluation of the neighbouring window is continued so far that its boundaries are completely found.

Then, these segments are verified by an analysis of the histograms and by the distribution of the edges / edge pairs as well as of the colour profiles in selected lines and columns. If there is a high number of colours, continuous colour modifications and only a few edges with large gradients or no systematic sequence of edge pairs, a classification to the class of photo-realistic image is being performed.

The procedure is repeated with a smaller window until all remaining segments, which are limited to the background by edges, have been analysed and marked. The edges which then are still not assigned to a segment, can show interferences or smallest structures which are not clear or areas which are not limited to photo-realistic areas by any contour line as well as graphical structures. When analysing these areas, only the above described procedure is used for the verification.

(3) Lines and Graphical Structures

Partial step 3.1   Building of segments with „thin" lines
„Thin" lines, which shall limit or highlight larger printing areas in the documents, have not yet been included in the segmentation process. In the areas, which had not been marked yet, gliding windows of 5 x 30 mm² and 30 x 5 mm², which contain at least 5 central points of thin lines, are marked as a segment of thin lines. In this case, all adjacent windows, which contain such a segment, are summarized to one image area.

Partial step 3.2   Building of segments with graphical structures
In the segments, which had probably been marked as graphical structures in the step (2) lines are mainly researched by edge pairs and centres of thin lines and for boundaries of homogeneous areas by edges.

Generally, for the rough segmentation it would be sufficient to describe all remaining areas where there are edges by the smallest possible rectangular and to show it as image class of graphical structures. But this would for instance lead to the fact that each remaining symbol (text character, dash) would build an isolated area and two vertically located lines would be summarized to one rectangular image. It is useful, to recognize already at that stage areas which are connected in content and to mark them. This evaluation is being performed in windows of 5 x 30 mm² and 30 x 5 mm², which are built by the non-overlapping tiles. It starts by the window which contains most of the edges, edge pairs and line centres. If this is a window of 5 x 30 mm², it may be assumed that it contains a nearly horizontal segment of a line or of a transition of homogeneous areas. In order to verify this, a window of 30 x 5 mm² is being superimposed on the centre of the horizontal window. Therewith, the edge pairs of broad lines, the general course of the lines and transitions as well as details of segment boarders are being derived.

The analysis is being continued step by step in the line to the left, then to the right until the segment borders are found. Then, the same procedure is being performed in all adjacent lines, which have not yet been analysed in the vertical window, until all region borders are found. When the segment is completely built, its borders are being described by a rectangular or by a polygon which marks the area and assigns the derived features.

The procedure is being repeated until all tiles of the image class which contain edges or lines are classified to graphical structures or are marked as interfering point. If a vertical window contains most of the edges and lines, the analyse is being started analogues to the described procedures in vertical direction.

(4) Detection of the Background Segments

After marking all regions which contain texts and photo-realistic or graphical images, only background segments remain for the further segmentation. They are composed of relatively small, but not unconditionally of connected areas which are located between the classified segments as well as between them and in the marginal areas of the document. The colours of the background are generally mainly bright (white, light grey, yellow) or very saturised (red, green) in order to realize high contrast to the text areas and to the graphical structures. The different colour combinations are selected in a way that they are distinctly different and the number of different colours in the background is quite little.

In order to determine that it belongs to a segment, in the majority of the documents it is sufficient to use the similarity or the modification of the colour values in comparison to the neighbouring. It had been decided that a general and firm procedure is the automatic cluster analysis [1], especially as the interferences by mixed pixels in the transition areas or by small structures cannot be excluded. In this cluster analyses, all colours of the central points of the non-overlapping tiles are imaged in the corresponding coordinates of the RGB colour space. Ideally, all colours of a „homogeneous" (monochrome) background are imaged in one point. The spreading of these values is building a cloud of points in form of an approximate rotation ellipsoid around this point. By using the frequencies and the distances in the coloured space, for each new assigned value it is controlled if it shall be part of the existing or if a new rotation ellipsoid shall be built. As before this step, any photo-realistic images and mixed pixels are mainly excluded, small rotation ellipsoids are built, which may easily be separated. The centres of the rotation ellipsoids are then unambiguously define the colours of the corresponding background.

Ellipsoids which are built by a few tiles show interferences or fine structures. These remaining areas are further examined after slight smoothing out in the fine segmentation.

4.3   Fine Segmentation and Finishing

In this step, mainly the texts and the graphical structures must be separated precisely from their surrounding background. Here, the characters and lines are assigned to uniform and correct colours and the line widths (as well that of the text elements) which correspond approximately to the original printing. Furthermore, the transitions between backgrounds have to be smoothed with different colours and to photo-realistic scenes, and that in a way that the original geometry is being copied. The last partial assignment is to forward not rectangular limited photo-realistic images and small structures in a suitable way to the printing program or to remove artefacts.

(1) Segmentation of Text and Background

A previous mixture of colours of the printing pattern is unavoidable. But there is the disadvantage that the majority of the texts is composed by thin lines and their colour values are being mixed with colours from the background when the influence of the dots is being removed at a certain size of the window. Before the segmentation is being performed, it is at least centred with a 3 x 3 filter. Already then, the colours of the text characters are dragged in direction of those of the background. The disadvantage is reduced by growing font.

But there are as well usable advantages for a segmentation:

- The colours of the background and of the text highly deviate from one another.
- There are always homogeneous partial areas, which allow to clearly determine the colours which are to be expected.
- The text blocks show only a few target colours beside the background colour, in general only one. Other colours will only be used to highlight single characters or words and distinguish themselves distinctly from the other colours of the text.

In the first partial step, the background colour is being determined. Therefore, the colours of all tiles in the colour space are being copied which belong to the lines which do not contain any edges. The central colour value of the therewith built rotation ellipsoid is being compared to the colour value of the background area surrounding the text block. If there is a sufficient similarity between these colour values, the colour value of the background segment is selected for the whole text block. Otherwise, the colour value which is determined from the lines between the text is being used.

In the second partial step, the colour values of the text blocks are determined and therefore transmitted to the colour space. Here it is expected that the different colours of the text are each imaged in distinctly separable clusters. If this is the case, the central point of each rotation ellipsoid is being determined. Otherwise, the procedure is repeated with a 5 x 5 filter. By the preset point of the background and the centres of the other rotation ellipsoids the straight lines are placed. In order to prevent from the influence of the colours which are to a high level mixed with the background, all colours in each rotation ellipsoid, which are projected to a straight line between the point of intersection of this straight line with its cover and its central point, are not included in the calculation of the target colour. The colours of the texts are then determined by the central points of the reduced clusters.

In the third partial step, the preparation of the segmentation is more centered with a larger filter (7 x 7 or 9 x 9 pixels), in order to completely eliminate the influence of the printing pattern. From the centred colour values, the ellipsoids are then again built and the separation of text and background is performed according to the described classification procedure [1]. In order to verify this separation, the colour values, which are located in the positions of the derived edges, are additionally included. Finally, all pixels which are assigned to the text are classified to the colour values which are determined in the second partial step by means of look-up-tables.

In the last partial step, if the background colours vary from text blocks and the surrounding, the course of the transition of the background areas are corrected pixel by pixel. Finally, the classified colours of all text blocks which show the same background and similar character structure are being compared. If the similarity criteria is fulfilled, these text blocks are assigned to an average colour.

(2) Finishing of Photo-Realistic Areas

In this image class, only the marginal areas of the segments are to be checked and eventually corrected. The colours of the pixels in the marginal areas of the image, which show colours of the background, are corrected. A further smoothing of the edge area of this region is renounced. This might lead to changes in the photo-realistic copy as its other pixels are transmitted to the printing process without any change.

In photo-realistic scenes which cannot be limited by a rectangle, but by simple geometrical structural elements (arcs, ellipses, splines), a corresponding approximation of the contour is taking place. An eventually remaining quantity of photo-realistic images are copied with a non-modified contour pixel by pixel.

(3) Segmentation of Thin Lines of the Homogeneous Background

The regions, which are pre-segmented with thin lines, separate or frame nearly exclusively printing colours or multicoloured background areas of the document. Therefore, there are almost only long axis-parallel lines, whereas even closely neighbouring and parallel lines, even with different colours, can be printed. Conditions and procedures correspond to those which had already been described in the segmentation of text and background so that we can renounce from a repetition in this place. Furthermore, the specific demands to the segmentation are described in detail under paragraph 3.4.

Compared with the text segmentation, the special conditions are:

- The lines are generally thinner as the elements of fine text structures, i.e. the colours are more mixed with those of the background. In this way, pixels which belong to thin lines could in the segmentation be assigned to the background colour. Variations of the line width are distinctly visible in the printed image. The course in a line segment is interpolished in a way that it is imaged as a sequence of adjacent pixels of the same colour with correct corners and uniform widths.
- The lines will have – apart from some exceptions – uniform colours between beginning-, end-, corner- and branching points and such points where the lines are distinctly widened (each called line segment). Changes in colours over the line course are checked in each line segment and if there are colour changes, these line segments are marked for a photo-realistic copy.
- Thin lines can pass over several background segments. By this change in colour, the colour of the thin line is as well modified. In this case, the line is being divided into segments and the changed colour value is being used for the reproduction.

All line segments with uniform colours and with the same width are marked as a segment of the class with thin lines and the derived attributes are being assigned.

(4) Segmentation of Graphical Structures

Areas which are marked as graphical structure, can show thin and broad lines, single text characters and/or words, homogeneous areas and small photo-realistic regions. Then, all graphical structural elements and colours can be overlapped, but as well classed separately with different portions. These classes, frequencies and reflections in an area depend on the kind of graphical presentation such as drawing or line diagram, surface diagram (for instance pie chart), whereas even here the most different combinations may occur. A pre-classification according to these kinds of presentations would lead to a high number of variations, but not to a general solution. Especially the demand in short periods in the treatment for an optimum printing copy, prevents from the use of such further classification. These segmentation assignments are useful, so that the graphical structures are as clearly arranged as possible for the viewer and therewith only a few colours and distinct transitions are favoured.

In the first partial step, another segmentation is being performed, but it is limited to the pre-classified area which is to be analysed and the expectation of the appearance of a high amount of homogeneous areas, where as well broad lines are counted among and a relatively little number of different colours. In general, the procedures which had been described above are being used.

The verification of the line structures is performed similar to the text segmentation described under step (1) for each connected partial region line graphic. The only difference to the text classifications is that the expectation values of the colours of the broad lines in the colour space do not have to be corrected, as in their centres there are sufficient values which are expected, which do not contain any mixed colours and that a line segment as well as a background region may show several colours. After the classifications, the contours of all lines and the colour values of the single pixels which deviate from the most frequent colour value are being replaced by it. If distinct colour differences are determined into a line segment, it is marked non-processed as photo-realistic region.

The line graphics can contain as well text segments. They show, apart from some exceptions, features, which allow us to distinguish between single words, characters and symbols of lines. Each character can describe a rectangle, where the size is being limited by the font. Additional features for the characters or other symbols are a high density of end- and branch points as well as of the curvature values. If characters are found, they are marked as such and it is tried to assign the same colour to each text block. Furthermore, from the order of the rectangle, the sense of the writing is roughly being derived which must not be parallel to the text lines in the graphical presentation.

(5) Corrections of Homogeneous Areas in the Printed Document

The contour areas of all homogeneous regions are checked pixel by pixel on their classification and if necessary, their classification is being corrected. All pixels are to be analysed, which are located in the tiles which build the contours of homogeneous areas as well as the adjacent pixels in photo-realistic areas and in transition areas to lines, if they do not belong to another region. This is being performed in an iterative way for each pixel and is limited directly to the contour which belongs to the background or which had been assigned to the background during an analysis. If the colour value is similar to the colour value of the background, it is assigned. Therefore, the colour changes of these suitable colour mixtures in the transition areas to the lines and other background areas are being taken into consideration.

In another partial step, it is checked whether there are included or adjacent smallest photo-realistic areas, they are then evaluated as artefacts and assigned to the homogeneous areas. The boundary areas between regions are smoothed by using edges and determined in previous steps. If necessary, approximated by straight lines or arcs.

In a final step, all background areas (without lines located in between) are included in the analysis of the colour spreading in horizontal and vertical lines after smoothing. Thereof, it is determined if in there areas there are continuous colour modifications (which may also have lead to the separation) or point out to systematic modification of textures. If that's the case, in these areas the corresponding features are additionally assigned. They can then be assigned as a photo-realistic image class or as homogeneous background by means of the preset parameters .

As a result of these steps, the document is completely segmented and the characteristics of the regions are described by features for an optimum copy or interpretation. Regions which are not unambiguously verified are assigned to the photo-realistic image class.

References

[1] Saedler, J.; Handschack, P.; Schlegel, J.: Analyse und Interpretation farbiger Dokumente, in Abschlußbericht READ (Förderprojekt 01 IN 503F), 1998
[2] Pischel, R.: Segmentierung Digitaler Bilddaten, Dissertationsschrift 1990, Institut für Kosmoswissenschaften
[3] Haralick, R., M.; Shapiro, L., G.: Image Segmentation Techniques, in Computer Vision, Graphics and Image Processing, 1985
[4] Rehrmann, V.: Stabile, echtzeitfähige Farbbildauswertung, Koblenzer Schriften zur Informatik, Band 1, 1994
[5] Eberhard, G.; Saedler, J.; Schlegel, J.: Farbbildverarbeitung für großformatige Dokumente, in Tagungsband zum 6. Workshop Farbbildverarbeitung der Gesellschaft zur Förderung angewandter Informatik e.V., Okt. 2000
[6] Patentschrift DE44 93 95: Verfahren und Einrichtung zur Analyse und Verarbeitung von Farbbildern, Graphikon GmbH, 1994
[7] Mandler, E.; Oberländer, M., E.: One-pass Encoding of connected Components in Multi-Valued Images, International Conference on Pattern Recognition, Atlantic City, 1990
[8] Eichhorn, N.; Osten, W.: An algorithm for the fast derivation of line structures from interferograms, Journal of Modern Optics, 1988, Vol. 35, No. 10, 1717-1725
[9] Kiesewetter, H.; Osten, W.; Saedler, J.: Automatische Ableitung und Verarbeitung von Linienbildern, Informationstechnik it, R. Oldenburg Verlag 1990, Heft 6, Seite 376-386
[10] Lange, T.; Gimsa, M.: Verfahren zur automatischen Trennung von Text- und Fotodokumenten in Bürodokumenten, Diplomarbeit, TU Magdeburg 1992
[11] Eichhorn, N.; Kiesewetter, H.: Grundsätze zur Detektion von Konturen, Bild und Ton 41, 1988, Heft 3, Seite 69-74
[12] Vectory 5.0, Nutzerhandbuch, Graphikon GmbH, 2002

Recognition of Short Handwritten Texts

Michael Boldt and Christopher Asp

AB+M GmbH, Haid-und-Neu-Str. 7,
76131 Karlsruhe, Germany
{mboldt, casp}@abm.de

Abstract. Building on our 10-year-experience with script recognition systems, a new reader generation was designed. Previously, only single handwritten words were compared against a dictionary. Now a short text is modeled and processed as a whole. The system does not proceed in a linear fashion anymore, but uses feedback between image processing, character recognition and syntactic alignment. The system features a new recognition kernel that works without prior segmentation and is based on geometric form descriptors.

1 Introduction

Automatic reading systems are now widely used in postal, office and even industrial applications. However, the recognition rate will reach really satisfactory levels only if all conditions are right: If the 'writing' is well localized, pretty much complete, undisturbed and easily separable from the background, and if the syntactical context is rather narrowly defined. All these requirements hold especially for the most difficult task – the recognition of handwritten text. And as always, users' demands are increasing faster than developers can deliver. Thus our task is the development of a much more flexible system, that adapts much more to the current context and that is not 'derailed' by small perturbations.

The first of the following sections introduces our framework for document recognition and embeds script recognition in that framework. Next we analyze the specific weaknesses of current script recognition systems and call for remedies. Summaries of our work in image processing, feature extraction, form recognition and syntax processing follow. Finally, the results reached so far are discussed.

2 Script Recognition as Part of a Document Recognition System

In addition to handwriting, most documents contain machine print, but also barcodes, logos and other graphical elements. A practical system should handle all these different objects in a unified manner, but this is beyond the scope of this paper. Instead we concentrate on the written parts.

A. Dengel et al. (Eds.): Adaptive READ Research Project, LNCS 2956, pp. 91–102, 2004.
© Springer-Verlag Berlin Heidelberg 2004

In order to construct a recognition system, we must understand the generating processes which takes us from the intention of the writer to the ink on the paper, i.e. the transformations from the contents (the semantics) to the appearance (the gestalt) performed by several syntactical and other formatting steps. Each transformation from a higher, more abstract to a lower, more concrete level usually offers many choices (and is prone to error). This multitude of possible representations and the fact that a lower level object can be generated from several higher level ones makes recognition so difficult to model and implement.

In the following we describe briefly the main abstraction levels. We use the term 'schema' (sometimes also 'model') for a description of all possible appearances of an object at one level. A specific example is called 'instance'.

Semantic schemata. This level relates to the meaning and describes the inner, logical structure of the content of a document class or a part thereof. It consists of a set of conceptual schemata (notions), which determine the kind of user data. In practice these are often defined by records in a data base. Each conceptual schema gets a name (e.g. 'address', 'family name') that is unique within a semantic schema. It constitutes an independent unit in respect of content. It is usually not atomic, but structured itself.

Let us look at the concept 'date' as an example. Let us assume that a document contains two dates, a date of birth and a date of issue. Both concepts build on the same schema 'date', which in turn builds on the schemata for day, month and year which contain knowledge about data types, valid dates, and possibly notion of earlier/later, calculation of time differences and so on. A precise description of the possible appearances or formats does not belong to this level.

The lower levels of schemata describe the possible external appearances of a document or a part of it. They represent a sequence of formatting steps which successively create more and more concrete forms down to the physical (i.e. sensory) level.

Natural language schemata. This level describes the possible syntactical and morphological representations of the concept schemata via natural language, including the formation of sentences, phrases, expressions, words and other linguistic entities. The transformation to written (as opposed to spoken) language occurs only at the transition to the next lower level.

Literary language schemata. This level describes by which character sequences the words or expressions can be represented, which abbreviations can be used, which alternative spellings are allowed (e.g. 'ue' for 'ü' in German), which punctuation rules apply, which possibilities exist for capitalization and so on. In other words this level handles the graphemes (and partially allographs).

Optical Gestalt schemata. This level contains allographs only and describes the ways text can be distributed in an area, i.e. the optical styles in terms of overall layout, columns, paragraphs, lines, hyphenation etc. and if required even things like paper formats. Most importantly, this level also specifies which graphical elements can be used to depict characters (fonts, writing styles). The shape of a character can depend on its neighbors (even in printed text, as in ligatures).

Physical schemata. This level models the effects that occur during writing or printing, which kind of perturbances can happen and what the imaging process is able to capture from the paper original.

For recognition, we need to build the inverse of the generating process. The task is to decode as accurately as possible the pictorial data and fill all the abstraction levels upwards. As background knowledge we have at our disposal the context given by the expected document schemata.

The decoding process is based on a repeated generation of hypotheses, starting from the image instance. Later on, each middle level will be influenced by the more concrete levels below (bottom-up) as well as by the more abstract levels above (top-down). The smaller the context, the more hypotheses must be generated and evaluated, of course. The resulting decoding of a document instance is the most likely overall hypothesis (except for the shortcuts taken by the interventions of the control algorithm).

All generating schemata are incomplete descriptions of the real world. This is even more so for the recognition algorithms, which are mostly based on statistics with incomplete underlying models. Some highly developed algorithms exist, though, while others are still more based on heuristics, especially if the environment is not clean and well defined. So one challenge is always to combine the obviously very heterogeneous, specialized knowledge levels, e.g. for hypothesizing the character class from a subimage or for hypothesizing the best phrase from a syntax description. We will discuss some of these processes later in more detail.

Finally, it should be noted that for a practical system, one must not forget to provide for flexible output format transforms (usually on several abstraction levels) which can vary widely between end users.

3   Practical Requirements

In this section we describe some typical shortcomings of script recognition systems and show ways of improvement. The biggest problem is the lack of feedback within the systems themselves and with respect to the environment as outlined in the previous section. This is also true for our previous script recognition system that is currently running in postal address readers.

3.1   Typical Shortcomings

The systems can usually handle only one word and assume that its image has been cut out correctly before being handed to the recognizer. Although this is quite often the case, it is fundamentally wrong in two aspects:

(a) The decision process about which parts really belong together is complex and inextricably interwoven with the recognition process. In fact a correct grouping, i.e. a correct segmentation is a *result* of recognition. This fundamental *segmentation problem* emerges not only at the image level but always when segmentation and recognition are carried out sequentially.

(b) An error at an early processing stage cannot be corrected later on. In a purely sequential way of processing each step must always produce a unique result by making a hard decision. This is always error prone. There is no feedback which could improve on the result, since these modules are pretty much encapsulated and unable to give hints for an external control system.

In a similar fashion, each of the usual basic steps like slant normalization, base line finding/normalization and upper/lower zone estimation can be erroneous and cannot be improved on. Also, the assumptions of common base line and writing zones even within one word are wrong in general. They should only be seen as initial estimates for a system using feedback.

The next step usually prepares the normalized image for feature extraction by generating a sequence of more or less vertical image strips or zones. This happens either by heuristic rules for likely character boundaries or simply by cutting off equally sized strips as if the image where a speech signal. Neither method finds the character bounds correctly in general. Again the partition is part of a sequential process without the possibility for answering a later request for a different setup, even if a later stage would suspect that some characters are interwoven.

The following step is feature extraction for each vertical zone (or zone combination), possibly followed by a vector quantization. Instead of adapting to the situation, depending on how simple or complex the underlying portion of the image appears, it always produces the same fixed number of features. The character- (or in the case of hidden Markov models shape-) classifiers put all the effort in carving up a fixed dimensional feature space but are unable to selectively 'grab' features and match them to a model as a true recognizer does.

The systems normally try to compare these data with a list of words (i.e. a dictionary) in order to find a best match. A dynamical combination of several dictionaries or the comparison with a context free grammar is not possible.

3.2   Improvements to Aim at

In order to arrive at a better system, all these problems - but especially missing feedback - must be tackled. This requires a completely new design.

Framework. The control structure must not be based on a straightforward process chain, in which errors can accumulate quickly, but must be organized much more flexible. It must allow for a clear and concise feedback between modules and be structured like a blackboard, on which each function can write references to its input data, parameter sets and results. If results are not satisfying, certain evaluation functions can determine a new parameter set for a recalculation. This way a core algorithm and the decision when and how to call it are clearly separated.

The management of alternative intermediate results should be unified as much as possible across the different representational levels. In order to achieve this, data structures must be standardized to a certain degree.

Viewed from a software engineering perspective, the framework must support both development and usage in the final product. I.e., after switching off the experimental outputs, the software should run unchanged on a production platform.

Gray level images. The recognition algorithms should not only work with binary images but also with gray level images. Since many algorithms on binary images exist, the first step is to introduce a locally adaptive dynamic thresholding process. In the future the feature generation should work on gray level images directly.

Features. Different feature detectors that respond to contours and areas should be developed. They should form the basis for geometric modeling.

Shape recognition. Techniques for a true recognition of characters or character parts should be investigated and developed further. I.e. the characters should not be segmented first and classified thereafter, but an active model match should be taking place. Models should be associated from certain features and then verified and mapped back onto the corresponding image areas thus determining their transformation parameters. It must be easily possible to curtail the geometric context by rules restricting relative or absolute positions, rotations etc.

The most important demands for such a recognition process are:

1. The recognition must work without prior segmentation.
2. The recognition must generate hypotheses, if parts of the character are missing.
3. It must generate hypotheses even if substantial disturbances occur close to the character.
4. It must be possible to recognize a character whose model was 'spontaneously' created (i.e. without prior training) at a different location of the image.

Grammar. The matching of character hypotheses must not be restricted to a dictionary. The syntactical context should be defined by general syntax graphs as well as dictionaries, and all of these should be connected via a context free grammar. In addition it must be possible to add semantic restrictions. These should be freely programmable and loadable via an interface to an interpreter.

4   Components of the System

This section presents short summaries of the main components that are available so far and some of the studies and experiments that went on during the development of the new algorithms and modules.

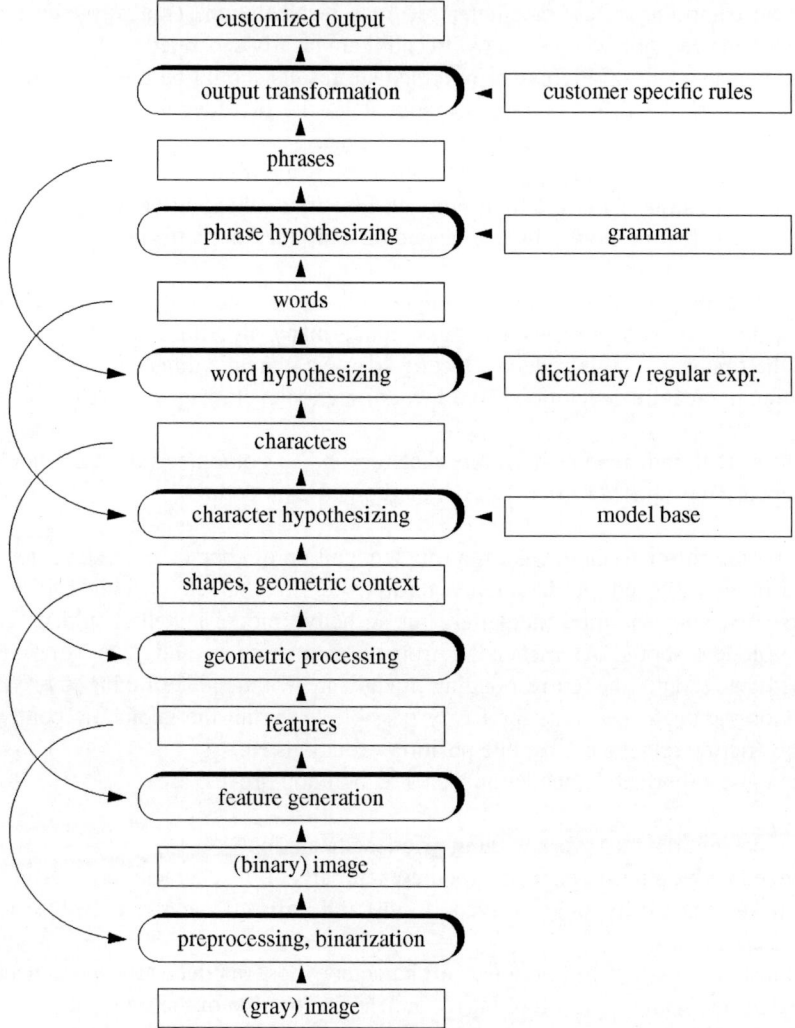

Fig. 1. Overview of major modules and data flow (including feedback)

4.1 Image Processing

Many algorithms still work on binary images because of run time restrictions. All commercial gray level image scanners can perform some kind of binarization and some image processing. The precise algorithms are kept as a secret though and are therefore difficult to parametrize. If one looks at the large contrast range to be found across documents during normal daily operation, the results are disappointing. But with today's cheap computer hardware it is possible to process gray level images entirely using software. More importantly, the recognition modules are then able to control the binarization locally for each image area.

A good binarization procedure must adapt to the local circumstances and be controlled by few parameters [1][2][3]. It is best to switch off all 'improvements' by the scanner like gamma and other contrast corrections and work on the raw gray level image instead. After collecting local statistics about contrast distribution and corresponding gray values, a local threshold is determined using a ranking filter. Local thresholds are then dilated or interpolated. Parameters are minimal contrast, neighborhood size and a filter parameter.

Gray level image processing should be tightly coupled with feature generation. One big problem is always to use the right scale, i.e. the right size of an operator. An approach to simplify this problem is to decompose the original image into a sequence of images, each of which containing information of a certain dominant scale. Then for each (scaled down) image the same operator can be applied.

We did experiments on the creation of image hierarchies based on image diffusion [4]. While these techniques are promising, they are still far too slow. For now the 'classical' approach of fast low pass filtering is more applicable [5]. A pyramid of successively smaller images is created by filtering and simultaneous subsampling (without violating the sampling theorem). An implementation using cascaded binomial filters guarantees an especially good transfer function [6].

4.2   Feature Extraction

The choice of the type of features depends on the recognition algorithm that uses them. Since we are interested in robust geometric matching later on, our features must be *local* (with respect to a certain scale) and of a *geometric nature*.

Features from binary images. Working on binary images has the advantage that many operations can be done very quickly and the disadvantage that these operations make hard decisions which cannot be readjusted as in gray level images. The sharpness of a binary image is merely an illusion subsequently paid for with incomplete or wrong features. Nevertheless binary images are currently to a large extent unavoidable.

Let us first consider one dimensional features, i.e. the description of a contour or other line-like object. Contours of connected components represent the most simple case. A principal axis fit of a sequence of contour points can detect locally smooth zones. The remaining patches can to some degree be described by a circle fit, but the curvature is usually rather uncertain and can only roughly predict the size of an object. These features are well defined only on points of the contour. The recognition methods that build on these features need to calculate many combinations of local features in order to get stable results. The smaller the primary features are the larger becomes the computing time. Therefore the contour is partitioned into pieces. It turns out that for matching the positional accuracy perpendicular to the contour is rather important while the positions of the points of partition are not. This is quite clear if the matcher is robust with respect to missing parts. We use an iterative partition which is quick, easily controlled and which guarantees a maximal perpendicular error.

Since contour based features are unstable if an object's border is frayed, we experimented with complementary, area based approaches. These features are based on the quick calculation of the approximate distance to a region's border ('chamfering'). A region is then described by a set of overlapping disks. Although the features are simple and easily matched, they are not yet stable enough.

Features from gray level images. The first kind of features are based on contours in the gray level image. The algorithms for contour approximation in binary images only have to be slightly adjusted for taking into account the more accurate positional information. Contours based on the well known Canny operator give reasonable results most of the time. Thin double sided step edges however suffer from the equally well known problem of wandering off quickly if smoothing is applied. We aim to remedy this in the future by the earlier mentioned nonlinear diffusion technique where we successively eliminate objects of a certain size *before* each smoothing step is applied.

We also studied and experimented with methods that calculate features directly in a scale invariant (scale space approaches [7][8]) or in a rotational invariant (parametric manifolds [9]) manner. It turns out that these methods are still at the research level and cannot realistically be used for recognition. Instead our operators are applied to a set of low pass filtered images. The required scale invariance is shifted entirely to the recognition end of the system.

Since gray level images produce features nearly everywhere, the number of features must be reduced to a manageable size. The locally strongest elements are chosen as initial candidates ('winner takes all'). The recognizer can later call for weaker elements if necessary.

4.3   Shape Recognition

Shape recognition is the match of a geometric model to a set of geometric primitives (features). One task is to make sure the match is meaningful, another to find the mapping parameters. We call a concrete match an 'instance'. The mapping is the more difficult to establish the more degrees of freedom are allowed. In our case a piecewise affine mapping should be sufficient. So far we have implemented similarity transformations only (translation, rotation and scaling). Of course the speed and accuracy increases if the parameter space can be restricted beforehand [10].

Several methods were studied and implemented. Graph matching must find a compromise between three contradicting requirements, if the computational time should stay reasonable: The search for matching features must happen in a local neighborhood of already found parts, it must concentrate on well discriminating relations and it must follow the best search path before other alternatives, i.e. it must execute a depth first as opposed to a breadth first search. This however makes it sensitive to disturbances. Graph matching does not realize early enough if different parts 'point' to the same instance.

The Hough transform (in its many forms) works diametrically opposed. All features vote for the instance with the best fitting transformation parameters. However this classic method is hardly ever directly usable. It becomes the slower and more uncertain the smaller (i.e. less restrictive) the features get, because a large subspace must be covered with votes. It will work well if the space is thinned out.

Newer model based approaches are appearance based matching, geometric hashing [11] and shape matching with context [12]. Our approach is a synthesis of elements from geometric hashing, shape matching with context and Hough transform. Building on contour based features we calculate quasi-invariants. These are used as triggers for the search after precalculated views of a model. This search works associative.

The results are strongly encouraging. A simplified version for rigid objects is already in daily use. The method finds even heavily disturbed objects without any prior segmentation and localizes them correctly. However it needs a contour that is at least partially intact.

4.4 Language Processing

This subsection summarizes the control of the higher levels of the recognition process by syntactical and geometric rules and conditions.

The possible contents of documents and their appearances can often be highly constrained in practice. This knowledge about norms, conventions and customer specific data like address or article lists should always be used in order to verify or correct character hypotheses in a larger context. A powerful system that profits from knowledge about literary language must fulfill the following requirements:

1. The specification of more complex syntactical structures must be supported in a manner that is simple to use.
2. The utilization of large dictionaries must be comfortable.
3. The matching algorithm must be fuzzy, error tolerant and efficient.

In coping with these demands a stochastic parser for context free grammars was developed. It determines the optimal mapping from a graph with character hypotheses onto a syntax graph based on the best-path-algorithm by Dijkstra. The parser supports finite deterministic automata for the efficient match with regular expressions and large dictionaries. These can be handled as partial languages and be embedded in complex context free structures.

The teaching of this system for a certain application consists of four tasks. The first three are of a purely lexical/syntactical nature, while the fourth states the geometric relations and expectations:

1. Definition of the basic lexical categories.
   These are the terminal nodes of syntax trees and must be supplied in terms of dictionaries (e.g. lists of first names, family names or street names) or regular expressions.

2. Definition of the syntactical categories and their assignment to a field of a database.

   In order for the recognition results to be of any use they must be mapped to the knowledge structure of the application. Such a structure is often realized as a set of fields in a database. For example, in an address recognition task fields for first name, last name and street name must be filled. Therefore, corresponding syntactical categories must be defined and linked to these fields.

3. Definition of the syntax specific to the application.

   These syntactical categories are used to construct the syntax. For example, it can be defined that a first name (in the sense of a field in the database) can be build from several first names (in the sense of 'elementary first name') and possibly single characters like dashes. It is useful to provide several alternative definitions which the recognizer can use successively. In the case of street names, for example, we should start with a list of names (including typical abbreviations) if the context is known. If this fails, we can try more general combinations like a string followed by a typical street name suffix.

4. Definition of the geometric arrangement of the syntactical categories.

   Many character and word sequences are linear. More complex cases require a description of possible geometric layouts, however, in order to safeguard and accelerate the recognition process.

Before the first use of the system these four descriptions must exist to a reasonable degree. Often they can be copied to a large extent from another project. If the system turns out to contain flaws, these partial descriptions must be corrected or enlarged accordingly.

4.5 Control and Feedback

This part of the system is not yet fully operational. Here we outline what is planned.

If there exists a description of the entire page or form, then a global control mechanism decides what kind of objects are to be expected in which zone. Some zones might require an image preprocessing step with a specific parameter setting, while others could be entirely ignored. Within each zone the recognition process runs bottom up at first and is improved by feedback cycles later on.

We illustrate this with the recognition steps for a single expression. We start with a bottom up sequence consisting of image processing (including binarization), feature extraction, shape recognition, determination of common transformation parameters, estimation of baseline etc., character recognition and syntactical matching. Each step is executed with a standard parameter setting. After this first attempt the feedback process is started. However this is currently possible only if there is some minimal result that can be improved on. The system must have some 'anticipation' of what is there. Otherwise we could only try again from the start with a completely different parameter set.

The system can now evaluate the intermediate results at different levels. It can then influence algorithmic steps 'lower down'. The syntactical match reports of weakly recognized characters and their positions. The character recognition is called again at that position with a new, more tolerant parameter setting. If the character recognition realizes that some parts are missing, then the shape finder is called again, which in turn can request a different feature extraction and so on all the way down to low level image processing.

The knowledge about the selection of parameter values as well as the direction and step size of their change during feedback will be determined empirically at first. Later on this will be automated.

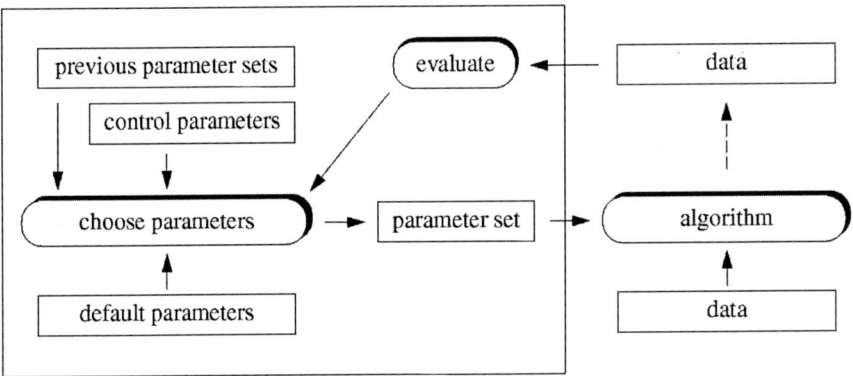

Fig. 2. Each module (algorithm) from Fig. 1 starts with a default parameter set. Parameter sets for future calls depend on the evaluation of higher level results, previous parameter sets and meta (i.e. control) parameters, which steer the next set into a certain direction

5   Conclusions

After analyzing the weaknesses of previous script recognition systems (our own and others), a completely new system was designed and implemented from scratch. A hugely beneficial side effect is a software that fits together at all levels.

Script recognition requires the integration of many techniques ranging from image processing to processing of knowledge at a syntactical/semantic level. This calls for a large system. Luckily almost all components can be used and tested in simpler systems like specific form recognizers. We are currently at that stage. The first spin offs are running very successfully at our customers.

References

1.   Zhang, Z., Tan, C. L.: Restoration of Images Scanned from Thick Bound Documents. Proceedings of the International Conference on Image Processing (2001)
2.   Savakis, A. E.: Adaptive Document Image Thresholding using Foreground and Background Clustering. Proceedings of the International Conference on Image Processing (1998)
3.   Tombre, K., Ah-Soon, C., Dosch, P., Habed, A., Masini, G.: Stable, Robust and Off-the-Shelf Methods for Graphics Recognition. Proceedings of the 14th International Conference on Pattern Recognition (1998)
4.   Weickert, J.: Anisotropic Diffusion in Image Processing. ECMI Series, Teubner, Stuttgart (1998)
5.   Burt, P. J., Adelson, E. H.: The Laplacian Pyramid as a Compact Image Code. IEEE Transactions on Communications, Vol. COM-31, No. 4 (1983)
6.   Jähne, B.: Digitale Bildverarbeitung. Springer-Verlag Berlin Heidelberg New York (2002)
7.   Lindeberg, T.: Edge Detection and Ridge Detection with Automatic Scale Selection. Int. J. of Computer Vision. vol. 30, number 2 (1998)
8.   Burns, J. B., Nishihara, H. K., Rosenschein, S. J.: Appropriate-Scale Local Centers: A Foundation for Parts-Based Recognition. Teleos Research Technical Report TR-94-05 (1994)
9.   Baker, S., Nayar, S. K., Murase, H.: Parametric Feature Detection. Tech. Rep. CUCS-028-95, Department of Computer Science, Columbia University (1995)
10. Grimson, W. E. L.: Object Recognition by Computer: The Role of Geometric Constraints. MIT Press, Cambridge, MA (1990)
11. Tsai, F. C. D.: A Probabilistic Approach to Geometric Hashing using Line Features. Computer Vision and Image Understanding, 63(1) (1996)
12. Belongie, S., Malik, J., Puzicha, J.: Shape Matching and Object Recognition Using Shape Contexts. Technical Report UCB//CSD-00-1128, Computer Science Division, University of California at Berkeley (2001)

Handwritten Address Recognition Using Hidden Markov Models

Anja Brakensiek[1] and Gerhard Rigoll[2]

[1] University Duisburg, Dept. of Computer Science,
47057 Duisburg, Germany
now: anja.brakensiek@odt-oce.com
www.fb9-ti.uni-duisburg.de
[2] University Duisburg, Dept. of Computer Science
now: Munich University of Technology, Inst. for Human-Machine Communication,
80290 Munich, Germany
rigoll@ei.tum.de
www.mmk.ei.tum.de

Abstract. In this paper several aspects of a recognition system for cursive hand-written German address words (cities and streets) are described. The recognition system is based on Hidden Markov Models (HMMs), whereat the focus is on two main problems: the changes in the writing style depending on time or regional differences and the difficulty to select the correct (complete) dictionary for address reading. The first problem leads to the examination of three different adaptation techniques: Maximum Likelihood (ML), Maximum Likelihood Linear Regression (MLLR) and Scaled Likelihood Linear Regression (SLLR). To handle the second problem language models based on backoff character n-grams are examined to evaluate the performance of an open vocabulary recognition (without dictionary). For both problems the determination of confidence measures (based on the frame-normalized likelihood, a garbage model, a two-best recognition or an unconstrained character decoding) is important, either for an unsupervised adaptation or the detection of out of vocabulary words (OOV). The databases, which are used for recognition, are provided by Siemens Dematic (SD) within the Adaptive READ project.

1 Introduction

Automatic recognition systems for handwritten addresses become more and more important for postal automation [30,22,32]. Usually, Hidden Markov Model-based techniques (HMM) are used for recognition of cursive handwritten words because of their segmentation-free recognition capability (see [26,33]). Although the performance of recognition systems has increased since several years, the error rate of recognizers for unconstrained handwritten address words is still quite high.

In general, words are recognized taking a dictionary of given size into account. With this kind of approach all words to be recognized have to be in the dictionary including all writing variants. For word images which contain a word not included in the dictionary, such a system will respond with the most similar word in the dictionary. Normally, the criterion for similarity is based on geometrical features, consequently the recognition

A. Dengel et al. (Eds.): Adaptive READ Research Project, LNCS 2956, pp. 103–122, 2004.

result can have a total different meaning. Thus, for practical usage, a reliability assessment of the recognized words will be necessary (compare [5]). It is cheaper to reject letters, which are recognized uncertain, and to label them manually, than to send them to a wrong address [13]. The decision, wether a recognition is uncertain or not, is done by confidence measures. A recognition result obtained by a neural network or a KNN-classifier, for example, can be interpreted as a confidence measure immediately, because it is a kind of posterior probability. In contrast to this, in a HMM-based system the confidence measures have to be computed additionally, because the recognition result itself is just a likelihood. Here, that word of the dictionary, which is the most probable, is selected. This leads to a further problem, if the selected dictionary does not contain the current word label (OOV: out-of-vocabulary). In postal applications the variety of words is so large, that a complete dictionary for all possible addresses is not really feasible. An address may contain all countries in the world (e.g. [34]), all their cities and streets and additionally all personal names of the recipients. Once the structure of the address is known, i.e. the words have been categorized (city, street), the size of the dictionaries can be reduced to sizes of 1000 words or less depending on the zip code. If it is not possible to decide, which line of the address block belongs to which category (e.g. no zip code, reverse writing order, foreign mail), or if the zip code is misrecognized or wrong, the recognition may be carried out with an OOV-dictionary. A rating of correctness depending on confidence measures is not only useful for the reject management in postal applications, but also for an unsupervised adaptation (mail streams) using automatically generated labels.

One possibility to handle the problem of unstructured addresses is a recognition of cities and streets without dictionary (compare also [4]). An alternative to a dictionary-based approach is the use of language models consisting of character n-grams [28]. This means, in a way, a recognition with an open vocabulary. The recognition process of a handwritten address could be realized in a two-step procedure using n-grams: In the first step a character n-gram based recognizer is used to convert the line images into a character stream. This stream can be parsed and if some keywords are spotted, the hypothesis for that word can be verified using a recognizer with a small dictionary. Another possibility is to match this stream with a full list of valid words, as it is done for machine printed addresses (standard OCR), if the recognition is based on single characters. Another field of operation for statistical language models is the recognition of personal names, which is important in case a person moved and the mail has to be forwarded. This topic is not examined in this paper, because a suitable database is not available.

Another aspect for optimization of a recognition system is the possibility of retraining or adaptation (compare [6]). But a HMM handwriting recognition system has to be trained by examples. The generation of labeled training examples is usually performed by humans, thus the generation of large training databases is expensive. Currently the recognition system is based on labeled training examples of only few post offices in Germany. However, it can be noticed that this general data is not really representative to the mail flow in concrete postal sites. Most of the mail which is delivered to a post office stays in that office, i.e. the mail has to be delivered to the same city or its surrounding. Therefore the recognizer has to process a lot of local mail. If the recognition rate on this local mail is high, the overall recognition rate in this post office will benefit. Here, the goal is to maximize the recognition rate for a special post office by adapting the baseline recognition system to the local mail stream. To increase the performance of a post office, the system has to be trained with local frequently appearing samples. A special training for each post office is time-consuming due to the problems in generating training material. A faster and cheaper way to increase the recognition rate would be to adapt a generic handwriting recognition system to the new task with few adaptation data. Changings in writing style over several years can be handled in principle in the same way. This aspect is not evaluated here due to missing data.

Here we want to present the recognition of single address words. The meaning of the recognition and the address interpretation, which leads to a specification of postal delivery points, has to be evaluated in further work. This paper just shows the possibility of using alternative approaches for some special problems in postal automation. Thus, in the following sections our address reading system (Sec. 2), the theory and some results, which are obtained by character n-grams (Sec. 3), by four different confidence measures using complete or OOV dictionaries (Sec. 4) and by three different adaptation techniques (Sec. 5) are described.

2   System Architecture

Our handwriting recognition system consists of about 77 different linear HMMs (see [26, 29]), using a semi-continuous (resp. tied-mixture) probability modeling structure with $J = 300$ Gaussian densities g_j (full covariance matrix). Here, the emission probabilities b_i for a state s_i can be computed as follows (ω_{ij} are the weighting factors) depending on the feature vector $\underline{x}$:

$$b_i(\underline{x}) = p(\underline{x}|s_i) = \sum_{j=1}^{J} \omega_{ij} \cdot g_j(\underline{x}) \tag{1}$$

We use one HMM for each character (upper- and lower-case letters, numbers and some special characters like '- / . ( )'), which consists mostly of three states (compare [6]), except for the special characters depending on their width. To estimate the HMM-parameters we use the Baum-Welch algorithm, whereas the recognition is performed by the Viterbi algorithm using city- or street-dictionaries or language models depending on character n-grams. In reality, the lexicon is determined and restricted in size by recognition of the zip code, which is easier to read than the rest of the address. To simulate this standard scenario, we use small complete dictionaries (no OOV), which are created artificially depending on the test set. Using these correct dictionaries, misrecognized words have to be rejected depending on the confidence measure. If it is not possible to decide, which part of the address belongs to the specification of the city and the street, a recognition using the wrong dictionary may become possible. This means a confusion of city and street dictionaries, which leads to an OOV recognition. In this case, all words have to be rejected using the same confidence measures and thresholds as for a correct specification.

The presented word recognition rates refer only to the recognition of cities (single words like 'Stuttgart' or short sequences like 'Frankfurt am Main') and streets and are independent of errors in zip code or street number recognition. To compute the character accuracy, the number of deleted and inserted characters have been taken into account, too.

The database of German address words, the extracted features and the basic principle of HMMs are described in the following sections.

2.1 Address Database

The database consists of handwritten address words (cursive or block letters, see Fig.1, compare also [6]). For our experiments we use two different kinds of databases: one general database of several post offices in Germany, which is used for the baseline recognition system to evaluate character n-grams and confidence measures, and four special databases of the post offices in Rostock, Stuttgart, Hamburg and Halle, which are used for adaptation. Each database is split randomly into training (resp. adaptation) and test set. The standard dictionaries contain always all labels of this database, which is currently tested.

Fig. 1. Examples of the database: cities and streets

General data. The baseline system is trained with about 20000 words, the test set consists of about 2000 words ($N = 935$ cities and $N = 1092$ streets). This implies a number of 7400 characters for the city test set (about 8 characters/city) and a number of 12026 characters for the streets (11 characters/street in average). The complete dictionaries for recognition of cities or streets contain all corresponding test-labels. This leads to a dictionary size of 421 for the cities and of 901 for the streets. The evaluated OOV-dictionaries consist of 100% out-of-vocabulary words. Here, the street dictionary is used for the recognition of cities and vice versa.

For our experiments we use a second kind of dictionary of about 20000 entries (separate city- and street-dictionary). These dictionaries are necessary, if it can be assumed that the structure of the address is known but no zip-code is recognized. The large city dictionary contains a list of all city-names in Germany (compare Sec. 3.2 for training the language model), the 20k street dictionary contains randomly chosen entries of all street-names in Germany (considering the test-labels, no OOV).

If it is not possible to detect the zip code and to decide, which part of the address belongs to the specification of the city and the street, a recognition without dictionary may be useful. Also, the recognition of names or country specifications in different languages will require an unlimited vocabulary. So, the third alternative for recognition is the use of character n-grams, which are described in Sec. 3. It should be noticed that in general a dictionary-based approach without OOV is superior, but in real applications it cannot be guaranteed that a dictionary without OOV is used - e.g. if one digit of the zip recognition result is wrong, the resulting dictionaries will not contain the correct entries.

Adaptation data. The adaptation set of the post office in Rostock (HRO) consists of about 1700 words for adaptation and 1550 words for testing using a (complete) vocabulary of 716 cities and 1240 streets. The second specific set of the post office in Stuttgart (STR) is quite similar. Here we use about 1500 words for testing and 1500 words for adaptation (vocabulary size: 637 cities, 1227 streets). For the post office in Halle (HAL) we use about 1580 words for adaptation and 1460 words for testing (vocabulary size: 736 cities, 1154 streets) and the recognition results for Hamburg (HAM) refer to a database of 1510 words for adaptation and 1500 words for testing (vocabulary size: 562 cities, 1220 streets).

2.2   Preprocessing and Feature Extraction

After localization and segmentation of the address words, the script samples are pre-processed and normalized according to skew, slant and height. The single steps of pre-processing have different purposes, such as the removal of inaccuracies or faults which arise during digitizing (compare also [8,11]).

After binarization of the image, the Binary Connected Components (BCC) are analyzed [19]. A BCC-Object consists of a contour-polygon (of the colors black or white), the surrounding rectangle, and a reference to inner context areas. The following feature extraction is based on the estimation of the baseline and the line above the lowercase letters, the ruler lines (compare Fig.2).

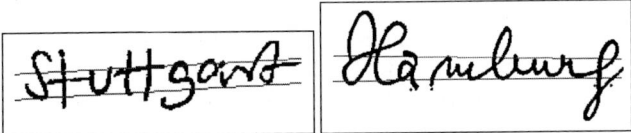

Fig. 2. Baseline estimation

Ruler lines are important for rotation normalization, detection of ascenders and descenders, and height-normalization. This estimation of the writing lines is computed in two phases (lower and upper baseline) on the unsheared BCC-Objects. For the baseline, a number of local minima with their width and weight are determined. Several linear regression analyses remove points of high variance and determine the baseline out of the remaining points. The top edge of lowercase letters determines the second writing line. A similar procedure determines local maxima. This results in an estimation of two straight lines, which are not necessarily parallel (e.g. fading size of the characters). The writing line model contains an implicit height-normalization on the basis of extracted characteristics by standardizing them on the given height on the writing lines.

After normalization, which includes also shearing and rotation of the pixel image, the feature extraction, which is based on a sliding window technique, can start. To compute the features, a small window is shifted from left to right over the normalized BCCs of the entire image. The windows overlap each other from one frame to another. Every sliding window is divided horizontally by the ruler lines in five overlapping areas, in which dashes, dots, cusps, upstrokes, curves and horizontal or vertical lines are detected to determine 20 features. Finally, a linear discriminant analysis (LDA) is performed on always three neighboring frames of these features and the resulting feature vectors $X = (\underline{x}_1, ..., \underline{x}_k)$ are reduced from 60 to 30 dimensions (see [6,4,5]).

2.3   HMM Based Recognition

The recognition problem using HMMs can be described by the following Eq. 2 using Bayes rule (with X is the sequence of feature vectors and W represents the class resp. word):

$$P(W|X) = \frac{P(X|W) \cdot P(W)}{P(X)} \qquad (2)$$

Here $P(W|X)$ represents the posterior probability, $P(X|W)$ is the likelihood, which is computed by the HMMs, $P(W)$ describes the a priori probability of the word W (using a dictionary or a language model, see Sec. 3) and $P(X)$ represents the a priori probability of the feature vectors.

Thus, the solution of our recognition problem is described by Eq. 3, because $P(X)$ is independent of W:

$$W^* \approx \underset{W}{\operatorname{argmax}} \, P(X|W) \, P(W) \qquad (3)$$

Disregarding the probability $P(X)$ the relative order of the best recognition results will not change. Thus for recognition only, this simplification is permitted. However, the probability $P(X)$ is important to compute the probability of correctness – the confidence – of the recognition result (see Sec. 4).

The recognition of a single word W^*, which is defined in a dictionary (assumption: the same a priori probability for each entry), leads to Eq. 4:

$$W^* \approx \underset{W}{\operatorname{argmax}} \, P(X|W) \qquad (4)$$

Here, the probability $P(W)$ is nonrelevant per definition.

3   Language Modeling

Language models (LMs) are used to enhance the recognition performance by considering statistic, linguistic or world knowledge (compare also [15,28]). A typical kind of a language model, which is well known in speech recognition, is the n-gram. Normally, word n-grams are used in combination with a dictionary. The goal is to model the grammar of word sequences using statistical methods. Alternatively, the dictionary can be replaced by a character n-gram. Our address recognition system can operate without any dictionary. To improve the recognition results when no dictionary is available or the vocabulary is unknown, we use backoff n-grams on the character level (compare also [4,3,7,25]).

3.1   Character n-grams

Character n-grams are statistical models, which influence the transition probabilities between trained character HMMs. It takes into account that, for example, in Germany the character sequence 'qu' is much more probable than 'qo'.

According to Eq. 3 the grammar or language model is presented by $P(W)$ (see also [1,38]). This language model is now described by a backoff n-gram of characters (not words) with $n > 1$.

The formula for estimating a backoff bigram (n=2) is the following

$$P(w_2|w_1) = \begin{cases} (N(w_1, w_2) \cdot d)/N(w_1) & : & N(w_1, w_2) > threshold \\ P(w_2) \cdot bo(w_1) & : & else \end{cases} \tag{5}$$

with $N(w_1, w_2)$ the number of times character w_2 follows w_1. The discounting coefficient d and the backoff factor bo are necessary to correct the probabilities for observed and unseen events (Eq. 6, see [16,9]):

$$\sum_{w_i} P(w_i|w_{i-1}) = 1 \tag{6}$$

The discounting strategy is to reduce the probabilities of common events and to raise the probabilities of rare and unseen events. Here, the linear discounting method is chosen to determine d:

$$d = 1 - \alpha \qquad with: \qquad \alpha = \frac{N_1}{N_a} \tag{7}$$

N_1 is the number of different events which occur only once and N_a is the total number of characters in the training text.

N-grams of higher context depth n can be computed analogously regarding the probability $P(w_k|w_{k-n+1}, ..w_{k-1})$. Examples for applications of language models are the use of n-grams of characters for word recognition, as described in this paper or n-grams of words in order to enhance sentence-recognition or document classification. One distinguishing characteristic of language models is the entropy (H) or perplexity (pp), which is a measure of surprise to see these characters or a certain string of characters. The perplexity depends on the language model as well as on the test-text (the better the language model fits the test-text, the lower the perplexity, see also [20]). Regarding a trigram, the entropy resp. the perplexity of a test-text with N_d characters is computed according to Eq.8.

$$H \approx -\frac{1}{N_d} \cdot \sum_{i=1}^{N_d} \log_2 P(w_i|w_{i-2}, w_{i-1}) \qquad and \qquad pp = 2^H \tag{8}$$

We generate several n-gram models ($n = 3, 5$ or 7) for the address recognition system by using the statistical character-sequences of different kinds of texts, which are described in the next section. The language models are trained with the CMU-Cambridge toolkit [9]. A detailed description of the stack decoder algorithm [23], which is used for this kind of language model with a very high context depth can be found in [38].

3.2   Text Corpus

Experiments are performed on a general German language model and some address-specific models.

The general language model (*n-gram: general text*, compare Tab.1:k) is trained with about four millions of words from several German web-pages. A main part of this text consists of broadcast news. This leads, e.g., to 195877 different 5-gram sequences (resp. 19505 trigrams or 610899 different 7-grams).

The address-specific language models can be subdivided into three classes: a specific model for cities, a specific model for streets and a general address model combining city and street names. The training text consists of a list of all valid city resp. street names in Germany. These are about 20000 city names and 500000 street names, not including the names of districts, which are often completed but not necessary for postal delivery. To improve the statistics of the cities, frequent city names like 'Berlin' or 'Hamburg' are additionally added to the original text-corpus depending on the number of inhabitants (*n-gram: c^*-list*). This procedure could not be performed with the list of streets (*n-gram: s-list*), because the information about the number of residents per street was not available. Another possibility is to combine the general city or street lists with frequent address words in a certain post-office, which means a kind of adaptation [6]. It can be shown, that most of the mail which is delivered to a post-office stays in that office, i.e. the mail has to be delivered to the same city or its surrounding. Thus, for experiments, language models are also trained on the labels of the entire (training and test) address-database (separate LM for cities and streets: *n-gram: city-data* resp. *n-gram: street-data*).

The general address n-gram (*n-gram: c+s-list*) trained by all valid city and street names (without frequency) is necessary, if it is unknown whether this part of the address belongs to the city or street (e.g. reverse order). This model leads to 490036 different 7-grams (26965 trigrams), compared to 20782 different 7-grams for the city-LM.

As a result we can create language models for specific purposes taking different kinds of training-text. Thus, the knowledge about the address structure can be considered. Language models trained on streets only should not be used for the recognition of cities, for example. The same applies to personal names and so on. Because of this, most experiments, which are presented in the following section, depend on the general list of cities and streets (*c+s-list*, compare Tab.1:d-f).

3.3   Experimental Results

The main reasons for using character n-grams instead of dictionaries are the unknown (or unlimited) vocabularies in some cases (e.g. names in a forwarding request, untypical notation of a city name) and the substitution of dictionaries with 'wrong' dictionaries, if the address structure is unknown (no zip code or reverse writing order of name, street, city and country).

The HMM-based recognizer using a dictionary always gives as a result an entry of this dictionary. This leads to a problem, if the 'wrong' dictionary (e.g. by mistaking cities for streets) or an incomplete dictionary is used. In general, but especially in this scenario, a good confidence measure is necessary to reject wrong or uncertain classified addresses (compare also Fig. 5). The following Tab.1 shows some word- respective character-recognition results using complete (no OOV) dictionaries of different sizes or language models of varying context depth and training-corpus. As can be seen, the recognition accuracy of 86.8% for the cities and 91.0% for the streets obtained by a small dictionary (Tab.1:a) decreases significantly by using very large dictionaries with 20000 entries (Tab.1:b) or character n-grams without dictionary (Tab.1:d-k). Only 2.5% of the cities and 0.4% of the streets are classified correctly using neither a dictionary nor a language model (Tab.1:c).

Table 1. Word recognition results (character accuracy) in % using different dictionaries or language models and perplexity of the test-database

method	cities	streets	pp_{city}	pp_{street}
a) small dict. (421c / 901s)	86.8 (92.2)	91.0 (95.2)	—	—
b) large dictionaries (20k each)	63.9 (81.8)	86.0 (92.3)	—	—
c) without dict, without n-gram	2.5 (45.2)	0.4 (45.8)	—	—
d) w/o dict, 3-gram: c+s-list	14.8 (58.5)	11.7 (65.9)	10.1	13.8
e) w/o dict, 5-gram: c+s-list	35.8 (67.4)	27.5 (72.9)	6.3	10.7
f) w/o dict, 7-gram: c+s-list	40.0 (68.4)	35.1 (75.2)	6.0	10.1
g) w/o dict, 5-gram: c^*-list	42.9 (72.7)	—	5.1	16.5
h) w/o dict, 5-gram: s-list	—	27.5 (72.8)	6.6	10.8
i) w/o dict, 5-gram: city-data	59.4 (79.8)	—	3.5	28.6
j) w/o dict, 5-gram: street-data	—	33.3 (74.4)	10.8	6.6
k) w/o dict, 3-gram: general text	8.0 (51.3)	2.5 (47.6)	21.7	23.8

Regarding the results obtained by language models, the accuracy increases by the context depth of the n-grams (see Tab.1:d-f) and by the similarity between test-addresses and training-corpus (Tab.1:*list*, *data* or *general*, compare Sec. 3.2) of the n-grams. So, using a 7-gram, which is trained on a complete list of all German cities and streets, the word accuracy increases to 40.0% for the cities and 35.1% for the streets (without postprocessing). These results imply a character recognition rate of 68.4% resp. 75.2% (Tab.1:f). Comparing different 5-grams, best results (59.4% resp. 33.3%) are obtained by the language model, which is trained on a text taking the word-frequencies of our address-database (not the frequency of inhabitants) into account (Tab.1:i,j). But this experiment requires a known address-frequency, e.g. in a special post-office. Nevertheless, regarding the results for the cities obtained by a LM trained on the general city- and street-list or the city-list including the number of inhabitants (Tab.1:e,g), the accuracy increases also significant by using a LM that better fits the test-words. These results are confirmed by the perplexity of the different language models, which is given in the last two columns of Tab. 1.

Admittedly, compared to a dictionary-based (no OOV) recognition, these word recognition rates are relative low, but the character accuracy is sufficient. However, a great advantage of n-grams is the possibility to process the result after recognition, because the similarity (e.g. measured by the Levenshtein distance) between correct and recognized word is relatively high. Several errors occur, because only one character of the word is substituted, deleted or inserted. Also, it should be noticed, that the dictionary-based results will decrease furthermore by using a larger vocabulary (streets: 82.4% obtained by a 30k dictionary).

The possibility of postprocessing using LMs is demonstrated in an experiment comparing the recognized strings with valid dictionary entries (e.g. delivery points). Aligning the recognized character sequences (obtained by the 7-gram) with the corresponding word list of the small dictionary (city or street), it can bee seen, that most of the matches are correct. 59.1% of the cities and 63.8% of the streets are rejected, because they are not absolutely identical with a dictionary entry. Then the error rate decreases to about 1%. And the comparison of the character sequences with the 'wrong' dictionary (e.g. street names instead of city names) leads to a rejection rate of 99.5%. In contrast to these results, a good confidence measure is needed to reject recognition results, which are obtained by a standard dictionary approach and the 'wrong' dictionary.

Thus, another aspect for comparison is the ratio of error-rate e and rejection-rate r (compare Sec. 4.1; see [4]). Using small complete (and correct) dictionaries, the error rate of 13.2% for the cities and 9.0% for the streets (compare Tab. 1:a) can be decreased to about 1%, if about 45% of the test-words are rejected using the 2-best distance as confidence measure (see Fig. 5 for city recognition). Compared to these curves the n-gram results without postprocessing do not seem to be so bad considering the ratio of error to rejection.

4   Confidence Measures

The likelihood $P(X|W)$, which is used for recognition according to Eq. 4 is not an absolute measure of probability, but rather a relative measure. Thus, we just know which word of a given closed dictionary is the most likely, but we do not know the certainty of correctness – the confidence measure $Conf$ – of this recognition result. For our handwriting recognition problem we compare four different confidence measures (compare [21,24,5]):

- the frame normalized likelihood $P(X|W)$
- the posterior probability $P(W|X)$ by approximating $P(X)$ using a garbage-model W_{garb}
- the posterior probability $P(W|X)$ by approximating $P(X)$ using a two-best recognition
- the likelihood $P(X|W)$, which is normalized by the likelihood $P(X|C)$ obtained by a character decoding without dictionary

The first investigated confidence measure, the likelihood $P(X|W)$, which is normalized by the number of corresponding feature frames is used as a reference. Here the computational costs are very low, because this measure exists in any case. Because of the dynamic of the HMM-based decoding procedure, in general these measures are computed as log likelihoods. Thus, in practice, the logarithm of the confidence measures are examined, which leads to a simple subtraction of the computed log likelihood values. The higher the normalized likelihood resp. the ratio of the likelihoods, the higher the reliability. If the confidence measure is below a threshold t, this test-word has to be rejected.

The following confidence measures take Eq. 2 into account. The posterior probability $P(W|X)$ will be an optimal confidence measure, if it was be possible to estimate $P(X)$ (here $P(W)$ is the same for each class, see also [39]):

$$Conf := \frac{P(X|W)}{P(X)} \qquad Conf \begin{cases} < t \rightarrow reject \\ \geq t \rightarrow accept \end{cases} \tag{9}$$

Thus, the second confidence measure, we tested, is based on a garbage-model (compare [27]). The garbage-model W_{garb} is trained on all features of the training-set independent of the character-label, which leads to an unspecific average model. Often, such a garbage-model is used for OOV detection in speech recognition, too. The confidence measure can be calculated using the garbage-model as an approximation of $P(X)$:

$$P(X) \approx P(X|W_{garb}) \tag{10}$$

To determine $P(X|W_{garb})$ the decoding procedure has to be expanded by an additional HMM, as it is shown in Fig. 3.

The third evaluated confidence measure depends on a two-best recognition according to Eq. 11 (see also [10]):

$$P(X) \approx \sum_{k=1}^{N} P(X|W_k) \cdot P(W_k) \quad \Rightarrow \quad P(X) \approx \frac{1}{N} \cdot (P(X|W_{1st}) + P(X|W_{2nd})) \tag{11}$$

This measure contains the difference of the log likelihoods between the best and the second best hypothesis for the same sequence of feature vectors. The approximation in Eq. 11 is valid under the assumption, that the likelihoods of the best and second best class are much higher than those of the other $(N-2)$ classes of the dictionary. Transforming this equation because of the dynamic range of the values, the new confidence measure $Conf^* = \frac{Conf}{N-Conf}$ can be defined as follows:

$$Conf = \frac{N \cdot P(X|W_{1st})}{P(X|W_{1st}) + P(X|W_{2nd})} \quad \Rightarrow \quad Conf^* = \frac{P(X|W_{1st})}{P(X|W_{2nd})} \tag{12}$$

Thus, this term is easy to compute, only the domain of $Conf$ resp. t has been changed. Again, for rejection the rule of Eq. 9 is applied.

The fourth method to obtain confidence measures is based on an unconstrained character decoding without dictionary (compare e.g. [40,14]), as it is shown in Fig. 3. The character-based likelihood $P(X|C)$ is used for normalization:

$$P(X) \approx P(X|C) = P(X|c_1, ...c_k) = \prod P(X_{f_i}|c_i) \tag{13}$$

A recognition without vocabulary leads to an arbitrary sequence of characters $c_i : 1 \leq i \leq K$ (K is the number of different character HMMs, X_{f_i} are the corresponding feature vectors per frame f_i) which is the most likely without respect to the lexicon. In general $P(X|C)$ will be greater or equal than $P(X|W)$. Additionally to this character-based likelihood, also the character-sequence itself can be regarded by calculating the Levenshtein-distance between W and C. The Levenshtein-distance describes how many changes are necessary to transform one string into the other.

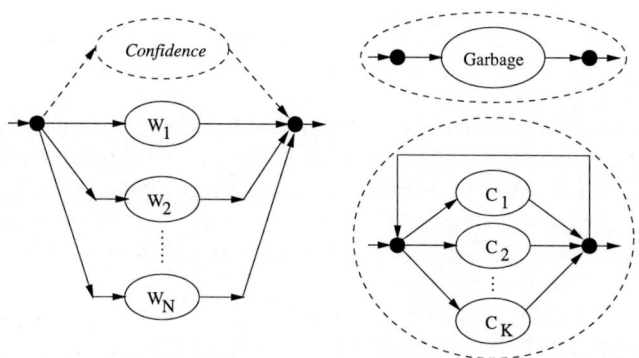

Fig. 3. Decoding configuration to obtain confidence measures: for recognition using a dictionary with the classes W a further path to compute the confidence (garbage model or recognition of characters c) can be added

These confidence measures differ significantly regarding the computational costs, the effectiveness and the application. Much more confidence measures especially for continuous speech recognition are described in the literature. But often, they take the grammar $P(W)$ of a sentence into account, which is not possible for single word recognition. A further error reduction in address recognition would be possible by taking the context of the entire address into account (holistic approach).

4.1   Experimental Results

In the presented experiments we examine the influence of four different confidence measures for handwriting recognition of single address words (compare also [6]). Additionally, we compare the effect of confidence measures using a complete or an OOV dictionary. Without rejection, a recognition accuracy of 86.8% for the cities and 91.0% for the streets is obtained by the respective complete dictionary. Fig. 4 shows the false acceptance rate FAR against the false rejection rate FRR for city and street recognition using different confidence measures and increasing thresholds. The usual terms FAR and FRR are defined as follows (Eq. 14):

$$FRR = \frac{FR}{FR + CA} \qquad FAR = \frac{FA}{FA + CR} \qquad (14)$$

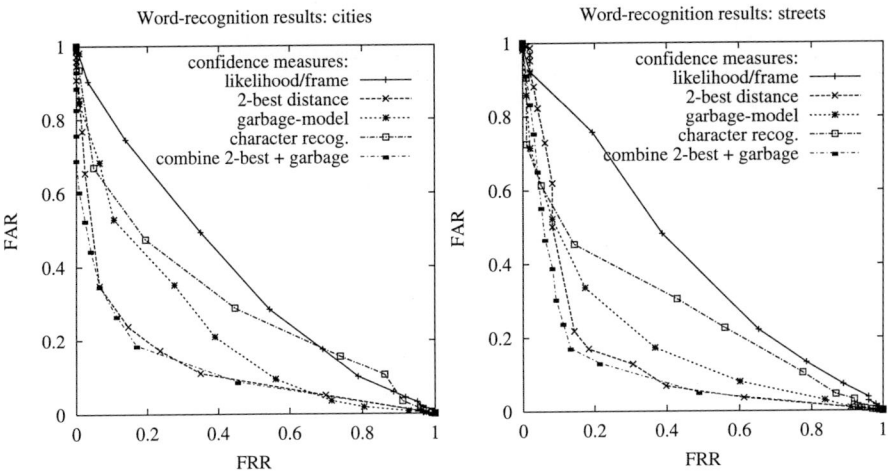

Fig. 4. ROC using complete dictionaries

Here, FR is the number of false rejected words (the result is correct but rejected), CA is the number of correct accepted words, FA the number of false accepted (the result is wrong but accepted) and CR the number of correct rejected examples with $FR + CA + FA + CR = N$. As can be seen in Fig. 4 (ROC: receiver operating characteristics), the best confidence measure is based on the 2-best distance of the likelihoods. And the frame normalized likelihood is the worst confidence measure, as it is expected. The analysis of the 2-best recognition considers the similarity of the entries of the dictionary, thus potential errors can be avoided. This means, that this confidence is highly dependent on the kind of dictionary (e.g. size, similar words like 'Hamburg' and 'Homberg', OOV). The 2-best confidence for the same test-word can be quite different using a dictionary without the second best hypothesis. Additionally, the ROC-curve using a simple linear combination (weighted sum) of the two best measures – the 2-best distance and the garbage-model – is shown. Here, the performance is only little better and this result is obtained by optimizing the parameters manually. Several other combination methods (other weights, maximum decision, AND-conjunction), which perform well on the city test-set, flop on the street-data and reverse. For evaluation of (automatic, more complex) combination methods (see e.g. [10,24]) a larger database has to be used to be more independent of the specific test-set.

The second aspect considered here is the behavior of confidence measures using OOV dictionaries. The presented results refer to the city- and street-database (see Fig. 5), whereas details are given for city recognition only.

Using the baseline system without rejection ($r = 0\%$) an error rate of $e = 13.2\%$ is achieved testing the city names. Sure, rejecting 100% of the test-data, the error will become zero (compare Fig. 5: left side). For comparison of confidence measures using complete and OOV-dictionaries another presentation – the ratio of error rate e and rejection rate r resp. threshold t – is shown using the following definition (N is the total number of words).

$$r = \frac{CR + FR}{N} \qquad e = \frac{FA}{N} \qquad (15)$$

These terms are used, because in a recognition using the wrong dictionary, it is $FR = CA = 0$. The recognition results, which are shown in Fig. 5, are determined using an increasing threshold $t = t0, ..., tn$. On the right side of Fig. 5 the corresponding error rates using a correct or wrong (OOV) dictionary at the same confidence threshold are presented. The left curve presents the rejection rate r referring to this error rate e using complete dictionaries (OOV: $r + e = 100\%$).

First, regarding the 2-best confidence: if any threshold t_k (or t_l) is chosen, such that $e_k = 1.9\%$ ($e_l = 0.8\%$) using the complete dictionary, the corresponding error rate for the OOV-dictionary is $e_k = 21.1\%$ ($e_l = 15.2\%$). Then the rejection rate for the complete dictionary is $r_k = 32.0\%$ ($r_l = 42.6\%$). Now some selected values obtained by the garbage-model (see Fig. 5): if a threshold t_u (t_v) is chosen, such that $e_u = 3.6\%$ ($e_v = 1.4\%$) using the complete dictionary, the corresponding error rate for the OOV-dictionary is $e_u = 4.8\%$ ($e_v = 1.1\%$). Then the rejection rate for the complete dictionary is $r_u = 40.0\%$ ($r_v = 57.6\%$). The 2-best confidence leads to curves for complete and OOV dictionaries, which run nearly parallel. Thus, for detection resp. rejection of OOV-words the garbage-model performs better than the 2-best confidence.

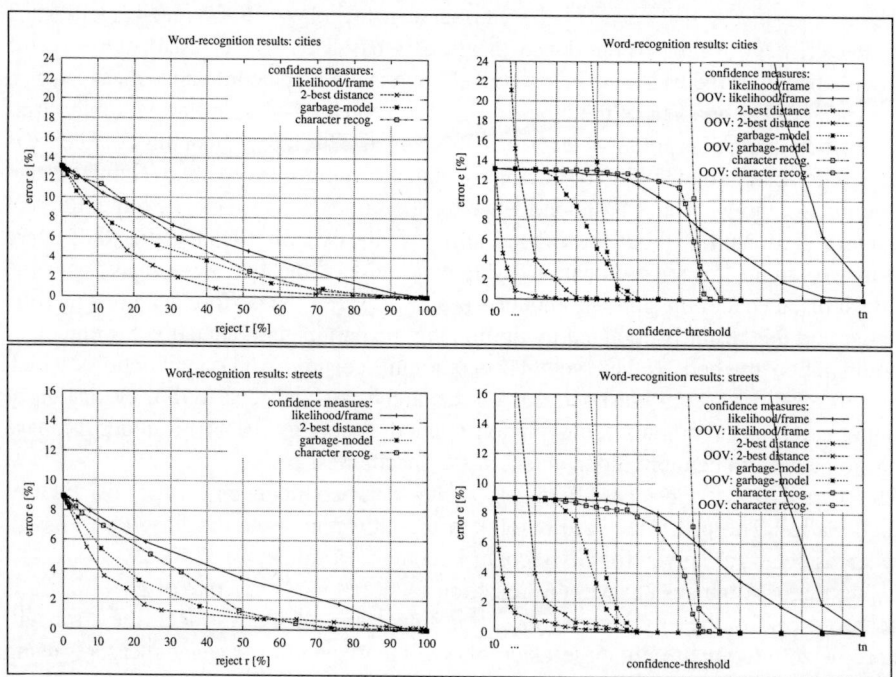

Fig. 5. Rejection management using a complete dictionary (left) and corresponding comparison of complete and OOV dictionaries using the same threshold (right)

5   Adaptation

In order to increase recognition results of different post offices, we tested some supervised adaptation techniques which are well known in speech recognition. The main difference between our approach (see [6]) and known approaches for speaker adaptation or handwriting adaptation (see for example [12,17,31,18,2,36]) is the kind of the adaptation database, which consists of several writers. The goal is to maximize the matching between the globally trained Hidden Markov Models (based on the general database) and some address words of a special post office by considering different writing styles and a different frequency of occurring addresses. We compare three different possibilities for adaptation: a retraining of the HMMs according to the maximum likelihood (ML) criterion (expectation maximization algorithm, compare [26]), the maximum likelihood linear regression (MLLR, see [17]) adaptation and a new discriminant adaptation technique called SLLR (scaled likelihood linear regression, see [37,35]). Often the amount of training or adaptation data is not sufficient for a standard (re-) training, then it is useful to update only a part of the HMM parameters λ, which consist of the Gaussian parameters (mean μ, variance) and also weights ω and transition probabilities.

5.1   Adaptation Techniques

Using the ML-criterion, all parameters can be estimated optionally, applying the MLLR- or SLLR-adaptation the transformation refers to the means only. To compare the standard ML-retraining (Eq.16) with the two further adaptation approaches, in the following the objective functions are given in principle.

$$\lambda_{ML} = \operatorname*{argmax}_{\lambda} P(X|W,\lambda) \quad : \quad \mu_{base} \overset{EM}{\to} \mu_{ML} \tag{16}$$

A similar transform can also be computed for the variances, weights and transitions of the HMM. In contrast to the ML-technique, in which a separate transformation of each Gaussian is performed, the sparse data problem has been taken into account by the MLLR/SLLR-approach by clustering several Gaussians into regression classes. From this it follows that models, which do not appear in the adaptation-dataset, can be adapted according to their regression class. Using the MLLR or SLLR adaptation only the means μ of the Gaussians are reestimated for each state s by transforming them with a regression matrix M (see Eq.17); the variances, weights and transition probabilities are unchanged.

$$\lambda \overset{M}{\to} \lambda_{MLLR/SLLR} \quad : \quad \mu_{MLLR/SLLR} = M \cdot \mu_{base} \tag{17}$$

This regression matrix M is computed using a gradient descend procedure (resilient propagation algorithm: RPROP), where the objective function differs comparing the MLLR (see Eq.18) and SLLR as follows:

$$\lambda_{MLLR} = \operatorname*{argmax}_{\lambda} P(X|W,\lambda) \quad \text{with} \quad P(X|W,\lambda) \approx \prod_{n} P(x_n|q_n = s_i, \lambda) \tag{18}$$

In contrast to the MLLR adaptation (W is the sequence of characters) which maximizes the likelihood according to Eq.18, the SLLR adaptation tries to maximize the conditional likelihood $P(X|W, \lambda)$ and to minimize the unconditional likelihood $P(X|\lambda)$ at the same time (see Eq.19).

$$\lambda_{SLLR} = \underset{\lambda}{\text{argmax}} \frac{P(X|W, \lambda)}{P(X|\lambda)} \quad \text{with} \quad P(X|\lambda) \approx \sum_{\text{best W}} P(X|W, \lambda)P(W) \quad (19)$$

Here we use an approximation for a frame-based discriminative training according to

$$P(X|\lambda) \approx \prod_n \sum_q P(q_n = s_i|\lambda)P(x_n|q_n = s_i, \lambda) \quad (20)$$

by estimating the state prior probabilities $P(s|\lambda)$ depending on their frequency in the training data. This approach with a discriminative objective criterion can be superior to ML based training functions, especially when the amount of adaptation data is small. Nevertheless, the SLLR adaptation is more time-consuming than the MLLR adaptation as can be seen by comparing Eqs.18 and 19. Although the experiments described in the following section mostly refer to a supervised adaptation (using correctly labelled adaptation data), also an unsupervised adaptation is possible. In this case, the labels of the adaptation data are received from the recognition output of the baseline system.

5.2   Experimental Results

We tested the influence of adaptation techniques for four different post offices (see [6]). The amount of streets and cities we recognized is quite similar for each post office. The baseline system, which is trained on several post offices in Germany, leads to a word recognition rate of 86.8% for the cities and 91.0% for the streets using a general evaluation database of different post offices (Tab.2:A, compare also Sec. 3.3 and Sec. 4.1). The recognition results of the adaptation databases on this baseline system are smaller (cities: about 80.9%, streets: about 85.4% in average), which can be explained by the use of a larger dictionary (see Tab.2:a, compare also Sec.2.1). Regarding the five best results (Tab.2:a, TOP 5), the recognition accuracy increases of about 4% in average. A lot of errors occur, if the test-word is very short or if the substitution of only a few characters generates another valid dictionary entry.

Table 2 shows word recognition results using different adaptation techniques. As can be seen, the recognition accuracy increases by adapting or retraining the system on special data (comparing line a with lines b-i). So first, it can be shown that an adaption to a writer independent dataset of specific post offices is useful, which is not absolutely expected. It can be noticed that the enhancement in recognition of cities is higher than the recognition of streets. This provides the assumption that not only the writing style in different German areas is responsible for these results, but also the higher frequency of special city names (the variance for street names is much higher), which can be trained very well. Table 2 shows two further facts: the influence of the amount of adaptation data and of the adaptation technique. If there is enough adaptation data available (*large*: whole training set of about 1500 to 1700 words) more parameters can be reestimated securely. So the results of the retraining using the ML criterion leads to the highest error reductions when means, transitions and weights are updated (compare Tab.2). When the

Table 2. Word recognition results (%) for various post offices (HRO, STR, HAL, HAM) comparing different adaptation techniques and the amount of adaptation data (large, small, very small)

A) baseline system	general data: 86.8% cities, 91.0%streets							
system/algorithm	adapt. HRO		adapt. STR		adapt. HAL		adapt. HAM	
	city	street	city	street	city	street	city	street
a) baseline system	82.1	85.0	81.5	85.3	80.2	85.7	79.6	85.6
baseline system: TOP 5	*86.1*	*89.1*	*85.6*	*89.1*	*85.4*	*88.9*	*84.4*	*89.3*
b) SLLR: μ, very small database	84.1	85.5	81.9	85.4	80.5	85.7	80.1	85.1
c) MLLR: μ, very small	82.3	85.3	81.8	85.0	79.8	85.9	80.0	85.8
d) MLLR: μ, small	82.5	85.4	82.3	85.6	80.1	85.7	80.3	85.8
e) ML: μ, small	82.4	85.3	82.1	84.8	79.8	85.0	80.3	85.8
f) ML: μ, large	83.0	85.4	82.1	85.4	80.0	85.3	79.9	85.3
g) ML: μ+transition+ω, large	84.2	85.5	84.4	85.9	82.2	87.5	81.4	87.5
ML: μ+transition+ω, large: TOP 5	*87.9*	*90.4*	*87.7*	*89.0*	*87.3*	*91.2*	*86.2*	*91.1*
h) ML: μ+transition+ω, very small	80.6	83.9	81.3	83.5	77.5	83.7	76.8	82.6
i) ML: μ+trans+ω, large, unsup.	83.2	85.8	83.7	85.0	82.1	86.3	80.4	87.3

adaptation set is reduced by choosing every 4th or 16th word (*small*: about 400 words; *very small*: about 100 words) the SLLR technique outperforms the ML reestimation and also the MLLR approach.

Nevertheless, in general, best recognition rates are obtained using a large adaptation database. So, in best case (large database of correctly labeled training words, Tab.2: g) the relative error is reduced by about 12% for city recognition in the post office in Rostock (HRO), 16% in Stuttgart (STR), 10% in Halle (HAL) and 9% in Hamburg (HAM) by retraining the system using the ML-approach updating the means as well as the weights and transitions of the HMMs. Testing the general data on an adapted system, the accuracy decreases slightly. The same applies to the specific post offices, as can be seen in Tab.3.

Table 3. Cross-validation: word recognition results (%) for STR and HAM adapting the system on 'wrong' data (ML-adaptation using a large database)

system	STR test-data				HAM test-data			
	adapt. STR	adapt. HRO	adapt. HAL	adapt. HAM	adapt. HAM	adapt. HRO	adapt. HAL	adapt. STR
city	84.4	81.5	83.3	81.2	81.4	79.1	80.6	79.8
street	85.9	84.8	85.3	85.3	87.5	86.9	87.0	86.0

A cross-validation, for example testing the data of the post office in Stuttgart on a recognition system, which is adapted (using the ML-approach) on another post office, results in lower recognition rates (compare Tab.2:g and Tab.3). This test proves the assumption, that the error reduction by adapting or retraining the system depends not only on the greater amount of data, but primarily on the specific adaptation data. In a first test it can be shown, that the recognition accuracy also increases, when an unsupervised ML-retraining (without confidence) is performed (see Tab.2:i). Because of this result (comparing Tab.2:g and i), it is expected, that a further error reduction can be obtained using a larger (the collection of unlabeled adaptation data is unproblematic) adaptation database and a confidence measure to select the available adaptation data.

6   Summary and Conclusion

We presented an HMM based handwriting recognition system for German address words with focus on language models, confidence measures and adaptation techniques.

First, we presented the comparison of dictionaries of different sizes and language models based on backoff character n-grams for the recognition of handwritten addresses. The dictionary-based approach leads to significantly higher recognition results, if the vocabulary can be restricted in size, e.g. by the zip code. If the used vocabulary is unknown, because the address structure cannot be recognized, the character error can be reduced by about 48% in average using a general address 7-gram (compared to the use of no language model). The second aspect of this work is the evaluation of confidence measures to reject uncertain results. Comparing four investigated confidence measures – based on the frame normalized likelihood, a 2-best distance, a garbage-model or an unconstrained character decoding – the best performance is obtained by the 2-best recognition. Regarding the same problem when using OOV-dictionaries the garbage-model based confidence and also the character decoding lead to some better results. Third, the effect of adaptation techniques is shown. We compared three different adaptation approaches using the ML algorithm, the MLLR and the SLLR estimation. The above experiments show, that it is profitable to adapt or retrain a general recognition system to the appearance of letters in special post offices. In this way a relative word error reduction of up to 16% can be obtained.

Acknowledgments. This work has been done in cooperation with Siemens Dematic.

References

1. I. Bazzi, R. Schwartz, and J. Makhoul. An Omnifont Open-Vocabulary OCR System for English and Arabic. *IEEE Transactions on Pattern Analysis and Machine Intelligence*, 21(6):495–504, June 1999.
2. Anja Brakensiek, Andreas Kosmala, and Gerhard Rigoll. Comparing Adaptation Techniques for On-Line Handwriting Recognition. In *6th Int. Conference on Document Analysis and Recognition (ICDAR)*, pages 486–490, Seattle, USA, September 2001.
3. Anja Brakensiek and Gerhard Rigoll. A Comparison of Character N-Grams and Dictionaries Used for Script Recognition. In *6th Int. Conference on Document Analysis and Recognition (ICDAR)*, pages 241–245, Seattle, USA, September 2001.
4. Anja Brakensiek, Jörg Rottland, and Gerhard Rigoll. Handwritten Address Recognition with Open Vocabulary Using Charcter N-Grams. In *8th Int. Workshop on Frontiers in Handwriting Recognition (IWFHR)*, pages 357–362, Niagara-on-the-Lake, Canada, August 2002.

5. Anja Brakensiek, Jörg Rottland, and Gerhard Rigoll. Confidence Measures for an Address Reading System. In *7th Int. Conference on Document Analysis and Recognition (ICDAR)*, Edinburgh, August 2003.

6. Anja Brakensiek, Jörg Rottland, Frank Wallhoff, and Gerhard Rigoll. Adaptation of an Address Reading System to Local Mail Streams. In *6th Int. Conference on Document Analysis and Recognition (ICDAR)*, pages 872–876, Seattle, USA, September 2001.

7. Anja Brakensiek, Daniel Willett, and Gerhard Rigoll. Unlimited Vocabulary Script Recognition Using Character N-Grams. In *22. DAGM-Symposium, Tagungsband Springer-Verlag*, pages 436–443, Kiel, Germany, September 2000.

8. T. Caesar, J.M. Gloger, and E. Mandler. Preprocessing and Feature Extraction for a Handwriting Recognition System. In *Proc. Int. Conference on Document Analysis and Recognition (ICDAR)*, pages 408–411, Tsukuba, Japan, October 1993.

9. P. Clarkson and R. Rosenfeld. Statistical Language Modeling Using the CMU-Cambridge Toolkit. In *5th European Conference on Speech Communication and Technology (Eurospeech)*, pages 2707–2710, Rhodes, Greece, September 1997.

10. J.G.A. Dolfing and A. Wendemuth. Combination of Confidence Measures in Isolated Word Recognition. In *5th Int. Conference on Spoken Language Processsing (ICSLP)*, pages 3237–3240, Sydney, Australia, December 1998.

11. J. Franke, J.M. Gloger, A. Kaltenmeier, and E. Mandler. A Comparison of Gaussian Distribution and Polynomial Classifiers in a Hidden Markov Model Based System for the Recognition of Cursive Script. In *Proc. Int. Conference on Document Analysis and Recognition (ICDAR)*, pages 515–518, Ulm, Germany, August 1997.

12. J.-L. Gauvain and C.-H. Lee. Maximum a Posteriori Estimation for Multivariate Gaussian Mixture Observation of Markov Chains. *IEEE Transactions on Speech and Audio Processing*, 2(2):291–298, April 1994.

13. J.M. Gloger, A. Kaltenmaier, E. Mandler, and L. Andrews. Reject Management in a Handwriting Recognition System. In *Int. Conference on Document Analysis and Recognition (ICDAR)*, pages 556–559, Ulm, Germany, August 1997.

14. T.J. Hazen and I. Bazzi. A Comparison and Combination of Methods for OOV Word Detection and Word Confidence Scoring. In *IEEE Int. Conference on Acoustics, Speech, and Signal Processing (ICASSP)*, Salt Lake City, Utah, May 2001.

15. Frederick Jelinek. *Statistical Methods for Speech Recognition*. The MIT Press, Cambridge, Massachusetts, 1998.

16. S.M. Katz. Estimation of probabilities from sparse data for the language model component of a speech recognizer. *IEEE Transactions on Acoustic, Speech and Signal Processing*, 35(3):400–401, 1987.

17. C.J. Leggetter and P.C. Woodland. Speaker Adaptation of Continuous Density HMMs using Multivariate Linear Regression. In *Int. Conference on Spoken Language Processing (ICSLP)*, pages 451–454, Yokohama, Japan, September 1994.

18. Z. Lu, I. Bazzi, A. Kornai, J. Makhoul, P. Natarajan, and R. Schwartz. A Robust, Language-Independent OCR System. In *Proc. 27th AIPR Workshop: Advances in Computer-Assisted Recognition (SPIE)*, pages 96–105, 1999.

19. E. Mandler and M. Oberländer. A single pass algorithm for fast contour coding of binary images. In *12. DAGM-Symposium, Tagungsband Springer-Verlag*, pages 248–255, Oberkochen-Aalen, Germany, September 1990.

20. U.-V. Marti and H. Bunke. Unconstrained Handwriting Recognition: Language Models, Perplexity, and System Performance. In *7th Int. Workshop on Frontiers in Handwriting Recognition (IWFHR)*, pages 463–468, Amsterdam, Netherlands, September 2000.

21. S. Marukatat, T. Artieres, and P. Gallinari. Rejection measures for Handwriting sentence Recognition. In *8th Int. Workshop on Frontiers in Handwriting Recognition (IWFHR)*, pages 24–29, Niagara-on-the-Lake, Canada, August 2002.

22. U. Miletzki, T. Bayer, and H. Schäfer. Continuous Learning Systems: Postal Address Readers with built-in learning capability. In *5th Int. Conference on Document Analysis and Recognition (ICDAR)*, pages 329–332, Bangalore, India, 1999.
23. D.B. Paul. An efficient A* stack decoder algorithm for continuous speech recognition with a stochastic language model. In *IEEE Int. Conference on Acoustics, Speech, and Signal Processing (ICASSP)*, pages 25–28, San Francisco, CA, March 1992.
24. J. Pitrelli and M. Perrone. Confidence Modeling for Verification Post-Processing for Handwriting Recognition. In *8th Int. Workshop on Frontiers in Handwriting Recognition (IWFHR)*, pages 30–35, Niagara-on-the-Lake, Canada, August 2002.
25. J.F. Pitrelli and E.H. Ratzlaff. Quantifying the Contribution of Language Modeling to Writer-Independent On-Line Handwriting Recognition. In *7th Int. Workshop on Frontiers in Handwriting Recognition (IWFHR)*, pages 383–392, Amsterdam, Netherlands, September 2000.
26. L.R. Rabiner and B.H. Juang. An Introduction to Hidden Markov Models. *IEEE ASSP Magazine*, pages 4–16, 1986.
27. R. Rose and D. Paul. A Hidden Markov Model based Keyword Recognition System. In *IEEE Int. Conference on Acoustics, Speech, and Signal Processing (ICASSP)*, pages 129–132, Albuquerque, New Mexico, 1990.
28. Ronald Rosenfeld. Two decades of statistical language modeling: Where do we go from here? *Proceedings of the IEEE*, 88(8), 2000.
29. E.G. Schukat-Talamazzini. *Automatische Spracherkennung - Grundlagen, statistische Modelle und effiziente Algorithmen*. Vieweg, Braunschweig, 1995.
30. M. Schüßler and H. Niemann. A HMM-based System for Recognition of Handwritten Adress Words. In *6th Int. Workshop on Frontiers in Handwriting Recognition (IWFHR)*, pages 505–514, Taejon, Korea, 1998.
31. A. Senior and K. Nathan. Writer adaptation of a HMM handwriting recognition system. In *IEEE Int. Conference on Acoustics, Speech, and Signal Processing (ICASSP)*, pages 1447–1450, Munich, Germany, April 1997.
32. M. Shridhar, F. Kimura, B. Truijen, and G.F. Houle. Impact of Lexicon Completeness on City Name Recognition. In *8th Int. Workshop on Frontiers in Handwriting Recognition (IWFHR)*, pages 513–518, Niagara-on-the-Lake, Canada, August 2002.
33. T. Steinherz, E. Rivlin, and N. Intrator. Offline cursive sript word recognition - a survey. *Int. Journal on Document Analysis and Recognition (IJDAR)*, 2:90–110, 1999.
34. C.I. Tomai, K.M. Allen, and S.N. Srihari. Recognition of Handwritten Foreign Mail. In *6th Int. Conference on Document Analysis and Recognition (ICDAR)*, pages 882–886, Seattle, USA, September 2001.
35. V. Valtchev, J.J. Odell, P.C. Woodland, and S.J. Young. Lattice-Based Discriminative Training for Large Vocabulary Speech Recognition Systems. In *IEEE Int. Conference on Acoustics, Speech, and Signal Processing (ICASSP)*, pages 605–608, Atlanta, GA, May 1996.
36. A. Vinciarelli and S. Bengio. Writer adaptation techniques in HMM based Off-Line Cursive Script Recognition. *Pattern Recognition Letters*, 23(8):905–916, June 2002.
37. Frank Wallhoff, Daniel Willett, and Gerhard Rigoll. Frame Discriminative and Confidence-Driven Adaptation for LVCSR. In *IEEE Int. Conference on Acoustics, Speech, and Signal Processing (ICASSP)*, pages 1835–1838, Istanbul, Turkey, June 2000.
38. D. Willett, C. Neukirchen, and G. Rigoll. DUCODER-The Duisburg University LVSCR Stackdecoder. *Proc. IEEE Int. Conf. on Acoustics, Speech, and Signal Processing (ICASSP)*, June 2000.
39. G. Williams and S. Renals. Confidence measures from local posterior probability estimates. *Computer Speech and Language*, 13:395–411, 1999.
40. S. Young. Detecting Misrecognitions and Out-Of Vocabulary Words. In *IEEE Int. Conference on Acoustics, Speech, and Signal Processing (ICASSP)*, pages 21–24, Adelaide, Australia, April 1994.

Adaptive Combination of Commercial OCR Systems

Elke Wilczok and Wolfgang Lellmann

Océ Document Technologies GmbH, Constance, Germany,
{Elke.Wilczok,Wolfgang.Lellmann}@odt-oce.com

Abstract. Combining multiple classifiers to achieve improved recognition results has become a popular technique in recent years. As for OCR systems, most investigations focus on fusion strategies on the character level. This paper describes a flexible framework for the combination of result strings which are the common output of commercial OCR systems. By synchronizing strings according to geometrical criteria, incorrect character segmentations can be avoided, while character recognition is improved by classical combination rules like Borda Count or Plurality Vote. To reduce computing time, further expert calls are stopped as soon as the quality of a temporary combination result exceeds a given threshold. The system allows easy integration of arbitrary new OCR systems and simplifies the determination of optimal system parameters by analyzing the input data at hand. Quantitative results are shown for a two-recognizer system, while the framework allows an arbitrary number of experts.

1 Introduction

Multiple classifier systems (MCS) have proven successful in many pattern recognition applications during the last decade: consulting several experts and combining their decisions in a suitable way usually leads to results which are more reliable than those produced by any single expert. Convincing examples from a variety of applications can be found in [KiRo00,KiRo01,RoKi02,WiRo03]. A short introduction into multiple classifier techniques will be provided in section 2.

Concerning OCR, combination methods have been widely used to improve the recognition of isolated characters. Little work has been done on combination at string level, i.e. the combination of words or lines usually resulting from OCR systems (cf. section 3). Sections 4 and 5 present an adaptive framework for the combination of OCR result strings, where *adaptive* refers to

- input data (handwriting or machine print, image quality, country...)
- number, type and performance of experts
- computing time (superfluous expert calls should be avoided).

Experimental results for a two-recognizer system are shown in section 6.

A. Dengel et al. (Eds.): Adaptive READ Research Project, LNCS 2956, pp. 123–136, 2004.

2   A Short Survey on Multiple Classifier Techniques

Essentially, there are two ways to construct highly-performant multiple classifier systems, namely:

- to optimize the classifier ensemble *(coverage optimization)* or
- to optimize the combination rule *(decision optimization)*.

Some approaches from literature will be sketched in the following.

2.1   Coverage Optimization

The success of a multiple classifier system strongly depends on the *diversity / independence* of its individual members [RuGa02,Akse03]: little improvement can be expected from combination strategies if all experts make the same errors. Diversity may be ensured by explicit construction of the individual team members *(ensemble creation)* or by choosing appropriate subsets out of a classifier pool at hand *(ensemble selection)*.

- *Ensemble creation:* Various strategies have been suggested to construct classifier ensembles with high diversity starting from a finite training sample. Typical examples are the manipulation of features, classification outputs or training examples [Diet00]. The last method (also called *resampling*) seems to be the most popular, including algorithms like *Bagging* and *Boosting*, in which component classifiers learn different subsets of the original training set [BaKo99]. While Bagging works with random subsets, Boosting iteratively concentrates on hard patterns, i.e. training data misclassified by the previously constructed experts. A well-known algorithm for feature manipulation is the *Random Subspace Method* [Ho98,SkDu01]. Multi-class problems are often tackled with *Error Correcting Output Coding* [MaVa02], i.e. they are reduced to a series of two-class problems the results of which may be interpreted as a binary code vector. Concerning the *accuracy* of the component classifiers, 'better than guessing' suffices for most ensemble creation methods. There are no restrictions on the underlying learning algorithms (e.g. whether to use neural networks or support vector machines). But usually all members of one ensemble use the same strategy - partially to simplify the training procedure, partially to guarantee controlled diversity.
- *Ensemble selection:* Given a (possibly large) number of arbitrary component classifiers and a special recognition task, it is rarely advisable to consult *all* classifiers and to combine their results blindly: one reason is computing time, another the risk of error accumulation. Fusing the outputs of the best individual classifiers is not a good solution, either: their errors need not necessarily be independent. A more promising approach is to compare the typical errors made by the candidate classifiers on a representative test set, and to choose teams according to diversity measures as proposed by [Akse03].

2.2   Decision Optimization

Given an ensemble of (hopefully diverse) experts, several strategies may be applied to combine their decisions. There is no unique categorization of combination (also called *fusion*) methods [KaWa03]. Some possible criteria are:

- *System architecture:* While *parallel* combination methods consult all experts independently, *serial* architectures include intermediate results to decide which classifier should be called next. Typically, coarse, simple classifiers are followed by highly-spezialized experts in serial (also called *multi-stage* or *hierarchical*) combination approaches. One example is the grouping of 'similar-looking' classes in multi-class problems.
- *Output information used for combination:* [XuKr92] introduced three levels of classifier outputs: *abstract, rank* and *measurement* level. Abstract level classifiers yield a single class label (also called a *crisp* decision), while rank level classifiers supply a sorted list of alternatives. Most information is provided by measurement level classifiers which add a *confidence value* to each proposal (*soft* decision). Depending on the output level of the component classifiers, various combination rules can be used [SuLa00].

  Combination methods suitable for abstract level classifiers are *plurality* and *majority voting*. The former selects the candidate class with the most votes as the winner, while the latter requires an absolute majority (i.e. more than 50 percent of all votes). Otherwise, decision is rejected [LiYa03]. Combination results may be obtained at measurement level, using the relative number of votes as a weight for the various proposals.

  Borda Count is the standard recipe for the combination of rank level decisions [ErSc00]: Assuming each classifier provides a fixed number n of alternatives, class label ω_k wins $n-i$ points ($i = 0,1,...$n-1) if ω_k is suggested as ith alternative by one of the component classifiers. Borda Count attributes weights to all class labels collecting the points suggested by the different classifiers.

  Sum-, Product-, Maximum-, Minimum- and *Median rule* are possibilities to combine classification results on measurement level [AlKi99,TaBr00,AlCa01]. Interpreting confidence values (after a suitable scaling) as approximations of a-posteriori-probabilities, product rule should theoretically perform best. In practice, however, it often appears too pessimistic, allowing single classifiers the power of veto. The scaling of confidence values resulting from different classification algorithms is one of the hardest problems in this context [LiDi98,BoGo99,AlDe02].

  Measurement level outputs may easily be transformed to rank level outputs. The first alternative in a ranking can be interpreted as an abstract level output. However, there is no way to enlarge the information content of a crisp decision. Consequently, given several classification results, the 'least informative' output determines the combination method to be used.
- *Data dependence: Fixed* combination rules like Majority Vote, Borda Count or Sum rule can be used directly to obtain quick recognition results for very general applications. Improved combination results may be achieved including a-priori knowledge about the behavior of the individual classifiers on the

data set under consideration. For that purpose, heuristical weights may be introduced in the combination rules described above, leading to methods like *Weighted Average* [FuRo03]. More sophisticated methods determine elaborate result statistics or interpret combination as an additional classification problem with the outputs of the single experts as feature vectors. However, those features induce unusual class distributions preventing the use of standard classification algorithms [KuBe01]. Consequently, new strategies have been introduced, like the *Behaviour Knowledge Space (BKS)* method, originally suggested for abstract level classifiers [RaRo03,CoFa01]: BKS decisions are based on a look-up table containing all classifier output combinations found on a training set, together with the corresponding 'true' class label. The latter is determined by the majority of training patterns leading to that special output sequence (ties may remain). Similar ideas applied to continuous measurement level outputs are the basis of *Decision Templates (DT)* [KuBe01]. *Trained* combination rules, like BKS or DT, work even in case of partially dependent component classifiers. However, large training sets are required to avoid overfitting.

Dynamic Classifier Selection (DCS) is an alternative approach based on the assumption that each component classifier is an expert in a local region of the feature space. Given a feature vector, DCS entrusts the decision to the single classifier seeming most capable for that task (referring to suitable test set statistics) [GiRo01] .

Obviously, coverage optimization has to be completed by some combination rule (or DCS), while combination rules may be applied to *arbitrary* classifier outputs. However, the higher the diversity of the classifiers constituting a team, the better results can be expected, even using simple combination rules like Majority Vote.

3   Multiple Classifier Methods for Optical Character Recognition

Optical character recognition (OCR), as understood in the following, is the whole process of transforming a document image (machine printed or handwritten) into a corresponding ASCII text. Many steps are necessary to perform this task, e.g. layout analysis, image preprocessing, line segmentation, character recognition, contextual postprocessing... Modifying one of them may lead to completely different results.

Multiple classifier approaches turned out successful in the context of *isolated* character recognition which is a standard classification problem: given a character image, one out of a finite number of class labels has to be determined (possibly with some additional alternatives or confidence values). Standard techniques may be used to combine the outputs of various character recognizers or to construct appropriate expert ensembles [LaHa97,DuTa00,WaYa00,SiHo02]. However, starting from commercial OCR devices, character results may not be combined so easily: typical outputs are words or text lines which may differ in length, due to alternative line segmentation strategies used. Especially for bad quality machine print or unconstrained handwriting recognition, a one-to-one correspondence between single characters is rarely achieved. Using dictionary-assisted recognizers (e.g. Hidden-Markov-based OCR systems) one can circumvent this problem: interpreting dictionary entries as new class labels, combination techniques can be applied on a higher level [VeGa01]. The consequence is a large number of classes, which may cause additional complications [GuBu03]. Furthermore, complete dictionaries are not available for many real-life applications.

Comparing string results produced by different OCR devices one may often find that no individual recognizer is completely correct, but that the correct result can be combined from substrings of the various suggestions. This motivates the following three-step approach for string combination (explained more extensively in section 4):

1. Find matching character geometries in the input strings. Administer them in a graph data structure, together with the unmatched substrings *(geometrical synchronization)*.

2. Use standard combination rules to get improved class rankings for matching character geometries.

3. Find the m best strings using standard graph search methods combined with suitable confidence measures.

Parallel segmentation/classification combination approaches have also been suggested by [Klin97,MaBu01,WaBr02,YeCh02]. The four articles differ in the strategies used for synchronization, expert weighting and best string search.

While experts created by coverage optimization usually distinguish in one single property (e.g. training sample *or* features), arbitrary commercial OCR systems may differ in many aspects, including learning algorithms or image pre-processing methods. However, OCR devices appear as 'black boxes' in most cases. Hence, differences are not explicitly known to the user. This means: there is some diversity potential in combining arbitrary OCR systems, yet diversity cannot be guaranteed. Consequently, combination rules need often be adjusted to get satisfying results. One important reason for the fusion of commercial OCR devices is software reuse allowing reduced implementation and training times.

4   A Three-Step Approach to String Combination

In the following, we describe the combination strategy used in this study.

4.1   Geometrical Synchronization

Given some string results, a so called *result graph* is built with nodes representing character geometries, edges representing segmentation decisions. The graph is directed and has some special nodes 'start' and 'end' containing no further information. Synchronization starts by completely inserting the first input string between start and end node. In all following steps, heuristically restricted breadth-first graph search is applied to integrate a new result string in the already existing result graph. Assuming string characters sorted by their horizontal positions (which may be ensured by suitable preprocessing), synchronization is performed from left to right, testing each string character for its horizontal overlap with some geometrically convenient subset of the graph characters. Two characters 'match' if their relative horizontal overlap succeeds a given threshold. No further criteria (e.g. vertical overlap, recognition result) are considered. Class labels corresponding to matching character geometries are enlisted in a common graph node. Substrings which cannot be synchronized that way lead to additional branches. A widely ramified result graph indicates large differences between the various segmentation strategies used. Confidence values provided by segmentation algorithms can be entered at the graph edges. Interpolation techniques may be used to guess missing character geometries.

A simple example is presented in the following. Given the string

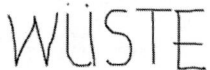

Fig. 1. Original string

two independent experts may suggest the segmentations

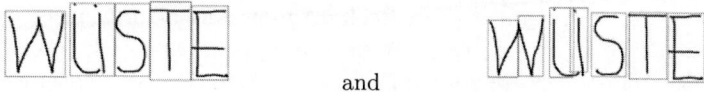

and

Fig. 2. Segmentation alternatives

leading to the recognition results
W (200) M (10) $|_{255}$Ü (180) U (100) $|_{255}$ S (190) 5 (30) $|_{200}$T (240)$|_{200}$
E (210) F (100)

and
V (110) U (20) $|_{150}$ V (115) U (18) $|_{250}$ I (190) $|_{130}$ J (110)$|_{210}$ S (219)$|_{210}$
T (220) $|_{190}$ E (240),

where each bar separates two character geometries. Between two bars, one finds all labels suggested for that geometry. The numbers in brackets (resp. bar-indices) denote the corresponding classification (resp. segmentation) confidence values on a scale 0 (=unlikely) to 255 (=certain). Geometrical synchronization yields the result graph shown in fig. 3. Broken lines indicate additional character transitions suggested by no single expert. It takes some time to compute them, however, and their influence on recognition rates seems rather negligible. Hence, they have been neglected in the following.

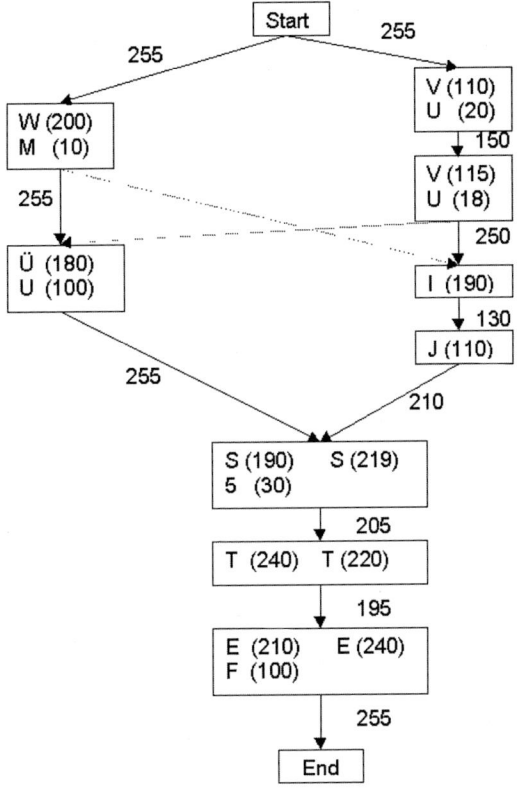

Fig. 3. Result graph

4.2   Combination at Character Level

Graph nodes containing more than one character recognition result after synchronization (hence, 'matched characters') may be associated with a single, improved class label ranking using standard combination rules like Plurality Vote, Borda Count or Sum rule. The system allows the explicit selection of a strategy. Otherwise, the most suitable combination rule may be chosen automatically, in accordance with the output types of the individual experts (abstract/rank/measurement level). Weights may be introduced to reflect strengths and weaknesses of the component classifiers (cf. section 5).

There is a common interface for all combination rules:

Input:
- an arbitrary number of (possibly 1-element) ranked lists of alternatives
(with or without confidence values)
- a look-up table with expert-specific class weights (cf. section 5)

Output:
a ranked list of alternatives with confidence values (independent from the types
of the single experts)

Plurality Vote leads to a (rough) confidence value on the scale $[0, MaxConfVal]$
using the formula

$$ConfVal(\omega_k) = \frac{number\ of\ votes\ for\ \omega_k}{number\ of\ experts} * MaxConfVal, \qquad (1)$$

which takes only three values for a two-expert system:
$MaxConfVal, MaxConfVal/2, 0$.
Considering a fixed number n of alternatives (the best ranked at position '0'), a
confidence value for Borda Count results may be computed as follows:

$$ConfVal(\omega_k) = \frac{inverse\ rank\ sum\ of\ \omega_k}{n * number\ of\ experts} * MaxConfVal, \qquad (2)$$

where

$$inverse\ rank\ sum\ of\ \omega_k = \sum_{experts\ i} (n - Rank_i(\omega_k)),$$

and $Rank_i(\omega_k)$ denotes the rank assigned to class ω_k by the i-th expert.

Combination strategies at measurement level, like Sum, Product or Maximum
rule, base their decisions on combined confidence values. Those may - the other
way round - be interpreted as confidence values for the combination results (an
appropriate scaling assumed).

4.3   Graph Search

Finally, the m best strings are selected from the result graph using standard
search algorithms. More precisely: given a suitable quality measure (usually
based on node and edge weights), the m best paths between 'start' and 'end' node
are determined using time-efficient incomplete depth-first graph-search. Various
string quality measures have been analyzed, e.g. average and maximum node
weight (or linear combinations of node and edge weights). Usually, 'node weight'
refers to the confidence value of the best alternative. All measures were chosen
string-length independent and may be completed with contextual information
like n-grams or dictionaries. One should be aware that contextual postprocessing performed by the individual readers will usually be destroyed by merely
geometry-based synchronization.

5   Design of an Adaptive Combination Framework

The strategy described in section 4 has been integrated in an adaptive combination framework. In doing so, one of the main requirements was a clear separation between application-specific, recognizer-specific and combination-specific program code to alleviate the customization of new problems, the integration of new experts and the test of new fusion strategies.

Experts were interpreted as special parametrizations of various commercial OCR devices. This allows the combination of various OCR systems, as well as the combination of e.g. handwriting and machine print version of the same recognition software. The latter may help to improve the recognition of bad quality machine print.

As for decision optimization, rapidly changing applications and small training samples prohibit the use of trained combination rules like BKS. However, strengths and weaknesses of single recognizers may be found heuristically and the combination framework should offer a chance to account for such additional knowledge. One extreme (but realistic) example is the combination of two classifiers trained on samples from different countries, e.g. a French and a German classifier. The first has never seen an 'ß', the latter is ignorant of 'ô'. Consequently, neither 'ß' nor 'ô' will ever get a full vote using standard combination rules, while good improvement may be achieved for characters 'a' to 'z' or numbers. To avoid such inconsistencies, *weighted character sets* have been introduced, which are manually composed for the moment. In combination with Sum rule, they lead to a class-specific Weighted Average method [WiRo03], but weights may be integrated in Plurality Vote or Borda Count as well, allowing single experts multiple votes or excluding them from certain decisions. In case of a 3-reader system, the character table may look as follows:

$$A \quad 1 \quad 2 \quad 1$$
$$B \quad 1 \quad 1 \quad 1$$
$$...$$
$$Ä \quad 1 \quad 0 \quad 2$$
$$...$$

Here, reader 2 is ignorant of 'Ä', while it seems perfect in recognizing 'A'. If applications show that some recognizers know more classes than originally expected, character weights are automatically updated.

While system architecture is mainly parallel, serial approaches may be included to save recognition time. Observing a string with high confidence value resulting from one of the first experts, further expert calls may be avoided, accepting the risk of over-confident individuals. Conversely, to suppress the influence of outliers, strings with extremely low confidence values may be excluded from combination. This may be interpreted as a kind of a-posteriori classifier selection.

Another heuristic classifier selection strategy for OCR applications is to analyze image quality (e.g. to count connected components or to measure stroke thickness) and to combine experts with corresponding image preprocessing parametrizations.

Selection is performed by some superordinate control unit.

Altogether, above considerations lead to the architecture sketched in fig. 4.

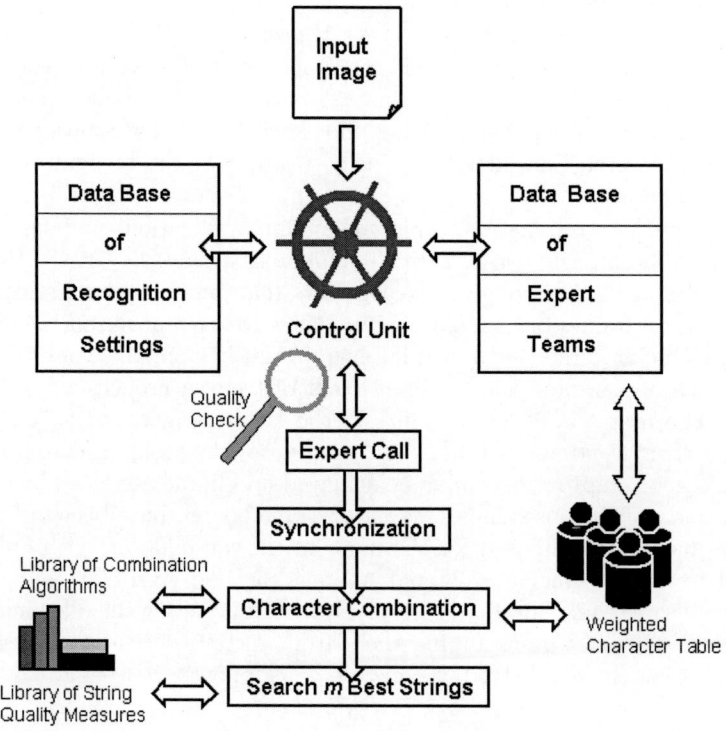

Fig. 4. Framework architecture

6   Experimental Results

Up to now, our investigations concentrated on various parametrizations of two commercial string recognizers based on pairwise hyperplane classification strategies at the character level. Both of them were trained independently using different data samples and features. Confidence values were provided at character level, reflecting inverse hyperplane distances. Additionally, both recognizers yielded character geometries. To clarify the influence of combination strategies, postprocessing steps (like n-grams or dictionaries) were suppressed for the individual experts. There was no contextual postprocessing for combination results, either.

Test samples originated from five real-life German handwriting applications (three numeral, two alphanumeric) and two alphanumeric machineprint applications. Single test sets consisted of 10000 to 50000 characters found in 800 to 3600 lines. Measurements were performed at character level using a reject threshold of 10, where confidence values ranged between 0 and 255.

Experiment 1 investigated different character combination strategies and their influence on string combination results, namely: Plurality Vote (PV), Borda Count (BC), median (instead average) based Borda Count (BCM), Sum rule (CVA = 'Confidence Values Additive'), Sum rule with special treatments of best alternatives (CVABA), Maximum rule (CVMax) and Product Rule (CV-Mult). Both OCR devices used corresponding parametrizations (e.g. both 'German handwriting'). There was no recognizer-specific weighting for single character classes. Results are presented in table 1. The first number in each column denotes the fraction of misclassified characters, while the second number denotes the fraction of rejected characters (in percent).

Table 1. Substituted / rejected characters (%) for different voting strategies

Strategy	Handwriting 1	Handwriting 2	Machine 1	Machine 2
Expert 1	20.73 / 0.78	11.85 / 0.68	9.17 / 0.59	5.76 / 1.82
Expert 2	25.99 / 0.51	22.48 / 2.23	11.29 / 0.26	7.15 / 0.89
PV	21.24 / 0.06	12.73 / 0.20	9.58 / 0.05	6.43 / 0.31
BC	20.82 / 0.06	12.41 / 0.20	9.15 / 0.05	6.23 / 0.31
BCM	21.28 / 0.07	12.57 / 0.08	9.57 / 0.05	6.41 / 0.32
CVA	19.12 / 2.74	13.33 / 0.55	9.27 / 0.13	5.65 / 0.42
CVABA	18.45 / 2.06	13.19 / 0.32	9.20 / 0.06	5.82 / 0.23
CVMax	19.26 / 2.50	13.33 / 0.55	9.32 / 0.13	5.65 / 0.42
CVMult	17.36 / 6.99	11.01 / 11.34	8.73 / 1.51	4.10 / 3.62

Strategy	Numerics 1	Numerics 2	Numerics 3
Expert 1	0.37 / 0.11	0.85 / 0.34	1.62 / 0.33
Expert 2	0.95 / 0.03	1.22 / 0.02	2.89 / 0.11
PV	0.40 / 0.00	1.04 / 0.03	1.62 / 0.02
BC	0.39 / 0.00	0.97 / 0.03	1.56 / 0.02
BCM	0.39 / 0.00	1.03 / 0.03	1.62 / 0.02
CVA	0.30 / 0.12	0.65 / 0.25	1.39 / 0.05
CVABA	0.31 / 0.08	0.67 / 0.20	1.38 / 0.02
CVMax	0.31 / 0.12	0.65 / 0.24	1.38 / 0.05
CVMult	0.31 / 0.24	0.60 / 0.53	1.24 / 0.82

Experiments show that confidence-free methods (PV,BC,BCM) tend to reduce rejection rate, while confidence-based methods (CVA, CVABA, CVMax) lead to less substitutions. Product rule is too overcautious, in general, which can be seen from its high rejection rate. This motivates experiments with smoothed

CVMult-versions (avoiding zero confidence values). Sum rule variants seemed most successful over all applications. The low reject rates of PV and BC(M) may be explained by the discrete confidence scales resulting from formulas as (1) or (2). Good recognizers could not be improved by much worse colleagues (e.g. on the difficult handwriting data), probably because of missing diversity. An analysis of typical recognition errors and the selection of corresponding character weights might help, but was not tested so far.

Experiment 2 investigated the effect of conditional combination: Further expert calls were abandoned as soon as the quality of the temporary string result exceeded a given threshold (150 resp. 200 on a scale [0,255]). Measures of string quality under consideration were: *average* and *minimal* confidence value of the best character alternatives in the string.

While minimum strategy guaranteed higher recognition rates using the same thresholds over all test sets and voting strategies, average criterion achieved higher time reduction (up to 33%) producing more rejects. The effect of time-saving strategies strongly depends on the test set under consideration. For difficult material (e.g. handwriting, alphanumerics) and a *two*-expert-system, the additional quality check may balance the time-savings achieved by avoiding a second expert call. Of course, the time-saving effect grows with the number of experts in the expert teams.

Experiment 3 concerned the dependency of recognition results on expert order (in case of conditional combination). Calling expert 2 before expert 1 using the minimum criterion with threshold 200 lead to a time-saving (up to 6%) on most test sets. Regarding recognition quality, slight improvements were observed as well as substitution rates growing with a factor 2.5, depending on the test set. This shows once more that combination techniques are no self-acting magic bullets, but highly sensitive algorithms which have to be tuned for special applications.

7   Conclusions

This study introduced an adaptive framework for the combination of OCR result strings originating from arbitrary commercial recognition systems. First quantitative results have been shown for a two-recognizer system using various combination strategies at the character level. Tests were performed to save recognition time using conditional combination. The performance of the various combination strategies turned out to be strongly data-dependent:

As for recognition rates, confidence-based combination methods lead to good improvements on numerics data. Combination was less successful on alphanumerics. Partially, this may be explained by missing contextual postprocessing (dictionaries, n-grams...) which supplements OCR in real-world applications.

Considering recognition time, conditional combination turned out to be most successful on numerics data, as well. For this quite simple material, one expert was reliable enough in many cases, while harder problems had to be tackled with both recognizers.

In a next step, the effect of recognizer-specific character weighting has will be tested. Experiments with more than two recognizers should be arranged. Up to now, combination strategies were assessed by character recognition rates. It would be interesting, however, to analyze the influence of geometrical synchronization separately.

References

[Akse03] Aksela, M., Comparison of Classifier Selection Methods for Improving Committee Performance, in: [WiRo03], 84-93

[AlCa01] Alexandre, L., Campilho, A., Kamel, M., On Combining Classifiers Using Sum and Product Rules, Pattern Recognition Letters **22** (2001) 1283-1289

[AlKi99] Alkoot, F.M., Kittler, J., Experimental Evaluation of Expert Fusion Strategies, Pattern Recognition Letters **20** (1999) 1361-1369

[AlDe02] Altinçay, H., Demirekler, M. Post-processing of Classifier Outputs in Multiple Classifier Systems, in: [RoKi02], 159-168

[BaKo99] Bauer, E., Kohavi, R., An Empirical Comparison of Voting Classification Algorithms: Bagging, Boosting, and Variants, Machine Learning **36** (1999) 105-139

[BoGo99] Bouchaffra, D., Govindaraju, V., Srihari, S.: A Methodology for Mapping Scores to Probabilities, IEEE Trans. Pattern Analysis and Machine Intelligence **21** (1999) 923-927

[CoFa01] Constantinidis, A., Fairhurst, M., Rahman, A., A New Multi-Expert Decision Combination Algorithm and its Application to the Detection of Circumscribed Masses in Digital Mammogramms, Pattern Recognition **34** (2001) 1527-1537

[Diet00] Dietterich, Th.G., Ensemble Methods in Machine Learning, in: [KiRo00], 1-15

[DuTa00] Duin, R., Tax, D., Experiments with Classifier Combining Rules, in: [KiRo00], 16-29

[ErSc00] van Erp, M., Schomaker, L., Variants of the Borda Count Method for combining ranked classifier hypotheses, Proceedings FIHR 2000, 443 - 452

[FuRo03] Fumera, G., Roli, F., Linear Combination for Classifier Fusion: Some Theoretical and Experimental Results, in: [WiRo03], 74-83

[GiRo01] Giacinto, G., Roli, F., Dynamic Classifier Selection Based on Multiple Classifier Behaviour, Pattern Recognition **34** (2001) 1879-1881

[GuBu03] Günter, S., Bunke, H., New Boosting Algorithms for Classification Problems with Large Number of Classes Applied to Handwritten Word Recognition Task, in [WiRo03], 326-335

[Ho98] Ho, T.K, The Random Subspace Method for Constructing Decision Forests, IEEE Trans. Pattern Analysis and Machine Intelligence **20** (1998) 832-844

[KaWa03] Kamel, M., Wanas, N., Data Dependence in Combining Classifiers, in: [WiRo03] 1-14

[KiRo00] Kittler, J., Roli, F. (Eds.), Multiple Classifier Systems, Proceedings MCS 2000, Cagliari, Springer Lecture Notes in Computer Science 1857, Berlin 2000

[KiRo01] Kittler, J., Roli, F. (Eds.), Multiple Classifier Systems, Proceedings MCS 2001, Cambridge, Springer Lecture Notes in Computer Science 2096, Berlin 2001

[Klin97] Klink, S., Entwurf, Implementierung und Vergleich von Algorithmen zum Merge von Segmentierungs- und Klassifikationsergebnissen unterschiedlicher OCR-Ergebnisse. Master Thesis, Kaiserslautern 1997

[KuBe01] Kuncheva, L., Bezdek, J., Duin, R., Decision Templates for Multiple Classifier Fusion: an Experimental Comparison, Pattern Recognition **34**, 299-314

[LaHa97] Lam, L., Huang, Y.-S., Suen, Ch., Combination of Multiple Classifier Decisions for Optical Character Recognition, in: Bunke, H., Wang, P.S.P. (Eds.), Handbook of Character Recognition and Document Inage Analysis, World Scientific, 1997, 79-101

[LiDi98] Lin, X., Ding, X., Chen, M., Zhang, R., Wu, Y., Adaptive Confidence Transform Based Classifier Combination for Chinese Character Recognition, Pattern Recognition Letters **19** (1998) 957-988

[LiYa03] Lin, X., Yacoub, S., Burns, J., Simske, S., Performance Analysis of Pattern Classifier Combination by Plurality Voting, Pattern Recognition Letters **24** (2003) 1959-1969

[MaBu01] Marti, U.-V., Bunke, H., Use of Positional Information in Sequence Alignment for Multiple Classifier Information, in [KiRo01] 388-398

[MaVa02] Masulli, F., Valentini, G., Effectiveness of Error Correcting Output Coding Methods in Ensemble and Monolithic Learning Machines, Preprint, Università di Genova, 2002

[RaRo03] Raudys, Š., Roli, F., The Behavior Knowledge Space Fusion Method: Analysis of Generalization Error and Strategies for Performance Improvement, in: [RaRo03], 55-64

[RoKi02] Kittler, J., Roli, F. (Eds.), Multiple Classifier Systems, Proceedings MCS 2002, Cagliari, Springer Lecture Notes in Computer Science 2364, Berlin 2002

[RuGa02] Ruta, D., Gabrys, B., New Measure of Classifier Dependency in Multiple Classifier Systems, in: [RoKi02], 127-136

[SkDu01] Skurichina, M. Duin, R., Bagging and the Random Subspace Method for Redundant Feature Spaces, in: [KiRo01], 1-10

[SiHo02] Sirlantzis, K., Hoque, S., Fairhurst, M., Trainable Multiple Classifier Schemes for Handwritten Character Recognition, in: [RoKi02], 169-178

[SuLa00] Suen, Ch., Lam, L., Multiple Classifier Combination Methodologies for Different Output Levels, in: [KiRo00], 52-66

[TaBr00] Tax, D., van Breukelen, M., Duin, R,. Kittler, J., Combining Multiple Classifiers by Averaging or by Multiplying? Pattern Recognition **33** (2000) 1475-1485

[VeGa01] Verma, B., Gader, P., Chen, W., Fusion of Multiple Handwritten Word Recognition Techniques, Pattern Recognition Letters **22** (2001) 991-998

[WaBr02] Wang, W., Brakensiek, A., Rigoll, G., Combination of multiple classifiers for handwritten word recognition, in: 8th Int. Workshop on Frontiers in Handwriting Recognition (2002) 117-122

[WaYa00] Wang, J., Yan, H., A Hybrid Method for Unconstrained Handwritten Numeral Recognition by Combining Structural and Neural "Gas" Classifiers, Pattern Recognition Letters **21** (2000) 625-635

[WiLe03] Wilczok, L., Lellmann, W., Design and Evaluation of an AdaptiveCombination Framework for OCR Result Strings, in: [WiRo03] 395-404

[WiRo03] Windeatt, T., Roli, F. (Eds.), Multiple Classifier Systems, Proceedings MCS 2003, Guildford, Springer Lecture Notes in Computer Science 2709, Berlin 2003

[XuKr92] Xu, L., Krzyżak, A., Suen, Ch.Y., Methods of Combining Multiple Classifiers and Their Applications to Handwriting Recognition, IEEE Transactions on Systems, Man and Cybernetics **22** (1992) 418-435

[YeCh02] Ye, X., Cheriet, M., Suen, Ch.Y., StrCombo: combination of string recognizers, Pattern Recognition Letters **23** (2002) 381-394

Component-Based Software Engineering Methods for Systems in Document Recognition, Analysis, and Understanding

Oliver Höß, Oliver Strauß, and Anette Weisbecker

University of Stuttgart, Institute for Human Factors and Technology Management, IAT,
Nobelstraße 12, 70569 Stuttgart, Germany
{Oliver.Hoess, Oliver.Strauss, Anette.Weisbecker}
@iat.uni-stuttgart.de

Abstract. Modern systems in the field of document recognition, document analysis and document understanding have to be built in a short amount of time, with a low budget and have to comply to the functional and non-functional requirements of the customers. Traditional software engineering methods cannot cope with these challenges in an adequate way. The component-approach promises to be a solution for the efficient development of high-quality systems. The paper describes the basics of the component-approach and its application to the area of recognition systems. Special attention is paid to component technologies, the integration of heterogeneous systems by using wrapping techniques and the central issue of component reuse. The works in this paper have been part of the project Adaptive READ which was funded by the German Federal Ministry of Education and Research.

1   Requirements for Systems in the Field of Document Recognition, Analysis, and Understanding

Software plays a constantly increasing role in today's value creation chains [1]:

- To support internal business processes
- To support inter-enterprise business processes (B2B)
- To support services for consumers (B2C)
- As an integral part of products (Embedded Software)

Therefore software is not only the key business area for companies in the computer industry but it is also a fundamental success factor for companies in the secondary industries like telecommunication, electronics or financial services.

A study conducted on behalf of the German Ministry of Education and Research [2] revealed that software on average accounts for about a quarter of the total development costs in the development of new systems and services.

Due to the high importance of software it is getting increasingly important for companies to develop the full potential that lies in the efficient use and development of modern software products.

A. Dengel et al. (Eds.): Adaptive READ Research Project, LNCS 2956, pp. 137–152, 2004.

This imposes high demands on the software which are not easily mastered by software developers and project managers [1]:

- Since the budgets in the majority of projects are very limited the projects have to be conducted under a high cost pressure.
- In order to reduce time-to-market new ideas have to be realized in a short amount of time which leads to high time pressure. This fact is also documented in [2] where the results show that around 70% of the software development projects have to be completed in an timeframe of less than one year (see fig. 1).
- In most cases systems are not isolated applications but have to be integrated with other, mostly heterogeneous systems. This puts high demands on the flexibility of the software and on its integration capabilities.
- In spite of high cost and time pressure the resulting systems have to comply to high quality standards in order to meet the demands of the users and to prevent system failures which may cause financial damage. The study in [2] showed that reliability and the fulfilment of the functional requirements are the two top quality attributes of complex software systems.

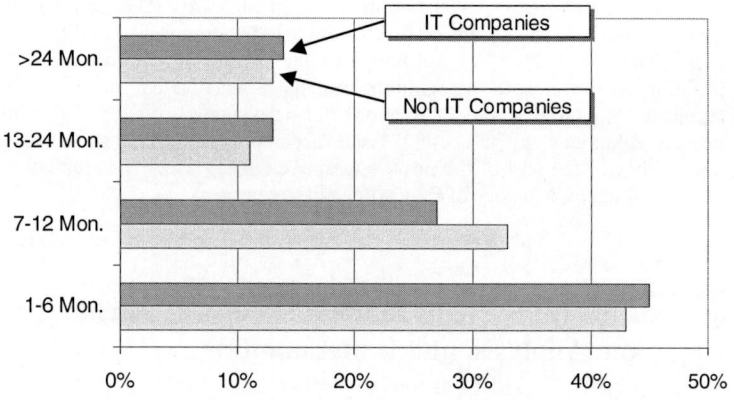

Fig. 1. Average project timeframe for software development projects [2]

The requirements portrayed above are especially valid for systems in the area of document analysis, recognition and understanding. These systems must have a modular structure, a high degree of adaptability and flexibility as well as the capability to integrate with other systems [3].

Thus two of the main objectives of the industrial partners in Adaptive READ were to reduce the engineering costs for the construction of individual systems and to increase the quality of the resulting systems (see fig. 2).

For example almost all large distribution centers in postal automation have automatic address recognition systems. The challenge for Adaptive READ was to develop methods and technologies for these kinds of systems that reduce the engineering costs needed to produce individually customized systems for smaller customers.

In the application domain of form processing one of the main tasks is the integration of form processing systems into the larger workflows of a company's IT systems.

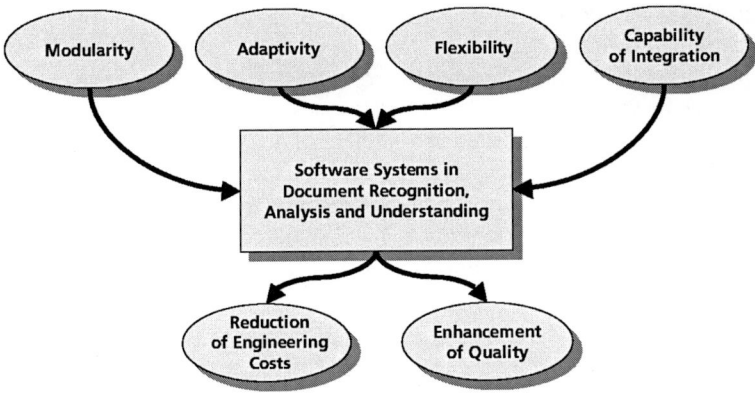

Fig. 2. Key success factors for software systems in document recognition, analysis and understanding

In other industries these challenges are met by reducing the vertical range of manufacturing, especially through the use of standardized components. Good examples are the automotive and electronics industries. Motor vehicles and electronic devices are assembled from a large number of components which are often provided by different producers.

Learning from these more mature industries it is reasonable to apply the component approach to software engineering, especially in the domain of document recognition, analysis and understanding. The goal is to combine the advantages of standard software with the advantages of individually developed software by assembling existing high-quality components to individual solutions for each customer. This "Componentware" approach promises the construction of software systems that fulfil the customer requirements to a high degree, can be developed with relatively low effort and meet high quality standards.

2   Component-Based Software Engineering

It is essential in component-based software engineering to define the term "software component". Remarkably the term "software component" and with it the idea of composing software from existing building blocks was already discussed in the sixties in the context of the industrial production of software systems [4].

In literature a variety of different definitions of the term "component" can be found (see e.g. [5], [6], [7]). These definitions are overlapping but by far not identical in emphasizing different aspects of the term "component" which are correct in only a particular context but seriously interfere with a universal definition.

Among other things the difficulty in finding a universal definition is based on the fact that the term "component" is used in contexts other than software engineering. A component simply represents a part of the whole (lat. componere: to put together).

Another difficulty lies in the multitude of aspects defining a component. A number of aspects of the term "component" are outlined in fig. 3:

- Components can occur as executable software, in source code form or only as a concept (e.g. a UML model).
- Components can be domain specific or can be used independently from an application domain.
- Components can be implemented in a number of different component technologies. This topic is elaborated in Chapter 3.
- Components can be located on the client-side or on the server.
- Components can be of different sizes, from small components, like elements of a GUI to large components, e.g. like SAP R/3.

Type	Executable Software		Source Code		Concept	
Domain Relation	Domain Specific			Domain Independent		
Technology	EJB	COM+	CCM	ActiveX	JavaBeans	...
Location	Client			Server		
Size	Small		Medium		Large	

Fig. 3. Different aspects of components

In the context of Adaptive READ only executable pieces of software are considered software components. To be able to use a uniform definition of a software component the following working definition is proposed, which summarizes the essential characteristics of a software component [8]:

- A component is a technically and functionally self-contained unit.
- A component offers its services only via well defined interfaces.
- Services of other components are as well used via well defined interfaces.
- Components can be aggregated to larger components.
- A component is developed with the intention of the subsequent reuse of the component in mind (see Chapter 5).

In some cases this definition may be adapted to the appropriate context. However the following three universal activities can always be identified when working with software components [8]:

- *Design for Component*: The initial development of software components with the objective of providing a defined functionality that can be used by other components or which can be integrated in more complex components and systems. In the optimal case the developed components are stored in a central component repository for a subsequent reuse (see Chapter 5).
- *Design from Component*: The incremental development of complex components or systems using pre-existing components.
- *Design to Component*: The transformation of conventionally developed, mostly monolithic systems into systems with flexible component-based software architectures.

The activities are visualized in fig. 4. In practice these three activities don't occur in isolation. For example the development of a complex application can rarely be accomplished exclusively by reusing pre-existing components (design from component). In most cases some specific components will be missing and have to be developed from scratch (design for component). Mostly the migration of monolithic legacy systems into component-based systems (design to component) includes the usage of pre-existing components (design from component) as well as the development of new components (design for component).

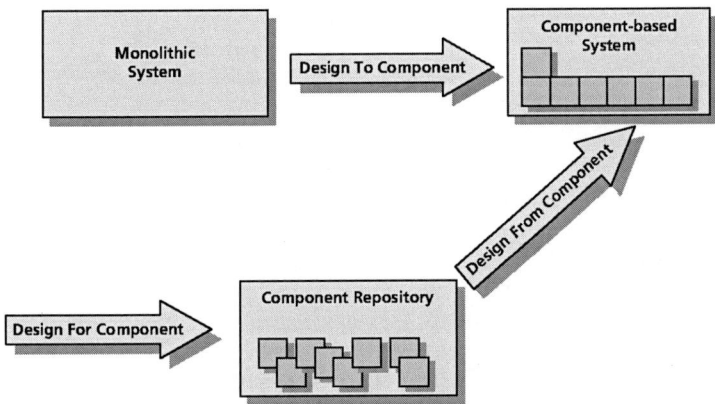

Fig. 4. Activities of component-based software engineering

3   Component Technologies

A standardized component technology constitutes an essential prerequisite for the technical coupling of different software components and for their reuse in other systems. It forms a technological basis by providing contracts, communication protocols and a standardized infrastructure that components can use to integrate with other components.

In the last years a number of standard component technologies and technology families were developed which are suitable to build complex systems from pre-existing components:

– The J2EE technology family from Sun (Java 2 Enterprise Edition)
– The .NET technologies from Microsoft
– The CORBA technologies of the Object Management Group (OMG)

Since these technology families were designed to implement component-based 3- or 4-tier application architectures they provide different technologies for the realization of the different layers of these architectures: the client layer, the optional server-side presentation layer, the server-side business logic and the data storage and integration layer (see fig. 4). The following sections will examine the three technology families in more detail.

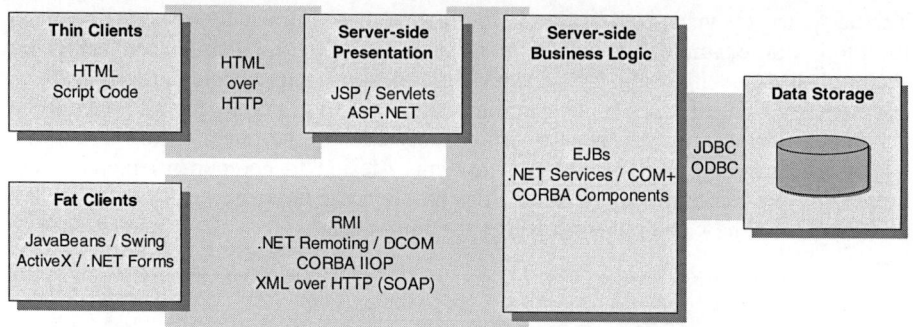

Fig. 5. Component-based 3- or 4-tier application architectures

3.1   Sun's Java 2 Enterprise Edition (J2EE)

The J2EE architecture [9] provides a component technology called Enterprise Java Beans (EJBs) for implementing the server-side business logic. This technology relieves the developer of a number of technical aspects like transaction support or the access to relational databases, so that the developer can concentrate on the implementation of the non-technical aspects of the application, i.e. the business logic.

The business logic provides services for different kinds of clients. If thin clients are used an additional layer, called server-side presentation layer, is located between the business logic layer and the client tier to dynamically generate HTML pages. This task is performed by so called Java Server Pages (JSPs) and Java Servlets.

The implementation of fat clients is supported by the JavaBeans component technology. In the base version of Java, the Java 2 Standard Edition (J2SE), Sun provides a number of JavaBeans components for the implementation of graphical user interfaces: the component framework Swing.

In order to operate a J2EE compliant application a J2EE application server is needed, which provides the runtime environment for J2EE applications. There are a number of commercial products available, e.g. IBM's WebSphere [, 10] or BEA's WebLogic application servers [11], but there are also high-quality Open Source alternatives like JBoss [12] which are suitable for use in production systems.

The standards J2EE and J2ME are complemented by a reduced version of the Java standard, the Java 2 Micro Edition (J2ME), which can be used to develop component-based applications for systems with restricted resources [13], e.g. embedded systems or PDAs (Personal Digital Assistants).

3.2   Microsoft's .NET Framework

Microsoft's counterpart to the J2EE standard is the .NET framework [14]. Similarly to the Java World a virtual machine, the Common Language Runtime (CLR), is used to execute byte code (the Microsoft Intermediate Language, MSIL), instead of real machine code to support cross platform deployment. Different programming languages, like Visual Basic, C++ or the newly developed language C#, can be used to generate MSIL code. In .NET it is even possible to use cross-language inheritance to support multi-language programming. Another feature which enhances the productivity in .NET dramatically is the existence of a class library, the so called Framework Class Library (FCL), which is available in identical form in all .NET development languages.

In .NET the server-side business logic is implemented using .NET Enterprise Services which are an enhancement of the older COM+/MTS technologies. Compared to the EJB standard of J2EE they provide similar functionality but are not as sophisticated. The server-side presentation layer uses the ASP.NET technology (Active Server Pages) to dynamically generate HTML pages to be displayed on thin clients. ASP.NET provides some very elaborate features to separate program logic from layout aspects which can also be used from all .NET languages.

To implement fat clients .NET provides a component framework similar to Sun's Swing, the .NET Forms, which can be used from all .NET languages in an identical way as well.

The counterpart of J2ME is the .NET Compact Framework which is a reduced version of the .NET framework for systems with restricted resources, like mobile devices.

3.3   CORBA Components

The CORBA standard (Common Object Request Broker Architecture) is defined and maintained by the Object Management Group (OMG). In its latest version CORBA provides a component technology for the implementation of server-side business logic, the CORBA Component Model (CCM). The CCM standard is similar to the EJB standard but it is not restricted to the use of Java as development language [15].

In contrast to Sun and Microsoft, who provide reference implementations for their standards, the OMG only provides a written description of the standard. The fact that it often takes a long time for someone to provide a working implementation of the standard led to the effect, that the CCM standard has been rendered almost obsolete by the latest developments in the field of J2EE and .NET. Until now there are no products available implementing the CCM standard.

3.4   Communication Protocols

The communication between components of different layers and sometimes also between components of the same layer is performed via standard communication protocols. These communication protocols provide services that enable components to implement method invocations on remote objects in a transparent way, i.e. it looks like a local method invocation.

In Java based environments the RMI protocol (Remote Method Invocation) is used, in .NET environments the .NET Remoting protocol is applied and in CORBA environments the GIOP (General Inter-ORB Protocol) is used, mostly in its representation for TCP/IP, the IIOP (Internet Inter-ORB Protocol).

All three protocols have very similar mechanisms, i.e. they use dynamically allocated TCP/IP ports for the communication between remote components. This can cause security problems in Internet applications. This fact and the necessity of communication in heterogeneous environments lead to the development of the SOAP protocol (Simple Object Access Protocol), which uses XML messages (Extensible Markup Language) over HTTP (Hypertext Transfer Protocol) connections to implement remote cross-platform method invocations in heterogeneous Internet environments. The services which are implemented using the SOAP protocol are now generally called Web Services. The standardization process and further developments in this area are coordinated by the World Wide Web Consortium [16].

3.5 Choosing the Right Technology

When the system architect is defining the component architecture of a new system for document recognition, analysis and understanding, he has to choose one of the component technologies mentioned above. Because of the lack of available products supporting the CORBA CCM model, it is mainly a choice between J2EE and .NET.

In table 1 the capabilities of the different component technologies are summarized. The J2EE technology family has advantages in the areas of completeness, platform independence and degree of use. In contrast to J2EE the .NET platform relies very strongly on the Windows platform which results in a very good integration into windows-based environments.

Table 1. Component technologies

	J2EE	.NET	CCM
Client-side components	●	●	○
Components for server-side presentation	●	●	○
Server-side components	●	◑	●
Degree of usage	●	◑	○
Platform independence	●	○	●
Independence of the development language	○	●	●

(● = feature available; ◑ = feature available for the most part; ○ = feature not available)

In many cases the decision is a matter of platform independence vs. integration into windows environments. Web Services as an integration technology may be used as technological bridge between two worlds.

4   Integration of Heterogeneous Systems

The use of the component technologies described in chapter 3 is not restricted to the implementation of systems for document recognition, analysis and understanding but extends to the integration of such systems into the IT infrastructure of the companies that want to use the system. This last point is one of the main tasks in today's projects.

The following two paragraphs outline the integration of a recognition system in different use cases.

4.1   COM+ Based Integration of a Recognition System into a Workflow System

In the context of Adaptive READ the Océ Document Technologies GmbH developed a component-based recognition framework called IDIS [3]. This system was integrated by the IAT into a workflow system called InTempo (see fig 6). Thanks to this integration the data extracted from paper forms by the IDIS system can be used to trigger and control workflows that support the company's business processes, e.g. applications for travel expense accounting or other processes based on paper forms.

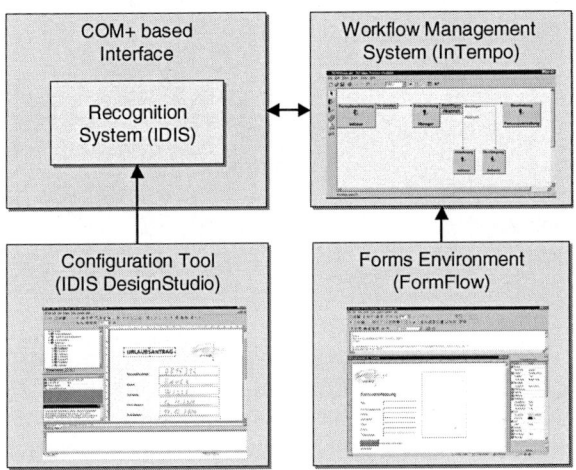

Fig. 6. COM+ based integration of a recognition system into a workflow system

The recognition system IDIS was equipped with a COM+ component interface since .NET Services were not yet available at that time. The workflow system is using this interface to access the data which was extracted from paper forms by the IDIS system. The process of enclosing a system with a component interface is called wrapping.

The IDIS system, the workflow system and the system used to map the paper forms on web-based forms (FormFlow) can be configured via graphical tools. This makes the whole system relatively easy to use (see fig. 6).

Although this example uses dedicated systems the principles can be transferred to all other systems in this area.

4.2   Integration of a Recognition System in a J2EE-Based Environment

In the last paragraph the integration of the IDIS recognition system into a workflow system was accomplished with Microsoft technologies. In the context of Adaptive READ another integration based on J2EE technologies was carried out. The objective of this integration was the development of an alternative platform independent configuration tool for the IDIS system. With this tool the IDIS system can be configured by defining the recognition operators and their corresponding parameters in a graphical way. The advantage of this configuration tool compared to the original tool is its platform independence due to the use of Java technology. However this prototypical tool does not comprise all functionality of the original.

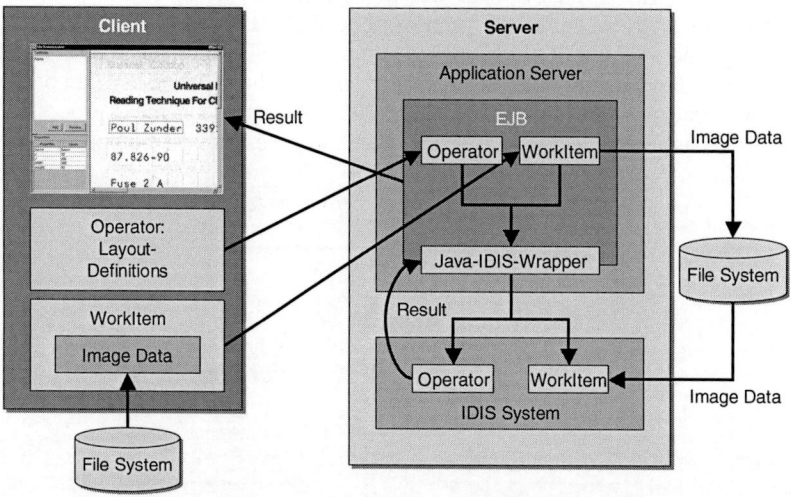

Fig. 7. J2EE-based integration and configuration client

In fig. 7 the configuration tool and the integration architecture is portrayed. In order to be able to access the data of the recognition system from Java applications a so called Java-IDIS-Wrapper was developed which uses JNI technology (Java Native Interface) to make calls to the IDIS system.

To provide this functionality in a standard way, another layer based on EJB technology was developed which offers Java methods over the RMI protocol in order to use the functionality of the IDIS system from any Java application.

The Java based client uses this EJB interface layer to enable the user to graphically define recognition operators and to integrate the functionality of the IDIS system.

5   Reuse of Software Components

The benefits of the component approach can only be fully utilized if there is a sufficient supply of high-quality software components and if they are being actually reused. Thus one of the key success factors in component-based software engineering is the reuse of software components.

The establishment of the component technologies described in chapter 3 has led to the development of a number of component marketplaces, like ComponentSource [17]. These marketplaces offer a large number of commercial and non-commercial components. Furthermore the Open Source community is another large provider of reusable software components. There are over 60000 Open Source projects located on SourceForge.net [18], the largest website for Open Source projects.

But despite of the component technologies and marketplaces the level of reuse in software developing companies is mostly not satisfactory [19]. In the following paragraphs we will therefore present a number of obstacles to software reuse as well as some measures to overcome them.

5.1   Obstacles to Software Reuse

The reasons for the lack of software reuse are multifaceted. They range from obstacles in the personal scope to obstacles which can only be solved on a more global scale (see fig. 8).

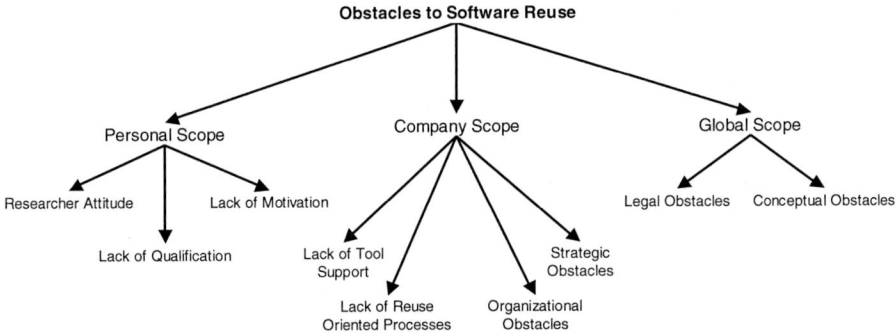

Fig. 8. Obstacles to software reuse [19], [20], [21], [22]

Personal Scope
In the personal area three main obstacles can be observed:

- Some developers have some kind of "researcher" or "do-it-yourself"-attitude, i.e. they don't want to reuse existing components but want to develop them by themselves.
- In many cases there's a lack of motivation to provide reusable software components to other developers, since reusable components require more development effort than normal software and the developers are under high time pressure in their own projects.
- Another obstacle is the lack of qualification, i.e. there's not enough knowledge about component-based software engineering among the developers and project managers.

These obstacles can be overcome by using incentive systems to encourage software reuse and additional education measures on the topic of component-based software engineering.

Company Scope

On the company level obstacles can be observed which go further than the personal scope:

- Often there's no support of software reuse by tools, like e.g. a component repository.
- The software development processes don't include activities concerning software reuse.
- There are organizational obstacles, e.g. there's no organizational unit responsible for software reuse.
- In some cases companies withhold from reusing software components from other companies for strategic reasons because they don't want to lose their unique selling propositions or because they don't want to be dependent on other companies.

Global Scope

There are also some obstacles which go beyond single persons or companies and which interfere with cross-organizational software reuse:

- Legal issues: A lot of legal problems are not ultimately solved yet, e.g. who is responsible if a systems fails due to the misinterpretation of the functionality of a subcomponent from another vendor?
- Conceptual issues: The basic concepts of the business processes in different companies have not yet been unified and maybe won't be in the near future which makes cross-organizational software reuse much more difficult.

In the following paragraphs we propose three measures to improve the level of software reuse which deal mainly with the obstacles on the personal and company scope.

5.2   Efficient Software Reuse through the Use of a Component Repository

The main measure to improve software reuse is the introduction of a company-wide component repository. It is the central library where the components developed in the company as well as external components can be stored and indexed for a later reuse.

Such a component repository should provide two basic services [23]:

- It should be possible to upload software components. This service should also include versioning and a quality assurance mechanism which ensures that the components are indexed using a standard classification scheme and are documented using well defined specification standards.
- It should be possible to search the components using different search mechanisms like tree search and keyword based search.

Besides these basic services a component repository should also provide a number of add on services, which produce an added value for the users of the repository [23]:

– Documentation of reuse: It should be obligatory for the reusing developer to document the reuse of a software component. This is necessary for generating notifications if a new version of this component is uploaded.
– Notification mechanisms: It should be possible for the users to register for notifications when new versions of certain components or new components in certain areas are uploaded to the repository.
– Support for an incentive system: The repository should support an incentive system which rewards the providers and reusers of software components and thereby encourages software reuse.

Additionally an optimal component repository should support the passive search for components and the gathering of metrics concerning software reuse. It should also provide some portal and community functionalities. A detailed description of the functionality of a component repository can be found in [23].

In the context of Adaptive READ a component repository was developed which implements the basic and value added services described above. In order to obtain a flexible component-based system architecture the repository was implemented using a 4-tier architecture which is compliant to the J2EE reference model (see fig. 9).

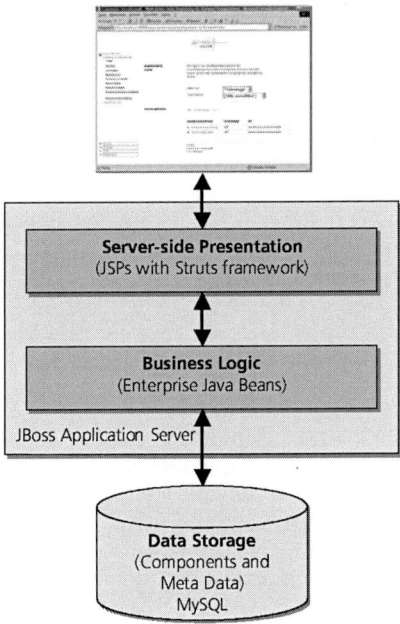

Fig. 9. System architecture of the component repository

The user interface was designed as an HTML based client to maximize the accessibility of the repository for the possible users. Java Server Pages (JSPs) are used to handle the dynamic generation of the HTML pages which form the server-side presentation layer. The JSPs additionally use the Open Source framework Struts [24] from the Apache Project to implement a Model-View-Controller pattern [25] which allows a clear separation of business logic, data and presentation code. The JSPs in turn use the services of the business logic layer which is implemented using Enterprise Java Beans (EJBs). The runtime environment for the JSPs and EJBs is provided by the J2EE compliant OpenSource application Server JBoss which is widely used due to its high quality and stability.

The persistence of the EJBs is implemented using the Container Managed Persistence (CMP) mechanism of the EJB standard. The advantage of this approach is that the mapping of the EJBs on relational databases is done almost automatically by the EJB container which is a part of the application server JBoss. The Open Source database MySQL is used as the backend data store.

5.3   Adaptation of the Organizational Structures

In order to successfully operate the component repository an organizational unit, a so called "reuse team", has to be defined which is responsible for the operation and maintenance of the repository. One of the main tasks of the reuse team is to ensure that the quality of the components stored in the repository remains on a high level. Additional tasks include:

- Identification of potentially reusable software components in the development projects of a company.
- Coaching the projects in architectural issues and software reuse issues.
- Keeping an eye on the external software market in order to find components which can be useful for the company.
- Controlling the software development processes under the aspect of software reuse.

These tasks are very time consuming so that it is not feasible to do them in addition to the day-to-day workload. Thus it is very important that the members of the reuse team can devote a large share of their working time on these subjects.

5.4   Adaptation of the Development Processes

Traditional process models like the Rational Unified Process [26] and Catalysis [27] or lightweight models like Extreme Programming [28] all claim to be component-based. But a closer look reveals that they all are based on the assumption that a new system is being built from scratch based on given requirements. The basic idea of component-based development is neglected: to use pre-existing components.

To successfully implement software reuse the software development processes have to be adapted:

- Integration of the component repository and the reuse team into the development processes.
- The search for and evaluation of pre-existing components must be mandatory before implementing new components.
- A company-wide software architecture has to be defined to lay the technical foundation of component reuse.

While all these measures seem to be common sense, they are far from being implemented in most companies. This is the main reason for the unsatisfactory degree of software reuse that can be observed today.

6 Conclusions

This paper described the foundations of component-based software engineering with respect to the development of systems in the area of document recognition, analysis and understanding as well as the basic technologies used in this area.

Based on these methodical and technical foundations some aspects of the work done in Adaptive READ in the fields of integration of heterogeneous systems and component reuse were presented.

Other fields of work in Adaptive READ like the classification and specification of components are out of the scope of this paper and can be found in the respective deliverables [29].

In summary it can be said that there are quite a few technological approaches to component-based software engineering. The work on system integration in the context of Adaptive READ is based mainly on these technological foundations.

However major obstacles to component-based software engineering and to software reuse can be found in the non-technical area. The work on component repositories done in Adaptive READ also addresses these non-technical aspects, especially through the value added services of the component repository.

In the future the emphasis should be put on the implementation of reuse-oriented processes and tools that support the day-to-day work of software developing companies. For the development of new methods in this area the focus should be put on the applicability in the practical work of these companies. Only when the concepts of component-based software engineering are applied and established on a broad scale the ideal of a "software component industry" can become reality, as it is known from other branches like the automotive industry [30].

References

1. Höß, O.; Weisbecker, A.: Componentware verspricht Erfolg im E-Business (Componentware promises success in E-Business), Computerwoche: CW 29 (2002), Special CeBIT issue, ISSN 0170-5121, pp. 50-51 (2002)
2. GfK Marktforschung GmbH; Fraunhofer-Institut für Experimentelles Software Engineering IESE; Fraunhofer-Institut für Systemtechnik und Innovationsforschung ISI: Analyse und Evaluation der Softwareentwicklung in Deutschland (Analysis and Evaluation of Software Development in Germany), final report of a study conducted on behalf of the German Ministry of Education and Research, December 2000, http://www.dlr.de/IT/IV/Studien/evasoft_abschlussbericht.pdf (2000)
3. Middendorf, M.; Peust, C.; Schacht, J.: A Component-based Framework for Recognition Systems. Published in this publication (2003)
4. McIlroy, D.: Mass produced software components. In: Naur, P.; Randell, B. (Ed.): Software Engineering, NATO Science Comitee Report, pp. 138-155 (1968)

5.   Turowski, K. (Ed.): Vorschlag zur Vereinheitlichung der Spezifikation von Fachkomponenten (Proposal for the unification of the specification of non-technical components), Memorandum of the GI working group 5.10.3: Komponentenorientierte betriebliche Anwendungssysteme (component-based information systems), Version February 2002, http://wi2.wiso.uni-augsburg.de/gi-files/MEMO/Memorandum-Februar-2002_2.34.pdf

6.   Herzum, P.; Sims, O.: Business Component Factory: A Comprehensive Overview of Component-Based Development for the Enterprise, Wiley, New York (2000)

7.   Szyperski, C.: Component Software: Beyond Object-Oriented Programming, Addison-Wesley, Harlow (1998)

8.   Weisbecker, A.: Software-Management für komponentenbasierte Software-Entwicklung (Software management for component-based software development). Habilitation, Jost-Jetter Verlag, Heidenheim (2002)

9.   Sun Microsystems: Java 2 Platform Enterprise Edition. Homepage, http://java.sun.com/j2ee, 10.International Business Machines Corporation: WebSphere Homepage, http://www.ibm.com/websphere

11. BEA Systems, Homepage, http://www.bea.com

12. JBoss Homepage, http://www.jboss.org

13. Sun Microsystems: Java 2 Platform Micro Edition. Homepage, http://java.sun.com/j2me

14. Microsoft Corporation: Microsoft .NET Homepage, http://www.microsoft.com/net

15. Object Management Group: The Common Object Request Broker Architecture. Homepage, http://www.corba.org

16. World Wide Web Consortium. Homepage, http://www.w3c.org

17. ComponentSource Homepage. http://www.componentsource.com

18. SourceForge Homepage. http://sourceforge.net/

19. Dietzsch, A.; Esswein, W.: Gibt es eine „Softwarekomponenten Industrie" ? Ergebnisse einer empirischen Untersuchung ("Is there a software component industry ? Results of an empirical study"). In: Buhl, H. U.; Huther, A.; Reitwiesner, B. (Ed.): Information Age Economy, 5. Internationale Tagung Wirtschaftsinformatik 2001 (5th International Conference on Information Systems), Conference Proceedings, Physika-Verlag, pp. 697 – 710 (2001)

19. Sodhi, J.; Sodhi, P.: Software Reuse – Domain Analysis and Design Processes, McGraw-Hill, New York (1998)

20. Reifer, D. J.: Practical Software Reuse. Wiley, New York (1997)

21. Jacobson, I.; Griss, M.; Johnson, P.: Software Reuse – Architecture, Process And Organization For Business Success, Addison-Wesley Longman, New York (1997)

22. Karlsson, E.-A.: Software Reuse – A Holistic Approach. Wiley, Chichester (1995)

23. Höß, O.; Weisbecker, A.: Konzeption eines Repositories zur Unterstützung der Wiederverwendung von Software-Komponenten (Concept of a repository supporting the reuse of software components). In K. Turowski (Ed.): Tagungsband des 4. Workshops Komponentenorientierte betriebliche Anwendungssysteme (WKBA 4) (Proceedings of the 4th workshop on component-based information systems). Augsburg, pp. 57-74 (2002)

24. Apache Software Foundation: The Apache Struts Web Application Framework. Hompage, http://jakarta.apache.org/struts

25. Gamma, E.; Helm, R.; Johnson, R.; Vlissides, J. M.: Design Patterns: Elements of Reusable Object-Oriented Software. Addison-Wesley: Reading, Mass. (1995)

26. Rational Unified Process Homepage. http://www.rational.com/products/rup/index.jsp

27. D'Souza, D. F.; Wills, A. C.: Objects, Components and Frameworks with UML: The Catalysis Approach, Addison Wesley, Reading 1998.

28. Extreme Programming Homepage. http://www.extremeprogramming.org

29. Adaptive READ Homepage. http://www.adaptive-read.de

30. Höß, O.; Weisbecker, A.: Wege zu einer Software-Komponenten-Industrie (Steps to a software component industrie) In: Engelien, M. (Ed.): Virtuelle Organisationen und Neue Medien 2002 (Virtual organizations and new media), Eul Verlag, pp. 365-386 (2002).

A Component-Based Framework
for Recognition Systems

Matthias Middendorf, Carsten Peust, and Johannes Schacht

Océ Document Technologies GmbH, Max-Stromeyer-Straße 116,
78467 Konstanz, Germany
{matthias.middendorf, carsten.peust, johannes.schacht}
@odt-oce.com
www.odt-oce.com

Abstract. The advantages of component-based software design have often been emphasized during the last years. This article describes the design and implementation of an object-oriented framework for document recognition systems. We use an operator-workitem-model for integrating numerous software components of various origins and written in different programming languages. This is done by defining two standardized interfaces, namely an operator-interface for the integrated recognition algorithms and a workitem-interface for all in- and output objects of the recognition algorithms. These conditions allow to arrange the operators in any successive order and any complexity to build a complete recognition system. For any choice and relative position of operators integrated, the framework provides facilities for parametrizing, testing and running.

The reported works have been part of the project *AdaptiveREAD* which was funded by the German Federal Ministry of Education and Research.

1 Why a Framework?

Reuse of software components offers a large number of advantages which have often been emphasized in the literature: reduced general complexity of the system, reduced costs for development and maintaining, a higher software quality by employing pre-tested and already optimized components, a higher portability of the complete system, and many others. But there are various ways how to realize component software in practice.

The classic and most elementary step towards designing component software has consisted in grouping the functionality into modules, or, in object-oriented terminology, classes, each of which is partitioned into an implementation which is hidden to the outside world and an interface which is public [Parnas 1972]. This leads to a system consisting of *n* modules with a limited, though still possibly high number of up to *n* different interfaces. In the consequence this approach necessitates a spontaneous combination of the reusable components for the needs of a current project, so that each new integration will be a unique problem to be solved individually. Further

A. Dengel et al. (Eds.): Adaptive READ Research Project, LNCS 2956, pp. 153–165, 2004.

more, reusing one of these modules in another context will in practice often make it necessary to change the interface, which may mean that the module will be changed or even that different versions of the same module will be created. The more complex a module is, and the more diverse the possible environments are in which it is going to be integrated, the less likely it is that its interface will be really reusable in different environments without major rework.

Attempts to refine the object oriented approach in order to alleviate this problem have a long history, one of the major steps having been the introduction of the concept of inheritance, which means that different versions of one module have a single implementation of their common features and need to separately implement only their delta changes.

But there is actually no ideal way to reconcile the two principally contradicting aims, on the one hand, to build multi-purpose components for use in various environments, and, on the other hand, to ensure at the same time that the components will remain usable without continual reworking and to possess stable, inexpensive procedures for integrating them into bigger systems.

As soon as we agree that our set of components is not going to be used for any possible task in the most diverse possible environments, a good option to deal with this problem emerges in form of defining a *framework*. A framework is a structured collection of components which is to some degree fixed and allows for integrating additional components only at well-defined „hot-spots" [Pree 1997: 7]. Thus while possibly still giving lots of possibilities for adaptation of the system, a framework admits only a limited degree of freedom. This is a realistic model of the real world where, within a given application domain, certain tasks recur in the same way and sequence over and over again, whereas typically only a subset of tasks needs to be reshaped according to actual changing demands.

A framework is therefore in fact an essential means of promoting and encouraging software reuse [Pintado 1995: 322]. It often pays to put effort into developing and maintaining a framework for integrating components, although this means that an extra effort is done beforehand which may be great; frameworks are definitely a long-term investment [Wallace 1996: 117].

It is then the task of the framework architecture to facilitate the use and integration of reusable components by exploiting knowledge about the application domain for which the framework has been designed. When the effort of constructing a framework has been invested, the system can be evolved more quickly and analyzed more reliably than an unstructured collection of components could ever be. While in unstructured object-oriented software systems, changes are generally made by some kind of programming, e.g. by inheritance, it is the goal of a framework to achieve changes solely by reordering the object composition, i.e. without programming [Pree 1997: 10], although, of course, additional possibilities for programming (scripting) may be welcome. The framework approach can therefore also be seen as a competitor of the traditional object-oriented approach, which has not always kept its promise to dramatically facilitate the construction of complex software systems [Nierstrasz 1995a, Szyperski 1998].

2   A Framework for Document Recognition Systems

2.1   Overview

In the following, we describe a framework which has been designed specifically for the domain of document recognition and processing. The purpose of this framework is to enable a quick and easy development and configuration of complex forms-based and free-forms recognition systems.

Not only can a single recognition engine be constructed relatively quickly with this framework. But also several products which due to their common architectural base are close enough to one another so as to form a product family can comparatively easily be created, which is one of the most salient advantages of framework based development [Fayad 1999]. Actually, several systems designed with this framework are currently in commercial production (the DOKuStar product family).

2.2   The Operator-Workitem-Metaphor

When a framework for components is going to be designed, an important architectural decision has to be made concerning the diversity of modules which the framework is supposed to handle. The theoretically infinite diversity of component interfaces has to be reduced to a small number of generic interfaces. This abstraction process, by which several components are defined as being equivalent with respect to their interface, is necessary to allow a flexible handling of the components within the framework and to make full use of the advantages that a framework can offer.

In our approach, all components are taken as representatives of two basic and very general concepts, called „operators" and „workitems". The recognition process is viewed as the successive transformation of workitems by operators into other workitems. Both the in- and output of all operators is provided with the same workitem-interface which ensures that, at least in theory, numerous rearrangements of the operators can easily be achieved within the framework. The „Operator-Workitem" paradigm strongly resembles the "Tools & Materials" approach [Lippert 2000], which has been well-proven in different applications like e.g. financial systems.

A workitem can be an image, a batch file, a set of document data, or anything else which serves as input (input-workitem) or output (output-workitem) of a recognition task. Workitem is just the base class, from which a number of specialized subclasses can be formed.

An operator represents an algorithm which is performed on a workitem as input and produces one or more workitems as output. The various types of operators will be described in more detail below.

Operators can combine to form more complex operations by using a "Sequence-Operator" which applies the single operators in sequential order, or by using a "Set-Operator" which splits processing into parallel paths (see Figure 1).

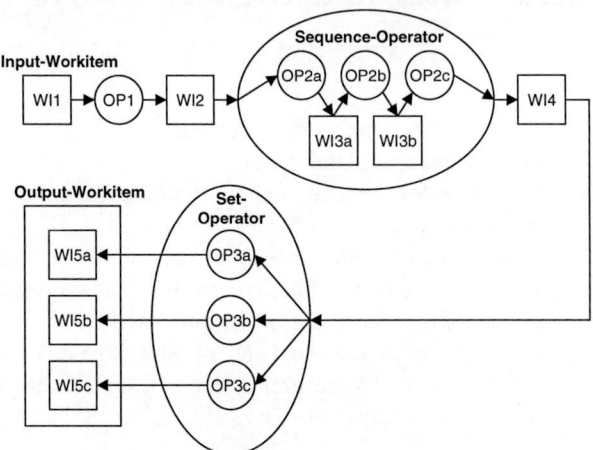

Fig. 1. The Operator / Workitem-metaphor

For creating objects, the framework, as conforms to current framework technology, provides a factory database mechanism. The factory database is a central repository that contains the names of all creatable classes together with some essential information (e.g. name of the base class for derived classes). The factory pattern makes it possible to create objects from external information such as, for example, a persistent XML project file, without explicit reference to the programming language in which the framework is implemented; new types of workitems and operators can be added by simply refilling the factory database without having to change the source code. Alongside with the factory database, the framework contains a number of additional central databases, among them the operator database (list of all operators allowed to be used in a given framework configuration) and a ressource database (containing country-specific message strings).

2.3 The Graphical Interface

A characteristic feature of the framework described here is its elaborate graphical interface („Design Studio"). The Design Studio allows to visualize, parametrize, test and run any object which is derived from the operator base class. The process of creating a recognition system, which implies to choose a set of recognition operators, arrange them into the desired order, parametrize, and test them, takes place here.

A graphical interface is not an essential part of frameworks at such, but has proven to be very useful for an intuitive adaptation of document recognition systems.

Apart from the design studio, the framework possesses a second graphical interface for displaying debug output. This tool is essential for quickly identifying problems which may appear while the system is in operation.

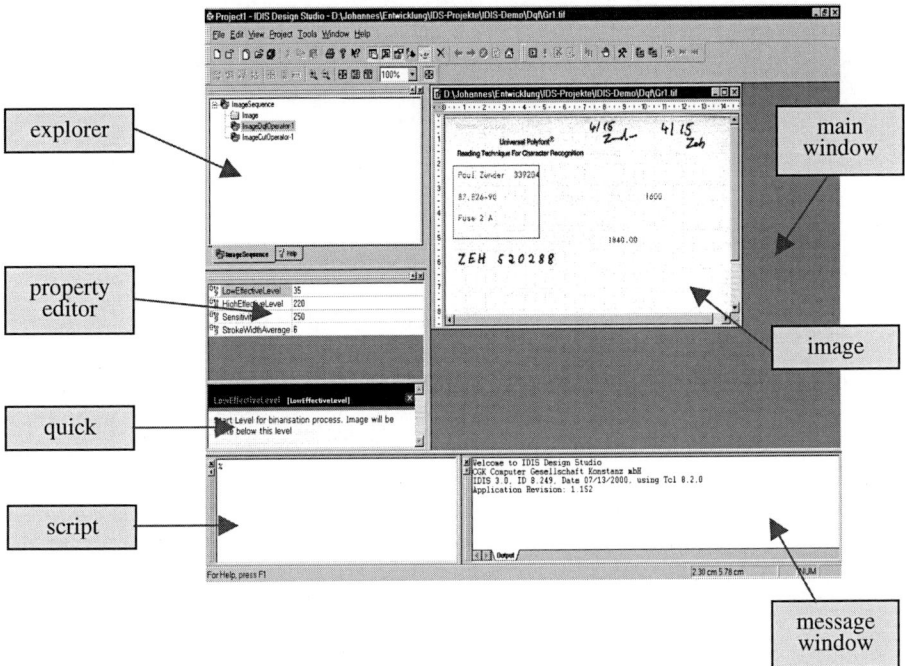

Fig. 2. The design studio

2.4 Workflow Integration

Another important requirement for recognition systems is the integration into the company's business processes. While the framework allows to construct recognition systems also as self-standing entities, they will in practice more often have to be integrated again into superordinate workflow systems. The easy integrationability into both recognition workflow management systems (e.g. Ascent Capture) and business workflows (e.g. SAP) was therefore one of the major focusses when the framework was designed.

An integration can be accomplished by developing specific interfaces between each superordinate system and the recognition system. This can be a very tedious task. By providing the recognition system with a generic interface using component technologies, this task can be simplified. It has therefore been decided to provide the interface with a standard component technology, as which COM has been chosen for the present period. The COM-layer allows different workflow-management-systems to integrate instances of document recognition engines. This COM-layer is currently being supplemented by a .NET-interface. One realistic scenario for the integration of a recognition system would be the automated categorization and processing of invoices as part of a procurement process.

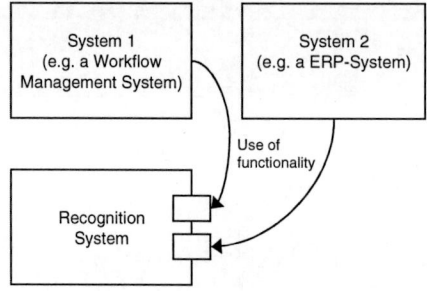

Fig. 3. Integrating a recognition system via component technologies

But the integration of the complete recognition system into a workflow management system is still a simplification of the demands that are often actually met. It is a more realistic scenario that subsets of the recognition system, e.g. the recognition engine in a narrower sense on the one hand and a component for manual validation on the other, are integrated as separate modules into the workflow. In this case, it is necessary to ensure that communication between the disentangled modules of the recognition system still works.

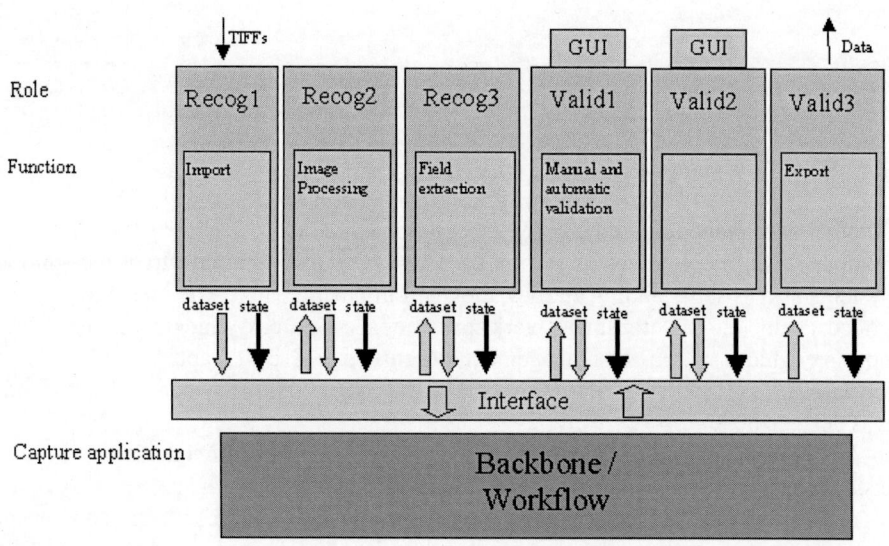

Fig. 4. A workflow with several integrated recognitionand validation components and one interface

This task can be simplified by defining a coherent data model for the whole framework. We have defined a generic data model („Dataset") in which any data state of a batch of documents can be represented. Each component works on an instance of the dataset and registers in it the modifications it performs. We then need only a single interface enabling the communication between the dataset and the superordinate workflow. Figure 4 shows a realistic workflow into which three recognition modules and three validation modules, two of which have an interface for manual validation, have been integrated. The design studio, by which the modules must have been parametrized beforehand, is not represented because it no longer plays a role at runtime.

3   The Components („Operators")

3.1   Overview

Alongside with the framework, about 30 operators have been created which offer various possibilities for extracting data from documents. We are not going to give here a detailed description of all of them, but we will only outline some of their general features.

The following shows an extract of the operator interface as defined in C++. The operator offers methods for validity check, initialisation, termination, and - most importantly - „work", by which the input workitem is transformed into the output workitem.

```
template <class BaseClass, class ImplClass>
class IDSOWP_API OperatorBase :
    public BaseClass
{
public:
    OperatorBase ();
    virtual bool checkRequirement (
        idskernel::StringVector* pMessages,
        bool bStop = false);
    virtual idskernel::Result init ();
    virtual idskernel::Result work (
        IWorkItem* pInputWorkItem,
        IWorkItem** ppOutputWorkItem = 0);
    virtual idskernel::Result term ();
    (...)
};
```

Fig. 5. The operator interface (extract)

Not all of the recognition components currently available in the framework have initially been designed with the purpose of a later reuse in mind. Instead, the idea of our approach was that already completed components written in different programming languages, as well as commercial components whose source code is unavailable, could also be wrapped as operators. The migration of existing software components to distributed object technology is done by writing a wrapper which translates their functionality into the operator methods and, if necessary, employing one of two currently available programming interfaces, a COM-interface and an iTCL-interface; a third .NET-interface is envisaged for the near future.

Since the operator interface is small, it is no great task to wrap as operators even components which have not been designed with the purpose of eventually being used within the framework. We have made this experience several times when integrating components of external provenance.

The operators differ considerably among each other: While some of them have a very specific, narrowly defined task (e.g. the pixel-count operator that checks whether or not a specific box is blank), others are big components covering a mighty functionality (e.g. the station for manual validation). Most of the operators can roughly be subdivided into two groups, namely the imaging operators on the one hand, which have the task of refining the input images in order to improve the results of the subsequent recognition, and the recognition operators on the other, which extract different kinds of information out of the documents. But there are also operators of other kinds, such as the validation operator, which will be described below, and the „composer"-operator, which is able to separate an unstructured batch of sources (images) into documents based on a fuzzy matching approach.

All operators can be parametrized by the user in the design studio. Parameters differ from operator to operator and may be integers, strings, boxes, or files. Box parameters are very typical for recognition systems, and to enable an intuitive handling and definition of them is one of the major tasks of the design studio.

All operators together with their parametrizations can be stored and reloaded in an XML-based persistence format.

3.2 Image Operators

There are numerous operators that optimize images before they proceed to the recognition, among them image crop (removal of black margins), correction of image orientation, removal of dot shading and lines, deskew, etc. The design studio allows to examine the effects of the operators on test images while creating the system.

3.3 Extraction Operators

Most extraction operators are OCR-based. Here belong, among others, operators for reading text, for localizing concepts essential in forms and documents such as dates, amounts, adresses and self-defined regular expressions, and for reading tables. Some operators do not need OCR such as the barcode recognizer and the logo operator which will be described below.

All these operators can be used in a search-and-extract mode, where they directly read the desired data, or in a search-only mode, where they are merely needed for determining the relative location of data on the document or for adapting subsequent operators which do the extraction in their turn.

In practical applications, some external knowledge about the expected content of documents is often available. One realistic case concerns the extraction of data from invoices, because an invoice is typically a reaction to an order put by the invoice recipient. If the ordering company keeps track of their orders in a business workflow system, this information can be of great help in understanding and checking incoming invoices. One particularly interesting matter is the identification of the invoice sender since for this purpose several features such as invoice sender name, address, bank account number, logos and the general layout of the invoice provide interrelated and partly redundant information, which is furthermore particularly likely to be represented in the ordering company's database.

In this case we employ a fuzzy-database operator which contains all the accessible information about possible invoice senders. Depending on the availability and the recognition quality of the various extracted fields, the system may in each particular case rely on different pieces of information to identify one and the same sender. This can be seen as a case of self-adaptation of the system to the peculiarities of the actual document which is being processed.

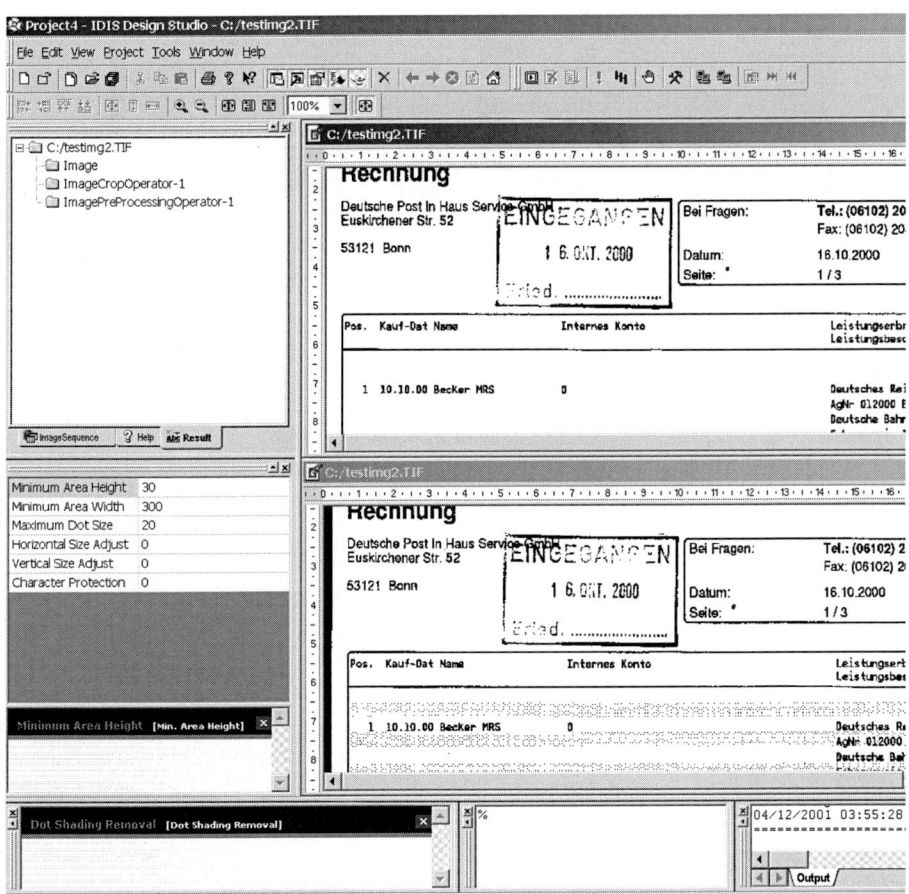

Fig. 6. Effects of crop and dot shading removal on an image as visible in the design studio

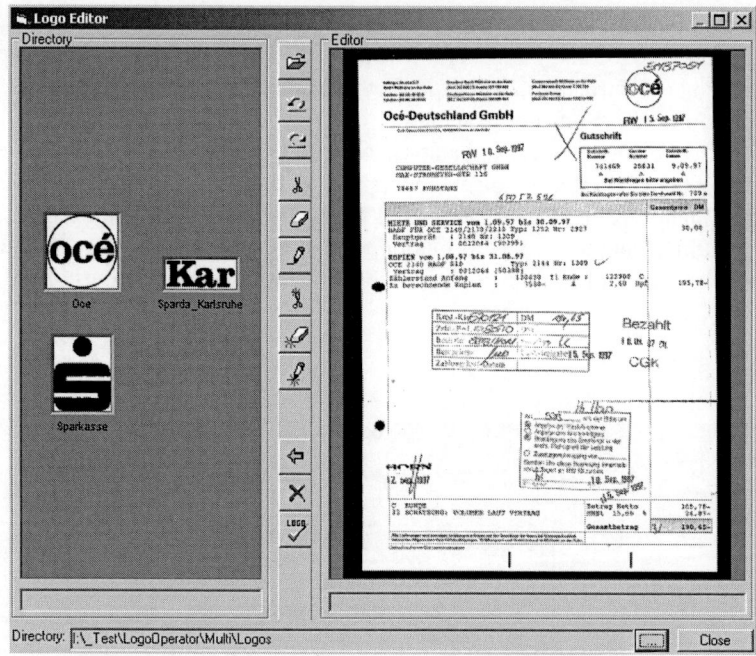

Fig. 7. The graphical definition interface of the logo operator

3.4 The Logo Operator

A recognition component which deviates in several respects from most other components used within the system is the logo-operator. Its aim is to recognize graphical
elements which appear frequently on forms or documents and can be useful to determine a form type even in extremely bad images where OCR results are unreliable.
The logo-operator differs from other recognition operators not only in its algorithmi-
cal function, but also poses special needs for parametrizing. We have supplemented
the logo operator with a specific graphical design tool, which comes integrated into
the general design studio. The logo design tool allows the user to choose and localize
logos on test images, modify them, and teach them to the engine. After having
learned a logo, the operator is able to find these structures also in different sizes or in
rotated form. It is thus an operator which is very robust and easy to parametrize at the
same time.

3.5 The Validation Component

The most complex single module within the system is a station for validating documents. This component allows the user to browse, verify, and correct reading results
whose confidence is under a given threshold. The validation can be performed manu-

ally on a separate graphical interface and/ or automatically by an event-driven VBA scripting interface, where, to name just one example, plausibility checks on amounts and summations within a document can be implemented. Even though this validation module is of a high complexity, it can still be viewed as an operator in the workitem-operator-paradigm because its task is to transform one workitem (a batch of documents with some extracted data) into another (a batch of documents with modified data).

4 Adaptiveness of the Framework

Adaptivity and flexibility is an important requirement posed on today's software. The framework described here has adaptive features on multiple levels.

First of all, the operators within the framework can adapt themselves at run-time based on the results of previous operators. For achieving this, the framework allows to define a control flow which, depending on the result of one operator, may call different subsequent operators or different operator configurations. The system can thus be taught to prefer certain search positions or OCR settings, or to load specialized keyword lists, after, for example, a specific invoice sender has been identified.

Still a different kind of adaptation is found in the treatment of logical interrelated data, as has already been explained above for the identification of the invoice sender. In this way, the system can largely remedy OCR failures or missing fields by focussing on different pieces of information in each particular case.

Furthermore, the operators can be internally adaptive, i.e. capable of learning. We currently employ one operator for localizing reading zones on a document based on a set of example documents. The performance of this location operator improves with the number of example documents it has been exposed to.

Finally, an important aspect of the adaptivity of the system is added by the focus that was put on the easy integrationability into superordinate systems and on the easy to handle graphical surface for manual adjustment to project specific needs. These non-algorithmic aspects of software systems are often underestimated but add a lot to the effectiveness of a software system in practical use.

5 A Case Study: An Invoice Reader System

In order to evaluate the framework together with its operators in a realistic application, we have used it to construct a complete system for processing invoices from German speaking countries. It was our intention to construct a general system which without much manual adaptation is able to extract data from invoices coming from a

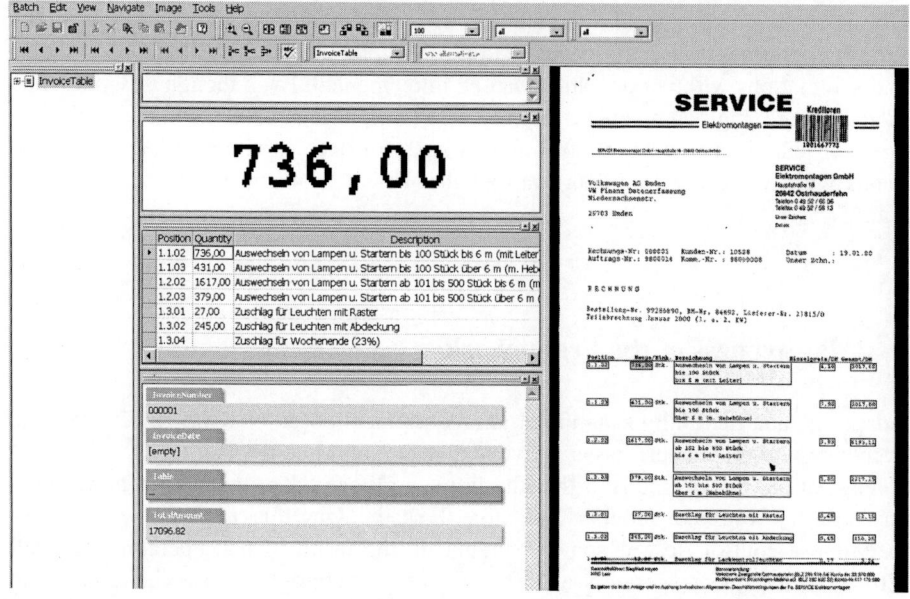

Fig. 8. The graphical surface of the validation studio. Here: Correcting a table.

huge variety of senders and in very diverse formats. The system contains a constellation of predefined general as well as highly specialized operators, which can be further adapted according to project specific demands. To the specialized invoice operators belong an amount-operator which extracts the net amount, VAT rate, VAT amount, and total amount from the document and performs arithmetical cross checkings, as well as an invoice sender operator which can work on a data base as described above. The system is completed by a configuration of the validation studio which is technically separated from the recognition components and communicates with them through the common data representation model („Dataset").

The probably most complex one of the invoice operators is an operator for automatically locating and extracting table structures, as are typical for invoices. The validation component as well provides specific facilities for displaying and navigating through a table, as is shown in figure 8.

Although the system works well already in its default configuration, it can easily be further adapted to project specific needs by modifying the operators in the design studio. For example, regulations about the VAT rate can be indicated, specific read options can be defined depending on keys such as logos detected on a document, or image preprocessing measures can be taken.

References

[Brown 1996] = A. W. Brown (ed.): Component-Based Software Engineering. Selected Papers from the Software Engineering Institute, Los Alamitos 1996

[Fayad 1999] = M. Fayad, D. Schmidt, R. Johnson: Building Application Frameworks - Object-Oriented Foundations of Framework Design, Wiley 1999

[Lippert 2000] = M. Lippert, St. Roock, H. Züllighoven: "From Documents to Applications via Frameworks: The Tools and Materials Approach", OOPSLA 2000 Companion, ACM press

[Nierstrasz 1995a] = O. Nierstrasz, L. Dami: Component-Oriented Software Technology, in [Nierstrasz 1995b: 3-28]

[Nierstrasz 1995b] = O. Nierstrasz, D. Tsichritzis (eds.): Object-Oriented Software Composition, London 1995

[Parnas 1972] = D.L. Parnas: On the Criteria to be Used in Decomposing Systems into Modules. Communications of the ACM, 15(12)

[Pintado 1995] = X. Pintado: Gluons and the Cooperation between Software Components, in [Nierstrasz 1995b: 321-349]

[Pree 1997] = W. Pree: Komponentenbasierte Softwareentwicklung mit Frameworks, Heidelberg 1997

[Szyperski 1998] = C. Szyperski: Component Software: Beyond Object-Oriented Programming, Harlow

[Wallace 1996] = E. Wallace, P. Clements, K. Wallnau: Discovering a System Modernization Decision Framework: A Case Study in Migrating to Distributed Object Technology, in [Brown 1996: 113-123]

smartFIX: An Adaptive System for Document Analysis and Understanding

Bertin Klein[1], Andreas R. Dengel[1], and Andreas Fordan[2]

[1] German Research Center for Artificial Intelligence (DFKI)
P.O.Box 2080, D-67608 Kaiserslautern, Germany
{dengel,klein}@dfki.de
[2] INSIDERS technologies GmbH
Brüsseler-Str. 1, D-67657 Kaiserslautern, Germany
A.Fordan@insiders-technologies.de

Abstract. The internet is certainly a wide-spread platform for information interchange today and the semantic web actually seems to become more and more real. However, day-to-day work in companies still necessitates the laborious, manual processing of huge amounts of printed documents. This article presents the system *smartFIX*, a document analysis and understanding system developed by the DFKI spin-off insiders. During the research project "adaptive Read", funded by the German ministry for research, BMBF, *smartFIX* was fundamentally developed to a higher maturity level, with a focus on adaptivity. The system is able to extract information from documents – documents ranging from fixed format forms to unstructured letters of many formats. Apart from the architecture, the main components and the system characteristics, we also show some results from the application of *smartFIX* to representative samples of medical bills and prescriptions.

Keywords: Document analysis and understanding, document classification, information extraction, table extraction, extraction optimization, extraction verification, industrial invoice processing

1   Introduction

About 1.2 million printed medical invoices arrive at the 35 German private health insurance companies every day. Those invoices amount to 10% of the German health insurance market and they are actually maintained by printed paper invoices. Figure 1 shows examples of such printed invoices. Until recently the processing of these invoices was done almost completely manually. In addition to the tedious task of initiating every single payment by transcribing a number of data fields from varying locations on the paper documents into a computer, this had the serious disadvantage that only a small number of inconsistent and overpriced invoices were discovered. Conservative estimates predict savings in the range of several hundred million Euros each year if this process could be automated reliably.

A. Dengel et al. (Eds.): Adaptive READ Research Project, LNCS 2956, pp. 166–186, 2004.

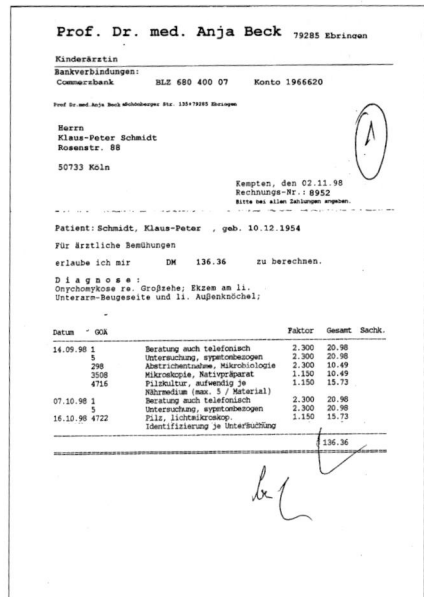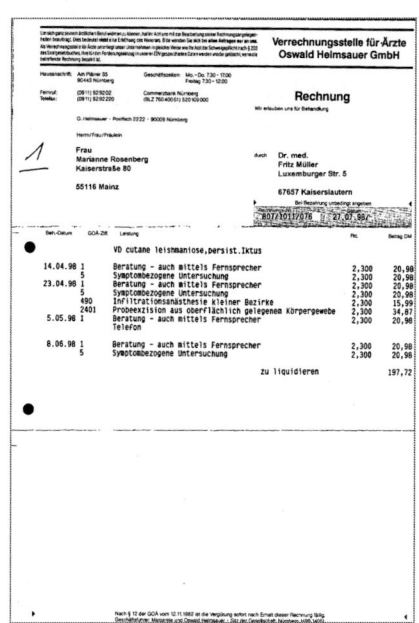

Fig. 1. Examples of medical invoices common in Germany

In 1999, a consortium of German private health insurance companies ran a public benchmark test of systems for Document Analysis and Understanding (DAU) for the respective private insurance sector. The benchmark was won by and proved the suitability of *smartFIX* (smart *For Information eXtraction*). This initial version of *smartFIX* was developed by a spin-off company of the DAU group at DFKI, INSIDERS (www.insiders-technologies.de, founded in 1999 by Prof. Dengel), thinking that the available DAU technology after a decade of focused research was ready to construct a versatile and adaptive DAU system [1, 2, 3]. After the premise of the identification of a viable type of application scenarios, the well-directed research on a feasible combination of available methods and completion with new methods could be successfully accomplished. This background probably explains the clear suitability of *smartFIX* for the project *adaptive Read*, which INSIDERS joined after the benchmark. Funded by the German ministry for research, BMBF, *smartFIX* was significantly extended and raised to a new level of ability to be adapted. The result of this project was further extended to several products for different industries, one e.g., in cooperation with four insurance companies for the analysis of printed medical invoices: *smartFIX healthcare*. In the meantime *smartFIX healthcare* has been established the standard product for the private health insurance sector. *smartFIX* was the result of several man-years investment. The brainpower in *smartFIX healthcare* can be estimated in a larger dimension.

The first two important facts about the target domains, in the following represented with the example of the health insurance domain are:

1. Invoices are more complex than forms.
2. Every invoice is inspected by a human operator anyhow.

Therefore, the DAU task for invoices requires more than the more simple methods that suffice for forms - a challenge for the DAU technology developers in the project. But at the same time, the insurance auditors can be assured, that the economic success does not only start after a distant breakthrough, but every little successfully implemented DAU step reduces the human operators workload right away. Every correctly recognized data item saves typing and can be logically and numerically checked. Diagnoses can be automatically coded into ICD 10 (the international standard code for diagnoses). Actually, even with no recognition results, the efficient user interface of the result viewer facilitates the processing of scanned invoices.

In general, *smartFIX healthcare* is not limited to the domain of medical bills but is applicable also to most kinds of forms and many unstructured documents. In the following, we will describe the major characteristics of the system including architecture, main components as well as some technical aspects. At the end of the paper, we will present run-time results of *smartFIX healthcare* applied to medical bills based on a recent evaluation of a large private health insurance company, which processes several tens of thousands of bills and prescriptions every day.

2   SmartFIX Healthcare

Nowadays, at least since the CommonKADS projects series [4], it is known how indispensable the analysis of the intended application is for successful knowledge-intensive software projects. Then the software has to be adapted in detail to the requirements. Facing the needs of a group of companies, this requirements-centered approach is even more important and challenging, e.g. the number of example documents, which the companies' representatives thought to convey their needs, rapidly grew to much more than 10000. It is important to understand what one can learn from these documents and alone their sheer number is obviously very challenging. So, the original ideas of our DAU researchers underlying *smartFIX* were refined with the needs of the insurance companies.

The insurance companies required from *smartFIX healthcare* (requirements which had certainly not been the primary concern in the ten years work of our DAU researchers):

1. Verified economic advantages (qualitative, quantitative)
2. Reliability (error recovery, error rate, error statistics)
3. Scalability
4. Plug-ability to their workflow (people, tasks, databases, archives)

The actual economic advantages were simply required to be tested. Actually, it turned out we had no problems at all to reach the required measures (see Results section). Generally, this seems to be not a problem also elsewhere: a questioning in German industry, which investigated the results of investments into DAU tools, indicates that companies typically hesitate to spend money first, but are very delighted about the achieved results (and return of investment) later. [12]

Scalability had already been targeted and was mainly available: *smartFIX* is a distributed system, CORBA on networked PCs, which can easily spread its single-analysis processes over many CPUs and still be controlled from one desktop. One aspect of reliability is achieved with a central transaction memory database. Thus, the only remaining tasks were to extend and adapt *smartFIX* to the insurers workflow requirements and to learn about reliability in terms of stable error-rates.

Extending the most basic principle that the design of DAU systems should not be technology-driven, but explicitly requirements-driven (and thus adapted to the users needs) [4], with our approach we came to the following guiding principles for the design of DAU systems:

1. **Compositionality:** A versatile system has to have a significant spectrum of different basic DAU components; one paradigm alone will almost surely fail to solve a real problem. – Complex methods, which at first glance are very hard to conceive, are obtained from deliberate, small combinations of simple methods. [3]

2. **Practice principle:** There is no way to get around errors. Thus it is important to help users to discover, judge, and either tolerate, or to correct errors. This is especially critical as the user in every day practice is left alone with the control of the system and the responsibility for its results. – The real DAU technology must be powerfully accompanied by technology for logging, tracing, visualizing, interactive testing, statistics.

3. **Epistemological adequacy:** The basic DAU components must be bundled to greater analysis building blocks (we call them "scripts" later in this paper), which are made available to the user. The user has to perceive document characteristics and map those to the scripts. Thus the scripts should be meaningful to the user, easy to memorize and use. Good script metaphors also guide the perception of the document characteristics. Later these scripts might report success or error messages. – This long standing AI principle implies that so-called "syntactic sugar" must not be taken lightly, but can actually make a difference. Beware of software engineers who disregard it.

4. **Constructivism:** The philosophic principle of constructivism says that every knowledgeable agent, human or machine, has a different account of reality and there is no objective truth at all. For a DAU system it means: (a) That every scenario will always require at least one aspect, which is outside of the capabilities of the system at hand. Thus it is important to allow users access to manipulate intermediate results. (b) That two persons at a time (and even often one person at two times) disagree on facts significantly often (cf. TREC human evaluators cross comparison [5]). Thus it is important that the DAU system gives feedback and continuously makes transparent, which information it receives from a user and how this information will be used.

3   System Architecture

The capabilities of *smartFIX healthcare* are diverse, and so is its architecture. The machinery alone to control the executables and configurations according to the needs of its owner – if smartFIX is locked up in a cellar or security zone, spread over several or many analysis computers, connected to company databases – is considerably tricky. However, in the end, and after having learnt many little but important details, e.g. that there are document analysis verifying personnel who cannot press

<Ctrl>+<F12> because they have only one hand: the familiar DAU methodology is still the heart of it all.

The architecture, i.e. the main components, are shown in Figure 2. This section's overview of main components and supporting components is succeeded in the following sections by a sketch of the *DocumentManager* through which the system is instructed and after that an explanation of the most central DAU component, the *Analyzer*. (*Analyzers* are mainly the component, which is cloned and spread over the CPUs of a networked system implementation.) The *Improver*, though part of the *Analyzer*, is focused thereafter in a separate section and finally also the *Verifier*, the module to check and correct the analysis results.

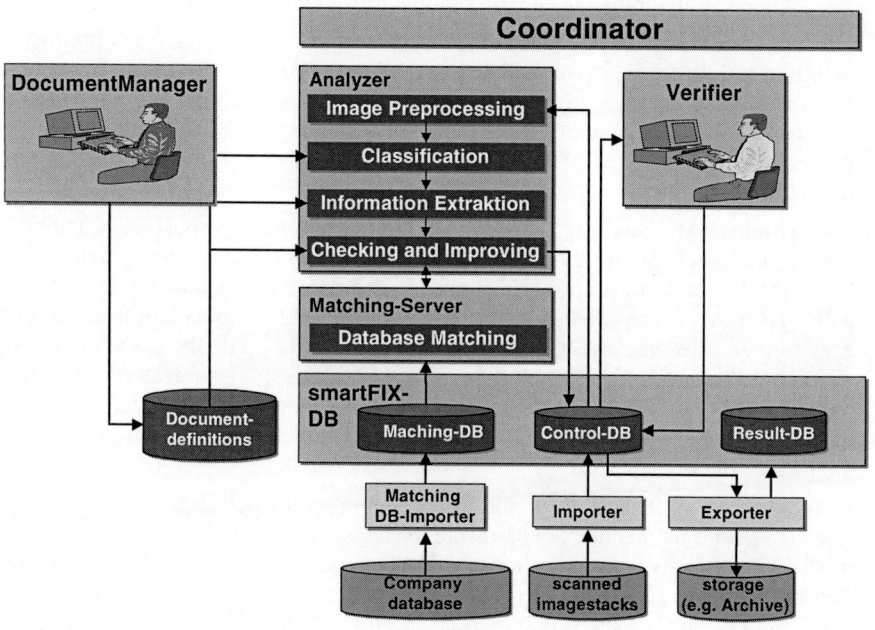

Fig. 2. System architecture of *smartFix*

3.1   Main Modules

In order to apply *smartFIX healthcare* to a new DAU problem, it is necessary to pin down the specific document types and the "what and how" of information extraction. The resulting "document information" –some prefer to call this the "processing knowledge"– is configured with the *DocumentManager*. (Section 4 treats the *DocumentManager* including a screenshot.)

Then the system can be started with the *Coordinator*: a control panel, from which DAU-processes, i.e. *Analyzers*, can be started on a freely-configurable network of PCs (so far we tested with over 60); one *Analyzer* per CPU as a rule of thumb. The *Coordinator* also starts some other processes, first now, two database processes used by the Analyzers: the *Matching-Server* provides very fast retrieval ("matching") on company knowledge from the *matching data base*. The *Matching Database*, mostly contractual data, is a working copy, which can be updated with a handy tool, the *Matching Database Importer*, from company databases. The *Control Database* is the central working memory of *smartFIX*. It could be regarded the blackboard of the whole architecture.

The *Coordinator* controls an *Importer* process, which transfers document images from a predefined source into the *Control Database*, together with possibly known information. Any idling *analyzer* will check out, process and check in again documents in the *Control Database*. Successful information extraction provided, human agents who are logged on with a *Verifier* process, are prompted the DAU results. With the database it is assured, that not a single bit is lost, even in the event of a power cut. Finished documents are transferred out of the system by an *Exporter,* typically into archive systems.

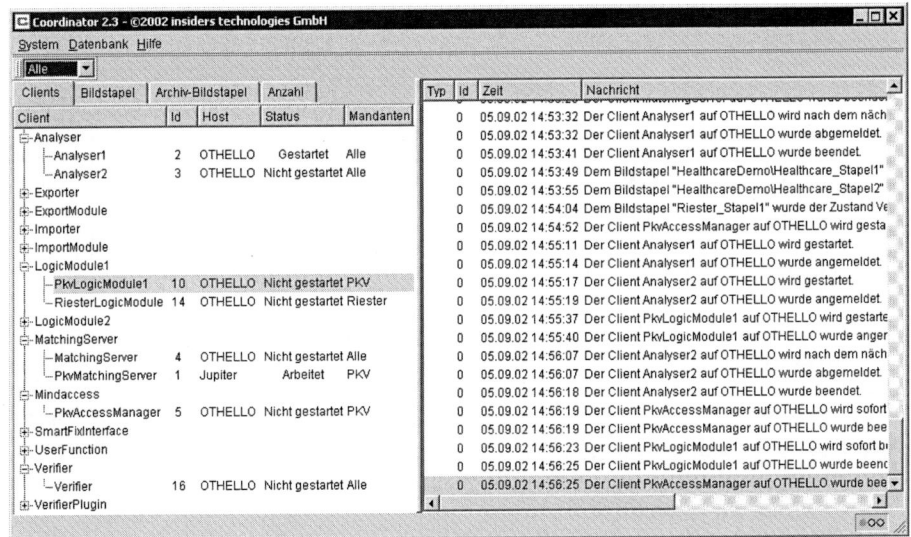

Fig. 3. The *Coordinator* controls the running and idling clients on remote hosts (left) and the status messages (right) of a productive smartFIX healthcare.

3.2   Supporting Components

The main architecture of *smartFIX healthcare* is completed with some more components, helping the user to direct and to understand the system. We briefly list some, but space prohibits to really elaborate on them.

The *Configurator* is a graphical editor for a number of global system values, e.g. a couple of parameters of image pre-processing, and for non-disclosure levels of document classes and user-groups.

The *DCAdmin* (Decision Classifier Administrator) is a graphical interface for the training of a classification component, called "mindaccess", which exploits machine learning methods to learn semantic similarity from examples (see Section 5.2). The contents of a document very often "tell" its class.

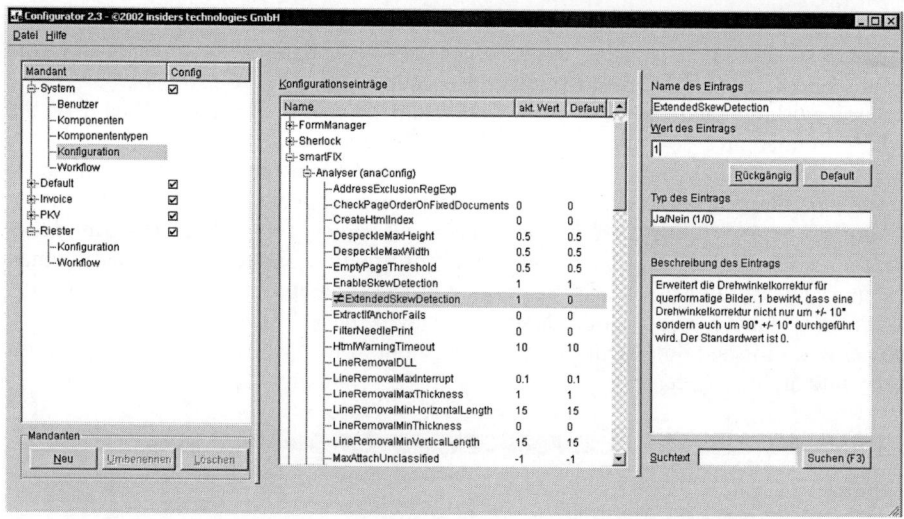

Fig. 4. The *Configurator* allows to create virtual sub-systems (left), to overview values and defaults of their sub-system-wide global system parameters (middle) and to edit them (right). The Figure displays the activation of "ExtendedSkewDetection" by setting it to 1.

All the different system modules adhere to one message format which can be visualized by *LogView*. This tool allows to log onto some module which runs somewhere in the system, on some of the possibly many host machines. It allows for a very efficient overview as well as debugging of the functioning of modules, due to its structural approach. It is equally used by our system developers and end-users.

The *Reporter* allows to query, display and print statistical data from the result database, like the number of pages, documents, and data fields read, the time needed for classification, extraction, the calculated reliabilities and also finally the actual reliability, i.e. the manual corrections.

The *Monitor* watches the system state by scanning all messages and can be configured either to mail, or to be queried by an SNMP management application or to send a so-called "trap"-message via SNMP if the system does not run stable.

The *StatisticTool* allows to run automatic regression tests, necessitating of course a set of ground truth documents. It is used to check and quantify the effect of system-changes (implementation or configuration). When the system configuration is changed one uses the *StatisticTool* to assure that the effect is positive and no degradations are unconsciously entered.

The complicated information for spotting and extracting tables is handled by a *TableTool,* which follows the approach we proposed in [10]. Amongst other things, the freely configurable workflow logic allows intermediate processing results to be externalized with a *user exit* process. The format is configurable, mostly XML. The intermediate results can thus be checked and changed with external software and then be reintegrated into regular processing. The workflow also allows for tricky DAU processes, where, for example, documents are analyzed to a first level and in a second run from the first level to a second level.

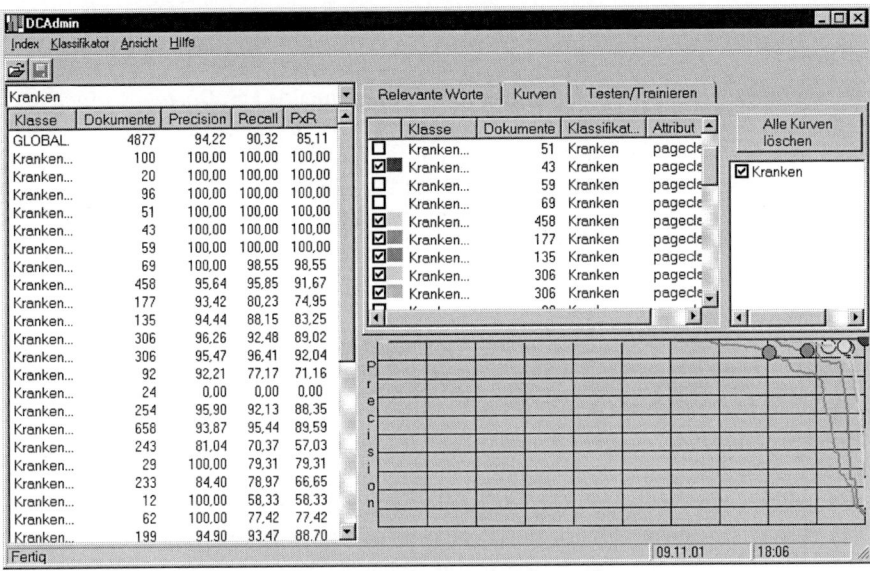

Fig. 5. The *DCAdmin* helps to supervise the learning of semantics of document content in order to classify future documents with significantly similar content.

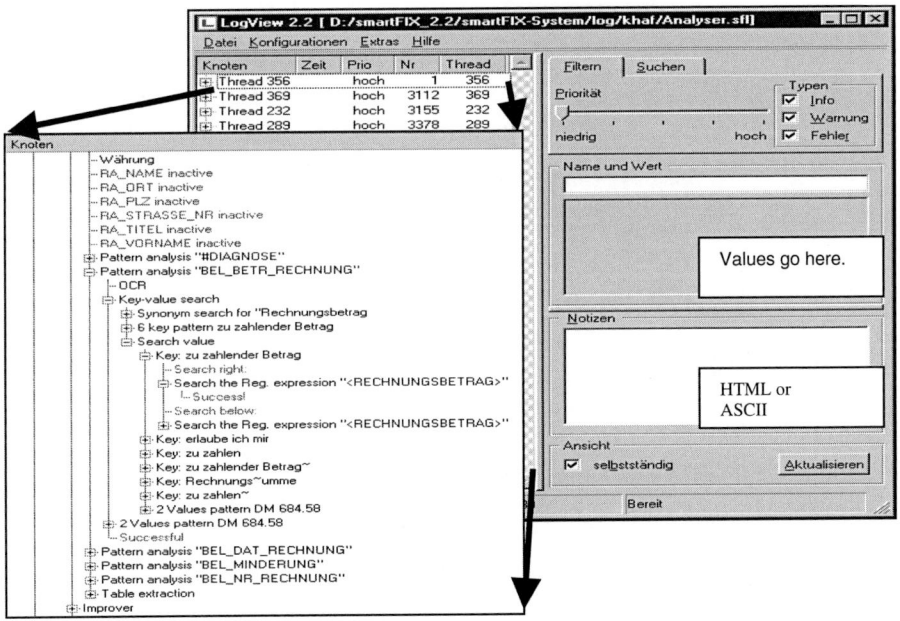

Fig. 6. *LogView* visualizes the messages of *smartFIX healthcare* modules. With a priority-slider messages can be suppressed depending on their priority. Messages can comprise values, e.g. an SQL statement, which caused an error, and can be augmented with arbitrary HTML or ASCII text, which is occasionally useful e.g. for messages from table extraction.

4   DocumentManager

Prior to going operative, *smartFIX* has to be programmed. The *DocumentManager* is a graphical editor with which the user defines document classes to distinguish, qualifies all necessary reference patterns, the analysis "recipe" and lets them be stored in a knowledge base of analysis configurations, simply called "document definitions". The *DocumentManager* is composed of five windows shown in Figure 3. On the right is a user-chosen sample document image, on the left:

- The directory of the different document classes and their aggregations
- The classification features
- The labels and the types of logical objects capturing the information to be searched
- So-called *Label Object Groups* (*LOG*), information on relations between objects

In order to configure *smartFIX*, example documents are loaded. In a first step, the user defines and links the corresponding document classes. He or she selects a region in the image where to search for a logical object of interest. This region of interest (ROI) is drawn with the mouse or selected to be the entire page wherever it is not sensible to constrain the region of search. To name the logical object, the user may either select the label from the existing list in the window or can add a new label. In addition, the user has to define the ROI type, which determines the type of analysis script which will be applied for the extraction of the contained information. *SmartFIX* offers various scripts. The most significant are:

- ADDRESS bases on a grammar of typical German addresses.
- CHECK BOX
- BAR CODE
- SEARCH PATTERN addresses a *key string* (including synonyms and acronyms from a configurable thesaurus) to which a corresponding *value string* has to be found. For example (see Fig. 4), the value of the logical object `<bill no.>` (in German `<rechnungs-nr.>`) is a numerical expression located within a certain relative distance in the image.
- ASSOCIATION skims with a whole database of known facts to find occurrences of them in the document.
- TABLE allows the extraction of tables and their logical structure, including many tricky features, e.g. interleaved columns.
- TEXT addresses objects which can be described with regular expressions and occur within free text, like "my insurance number is BG/1495-H".

All logical objects, which are defined, are related to ranges of values, e.g. lexical knowledge, regular expressions, or numerical constraints, depending on their type. For example, columns of a table are linked to sets of values, i.e. the logical object `<product>`, which represents a table column name, can be linked with all valid product names in a data base.

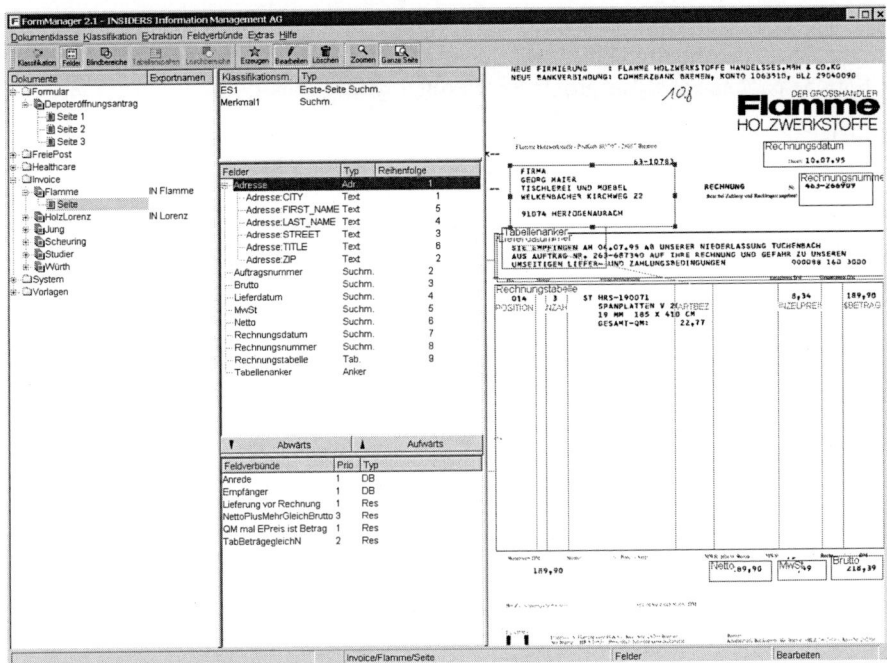

Fig. 7. The DocumentManager

After the definition of logical objects and corresponding ROIs, it is possible to support the analysis further with *LOG*s. A *LOG* relates a named set of scripts which depend on each other, e.g. a LOG <SERVICE SUBJECT> could be composed of <insurance number>, <person>, and <address>, while the latter two again consist of <first name>, <last name> as well as <zip code>, <city>, and <street name>.

Finally, all information is stored in a knowledge base of document definitions to be used later for the analysis of documents.

```
Kempten, den 02.11.98
Rechnungs-Nr.: 8952
```

Fig. 8. Typical constellation of numerical data close to a meaningful keyword.

5   Analyzer

A number of *Analyzer*s actually accomplish the real DAU processing. Every running *Analyzer* polls the brain of the system, the *control data base,* for documents to process. After finishing with a document it is labeled and put back into the *control data* *base.* The label is like the address of the next necessary processing stage, e.g. *Verifier*, and the labels flexibly implement the internal workflow.

For one page the analysis progresses in roughly four stages:

1. Image pre-processing   (Section 5.1),
2. Classification   (Section 5.2),
3. Information extraction (Section 5.3),
4. Improvement   (Section 6).

OCR is called lazily, i.e. it is called for segments only when their character content is needed. As a matter of fact, the four phases are not always clearly distinguished. E.g. after the classification it is possible to have found that the image must be scaled. Newly, for classification, all methods out of the information extraction toolbox are usable. The first three steps are explained in the remainder of this section. Improvement, because of its probable novelty to the reader, is the topic of the next section.

5.1   Image Pre-processing

Image pre-processing consists of five optional steps. Each step can be individually switched on and off, tuned with parameters, and be required for the whole page or arbitrary regions.

1. Removal of graphical lines (vertical and horizontal)
2. Optimization of matrix printed characters
3. Despeckle
4. Deskew (±10° landscape and portrait)
5. Correction of upside-down

The pre-processed images are stored for the later visualization of the extraction results.

5.2   Classification

The classification runs in predefined phases and searches the following features until a class is determined:

1. Layout similarity [7, 8]
2. Recognized tables [6]
3. User-defined or machine-learned patterns (including Not-patterns)
4. Machine-learned semantic similarity [11]
5. Document size
6. Barcodes, signatures, vertically oriented patterns

The known classes and their features are configured using the *DocumentManager*. The classes can be structured decision-tree-alike, so that the classification can at least narrow down the alternatives whenever no single class can be determined. The classes can be set up so that non-classified documents are sent to a *Verifier* for manual classification, or run through a default information extraction first.

The classification also has to deal with the collation of pages to documents. The most reliable method, interspersing different documents with easy-to-recognize dividing pages at scanning, is sometimes not possible. Therefore *smartFIX healthcare* provides a collation-machinery, which is not really sophisticated but confusing to explain without using many examples.

The classification can utilize if document pages are entered into the system accompanied with pre-information, in the form of attributes, which perhaps codes the source of documents like scanner type, scanning location, personnel or the like. One important consequence of this is that it allows for one aspect of SAP-compatibility: documents from different sections of a company can be attributed as such, thus distinguished in the system and thus be processed on one and the same hardware. So two or more systems can share one hardware.

The class of a document fixes its further path through the system. Different classes are often handled totally different, including their export out of the system to different target systems.

5.3   Information Extraction

Information extraction is performed according to the "scripts" which –with the *DocumentManager*– were individually configured for the respective document class. Scripts have a type and a name. According to their type, scripts perform a specific action referring to the page at hand, after which they provide a value under their name. Where this is important, scripts can be assigned priorities to constrain the sequence in which they are run. Simple extraction scripts search the image of the page. The complex extraction scripts use complicated user-provided and built-in knowledge. The data scripts are simply providing access to logical page data. These three categories of script types are explained in the following.

Simple Extraction Scripts Types

1. "Text" and "Combination": extract characters in a specified area. The combination script sends the extracted characters later to have it split into components with the support of database lookups. It is possible to have the area initially cleared from form preprints.

2. "Checkbox": two different algorithms can be chosen, to determine whether a checkbox area is ticked.

3. "Pattern search": either on the whole page or in an area, a regular expression is either searched directly, or searched in the configurable surroundings (direction and distance) of a prior regular expression match or thesaurus synonyms match.

4. "Address": a specific script for the extraction of German addresses, split into standard pieces. A regular expression may be used to exclude strings from the search space.

5. "Anchor": does a pattern search and after matching it triggers other linked scripts, which then run in an area relative to the position of the match.

6. "Format": currently simply measures and evaluates to A4, A5, or A6.

Value Script Types. With the choice of one of the following scripts it is possible to access page information: "Document class": Evaluates to the result of the classification. "Document ID": evaluates to the unique identifier of the document (which often allows access to further related external archive data). "Task ID": evaluates to the task which the document belongs to.

A "free value script" does nothing, but can be set later with a value from a database lookup. This might be helpful as a variable for further database lookups, for automatic checks, or as an additional information for human Verifiers.

Complex Extraction Script Types. "Association": skims for occurrences of patterns from a possibly huge database. Several fields of the database can be mixed. Prior successful scripts can be used to restrict the search space of database field combinations. This is a powerful tool e.g. to find exceptionally formatted senders' addresses, if they are only known in a customer database.

"Fixed table": extracts a table according to user-defined layout rules.

"Free table": is a comprehensive Analyzer in its own right. According to a complex knowledge configuration with the *TableTool*, this script extracts tables of different layouts, even spanning more than one page, rather intelligently. Extracts also table-related data like sum total. [6]

6   Improver

The improving module, based on the Symbolic AI technique of constraint solving, checks consistency, searches optima, and fills in deducible information. The main idea is that the results of all the single scripts, which are fuzzy and unsafe, can be constrained step by step to more specific and reliable results, with local auxiliary conditions and interdependency conditions. In detail the improving module is described in [9].

The improving module employs a unique formalism to cope with the manifold alternatives generated by almost any component used in DAU. As far as we know, there are no comparable systematic DAU optimizations yet, and the *smartFIX healthcare* system is the first to integrate database and other constraints, and to profit from the theory of constraint solving. Optical Character Recognition (OCR) is still the slowest and weakest processing step in our application domain. As a rule, 1-10% of machine font characters are not read correctly; even more in cases of bad scan quality. Most OCR implementations return lists of alternatives to express ambiguity, but for the assessment of the quality of the alternatives, it can be hardly relied on the quality values returned by the OCR. A much safer approach is to exploit some context knowledge to exclude inadequate interpretations. E.g. the results of two scripts like for a name and a contract number are rather unsafe after simple extraction. But their combination most often allows the determination of the one right name and contract number.

The execution time for the constraint solving process e.g. of one medical invoice including a table with a couple of cells rarely exceeds one second. The error rate for fields that are marked *safe* is not allowed to exceed 1/1000. On average, roughly 70-90% fields can be presented *safe* to the user.

Context knowledge adds a flexible power of modeling to *smartFIX healthcare*, because its specification is substantially faster than a re-implemention of the document analysis for a certain domain. Moreover, the same knowledge serves as a correction mechanism later in the *Verifier*, so that after the typing of missing information, deducible information is provided by the system.

6.1   Constraint Solving for Exploiting Context

Context knowledge in document analysis can be denoted as constraints, i.e. as relations among the text fields. The variables in DA are the regions of interest (ROI). The fuzzy set of OCR interpretations can be seen as the natural domain for fields. In this way, document understanding becomes a matter of constraint solving and optimization.

A search pattern that identifies the invoice date, for instance, will generate several potential locations on the page. Constraints can eliminate inconsistent date alternatives like those before the date of the last medical treatment. Another practice example is the *hospital invoice* where *smartFIX healthcare* is supposed to find the hospital address. Different hospitals have different typical rates for certain services. Ambiguous address matches can exploit the special rates help identify the correct address and vice versa.

The constraints that the improving module exploits are the user defined *Labeled Object Groups* (LOG), user-provided auxiliary conditions and it also finishes the "Association" scripts, heavily using the *matching server* process. LOGs relate different scripts (i.e. their values) together, by a reference to databases. Also the "Combination" scripts, introduced before, are processed in this module. In their case, the difference is only, that name and number and perhaps more data are concatenated in one string, possibly permutated. The "Association" scripts skim a whole region or entire page whether any of the facts from a whole database trigger an association and where, e.g. whether and where on a page one or more out of perhaps 10000 known company names can be found. With the local auxiliary conditions the system estimates levels of reliability for every single piece of extracted information, which is used in the *Verifier* as colored backgrounds green, light blue, blue, to direct the attention of human operators.

Auxiliary conditions need not only be monadic operators, but can also relate two or more script values analytically, then resembling LOGs. E.g. all the fields in a summation column sum up to the sum total below the column. Available predicates and functions address arithmetics, dates, checkboxes, strings. Some of the auxiliary conditions can generate correction hypotheses or fill empty fields (e.g. a wrong or empty OCR result in a summation column) others only work as a filter. Via CORBA or COM users can also call user-implemented condition functions (returning a string).

There are a number of important differences to classical constraint solving.

- There is no discrete truth model for the constraints. We have to deal with probabilities. Even a perfect match of OCR and database does not give 100% accuracy as we never know about the correctness of the OCR.
- In DA, we are not focused on the question of consistency. Classical logic will return *false* or *no* in case of inconsistency. But the typical application in DA does not know a thing like an inconsistent document. Rather, inconsistent constraints are omitted such that the remaining values can be proposed to the user.
- The result of the DA is supposed to be corrected by verifying personnel. In order to accelerate the correction, the system returns a *rating* for any field which is one of (a) safe, (b) proposal, or (c) OCR result. The user is not supposed to check the safe values (although he can).
- There are at least two kinds of *truthes*: (a) the truth from the viewpoint of the author of the document, and (b) the so-called ground truth, i.e. the mathematical arithmetics, respectively the database.

6.2 Relating OCR Values with Constraints

The domain of the variables is the *fuzzy* set of OCR interpretations. Matching it to some database values or confirmation by another constraint, changes it from fuzzy to *exact*, which means its reduction to a finite table of possible values (exact values are more tractable). This implies that results may vary depending on the order of evaluation. However, the performance gain is too big to be wasted and *smartFIX healthcare* allows for a priority setting to give control of order to the user if necessary.

Any constraint has access to the document fields, which are considered the variables here. Alternative values are assigned a quality. This quality is computed as the average Levenshtein similarity of the new alternative values and their associated OCR graphs. Lines are only kept if they are better than configurable thresholds.

A database constraint takes the fuzzy or exact alternatives from its variables and builds a database query. As this query may be fuzzy, this cannot be achieved with SQL. The wanted result consists of those DB lines that are the most similar to the OCR values. The *smartFIX healthcare* system thus comprises a complex tool called *Matching-Server* which exploits Levenshtein editing distance, Trigram search, and other methods to efficiently scan large databases for fuzzy matches. For *Association* fields, the locations are initially unknown, so that the task of the *Matching-Server* there is to find location as well as contents. A realistic size for an address database is roughly 100 million entries on a standard PC with 1 GB RAM attached.

A successful database constraint chooses one or more table lines and writes the results back into the table of alternatives. Exact variables provide a *hard* selection like the WHERE clause in a SQL SELECT statement. Consequently, all result lines satisfy this selection. In contrast, fuzzy variables provide a *soft* selection. Thus they may be changed to a considerable degree if the whole line matches well. Empty variables do not give any selection. Rather, all possible results are returned. A typical query would be the following:

Field	Value	State
Last name	`M6yor'	fuzzy
First name	`J0n'	fuzzy
Account no.	`'	fuzzy
City	`London'	exact

Note that the values are OCR results in the case of fuzzy fields while exact values may have another origin. After the query, the table of alternatives could look as follows:

Quality	First name	Last name	Account no.	City
0.8	John	Mayor	12345678	London
0.7	Joe	Major	87654321	London
0.5	John	Maiden	18181818	London

Arithmetic constraints are potentially infinite relations, requiring a different approach. First, the exact variables are regarded, by running the algorithm for any possible combination of exact input values. (This calculation possibly explodes and thus the system has configurable limit, above which it gives up.) Second, if the constraint is satisfied an alternative line is generated. Otherwise, it is tried to correct one of the fuzzy variables. Often one can create sensible proposals for the variables, written into the table of alternatives.

A special case is an *assignment*. This is an equation with one empty fuzzy variable. Assignments are a perfect fit, but will never be rated *safe*.

As an example, suppose that the OCR has read 4.8 as a value for x and 2.3 for y and there is a constraint [x] = [y] * 2. The solver would then create two alternative solutions for this constraint:

Quality	X	y
0.833	4.6	2.3
0.833	4.8	2.4

Recall the example alternative table given in the last section. A constraint like [Account no.] ≥ 20000000 would eliminate the records `John Mayor' and `John Maiden'. So would SUBSTR([Account no.], 0, 1) = '8'. So would [First name] = 'Joe'. Suppose that there is no OCR input for field X. Then the constraint [X] = [First name] would generate the following alternative table:

Quality	X	First name
1	John	John
1	Joe	Joe

It should be mentioned that *smartFIX healthcare* offers a full range of constraints like =, <, >, ≥, ≤, plus linear arithmetics, and a number of constraints for checkboxes, for strings, and for dates. A user-defined function is available which can be implemented in a CORBA object. Also, some extra-logical predicates like IF-THEN-ELSE are available.

6.3   Propagation and Rating

Once the constraints have generated their alternative tables, they start a classical propagation. This ensures eventually that every constraint on a variable x will contain exactly the same set of values for this variable. The only exception is an empty alternative table. Empty tables do not propagate to prevent the whole system from being emptied and possible proposals from being deleted.

After the propagation the labeling stage begins. Obviously, this is a critical step w.r.t. optimization. We use heuristics to find an order to process the constraints. As opposed to regular labeling, we select one alternative line per constraint rather than one value per variable, since we administer the domains in the constraints rather than in the variables. For any constraint we select the regionally best alternative, assign the results to the variables, and then propagate.

The final step is the rating of the fields. Recall that alternative lines contain a quality rating. One of the lines has been selected after labeling. If its rating exceeds a `success' threshold, the constraint is considered *successful*. If there is no other alternative line within a `distance' threshold, it is considered *unique*. If at least one constraint over a field is successful and unique, the field is rated *safe*.

In classical CSP, constraints are usually seen conjunctively i.e. connected by *and*. This is the expected behavior w.r.t. the ground truth, too. *And* logic implies that the basic assumption is true (i.e. *safe*) and constraints can contradict (respectively weaken) this rating.

This is anticipated by our *confidence* that what we read is really what the author wrote (or intended to write). Pure OCR gives a very low confidence state, in fact the least in our three-step rating scheme. Only when a constraint has confirmed the OCR result, the rating becomes stronger. This corresponds to a classical *or* logic.

Both logics *and* and *or* are justified and thus we decided to combine them. In classical logics, there is no `combination' of *and* and *or*, but it has proven a very useful heuristics. We use the *or* scheme during the evaluation and only as a final step, we introduce an aspect of *and*. This is achieved by making sure that no unsuccessful constraint is rated completely *safe*, i.e. if all fields of an unsuccessful constraint are rated safe, we reset the ratings.

7   Verifier

Verifiers automatically poll the result database for documents after analysis, in the status to be verified. The original page is displayed, also, zoomed, the source area of an extracted data item, and the extraction result. Focus jumps to the next data item, as soon as the first was acknowledged or corrected. Colored areas can be configured for document classes to support the eyes finding zones on pages (like the field in the background in Figure 9, right below the address, the area to typically find a textual diagnosis), "safe" estimated result data are automatically coded green, the results less safe are coded light blue and blue. Manually typed data is immediately used to fill up and cross check deducible data, perhaps insurance number and first name, after the correction of a date of birth. Thus, the *Verifier* allows to check and correct the extraction results one after the other rather efficiently.

Verifiers are a crucial part of *smartFIX healthcare*, as they serve an intrinsically critical task of DAU: the re-integration of computed DAU results into the world of business processes and humans, where these results represent monetary values. Tasks that a) affect values and b) are delegated to somebody else, in this case even a mainly dumb system, rely very much on a significantly high chance to find errors wherever they might origin from.

Verifiers can have different priorities and rights assigned and can log the user-actions.

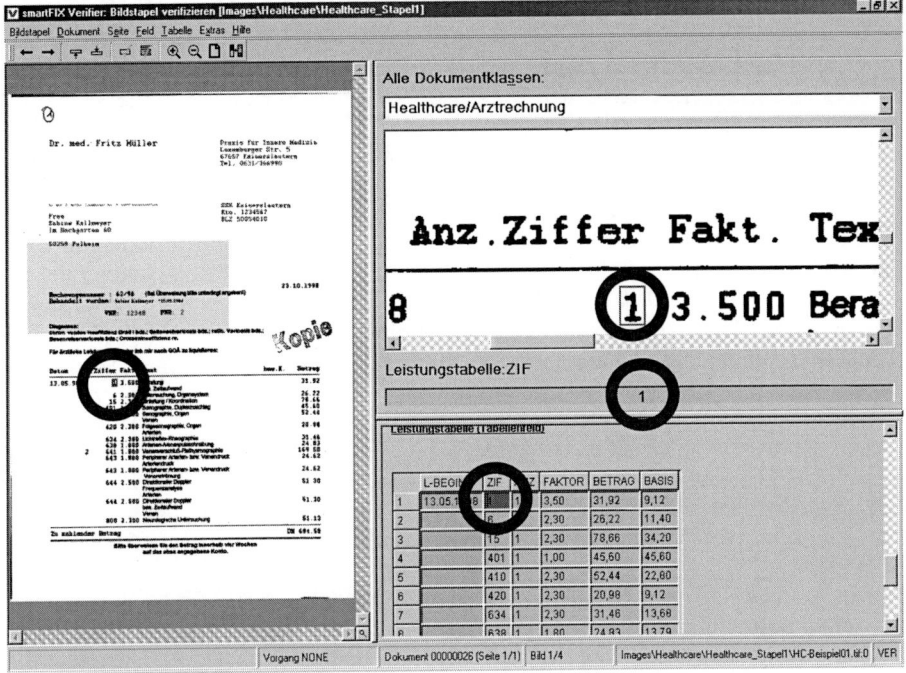

Fig. 9. The *Verifier*: four synchronized views on the same data for efficient checking

8 Results

smartFIX healthcare was installed at the insurances' sites and connected to their workflow successfully, i.e. adapted to the specific requirements at hand. It was configured to distinguish about 50 different types of mostly unstructured documents, like hospital bills, dentist bills, medicament bills etc., all coming with data which trigger and control processes. Most of the processes are directly involving money transfers.

Information items for which *smartFIX healthcare* was configured comprise: (a) insurance number, (b) name of patient, (c) date, (d) service period, (e) diagnosis, (f) medical services table, (g) duration of treatment, (h) name and address of doctor, altogether a number of 107. Out of this base set, about 20 are to be found on one type of document on average.

For an evaluation, we considered a representative stack of 525 documents as they arrived at one of the largest health insurance companies in Germany. The test comprised of classification into classes reimbursement form (RF), prescription (P), dentists bills (D), hospital bills (H), bills from medical doctors (M), and others (O) while the latter ones had to be sub-classified into another 20 classes. The following Table 1 shows the classification results:

Table 1. Classification results of *smartFIX healthcare*.

RF	95%	D	100%	M	92%
P	96%	H	94%	O	73%

The classification rate over all classes was 92%; the human workload is thus reduced by 92%. The remaining rejects are sent to personnel at a Verifier. Another key measure, the systems error rate was less than 0.1%.

After classification, the instructed ROIs were searched and their information content extracted. For the evaluation, two aspects were important: The extraction rates as well as savings in time. The extraction rate for all fields (a) to (h) was 81 % and saved an average of 64% of time compared to manual input. (Other numbers from a couple of other customers and scenarios mostly even tend towards roughly ¾ of savings of time.)

Special add-on modules (included in *smartFIX healthcare*) can recalculate the figures on the invoice, to check its correctness. This implies a check of the single service fees, allowed multiplications with so-called factors, and the sums and their final addition on the invoice. Finally, *smartFIX healthcare* can check whether the service positions on each invoice adhere to the German scale of charges and fees, the so-called GOÄ.

This result is just one example presented to the reader. *smartFIX* runs at more than a dozen of customers sites, with very different configurations. A huge number of very different documents were classified and their information extracted to date. Note for example, that at one company the classification rate went down to 30 % last year. They were happy. Without changing the system configuration, they strained the system with a variety of new and complicated input documents, which could of course not be classified; and which should not be classified. And this is what *smartFIX* did not do, correctly. Our statistics are not important to us, the customers satisfaction is.

9   Summary

We have given an overview of a commercial document analysis system, *smartFIX*, which is the result of the exploitation of research results from the DFKI, their non-trivial combination and additional research by the spin-off company INSIDERS. The system is able to process stacks of mixed-format documents including forms, invoices, letters, all of which may contain machine-written or hand-printed information. The system is installed at about two dozens of customers analyzing several hundred thousands of document pages every day. The purpose of *smartFIX* is in the distribution (classification) of scanned incoming mail and the extraction of information relevant for the user or customer. *smartFIX* has some special features. It processes unsorted incoming mail of any format and independent of the degree of structure or preprints. Furthermore it is not limited to a small number of sorted and separated document types. *smartFIX* classifies all documents and therefore is independent of pre-sorting. Images are combined automatically into single- or multi-page documents. Documents from different sections of a company can be attributed as such, distinguished in the system and thus be processed on one and the same hardware. So two or more systems can be run on one hardware.

A special feature of *smartFIX* is its dedication to what we call *adaptivity*. *Adaptivity* aims to reduce the (human) effort to maintain applications and to configure the system for new applications. Thus the requirements of adaptivity are a dedicated interfacing machinery to both computer/hardware environments and human/business environments. Not only are modules required to technically connect the system to fixed computer infrastructures. The system was also re-constructed more modular, so as to allow for a greater variety of possible configurations. And last, adaptation requires to help the human instructor in his task to assess the scenario and find the best system configuration to adhere to it. Thus, we have developed learning tools and domain assessment tools. Learning tools aid, because it is simpler to just provide examples, than determine the right features and explicate them to the system. Domain assessment tools aid determination of relevant features, by allowing the evaluation of e.g. the average distance between two consecutive words on 1000 sample documents. During the research project "adaptive Read", funded by the German ministry for research, bmbf, *smartFIX* was fundamentally furnished with the respective adaptivity-features.

Recently, we have been working on some improvements and additional features of *smartFIX*. The first addresses the restructuring of the system into even smaller modules which then allow for more flexible mixing, which in turn allows to serve new and more complex application scenarios.

The second addresses a new paradigm for the *DocumentManager* with full access to all *Analyzer* features, so that the effect of every single configuration-information can be immediately tried out interactively. This will look and feel like a software engineering environment with full debugging support.

References

1. A. Dengel, R. Bleisinger, R. Hoch, F. Hönes, M. Malburg and F. Fein, OfficeMAID — A System for Automatic Mail Analysis, Interpretation and Delivery, Proceedings DAS94, Int'l Association for Pattern Recognition Workshop on Document Analysis Systems, Kaiserslautern (Oct. 1994), pp. 253-276.

2. S. Baumann, M. Ben Hadj Ali, A. Dengel, T. Jäger, M. Malburg, A. Weigel, C. Wenzel, Message Extraction from Printed Documents A Complete Solution. In: Proc. of the 4.th International Conference on Document Analysis and Recognition (ICDAR), Ulm, Germany, 1997.

3. A. Dengel and K. Hinkelmann, The Specialist Board – a technology workbench for document analysis and understanding. In M. M. Tanik, F.B. Bastani, D. Gibson, and P.J. Fielding, editors, Integrated Design and Process Technology – IDPT96, Proc. of the 2nd World Conference, Austin, TX, USA, 1996.

4. G. Schreiber, H. Akkermans, A. Anjewierden, R. de Hoog, N. Shadbolt, W. Van de Velde, and B. Wielinga. Knowledge Engineering and Management – The Common-KADS Methodology. The MIT Press, Cambridge, Massachusetts, London, England, 1999.

5. http://trec.nist.gov/

6. B. Klein, S. Gökkus, T. Kieninger, A. Dengel, Three Approaches to "Industrial" Table Spotting. In: Proc. of the 6.th International Conference on Document Analysis and Recognition (ICDAR), Seattle, USA, 2001.

7.   A. Dengel and F. Dubiel, Computer Understanding of Document Structure, International Journal of Imaging Systems & Technology (IJIST), Special Issue on Document Analysis & Recognition, Vol. 7, No. 4, 1996, pp. 271-278.

8.   F. Dubiel and A. Dengel, FormClas — OCR-Free Classification of Forms, in: J.J. Hull, S. Liebowitz (eds.) Document Analysis Systems II, World Scientific Publishing Co. Inc., Singapore, 1998, pp. 189-208.

9.   A. Fordan, Constraint Solving over OCR Graphs. In: Web-knowledge management and decision support. 14th International Conference on Applications of Prolog (INAP), Tokyo, Japan, 2001, Revised papers. LNAI series, Springer 2003.

10.   T. Kieninger and A. Dengel, A Paper-to-HTML Table Converting System, Proceedings DAS98, Int'l Association for Pattern Recognition Workshop on Document Analysis Systems, Nagano, Japan, Nov. 1998, pp. 356-365.

11.   M. Junker and A. Dengel, Preventing overfitting in learning text patterns for document categorization, ICAPR2001, 2nd Intern'l Conference on Advances in Pattern Recognition, Rio de Janeiro, Brazil, March 2001.

12.   C. Altenhofen, M. Stanišic-Petrovic, M. Junker, T. Kieninger, H. Hofmann, Werkzeugeinsatz in der Dokumentenverwaltung (German), in: Computerworld Schweiz, Nr. 15/2002, April 2002, S. 6-11,
http://www.kodok.de/german/literat/artikel/index_artikel.html

How Postal Address Readers Are Made Adaptive

Hartmut Schäfer, Thomas Bayer, Klaus Kreuzer, Udo Miletzki,
Marc-Peter Schambach, and Matthias Schulte-Austum

Siemens Dematic AG, Konstanz, Germany,
{Hartmut.Schaefer, Thomas.Bayer, Klaus.Kreuzer, Udo.Miletzki,
Marc-Peter.Schambach, Matthias.Schulte-Austum}@siemens.com,
www.siemens-dematic.de

Abstract. In the following chapter we describe how a postal address reader is made adaptive. A postal address reader is a huge application, so we concentrate on technologies used to adapt it to a few important tasks. In particular, we describe adaptation strategies for the detectors and classifiers of regions of interest (ROI), for the classifiers for single character recognition, for a hidden Markov recogniser for hand written words and for the address dictionary of the reader. The described techniques have been deployed in all postal address reading applications, including parcel, flat, letter and in-house mail sorting.

1 Introduction

The address reader from Siemens Dematic AG has been designed to read virtually all forms of addresses in any country of the world. However, to reach this ambitious target, many complex tasks had to be solved. For example, an address block within a complex and changing text-image-graphics layout has to be found. This is a difficult task that requires statistical modelling. Within the address block, the structure and the style of handwriting have a wide range of variation, which can only be coped with by introducing adaptive models. The address logics and the dictionary structures are in continual flux and therefore need to be adaptive, and so forth. Indeed, the address reader needs to be highly adaptable in many respects. This chapter describes solutions for some individual components of the address reader as well as for the system as a whole.

An address reader needs a fair amount of adaptation for each address type it must recognize. As the adaptation costs must be spent whether a customer needs just one address reader or hundreds, this effort is highly expensive for small countries with a small number of readers. Thus, one of the main goals of Siemens Dematic is to make the adaptation process cheaper by automation, resulting ultimately in a self-adapting system, able to improve itself by continuously learning from daily live mail. During the *Adaptive READ* project, Siemens Dematic AG has made a big step forward towards this goal. An overview of the techniques used to automate the adaptation process will be presented in this chapter.

Besides reduced costs for adaptation, the postal address reading market is seeking new capabilities such as "forwarding" and "revenue protection". "Forwarding" means the ability to detect as early as possible obsolete addresses for recipients whose address has changed, and to send the mail directly to the new address. "Revenue protection"

A. Dengel et al. (Eds.): Adaptive READ Research Project, LNCS 2956, pp. 187–215, 2004.

is the ability to detect mail pieces with missing or incorrect franking and to treat these mail pieces according to certain rules (e.g., "return to sender"). For both features, the address reader needs to be able to read much more than just the standard target address block. It must also read the full return address, including names and nicknames, and determine the mail class. To do this, the address reader must identify various types of franking (e.g., stamps, barcodes), and it needs to recognize a huge variety of additional remarks that may appear on the mail piece. For this purpose, during the *Adaptive READ* project, the address reader was extended by a set of new recognition algorithms and more flexible interpretation and control algorithms. The result is a highly adaptable reader, which is able to perform the tasks "forwarding" and "revenue protection", as well as "multi-Lingual" reading and many more. Some of the most remarkable goals reached during *Adaptive READ* will be described in the following sections.

The state-of-the-art Siemens Dematic Reader Systems typically are optimised 'back-stage' once before delivery using a set of adaptive algorithms and a set of well defined learning data, extracted from the customer's daily mail stream. Various optimisation methods have been developed so far for the individual steps of reading, the so-called pre-processing, the recognition, and the post-processing steps. These have matured over the decades and were substantially refined during first *READ* research and development programme, funded by the German Federal Ministry for Education and Research (BMBF) from 1997 to 1999.

Yet what these methods lacked was on-site adaptiveness, i.e., learning algorithms directly implanted in the product itself, able to learn from weaknesses and errors throughout the product life cycle. The reason for the late introduction of this type of improvement was the heavy structural alteration of the system that was necessary, and the big effort associated with it. Therefore this major improvement was postponed to *Adaptive READ*, the results of which are explained here in detail.

Within this project, the generic reading system as a whole was analysed and investigated in respect of adaptiveness. Wherever constant parameters or fixed rules for decision processes were found, they were changed into variables and made available to learning algorithms, which optimise them during the learning phase in terms of error and recognition rate.

Considering the main flow of data from the scanner to the imprinting of a destination code, a number of processing points are candidates for adaptive optimisation. Four important adaptive optimisation strategies are described in the following sections.

Section 2 describes how new methods for adaptive object finding and segmentation were implemented. As mentioned above, customers are no longer exclusively interested in receiver addresses, but also require information from return addresses, as well as stamps, indicia, logos etc., in short, all iconic objects that contain information relevant to postal mail processing. Learning stamps and indicia means being able to control postage charges and helps ensure this source of revenue to the postal services. Learning icons may help to identify the sender, if the sender's address is not written explicitly on the envelope. Object finding now includes nearly every kind of block on the mail surface except – up to now – advertisements.

In future, postal services may offer selective delivery of non-addressed mass mailings, based on the type of advertisement shown. This will make it necessary to recognize the advertisement and to use the reader system inversely as an addressing machine, printing appropriate addresses on the non-addressed mail according to individual profiles of the postal service's end customers. Selective delivery of mass mailings can make them more cost-effective, since it avoids the cost of sending unwanted ads to uninterested customers. Since new advertisement objects will appear frequently in the mail stream, this type of service can make good use of the results of *Adaptive READ*.

Once the relevant objects on the mail piece are detected, the reader software must distinguish between image blocks containing text and image blocks containing other symbols, graphics or pictures. Within each text block, the character objects must be converted into numeric character codes (ASCII, Unicode, etc.); in other words, the image blocks have to be reduced to their meanings by use of OCR-classifiers. These statistically based classifiers are one of the core technologies for the general conversion of pixels to meaning, and contain several hundred thousands of free parameters, defined in an off-line learning process during the development phase. This procedure works quite well for a time, until new fonts and character shapes begin to appear in the mail stream. Then an update of the reader software becomes urgently necessary – too late to be optimal, resulting in a typical two-threshold or "bang-bang" reaction: system degradation must have occurred before any action will be taken.

Section 3, on character classifier adaptation, shows in detail how character recognition can be made adaptive on-site. As part of *Adaptive READ*, the Stepwise Improvement Classification method (SIC) has been developed to improve on-site character recognition. It carries out adaptation in small steps, and can be interrupted at any time, learning new shapes character by character, instead of by the time consuming, complex and expensive off-line method, which needs to generate moment matrices and subsequent matrix inversions, learning all characters samples at once.

The SIC method is applicable wherever text can be properly segmented into its character elements. Where this is not the case, which mainly is true for script words as well as for non-segmentable machine printed words, techniques are deployed that can recognize words or phrases like *Stratford upon Avon* as unitary images. These work quite well with distinct, hand printed characters or neatly written script. However, these state-of-the art word recognisers utilize models having relatively uniform complexity, no matter how simple or complex the internal character structure of the word or phrase is. This handicap becomes especially evident especially when trying to read 'natural' handwriting.

Section 4 describes how an extended Hidden Markov Model based method, called HMAM, was developed to overcome this drawback. It is able to model words automatically using adaptive model structures for the individual characters, the number of states used depending on their complexity. Based on this form of character recognition, word recognition is made more tolerant of the idiosyncrasies of human writers.

Section 5 shows that another important application of adaptive techniques is dictionary correlation. Even if all characters and words within an address have been recognized perfectly, the result will be rejected if it cannot be verified against an address directory as a unique and valid address. Such directories or "dictionaries" are usually generated according to a rule base and must be periodically updated. However, postal customers do not always follow the addressing rules and write addresses with certain deviations.

In this Section a new dictionary learning method is introduced, which is able to find the most frequent deviations in the daily mail stream. In case of uniqueness, these deviations can be learnt and accepted and lead to successful read results. In some cases, when entirely new names or addresses appear, or old ones disappear, the dictionaries can be changed on-site, without waiting for the next update. These techniques help adapt address interpretation to current conditions.

Last but not least, it is not enough to make all the components of the system adaptive. They must also communicate with each other concerning overall parameters, and they must be adapted and tuned as an ensemble; otherwise the components may improve, while system performance degrades. Therefore, a method for optimisation of a cascade of components of a complex system has been developed to ensure best possible system performance. In this way the system as a whole is made adaptive.

The reader's adaptiveness has been demonstrated in applications throughout Europe, in Australia, New Zealand, U.S.A. and even Cyprus with a Greek alphabet, Dubai with an Arabic alphabet and in several countries in eastern Europe that use a Cyrillic alphabet. These non-Latin alphabets typically need to be recognized side-by-side with the Latin alphabet, because in these countries Latin characters are used as well, especially for international business mail. Thus the reader has become "Multi-Lingual", a process to which the *Adaptive READ* project made an important contribution.

Although the described postal address reader is already highly adaptive and the adaptation process can be automated to some degree, Siemens Dematic AG will continue to make the adaptation of the postal address reader more comprehensive, cheaper and faster, ultimately resulting in a self-learning system. This will remain a challenge for the coming years.

2   How Pre-processing Is Made Adaptive

One of the most challenging tasks in document analysis of complex postal images is to detect and identify all image regions relevant for mail processing. Such relevant regions (Regions of Interest - ROIs) are areas like the receiver address block, the return address block and indicia objects like stamps or meter impressions.

To identify these regions correctly one has to consider different types of mail piece layouts along with information implied by spatial relationships among the regions. To cope with the great variety of possible layouts an adaptive technique has been developed that allows semi-automatic training of the region evaluation system. This technique is described in this Section.

2.1   Block Generation

A preliminary step in block evaluation is the identification of possible text blocks. Within the image processing component (the Region Of Interest function or ROI) there is a text block generation component that delivers regions suspected to contain text blocks.

After generation, these suspected text blocks are evaluated by computing layout-related features. A simple way to find a receiver address is to use logical layout rules to select the correct area. For example, "take right block before taking the left", "take lower block instead of the higher block" or "the block in the top left corner is the receiver block" are some rules which have been quite good for the layout of standard mail envelopes.

Such simple rules are reliable only for a limited range of mail piece styles. The effort required to refine and maintain the block evaluation rules increases with the variety of mail piece layouts that must be analysed. Some existing mail piece layouts even have no obvious rules.

2.2 Generating Statistical Data

To overcome the problem of adapting rules to a nearly infinite variety of mail piece layouts, a basic statistical instrument for evaluating blocks has been developed. Large samples of test images have been recorded (>10,000 images) and the block generation system has calculated the address block positions and features over this data. The statistical data for each of the text block features used is transformed into a feature diagram, or histogram, where the probabilities for each of these features are documented. Basic text block features are:

1. position on the mail piece on a 8x8 grid
2. text is left, centred, or right aligned.
3. ratio of width to height
4. block is handwritten, or typewritten, has constant spacing or not
5. number of lines inside the block
6. has a lower right neighbour

A value is assigned to each of these features, giving a feature vector that can be used to classify the block.

2.3 Block Evaluation

With the trained block evaluation statistics histogram it is possible to calculate a probability that a given text block is, for example, a receiver address block. Comparing the blocks against one another, the most probable receiver address block is selected, ensuring an optimal read rate and minimal error rate.

The block evaluation starts by calculating feature values for each text block generated by the block generation. The features give a vector, which is classified using the statistics histogram to produce a confidence value for the class receiver address. The resulting confidence is compared with a given minimum threshold. If the confidence is higher, the block is selected and returned as a candidate receiver address. If the confidence is below this threshold the text block will be rejected. The resulting probabilities of the remaining text blocks are then compared. The block with the highest probability will be submitted as the receiver address and will be sent on for further OCR processing steps.

To deal with multiple layout schemes, it was found necessary to discriminate standard layouts and complex layouts. For standard layouts the probability of a receiver address in the top 2/8 of the 8 by 8 grid is very low, and in our current configuration we set it intentionally to 0, so that text blocks found in this area will be ignored. This helps reduce misclassification of return address blocks, because these often reside in the top area of the mail piece.

If only one address-like block is found, it can usually be classified as a receiver block. But it may happen that, for example, a smeared or hand-written receiver text block is not generated as a text block, so that the only candidate generated is the return address. For these cases we need the ability to reject a single block in the typical return address position. The exact criteria depend, however, on the layout type of the mail piece, and for each layout type a separate block classifier must be learnt.

Take, for example, standard flats with machine style written text. For evaluating the position feature of a text block, two 8 by 8 matrices of histogram values must be learnt, one for blocks in horizontal positions and one for blocks in vertical orientation. A position histogram is selected according to the orientation of lines in the analysed text block. The centre of the address block under consideration is located on the 8 by 8 grid and compared to the corresponding histogram value to obtain a value for the position feature. For a horizontal block the top 2/8 of the mail piece and the left 1/8 of the mail piece are zones where all detected blocks are rejected. For a vertical block this behaviour is a bit different.

For the following types of mail pieces separate configurations are being used:

- Letter
- Flat
- Parcel
- Hand written
- Machine print
- Newspapers

2.4   Training the System

Thus, block classification is not based on logical rules but on scalar parameters that can be learnt semi-automatically. A typical training or tuning phase for such a system follows these steps:

1. Capture a representative sample of images (mail pieces with different layouts).
2. Run a standard OCR engine over these images.
3. Generate statistical data over the block features of the mail pieces.
4. With the aid of reference data, select the images with correct read results.
5. Transform this statistical data into a loadable histogram.
6. Run the OCR engine with a block evaluation controlled by this new histogram again.

The tuning process may include a number of iterations that change the histogram until performance reaches an optimum value.

2.5   Conclusion

Adaptive block evaluation has made it possible to adapt the OCR engine quickly to new layouts. It has also improved the read and error rate in most applications. A drawback of this system is that is not always obvious how a given block classification is obtained. By comparison with strictly rule-based systems, statistical block evaluation may occasionally contradict obvious rules, like "take right text block before the left block" as the receiver address. In most cases the statistical block evaluation will conform to this rule, but if for example the combined feature probabilities of the two blocks are very close together, some feature other than position may be decisive. A solution to this problem has been found by introducing a number of layout models with different statistical block evaluation engines.

3   How Character Recognition Is Made Adaptive

In a certain sense practical character recognition is of necessity already adaptive – no one could analyse and describe all the possible variants in a given character class. But current techniques are based on a computationally expensive process that is normally performed off-line, at a fixed point in time, so the classifiers cannot adapt to changes in printing or writing styles.

3.1   How Can Character Recognition Be Made Adaptive?

Character recognition is a process that takes as input a character image and gives as output the character's meaning. Modern character recognition techniques always involve some form of statistical learning. That is, the process makes use of classification parameters that need to be trained against statistical samples of character images to meet performance requirements for the process. Some common performance requirements are high recognition rate, low error rate, low consumption of computer resources, i.e. processing time and memory, and, of course, a set of character meanings (classes) that are to be recognized. Training *is* the adaptation to meet these requirements. In this sense character recognition is already adaptive.

So how can character recognition be made more adaptive?

The tuning or adaptation of the parameters of the recognition process is itself a process. It takes as input character images from a learning set where the meaning of an image is known and gives as output adjusted parameters for the recognition process. The crucial disadvantage of the classical training process is the point in time when it is carried out: The parameters are adjusted once and the recognition process uses them unchanged, for as long as the character classifier is deployed, regardless of how actual printing and writing conventions evolve.

Making character recognition " adaptive" means in this context that an adaptation process is integrated into the recognition process. The parameters are adjusted during the recognition phase.

3.2   Making Recognition More Adaptive

To make on-line tuning possible, both the adaptation and the recognition process need to be redesigned. The adaptation process must now also comply with requirements of the recognition process and the recognition process must also provide input to the adaptation process.

The inputs of the adaptation process are character images with their correct meanings. The recognition process receives images and returns a meaning for each image. But is it the correct meaning? Another process must be introduced to provide the correct meaning or to decide if the meaning returned by the recognition process is trustworthy enough to be learnt or adapted.

Such a process can use context information, dictionaries or even human expertise (from video coding stations). If there are time and memory constraints on the recognition process, then they must be met by the adaptation process. In particular, it will not be possible to collect and hold all the statistics of all classes from the learning set and add the new learning element to approximate the optimal parameters for this enlarged learning set. What is needed in this case is a quick and cheap way of learning.

3.3   An Answer to Quick and Cheap Learning: SIC

Quick and cheap in this context means moderate CPU and memory requirements. The idea is to take the existing parameters and alter them appropriately by considering the new image with its meaning as if it had been part of the learning set. J. Schürmann described this idea as *Recursive Learning* [8].

This incremental way of learning is implemented in the Stepwise Iterated Classifier (SIC). In most applications the SIC method is fast enough to run during the recognition process and is moderate in its use of memory resources.

The SIC method can enhance the recognition rate and can reduce the error rate on the learning set, but it is not as good in initial training as the direct method. There are some parameters of the method which have to be chosen carefully to avoid overlearning and unlearning of classes. It depends on the frequencies of the different classes within the learning set.

3.4   Applying SIC to Complex Structured Classifiers

A 'plain' classifier maps directly from a pixel image to a character meaning and is constructed with a single set of parameters. In the initial adaptation process the learning set is arranged to guarantee that all character classes are well distributed over the learning set to comply with the requirements of the SIC method. Plain classifiers adapted or iterated by this method give good results.

However, performance requirements have lead to the introduction of more complex, structured classifiers. A tree of plain classifiers, for example is able to handle large sets of classes faster. As the classification process descends the tree, each node selects an ever-smaller subset of the classes, until a final node selects the character meaning. A net structure is useful for high recognition rates when time restrictions are not so strong and the number of classes to recognize is not too high. The final decision is derived from the decisions of a set of classifiers with two classes.

Applying the SIC method to these complex structured classifiers did not result in the expected improvements at first, and raised doubts as to whether the SIC method could be applied to them.

3.5   Applying SIC to Complex Structured Classifiers

Tree and net classifiers are composed of plain classifiers. To apply the SIC method to these complex structured classifiers one must apply it to every plain classifier of the composition. If each plain classifier improves, the whole classifier should improve. There is no reason why the SIC method should not work as well for the complex structured classifiers as for the plain classifiers. The code to decompose a complex classifier into plain classifiers and the recomposition after the iteration is easy to verify and, in our experiments, showed no hint of a problem.

After searching fruitlessly for implementation bugs, we realized that since the SIC method is sensitive to the arrangement of the elements in the learning set, there has to be a special arrangement of the training data for every plain classifier of the classifier composition. To verify this idea the software had to be redesigned.

3.6   Software Redesign Needed

Since the SIC method depends on the frequencies of the different classes within the learning set, there has to be a function that distributes the different classes properly over the whole learning set.

Originally, this function was called before the decomposition of the complex structured classifiers. After redesign, it is called for every plain classifier of the classifier composition, and the rearrangement can be different each time.

Think of a tree classifier for the digits $\{0\ 1\ 2\ 3\}$. A higher-level classifier node has to decide between two subsets of these digits. Let l be the left subset $\{0\ 1\}$ and let r be the right subset $\{2\ 3\}$. Finally let the learning set be sorted in a way that is not good for the SIC method $\{0\ 0\ 1\ 1\ 2\ 2\ 3\ 3\}$. The classifier learns these elements simply as l and r. To keep track of the meanings learnt, we notate the digits as subscripts to the higher-level classes, as in l_0.

One can think of two ways to rearrange the learning set for this node. Rename the digits first, giving $\{l_0\ l_0\ l_1\ l_1\ r_2\ r_2\ r_3\ r_3\}$ and then arrange l and r elements to be well distributed, giving $\{l_0\ r_2\ l_0\ r_2\ l_1\ r_3\ l_1\ r_3\}$. One observes that in the second half there are no elements which came from $\{0\ 2\}$.

The other possibility is to distribute the elements as $\{0\ 1\ 2\ 3\ 0\ 1\ 2\ 3\}$, rename them $\{l_0\ l_1\ r_2\ r_3\ l_0\ l_1\ r_2\ r_3\}$ and finally rearrange them $\{l_0\ r_2\ l_1\ r_3\ l_0\ r_2\ l_1\ r_3\}$. Here we find every class in both halves of the learning set sequence.

For this case, it turns out that the second variant shows better results.

3.7   Summary and Outlook

On-line adaptable character recognition requires an adaptation method that is quick and cheap in terms of processing. The SIC method is suitable for this task and can be applied to simple and complex structured classifiers if one takes care to rearrange the learning sets well.

Further investigations are necessary as to how this rearrangement can be achieved during the recognition process. It cannot be expected that characters on the incoming images are distributed well enough to be used directly. The process that decides what elements are trustworthy enough to be adapted might be elaborated to implement this restriction.

The new approach of the SIC method is an important stepping-stone to making character recognition adaptive.

4   How Word Recognition Is Made More Flexible

When building a system for cursive handwriting recognition, an important step is finding the right *model* that best describes cursive script. Many recognition systems are based on Hidden Markov Models (HMMs). In these systems, much attention has been given to training of HMM *parameters* to gain best recognition performance. To improve the flexibility of word recognition, the adaptation of the underlying HMM *structure* has been added to the training of the system (Fig. 1). Modelling the structure is the first step in building a recognition system and is normally done manually. In the system presented, this task has been automated.

When modelling script, an important decision concerns the question of how many writing variants, or *allographs* of each letter have to be considered to get a model representative for all writing styles that may appear. Mostly, these decisions are made manually, based on guesses about the writing conventions. Thus, upper and lowercase letters are usually distinguished, as well as hand block and cursive writing styles. But a good model has to consider the variants that really occur, especially if detailed knowledge about writing styles is not available. Another decision is about the number of HMM states used to model each variant. It mirrors the complexity of the letters.

It is useful to determine the writing variants and complexities automatically, especially in postal automation systems, where recognition systems specific to different countries with different writing styles and even alphabets have to be developed. The HMM structure is determined by analysing the same sets of training data that are already available for setting the recognition system parameters.

4.1   Recognition of Cursive Script with HMMs

The script recognition system is based on linear left-to-right HMMs, with a semi-continuous, tied-mixture probability modelling structure [1]. The script model is defined by a set of *graphemes* (letters, numbers and special characters). Different writing variants of a grapheme – *allographs* – are combined in a *multipath letter model* with multiple, parallel state paths (Fig. 2).

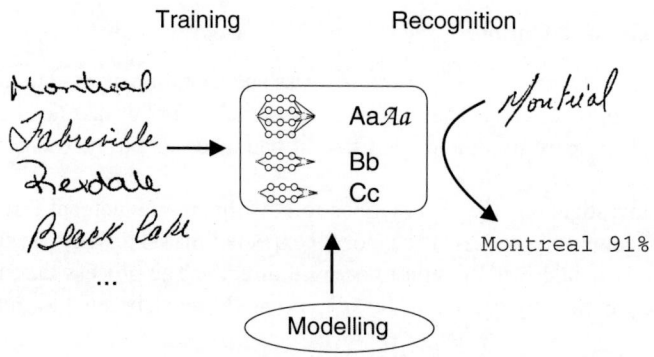

Fig. 1. Flexible word recognition by modelling of the HMM structure.

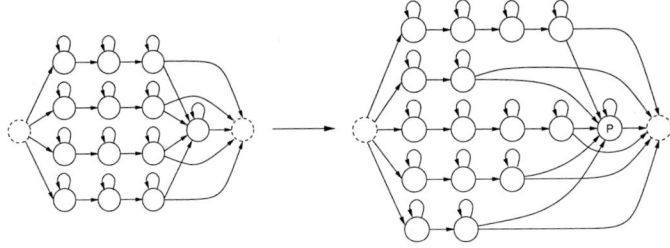

Fig. 2. Improving the flexibility of HMM model structures

The system has been applied in postal automation systems to recognition tasks in cursive script, hard-to-segment hand block and machine print, and Arabic script recognition. For testing the algorithms, eight configurations from different countries have been selected: Canada, Germany, the USA, and the United Arabic Emirates. Word recognition tests have been performed with dictionaries of about 150 words for country, city and street names, and about 40000 words for postal codes.

4.2   Model Length Adaptation

Trying to find the optimal number of states for each of the letter HMMs, one is faced with the following problems: Under the condition that no letter boundaries are labelled in the training data, every change in model length influences the other models during training. Adapting the number of states of each model separately also results in high computational costs. An algorithm has been developed that is able to adapt all models at once in one iteration, so only a few iterations are necessary [3].

Algorithm. The model length adaptation is done iteratively, and all letter models are optimised at the same time. The starting point is a trained standard system with default path lengths. In every iteration, different model alternatives are generated, all models are trained, and finally the best model is chosen. The following steps are performed:

- In case of multipath models, assign fixed writing variants to the training data and separate the models into singlepath models.
- Expand each allograph model by adding parallel state paths with ± 1 states (Fig. 3). The new state paths do not represent writing variants but realize alternative model lengths.
- Perform parameter training (*Baum-Welsh* algorithm [4]) with the expanded models.
- Select the "best" path, representing the new model.
- Retrain the HMM parameters, including a new vector quantizer, without fixed assignment of writing variants.

Two criteria control the termination of iterations. The first criterion is that no more improvement in likelihood of training data takes place. To avoid being stuck in suboptimal configurations, a second criterion has been added, which stops the iterations only

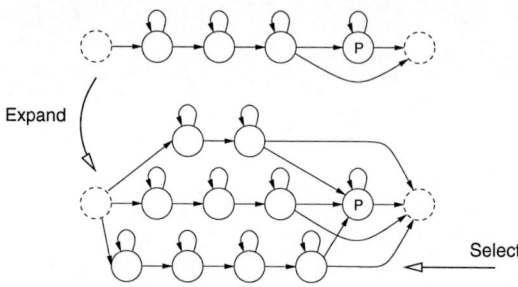

Fig. 3. Learning the model length

when no further change in model topology occurs. Better recognition results have been achieved this way.

Path selection criteria. The choice of the "best" path during iterations has great impact on the algorithm performance. A two-step mechanism has been developed. First, the state path which has been selected most frequently during training is chosen; this is indicated simply by the transition probabilities to the first states of each path. Then, after retraining the paths selected this way, the average likelihood for the new letter models is calculated. Only in cases when this likelihood is improved is the new model length kept. The second step is important to gain better recognition performance.

Results. By applying the algorithm on the tested systems, the average length of model state paths is increased. As the modelling becomes more fine-grained and better adapted to the data, the recognition performance is improved by about 2.1 percent. Analysing the relation of performance on training and test data, an increase in the generalization capabilities of the system can also be seen: Results on independent test data converge to those that are achieved on training data.

4.3   Allograph Adaptation

To adapt the HMM script model automatically to the best number of writing variants, a similar, iterative algorithm has been developed.

Starting from a trained system with a default model, the allograph clustering algorithm iteratively adds and removes allograph models. In every iteration, the following tasks are performed:

- Select allograph state paths for modification. Different strategies have been developed and tested. They are described in detail below.
- Modify the selected allographs. Remove a state path by deleting or mixing similar paths, or add one by modifying a selected, existing path.
- Retrain the HMM, including codebook calculation.

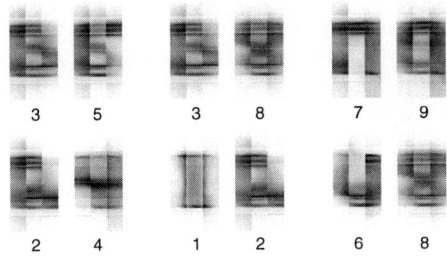

Fig. 4. Visualization of HMM-Parameters for model pairs with smallest (top) and highest distance (bottom) in a recognition system for German postal codes

Iterations are terminated when a maximum or minimum size of the allograph model is reached, or when a given maximum of iterations has been performed. The final script model is selected by Bayesian model selection criteria.

In the following Section, the different model selection strategies (used within the iterations) are presented and discussed. Then, the final model evaluation method is presented. For practical use, a variation of the algorithm will be developed, and finally, results are shown.

Strategies for selection and modification. Four strategies for allograph selection and modification have been developed. A subset of three is used for adding and another subset of three for removing allograph models.

Model similarity – Determining the writing variants in script samples means clustering the training data. For clustering, it is necessary to define a distance between objects, in this case between allograph HMMs. The distance proposed is calculated for left-to-right allograph models, but it can also be applied to multipath letter models. The calculation method is called *Statistical Dynamic Time Warping* and is described in [2]. It is possible to calculate distances between models even if they have differing numbers of states. Similar allographs within a single letter model represent the same data and are therefore candidates for merging. Using the proposed distance measure, the grapheme model with the pair of paths closest to each other is chosen and the respective paths are joined.

The quality of the distance measure proposed is examined by visual inspection. A method for visualization has been developed and is presented in [3]. Figure 4 shows some examples of letter models with smallest or highest distance; the results correspond quite well to human perception of similarity. Additionally, it could be shown that the recognition system also confuses similar models more frequently.

Model quality – To test whether it is useful to model allographs, an independent measure for model quality has been developed. For semicontinuous HMM systems, an easy measure is the entropy of emission weights. No properties of the classes themselves are considered, but for well separable classes, the value indicates how well defined the model states are. The letter model quality is defined by averaging the entropy of all states. The worst model, indicated by the highest allograph entropy, is chosen to have an additional writing variant. As initialisation, the best allograph, i.e. the one with lowest entropy, is doubled, and emission weights are shifted randomly.

Model likelihood – The effect of grapheme modelling within the recognition system can be given by model likelihood. This is the contribution of a particular letter model to training data likelihood, and it can be calculated from the Viterbi path, where likelihood is assigned to each model state. To remove an allograph, the one with the overall worst contribution in likelihood is chosen. Model likelihood also can be used to add allographs: the grapheme with the average worst likelihood of all allographs is chosen, and the allograph with the highest likelihood variance is doubled.

Amount of represented data – A pragmatic approach to improving the recognition system selects model detailing by frequency in training data. Graphemes that appear more often have higher influence on overall performance, and are modelled with more allographs. The allograph frequency is defined by the product of number of occurrences of the grapheme in training data and the transition probability to the first state in the allograph state path. Allographs with low frequency are removed; those with high frequency are doubled.

Discussion of selection strategies. For each of the eight configurations tested (see Section 4.1), experiments for all six selection and modification strategies have been performed [5]. Inspecting images of the final grapheme models gives interesting insights into the properties of the different selection strategies. When adding allographs, selection by entropy gives the best visual impression. Adding allographs by frequency results in best recognition performance, but the modelling is non-intuitive. The best mixture of performance and good visual impression is given by selection by likelihood. Regarding the iterations where allographs are removed, the best visual impression combined with good recognition performance is obtained by removing by distance.

Evaluation of models: Bayesian selection criteria. After adaptation iterations, the best script model has to be selected. Generally, when trying to find the "right" model, the danger of over-adaptation to the available data exists. In our case, more allograph models could result in worse generalization to test data. Bayesian model selection criteria are a general approach to deal with this subject. Different selection criteria like the *Akaike Information Criterion* (AIC), the *Bayesian Information Criterion* and *Cheeseman-Stutz Approximations* [6] have been applied. They differ slightly in the terms penalizing high model complexity. Figure 5 shows that the criteria predict quite well the generalization capability of the models.

Fixed complexity. However, none of the criteria could really be applied to final model selection, because the generated models have been too big with respect to time and memory constraints of real world applications. Therefore, the adaptation process had to work with a given, fixed overall model complexity, allowing only zero-sum changes between models. An adaptation algorithm with alternating steps for adding and removing allographs has been developed. The selection criterion was given by a ranked list of likelihood, distance and frequency, to take full advantage of all different selection strategies.

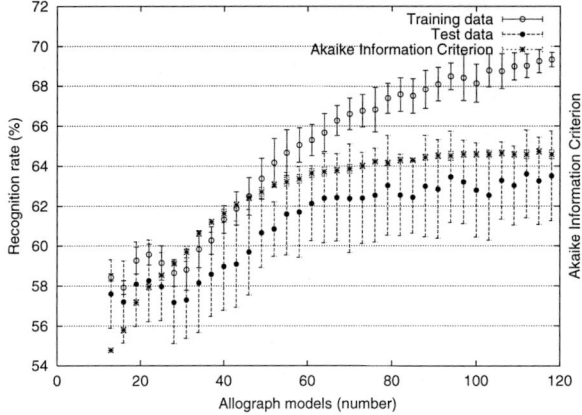

Fig. 5. Saturation of test recognition rate when continuously increasing model complexity. The *AIC* predicts the effect quite well

Table 1. Word recognition rates (forced recognition) for different adaptation methods

Project	Baseline	Length only	Allographs	Combination
Arab Emirates	76.9 %	85.5 %	86.4 %	86.4 %
Canada (address)	93.4 %	93.4 %	95.4 %	95.5 %
Germany (address)	92.8 %	93.3 %	94.5 %	94.7 %
Germany (ZIP)	69.1 %	72.1 %	78.3 %	76.0 %
USA (address)	81.2 %	82.7 %	84,6 %	84.4 %
USA (ZIP)	60.8 %	62.9 %	70.7 %	71.4 %
CEDAR (cities)	84.2 %	84.2 %	85.1 %	86.3 %
CEDAR (ZIP)	58.2 %	59.5 %	68.3 %	71.7 %
Average	77.1 %	79.2 %	82.9 %	83.4 %

Experimental results. Recognition rates are shown in Table 1. Eight recognition systems have been adapted and tested with independent data. With adaptation of model length only, an improvement of 2.1 percent could be obtained, while allograph adaptation alone gave an improvement of 5.8 percent. Both methods have been combined by serial execution, which resulted in an overall improvement of 6.3 percent. Thus, the approaches proved to be "orthogonal" (i.e. independent of each other, concerning their effects), as the different degrees of freedom in the model images (Fig. 2) also suggest.

4.4 Application to Practice

The algorithms developed for adaptation of HMM model structure are used for fine-tuning word recognition systems for new and existing applications in postal automation. By determining the model structures automatically, engineering efforts for model selection could be reduced. Because improvements in recognition can be obtained that hold the overall model complexity constant, computational costs increase only in off-line training, not during the crucial recognition phase. Thus, the adaptation system can be used for real world applications.

5   How Address Interpretation Is Made Adaptive

Address reading systems need information on the content and syntax of addresses in order to be able to extract data needed for sorting, such as town, postal code, first and last name, etc. The permissible content of individual address elements is described by means of a dictionary (list of permissible strings) which, conventionally, is built up from current information sources such as a postal directory or a list of employees of a company. However, the application domain changes with time, so that a dictionary created at a particular point in time gradually becomes inaccurate. A reading system used for mail distribution within a company can experience considerable change: employees leave the company, new employees are added, employees change their department or last names due to marriage, etc. Thus, required entries will be missing in the dictionary, and there are entries that are no longer valid. The more the set of words currently used deviates from the lexicon, the more the recognition performance of the reading system drops.

To maintain performance, changes have had to be manually transferred to the dictionaries at frequent time intervals, imposing additional maintenance costs on the customer.

In the following a system will be described that is able to add words or word sequences to the dictionary automatically and detect no longer used words or word sequences in order to remove them. The first section will give an overview of the system, its operational principles, and some possible variants. The second part will describe a concrete system with examples.

5.1   Overview

The goal of the described system is to automatically construct and/or automatically update a dictionary for reading addresses. It is based on the idea of temporarily storing the results of the current reading processes, evaluating, and using them to automatically build or update a dictionary. During address recognition and analysis, the address is marked to indicate whether it has been read successfully or whether it has been rejected because it could not be found in the existing dictionary. If a dictionary is to be newly created or if new addressees are to be entered in the existing dictionary, the rejected reading results (results that could not be found in the current dictionary) are utilized. Items in the dictionary that are not regularly found in the mail stream are eventually deleted.

The dictionaries are directed graphs where each node contains a word of a certain type (first name, last name, street, city etc.). A path through this graph represents a valid address. However, as found on mail pieces, addresses can vary from the normalized form in the dictionary: some words appearing in the dictionary graph may be missing, and other words not belonging to the dictionary graph may be interspersed in the address.

A dictionary can be constructed or updated automatically on the basis of read addresses by forming classes of words or word sequences which have a fixed minimum measure of similarity with respect to one another, and including at least some representatives in the dictionary at the associated address areas, so that new address information can be added at the correct node in the dictionary.

An important step in updating is to form classes of non-correlated words or word sequences so that – so far as possible – only the correctly written word or word group will be added to the dictionary, rather than misspellings or strings containing recognition errors. To do this it is advantageous to create a list of all words or word groups of non-correlated reading results, sorted in accord with their frequency. Beginning with the most frequent word or word group, the factor of similarity with all remaining words or word sequences is determined and entered in a similarity list. All words or word sequences in the similarity list having a similarity factor above a fixed threshold are then allocated as a class to the current word or word group. It has proved advantageous to determine the similarity factor for words and word sequences by means of the Levenshtein method (see [9]). Subsequently, the words or word sequences of the class are removed from the frequency list. In order to find the correctly written word or word group in the class, a representative or 'prototype' is identified. The prototype can be often identified as the shortest or most frequent word or word group.

To prevent irrelevant words from being introduced into in the dictionary, they can be checked against a special list of irrelevant words. A useful heuristic is to avoid introducing words having few letters (exclusive of a full stop).

To identify words or word sequences in the dictionary that must be changed or removed, it is advantageous to statistically analyse those addresses that can be read unambiguously, maintaining frequency values for words and word sequences that can be correlated with the dictionary. If the correlation frequency for a word or word group drops below a certain threshold for a predetermined time, the word or word group is removed from the dictionary.

A number of variations on this basic scheme are possible. To permit address interpretation in as detailed as manner as possible with the aid of the dictionaries, it be could advantageous to include, in addition to the prototype words, the variant forms of the associated classes with their similarity factors and frequencies.

A further possibility is to identify and store addressing 'collocations'. These are sequences of words occurring frequently together but not appearing contiguously, having n words belonging to the collocation, mutually separated by irrelevant m words. Collocations can be identified by searching the address text with windows having a width of $n + m$ words, starting at the some individual word destined for the dictionary. Once the further $n + 1$ individual words with the interspersed m words have been determined, this word group and its frequencies are included in the corresponding group dictionary.

To avoid errors from automatic updating, it can be useful to first store and categorize the updating proposals, and to have a human operator confirm them at a manual coding station, before they are incorporated into the corresponding category. Alternatively, the updating proposals can be validated against a file in which characteristic, generally applicable names or at least strings related to the proposed updating category (first name, last name, department) are stored.

5.2   Example of an Implementation

This Section explains in greater detail how automatic updating can be realized, illustrating with a simple implementation. The aim of this implementation is to detect previously unknown last names ($n = 1$) or pairs of unknown first and last names ($n = 2$) or combinations containing last and/or first and last names as well as department names of employees of a company. It will add these to the dictionary, and it will also identify

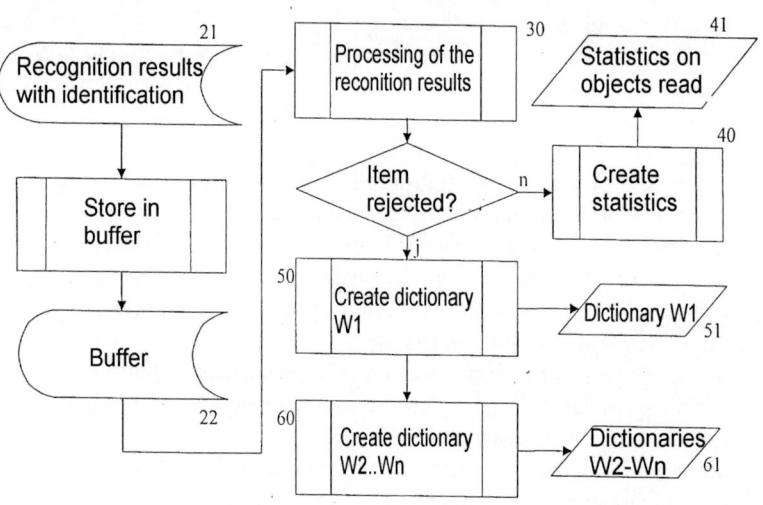

Fig. 6. Flow structure of a monitor process for monitoring and controlling the updating of the dictionary

corresponding, no longer valid names or name combinations, deleting them from the dictionary.

In daily operation the address reader generates word proposals from corresponding snippets of the mail piece image; it then segments each word snippet into characters. For each individual character pattern, the reading system generates a ranked list of possible character meanings. Together with data about the snippet's geometry and layout, these data make up the "pattern" of the item. The reader checks the resulting word proposal against the dictionary to see if the dictionary contains a similar string. Subsequent processing steps determine whether the address as a whole can be validated by finding a possible path through the dictionary graph.

To update or even learn dictionary entries, the set of items processed must be separated into two subsets, into the set of items read automatically (but not necessarily correctly) by the reading system and the set of rejected items. The set of items read automatically will be used to identify dictionary entries that are no longer valid; from the set of rejected items, new dictionary entries will be derived.

The example system consists of five modules: a monitor process (Fig. 6), processing of the recognition results (pre-processing, figure 7), two dictionary generation methods (figures 9 and 9) and a proposal administrator (figure 10).

Monitor Process. As shown in figure 6, the monitoring process monitors and controls the dictionary learning. The recognition results 21 for each pattern of an item, together with an flag indicating "read successfully (correlated)" or "rejected", are transferred from the reader to the monitor. Additional information on the type of mail piece (letter, large letter, in-house mail form) and other features relating to the individual objects of the recognition results such as ROI (Region of Interest), line and word hypotheses, disassembly alternatives and character recognition results can also be transferred. These recognition results are stored in a buffer 22 in the monitor until a sufficiently large amount of data has accumulated (e.g. after 20 000 items or after one week of operation).

In the simplest case, only the first alternatives of the character recognition results together with the best segmenting path is stored in a buffer. In a more complex case the complete segment graph or a subgraph with several alternative character recognition results could be stored. In our example system we have implemented the simplest case. In this system, the buffer contents could appear as follows (note the recognition errors):

```
====================================================================
<Recognition Results>               <Identification>
: ...
1017921 PMD 55
recognized
MR. ALFRED C SCHMIDI
EXCCU1LVE DIRCC1OR, OPCRA1IONS
DCVC1OPMENT
MyComp, INC
1 MyStreet


MyCity, 12345


PO11Y O/BRIEN                       rejected, not in the
                                    dictionary


MANAGER, COMMUNITY AFFAIRS
MyComp INC
1 MyStreet
MyCity, 12345


PO1LY OBRIEN                        rejected, not in the
                                    dictionary


MANAGER, COMMUNITY AFFAIRS
MyComp, INC
1 MyStreet
MyCity, 12345


MS ME1INDA DUCKSWORTH
recognized
MyComp, INC
MAI1 CODE 63-33
1 MyStreet
```

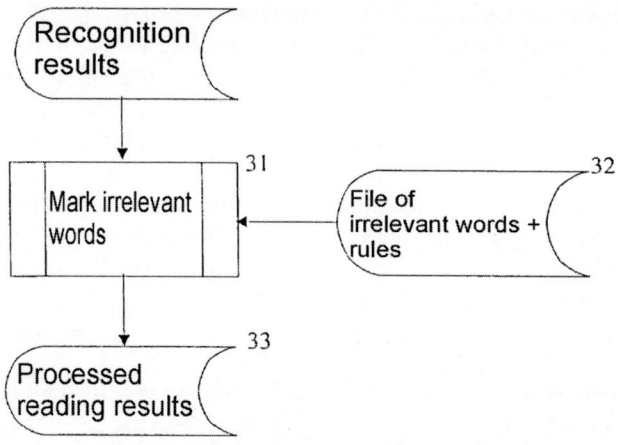

Fig. 7. Flow structure for determining and marking a irrelevant words

```
MyCity, 12345


*********AURO**MIXED AADC 460        Rejected, not in the
                                     dictionary


MIKO SCHWARTZ
O AND T 26-00
1 MyStreetMyCity, 12345


...
==================================================================
```

Once sufficient results are available, the rejected recognition results are transferred to a processing unit 30 and forwarded to the two subprocesses for dictionary training for single words 50 and word groups 60. In the case of successful automatic recognition, the results are transferred to a statistics module 40. When all items have been processed, the word and word group lists 41 of the statistics module and of the dictionary training processes 51, 61 are collected and presented to an operator for confirmation by means of a suitable graphical user interface.

Marking irrelevant words. The processing unit 30 identifies irrelevant words in the rejected recognition results. These are not taken into consideration in the subsequent text analysis (compare Figure 7). They are marked as not relevant, but they are not deleted since the word neighbourhood can be of importance for the subsequent extension of the dictionary.

In the step marking irrelevant words 31, short words are marked from the set of word hypotheses, for example those words which are less than 4 letters long and, at the same time, do not end in a full stop, and those in which less than half of the characters are alphanumeric. Furthermore, those words are marked which appear in a special file 32, which contains frequent but irrelevant words for this application. In the reader for in-house mail distribution, for example, this special lexicon can contain the company's own name, city name, street name, post box designation etc. The results of the processing are written back into a buffer 33.

After this pre-processing, the results appear as follows:

```
=====================================================================
<title MR> <first-name ALFRED> <last-name SCHMID>
<role EXECUTIVE DIRECTOR OPERATIONS>


PO11Y O/BRIEN
MANAGER, COMMUNITY AFFAIRS
<irrelevant MyComp, INC>
<irrelevant 1 MyStreet>
<irrelevant MyCity> <irrelevant 12345>


PO1LY OBRIEN
MANAGER, COMMUNITY AFFAIRS
<irrelevant MyComp, INC>
<irrelevant 1 MyStreet>
<irrelevant MyCity> <irrelevant 12345>


<title MS> <first-name MELINDA> <last-name DUCKSWORTH>


<non-alpha *******AURO**MIXED> AADC <short 460>
MIKO SCHWARTZ
<short O> <short AND> <short T> 26-00
<irrelevant MyComp, INC>
<irrelevant 1 MyStreet>
<irrelevant MyCity> <irrelevant 12345>


...
=====================================================================
```

Determining previously unknown words. As shown in Figure 8, from the processed rejected recognition results, a frequency list FL 53 of all words occurring there is created in a first step 52, sorted in accordance with descending frequency and stored in a buffer. For the above example, the frequency list FL 53 could appear as follows:

```
=====================================================================
...
AFFAIRS                 37
MANAGER                 37
COMMUNITY               37
```

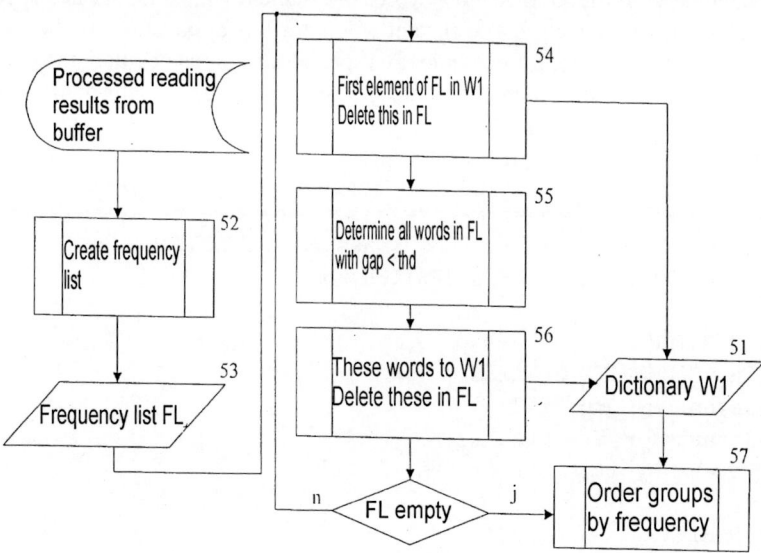

Fig. 8. Flow structure for determining previously unknown single words (n = 1) (last names)

```
OBRIEN       20
O/BRIEN      17
SCHWARTZ     15
MIKO         12
POLLY        10
PO11Y         8
PAULA         8
PO1LY         5
MIKO          3
...
```
==

From this list, an update dictionary W1 of relevant words 51 is built up step by step. For each word in the frequency list FL 53, the distance d to all words in this frequency list is determined. One method for measuring the distance between two strings is the Levenshtein method which calculates the minimum distance between two strings referred to 3 cost categories, based on costs of replacing one character, an insertion and a deletion operation. In addition to the string, other features of the recognition result, for example the character alternatives, the segmentation alternatives, etc., can be used for calculating d.

The first word in the frequency list FL 53 (currently the most frequent one) is included in the dictionary W1 51 and deleted 54 from the frequency list FL 53. All words from the frequency list FL 53 having a distance of less than a predetermined threshold *thd* are allocated 55, 56 to the current word in the dictionary W1 51 with their frequency. At the same time, these words are deleted from the frequency list FL 53. The iteration stops when the frequency list FL 53 is empty. This forms word classes which do not exceed a distance *d* between each other or, respectively, do not drop below a corresponding similarity factor.

When all words have been processed, the update dictionary W1 51 consists of a set of word classes. The shortest word of a word class is called the representative or 'prototype' of the group. Each word class contains words which are similar to each other, with the associated frequencies and distances from the class prototype. The prototypes of word classes in the dictionary W1 51, and thus also the word classes, are sorted 57 in accordance with descending frequency. The frequency of a word class is composed of the frequency of the prototype and the frequencies of the elements of the word class. Word classes with a frequency which drops below a particular threshold are deleted from the dictionary W1 51. In consequence, the following dictionary W1 51 is formed from the above list:

```
===================================================================

<Word class>              <Frequency>              <Distance>

...

AFFAIRS                       37
MANAGER                       37
COMMUNITY                     37
OBRIEN                        37
            O/BRIEN           17                    (d = 1)
POLLY                         23
            PO11Y             8                     (d = 2)
            PO1LY             5                     (d = 1)
SCHWARTZ                      15
MIKO                          15
            MIKO              3                     (d = 1)
PAULA                         8



...

===================================================================
```

The formation of prototypes can be supported by further knowledge, depending on the application. Thus, a word can be mapped either onto a number or onto an alpha sequence by using OCR replacement tables which define interchangeable pairs of characters such as 1 - L, 0 - O, 2 - Z, 6 - G etc. If, in addition, alternative sets for word classes to be learnt are known, for example nicknames for first names such as Paula - Polly, Thomas - Tom, etc., these replacements can also be performed. Both steps can be applied to the dictionary W1 51 which leads to a further blending of word classes.

Finally, all words occurring in the dictionary W1 51 are marked in the recognition results and supplemented by their prototype. In the text which follows these words will be called W1 words.

At the top of the dictionary W1 51, the most frequent, previously unknown word forms are located and the word classes contain spelling variants thereof. Thus, in the

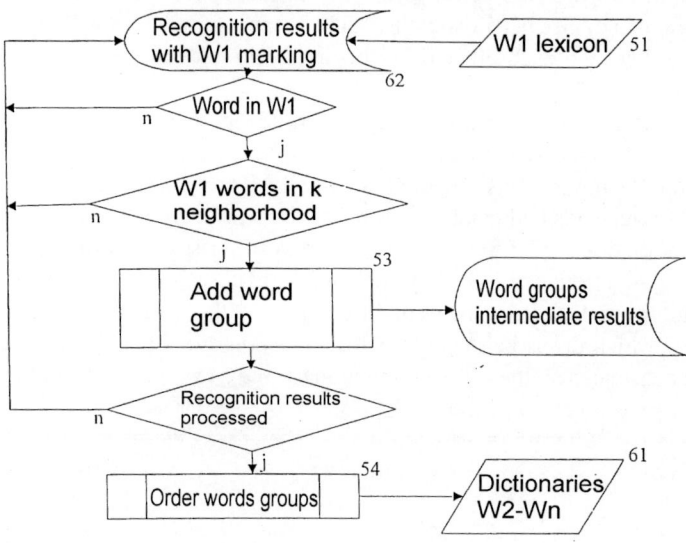

Fig. 9. Flow structure for determining previously unknown word sequences starting with the single words

application of in-house mail distribution, previously unknown first and second names and parts of departmental designations will be now be stored in the dictionary W1 51. In addition, their word classes contain spelling variants or variants which have arisen due to the characteristics of the reading system.

Finding unknown word sequences. Starting with the prototypes of the word classes in the dictionary W1 51, which are marked as such in the recognition results, word sequences of length 2 to n are determined in the next step according to Figure 9. The neighbourhoods of W1 words of the recognition results 62 are examined. For each W1 word, the right-hand neighbourhood is searched within a window of width $k <= n$ to see whether it contains further W1 words. The so created groups of words are stored in lists we call collocation dictionaries. Initially $n-1$ empty collocation dictionaries are set up in a buffer and filled step by step. An n-tuple is then included in a word group buffer 53 when n W1 words have been found and there are fewer than m further non-W1 words between these n. As in the case of the dictionary W1 51, the frequency of occurrence of the individual word sequences of length n is stored here, too.

The choice of the values of m and n depends on the actual application. For values of $n > 4$, no further significant frequent entries can be expected in the application of reading addresses. $m = 0$ means that all n W1 words follow one another directly. In the case of pairs of first and last names, however, in particular, a second name can occasionally interrupt the direct succession, just as segmentation errors of the automatic reader can generate supposed word hypotheses and thus prevent a direct succession. In

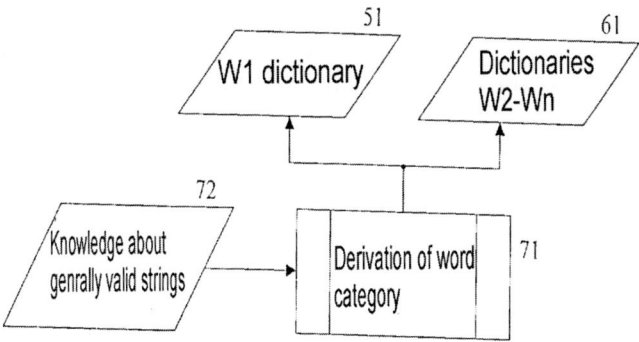

Fig. 10. Flow structure for updating the dictionaries, taking into consideration the word categories

consequence, $m = 1$ and $n = 3$ are suitable values for the application described. In this step, in consequence, $n - 1$ dictionaries Wn 61 containing frequent word sequences with the frequencies for pairs, triplets etc. up to n-tuple are generated from the word group buffer. In each dictionary Wn 61, the frequencies of the n-tuples are included with the frequencies of the W1 words of the n-tuples to calculate a dimension. Each dictionary Wn 61 is sorted in accordance with descending dimensions so that the most significant word sequences are again at the beginning of each dictionary Wn 54.

For the above example, the dictionary W2 appears now as follows:

```
W2
===================================================================
COMMUNITY AFFAIRS              37
MANAGER COMMUNITY              37
POLLY OBRIEN                   23
MIKO SCHWARTZ                  15
PAUL OBRIEN                     8
===================================================================
```

The dictionary W3 has 3 entries, provided that the name POLLY OBRIEN always occurs in combination with the designation MANAGER COMMUNITY AFFAIRS and that a line break is allowed in an n-tuple.:

```
W3
===================================================================
MANAGER COMMUNITY AFFAIRS      37
POLLY OBRIEN MANAGER           23
OBRIEN MANAGER COMMUNITY       23
===================================================================
```

Group dictionary update. As described, the word proposals of the dictionaries Wn 61 (W2, W3, etc.) are now presented to an operator for validation according to Figure 10. Knowledge about the word units 72 to be learnt makes it possible at this point to categorize 71 entries in the dictionaries W1, W2, ... Wn 51, 61 semantically. Thus, in this application, entries can be allocated to the semantic class <Name> by looking at generally applicable lists of first names. This applies similarly to the semantic class <Department> which can be derived from keywords such as *Department*. Naturally, this process can also be carried out automatically without an operator by comparison with the entries of these lists.

Detecting obsolete words or word sequences. For addresses successfully correlated, the address elements required for this have been found in the dictionary and are identified as such in the recognition results. If, for example, each time a last name and first name are successfully read by the in-house mail reader, these results are recorded in a corresponding statistics table; in particular, the frequencies of the extracted words, pairs, generally of n-tuples over defined time intervals td, e.g. for a week, are stored and it is possible to take into consideration the type of item. As a result, a distribution of the address elements to be extracted for a sequence of time intervals is obtained:

```
================================================================
Time 1


MELINDA DUCKSWORTH       123
ALFRED SCHMID                              67
...


Time 2
MELINDA DUCKSWORTH         1
ALFRED SCHMID                              85
...


Time 3
MELINDA DUCKSWORTH         2
ALFRED SCHMID                              72

...
================================================================
```

From the distribution thus found, it is possible to decide whether dictionary entries should be deleted: the entries are inserted into a list for removal from the dictionary if their frequency abruptly decreases from time point tdi to $tdi+1$ and stays at this level in successive time intervals $tdi+k$ (e.g. $k = 4$). Thus, the person MELINDA DUCKSWORTH in the above example is deleted from the dictionary. This decision can additionally be submitted to a confirmation process.

5.3   Conclusion

The described system has worked well for the in-house mail sorting application and national mail sorting as well. It was able to detect missing entries. However, besides the correctly identified missing entries, the system has also identified words or word sequences as missing which in fact had mail-sorting relevance, but not meanings belonging to the address. This happened, for example, for "postage paid". The next steps will be to refine the single processing steps in order to have them ready for daily use.

6 Summary and Economic Benefit

6.1 Technology Advances

In this chapter it was shown how recognition methods can be generalized and how the individual components of a postal address reader as well as the total system can be made adaptive as a whole.

It was shown how finding regions of interest could be improved by statistical learning methods, namely by an adaptive histogram classifier.

It was also shown how character recognition can be adapted to new fonts and writing styles in the target system by means of a new method, called the Stepwise Improvement Classifier, or SIC method. This method enables the system to be self-adaptive, which is important for learning new fonts and handwriting idiosyncrasies at once.

Another important contribution to better adaptiveness was described in detail: the HMM method with adaptive model structure, which proved to be a major breakthrough in recognition of handwritten words. While in state-of-the-art systems, only the parameters of models having fixed structure can be adapted, in the method developed here, both the parameters, and the model structure itself will be adapted to the word learning set according to the complexity of the reading task. As a result, in an average over several country applications, an improvement of more than 6 percent read rate was reached, which is significant.

Last but not least, the Learning Dictionary method developed under *Adaptive READ* has shown how to find and automatically delete obsolete dictionary entries and introduce new valid ones, which can be offered in two ways: As an address data base improvement service and/or as a read improvement, since an updated address database is coupled with higher read performance.

6.2 Economic Potential

Despite the warnings of Internet enthusiasts wanting to make us believe that physical mail will decrease or even vanish, to be replaced largely by electronic data transfer, there is no way to replace the mailing of physical goods. Forecasts for the next decade from the Universal Postal Union and other institutions dealing with the postal future tell another story:

On average, physical mail will show an annual increase of two percent in industrial countries, even four percent in developing countries such as China. This seems rather plausible in light of the recent development of e-purchasing and the heavy increase in flats and parcels caused by it.

Thus, total mail volume will increase moderately; however, the mail mix and postal logistics will change dramatically due to new market tendencies. This in turn presents new and challenging requirements for postal reading and sorting technology. Thanks to the advances in automatic pattern recognition and machine learning achieved in the project *Adaptive READ*, Siemens Dematic is well armed for these future challenges, as there are:

- Omni – Mail format processing, including letters, flats, parcels, bundles, newspapers; in short: standard and non-standard mail.
- Omni – Image Object Finding, which means finding every relevant information block, like target address, return address, stamps, labels, stickers, logos, endorsement lines for forwarding, etc.; in short, every type of information block except advertisement.
- Omni – Country Application, which has been practised now for more than thirty countries, and will be potentially applicable for all UPU members.
- Omni – Alphabet Reading, adding to global Latin all the other local alphabets which are relevant in a global postal network as well, like Arabic, Cyrillic, Hangul, Chinese, Hindi, etc.

Adaptive READ also brought an essential impetus to new business through new functionalities such as Automatic Forwarding – also called redirection – and revenue protection, and in future possibly also business reply mail.

Thanks to the *Adaptive READ* project, a set of new business ideas have appeared on the horizon, such as web-based Reading and Coding services: The customer contracts with a supplier like Siemens Dematic for a service that lets him upload images of his daily mail, and depending on the chosen service level, the read results for 100 percent of the images or less are returned within seconds to hours. Thus, smaller private postal offices, which cannot afford expensive reading and sorting equipment, can also benefit from this sophisticated technology.

In the same way, large postal services can benefit from a reject analysis and improvement service: A representative sub-sampled set of mail images is uploaded to the Reading and Coding web-center and the analysis results and improvement proposals are returned.

Another very promising service is the automatic address database clean-up service, using address interpretation and learning dictionary methods to search out obsolete data entries as well as new valid aliases for improving efficiency of the reader system.

References

1. C. KALTENMEIER, T. CAESAR, J. GLOGER, AND E. MANDLER. Sophisticated topology of hidden Markov models for cursive script recognition. In *Proc. of the 2nd Int. Conf. on document analysis and recognition*, pages 139–142, Tsukuba Science City, Japan, Oct. 1993. IEEE Computer Society Press.
2. C. BAHLMANN AND H. BURKHARDT. Measuring HMM similarity with the Bayes probability of error. In *Proc. of the 6th Int. Conf. on document analysis and recognition*, pages 406–411, Seattle, WA, Sept. 2001. IEEE Computer Society Press.
3. M.-P. SCHAMBACH. Model length adaptation of an HMM based cursive word recognition system. In *Proc. of the 7th Int. Conf. on Document Analysis and Recognition*, Edinburgh, Scotland, August 2003.

4. L. R. RABINER. A tutorial on hidden Markov models and selected applications in speech recognition. *Proceedings of the IEEE*, 77(2):257–285, February 1989.

5. M.-P. SCHAMBACH. Determination of the number of writing variants with an HMM based cursive word recognition system. In *Proc. of the 7th Int. Conf. on Document Analysis and Recognition*, Edinburgh, Scotland, August 2003.

6. P. CHEESEMAN AND J. STUTZ. Bayesian classification (AutoClass): Theory and results. In U. M. Fayyad, G. Piatetsky-Shapiro, P. Smyth, and R. Uthurusamy, editors, *Advances in Knowledge Discovery and Data Mining*, pages 153–180. MIT Press, 1996.

7. M.-P. SCHAMBACH. *Automatische Modellierung gebundener Handschrift in einem HMM-basierten Erkennungssystem*. Proposed Dissertation, Universität Ulm, 2003.

8. JÜRGEN SCHÜRMANN. PATTERN CLASSIFICATION A Unified View of Statistical and Neural Approaches, Chapter 6.14 *Recursive Learning* pages 165–182. Wiley-Interscience, 1996.

9. K. OKUDA, E. TANAKA AND T. KASAI. A Method for the Correction of Garbled Words, based on the Levenshtein Metric IEEE Transactions on Computers, Vol. c-25, No. 2, February 1976

A Tool for Semi-automatic Document Reengineering

Jens Drawehn, Christoph Altenhofen, Mirjana Stanišić-Petrović, and
Anette Weisbecker

University of Stuttgart, Institute for Human Factors and Technology Management,
Nobelstraße 12, 70569 Stuttgart, Germany
{Jens.Drawehn, Christoph.Altenhofen, Mirjana.Stanisic,
Anette.Weisbecker}@iao.fraunhofer.de

Abstract. Marking-up of documents that only contain a layout-oriented structure (e.g. documents created by an ordinary word-processor) becomes more and more important for the future of information management in modern companies. That's because only after the document has been marked up with logical elements, those additional information can be used for example to implement single-source publishing or to enable content-oriented retrieval. Today the process of marking-up layout-oriented documents usually has to be done manually what leads to high costs for the companies.

In the project "Adaptive READ" the Institute for Human Factors and Technology Management (IAT) of the University of Stuttgart has developed a semi-automatic approach to solve this problem of marking-up documents that only contain a layout-oriented structure. The main issues of this development are discussed in the following article.

1 Introduction

1.1 Initial Situation / Motivation

Generally, documents consist of 3 levels. The *logical structure* describes the logical elements of a document and how they are correlated. For instance, a business letter may contain the elements "sender", "receiver" and "body". The *content* is the actual information of the document. The *layout* information determines the appearance of the document.

These three levels form a whole and are relevant for processing the document. The layout information is only necessary to display the document in a human-readable format, enabling users to access the content of a document by recognizing the logical structure.

For the automatic processing of a document, e.g. in complex information retrieval systems, the logical structure is much more important. A document containing strong layout information can make the automatic processing more difficult. This is valid particularly if the document is to be processed further on different media or to be divided into components that will be put together building up new documents. The last aspect can be found in the field of technical documentation, where documents increasingly are built up from modules.

Most documents currently are created by layout-oriented tools, e.g. Microsoft Word. These tools provide many ways to form new documents with the focusing only

A. Dengel et al. (Eds.): Adaptive READ Research Project, LNCS 2956, pp. 216–234, 2004.

on their layout. With these tools, the logical structure cannot be represented explicitly. Thus, building up documents that enable the automatic recognition of their logical structure requires a high expense.

However, such a structuring of the content is necessary in the following cases:

Document re-use: Parts of documents shall be reused in other documents. In this case, savings can be achieved since identical contents are created only once and can subsequently be used in several documents, for example in the field of technical documentation. The maintenance of the documents is facilitated as well, because changes have to be done only at one place and take effect on all concerning documents.

Personalization: Documents shall be tailored to the needs of the reader. This includes the localization, that is, the adaptation of documents to country-specific conditions like language for example.

Single Source – Multiple Media: This concept implies the display of documents on different media without any changes of the document.

Directed search: The logical structure can be used to improve document retrieval.

In the following sections, our approach of *document reengineering* for documents created with word processors is presented. The objective of this approach is a process, that allows companies and organizations to transform large collections of documents with a minimum of manual effort into a structured format, that permits automatic processing of the documents taking into account their logical structure.

1.2   The Concept of Generic Coding

As explained above, current word processors rest upon the WYSIWYG[1]-approach. This implies that a document is created and printed out in the same form. At this, the emphasis is on the visible layout of the document. If documents are created following the WYSIWYG-approach, the information about the logical structure of a document is not saved. It is accessible for human readers through the layout, but largely hidden for computers. Thus, humans recognize headings through the highlighted presentation and incorporation of the context. The computer, on the other hand, processes them as simple text strings with particular typographic markup.

The fundamental idea of *Generic Coding* picks up this problem. Already at the end of the 1960ies, William Tunnicliffe [1] proposed to separate the information content of a document from its format. This and other proposals led to the concept of *Generic Markup*.[2]

Instead of format instruction, the markup should now contain information about the nature of the marked location [2]. Then, headings, chapters, citations and warnings are identified, thus giving the document and its parts an explicit semantic and logical structure. The graphical representation of a certain part of a document is determined,

---

[1] WYSIWYG: Acronym for 'What You See Is What You Get' from the field of word processing, whereupon the print output exactly corresponds to the image displayed on the screen.

[2] Markups are items, originally used to write typographic information into manuscripts, afterwards interpreted for printing.

when the document is displayed. The advantage of this method is the possibility to generate different outputs for several media from one single marked up document without the need to change the document. This principle is known as *Single Source - Multiple Media* [3].

1.3   The Use of Extensible Markup Language (XML)

Since its publication, the standard XML - other than SGML (Standard Generalized Markup Language) – has quickly become successful. A look at the book market shows clearly the interest in XML: Within four years, several hundred books dealing with XML were published, whereas significantly less books about SGML came on the market.[3] One reason for the popularity of XML is the reduction of complexity in comparison with SGML, leading to simpler tools and better handling and a positive impact on automatic processing as well [4].

In addition, numerous applications of XML exist in various branches and areas of application, that enable the exchange of data through the use of publicly available Document Type Definitions (DTDs).[4] MathML[5] (Mathematical Markup Language) for the description of mathematical expressions, UIML[6] (User Interface Markup Language) for the description of user interfaces and WML[7] (Wireless Markup Language) for displaying of WAP documents on mobile devices are only a few examples. In the field of business relationships, with BMEcat[8] and openTRANS[9], exist widely accepted standards for the exchange of catalogue data and business documents. Both standards are developed with participation of the Fraunhofer IAO, that is working in close co-operation with the IAT of the University of Stuttgart. Beside it, XML has become a standard format for the interchange of structured data between different database systems.

In summary, the use of XML has significantly altered the handling of information in many areas. However, a new technology cannot solve all problems. Only with a combination of technology and affiliated organisational changes, the current drawbacks, e.g. concerning the interchange of information across companies, can be eliminated.

2   State of the Art

In this chapter, the state of the art in the field of document reengineering will be presented. Scientific approaches are discussed in section 2.1 and available products in section 2.2.

---

[3] A search in the KNO Buchkatalog in January 2003 resulted in 326 hits for a keyword search for XML, the search for the keyword SGML resulted in only 4 hits.

[4] A good overview can be found on the cover-pages of OASIS-Open [5]. Currently there are listed more than 550 XML applications.

[5] http://www.w3.org/TR/REC-MathML

[6] http://www.oasis-open.org/cover/uiml.html

[7] http://www.oasis-open.org/cover/wap-wml.html

[8] http://www.bmecat.org

[9] http://www.opentrans.org

2.1   Scientific Approaches

Many approaches located in the scientific area can be assigned to the field of text mining. These approaches aim at extracting information from documents and are not made for bringing structure into the documents. The article of Soto gives an application-oriented introduction into the field of text mining [6].

The article from Ahonen [7] also discusses the field of text mining. The described approach uses already extracted phrases. The first step is a conversion from the source format to a SGML format. From this format, information is extracted through the use of regular expressions, whereby it is quite complicated to define these expressions.

In contrast to this, Ahonen deals with the structuring of documents. In [7], she gives a good overview of topics related to automatically generate DTDs. In particular, the expense for a fully automatic solution is set in proportion to its runtime behaviour. Ahonen arrives at the conclusion that a fully automatic solution is only practicable with limitations for complexity or demand of time.

A specific problem of the automatic generation of structures, e.g. DTDs, is the avoidance of ambiguity. This issue is discussed in a second article of Ahonen [8]. Although the perspective of Ahonen is the automatic generation of DTDs, what does not belong to the work within Adaptive Read, the considered aspects can be used for our considerations referring to the automatic structuring documents.

Both aspects (automatic generation of DTDs and avoidance of ambiguity) are discussed as well in the doctoral thesis of Ahonen [9].

In [10], the concept *microdocument* is introduced. Microdocuments are defined as logical units within a document, which are used to access the information contained in the document. To detect these microdocument structures, an automatic process is suggested, which uses layout information as well as the frequency of terms in different sections of the document. With this, the microdocuments are defined and can be used subsequently for retrieval. Thus, the objective of this approach is to support information retrieval and not to give documents a logical structure. Nevertheless, the article provides an interesting basis for the markup of text segments.

Klein and Fankhauser [11] deal with the automatic structuring of documents as well. For this purpose, they introduce the *document structure description* (DSD). A DSD is an extension of DTDs, providing additional elements for the definition of simple content definitions, e.g. string patterns and operators for manipulations of the document. The creation of the DSD is complex and has to be done manually. The approach, which is put into practice in the prototype DREAM of the Fraunhofer IPSI, does not support learning.

In 1998, Ahonen turns closer towards text mining. Thus, in [12] general approaches of data mining are discussed and their transferability to the field of text analysis are explained. The focus of this article is the extraction of information from unstructured documents, what is discussed within other work packages of Adaptive Read.

In 2000, Barabara Heikkinen describes in her doctoral thesis [13] the assembly of documents from components. For this, a conversion of the existing structure of a single document into a generic DTD takes place, so that the entire document becomes homogenous.

Oliver Zeigermann deals in his diploma thesis [14] with the aspect of transforming documents. Different kinds of transformation are introduced, whereby connections to the construction of compilers are established. The approach concentrates, like several of the other approaches mentioned above, at the syntax-driven conversion and does neither contain a comfortable component for defining the conversion nor a graphical user interface for a user-driven conversion.

In summary, techniques for the automatic structuring of documents are discussed in the scientific community. The applicability of these approaches is restricted to situations, where a fully automatic conversion is possible. Within the considered articles dealing with text mining, the focus is more on the automatic extraction of information from documents than on the structuring of documents.

Thus, the existing approaches do not cover all aspects that are necessary to identify the complete structure of documents. For this reason it can be stated, that the considered articles provide useful requirements, but cannot be taken as a basis for the further conception.

2.2   Available Products

Products Supporting the Structuring of Documents

An available product that covers all aspects of our approach is not known. Subsequently, implemented examples and different approaches are described.

The product or framework *SmarteningUp* from SPX/Valley Forge [15] is the most similar product to our approach. SPX/Valley Forge is an enterprise that provides and implements publishing solutions for technical documentation in the automotive industry. The above mentioned product consists of several components and can be characterized as a framework. The product processes SGML and XML data and the process' objective is – similar to our area of work in Adaptive READ - the transformation of weakly structured documents into documents that are marked up according to their logical structure. For this, a rule based procedure was developed, in which the rules had to be created manually. Consequently, the implemented process requires high administrative expenses, even if there is a rule-learning component that detects deviations or problems with the defined rules. Rules are created by using pre-defined keywords and simple layout aspects. The product implements a fully automatic approach. In case there is a heterogeneous set of documents (what is the normal case for documents created by word processors), it will lead to increasing problems. Further on, the product does not support an automatic adaptation to new or altered document types and provides no graphical interface for a user-driven conversion.

Another approach for marking-up layout-oriented documents, based on a translation memory system, is offered from DocConsult [16]. Thereby, the association from layout elements to logical structures is based on a combination of content and formatting. This approach restricts to the mentioned aspects and does e.g. not pay attention to previous and following segments. A graphical interface for the definition of the associations does not exist and the system is not able to learn.

The product *DynaTag* from Inso with a similar objective is no longer available on the market. Inso was taken over from Stellent [17]. This product was designed for the conversion of word processor documents into another product of Inso, *DynaText*. *Dynatext*, as well no longer available, displays online books that are based on SGML or XML. *DynaTag* possessed a graphical user interface for the definition of mapping from templates to XML elements. The definition of mapping rules could not contain dependencies to previous or following segments and did not permit combinations of content and templates.

A product from the field of text mining is the *KnowledgeServer* from Autonomy [18]. The objective of the product is the automatic classification of documents. It does not support the structuring of documents and is left out of consideration. Another text mining tool is the *Intelligent Miner* from IBM [19], that classifies documents based on extracted keywords and provides retrieval functionality. This product does not support the structuring of documents, too. The *Insight Discoverer* suite of Temis Group [20] contains tools that extract contents from documents and classifies documents into pre-defined classes. To the same category of tools belongs the product *LinguistiX* from inxight [21] described in [22]. This product is as well a tool for extracting information from documents, whereby it follows a linguistic approach. Like the other mentioned products, *LinguistiX* [23] does not support the structuring of documents.

Products Supporting Single Steps of the Process
An observation of products that support single steps of the process results in the following view.

A widespread tool for conversions, i.e. the transformation of structures, is *Omnimark* from Omnimark [24]. This tool was originally designed to support conversions of SGML documents. It provides its own language for defining conversion rules. The rules are not restricted to SGML, it is also possible e.g. to define rules for transforming RTF documents to SGML. *Omnimark* supports the automatic conversion of documents, whereby it has no graphical interface for the definition of conversion rules. Further the product is restricted to the definition and execution of the rules, learning is not supported. Consequently, the product could be used within our approach as one component of an aggregated system. It is suitable to transform documents from proprietary formats into a working format, as it is described in chapter 4.1.

Another tool for the conversion of documents is the public source product XTAL from Zeigermann, meanwhile substituted from XPA [25]. It was created in the context of Zeigermann's diploma thesis [13]. The product is based on ANTLR, a publicly available java translator and compiler generator [26]. The definition of the conversion rules follows a java-oriented syntax, that is complex to learn and error-prone. The product has no graphical interface for the definition or control of the conversion and does not support learning.

In conclusion, a complete system that accomplishes all requirements of our approach does not exist on the market yet.

3   Structuring Documents

Existing approaches that implement an automatic conversion of documents lead to high expenses for manual post-processing, in the case the documents are heterogeneous. Therefore, we suggest a semi-automatic approach, that combines both tasks, *automatic conversion* and *manual control*, reducing the overall expenses for

222   J. Drawehn et al.

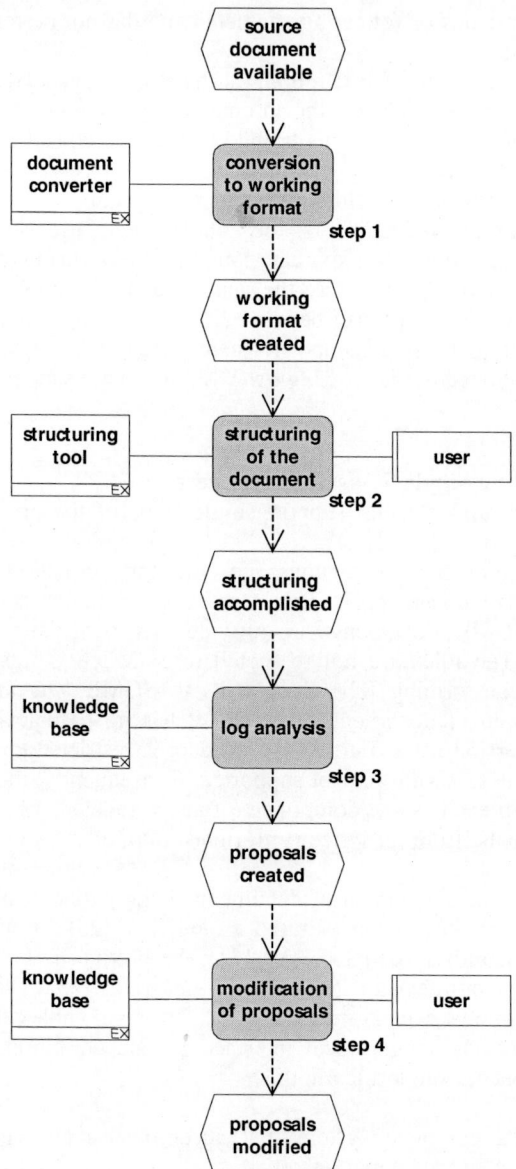

Fig. 1. Overview of the process

preparing automatic conversion and carrying out manual tasks. In the following, the process of structuring documents is described. Figure 1 gives an overview of this process.

In practice, there is a large number of document formats. These are proprietary formats (e.g. MS Word 97) as well as publicly available formats (e.g. PDF). The first step (see figure 1, step 1) is the conversion of these different formats into one *working format*, so that we subsequently does not have to care about different formats. This conversion extracts all information from the document, that is necessary for the further processing.

The next step (see figure 1, step 2) is the association from content and logical structure. For that, a user opens the document and creates the associations manually. It is necessary to know into which structure the document is to be transformed. This target structure corresponds to a DTD known from the SGML/XML context. In addition, the system supports the user by suggesting appropriate associations for the structuring of documents and displays them to the user. These *suggestions* rest upon a knowledge base, that contains all associations that took place in the past. All actions of the user are written into a log und are subsequently used to derive new proposals.

In the next step (see figure 1, step 3), the log is analysed. The analysis component uses additional information, e.g. a domain specific thesaurus, which is useful to notice relations between terms and so thus improving the quality of the newly generated proposals.

The new proposals are presented to the user with another tool (see figure 1, step 4) and can then be modified, if necessary. In this step, the user can accept, change or reject proposals. The results are then stored in the knowledge base and are subsequently used for structuring documents of the same type.

An exemplary process shall illustrate our approach. The chosen scenario is the transformation of catalogue data, assumed that they are available as an electronic document.

If documents of this type have already been transformed, the tool used for structuring the documents may involve information about former associations, execute the appropriate actions and present them to the user. If the document is the first of its type, i.e. if nothing is known about this document, the user has to carry out all associations manually. When he or she associates segments of the document to logical elements of the target structure, e.g. the qualification of a paragraph to the element 'description', the users' actions are logged.

Directly after the logging, these data is analysed with regard to the derivation of association rules. If the user has associated several paragraphs of the template 'indentation', that starts with the string 'description', to the element 'description' an appropriate association rule can be derived and subsequently used for further work.

The created association rules are presented to the user and can be changed or rejected. Through this, it can be guaranteed that the processing of documents, that are considered to be rare exceptions, does not lead to a degeneration of the rule set.

4   Implementation

4.1   Conversion from Proprietary Word Processing-Format to XML

As mentioned above, the process of structuring documents shall be independent from the application used to create the original document. For this reason, the first step is the transformation of the document from the layout-oriented format into the working format, that is based on a XML DTD. This was one reason not to choose one of the available XML export functions of a word processor. The result would then not be independent from the application. Instead, we used the publicly available Rainbow DTD [27], that was designed for mapping documents created by word processors to an application independent format. The first task was the manual transformation of the SGML DTD to a XML DTD, which was trivial because of the minimal differences between SGML DTDs and XML DTDs. Beside the transformation, we modified the DTD to a minor degree. We added elements for lists and the according format information, e.g. the element 'liststyle' to mark the used list signs.

Figure 2 shows a graphical representation of the modified Rainbow DTD, which consists of three fundamental parts:

– the head (element 'fileinfo') containing information about the version of the DTD and the application
– a style area (element 'styinfo') containing the paragraph and character templates of the document
– the content of the document (element 'doc')

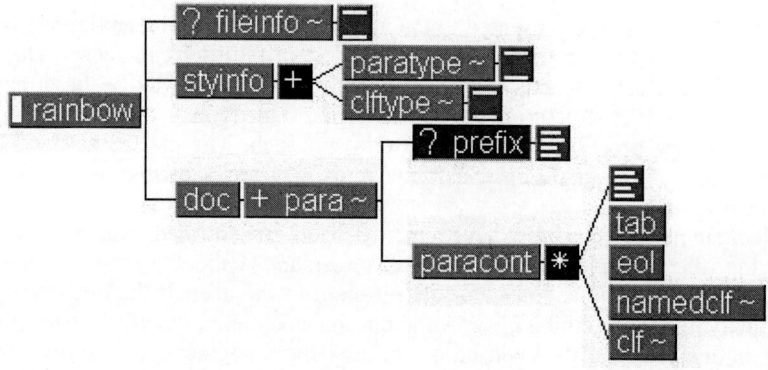

Fig. 2. The modified rainbow DTD

The structure of the rainbow DTD is layout-oriented, i.e. the markup has the purpose to map features of the original documents directly. The mapping does not change the structure of the document. In practice, large differences between the single documents will arise, caused by different use of the word processor and the know-how of the users. For instance, text formatting can be done through the use of templates or depending on the situation through manual formatting. These differences could be easily observed in the realized test scenarios.

As a prototype, the conversion from word documents to the rainbow format was realized through the use of VBA macros. An advantage of this method is the direct access to the object model of the application, a disadvantage the poor performance.

Because the execution does not involve user interaction, the process is nevertheless feasible and large sets of documents can be converted in one step.

So far, the prototype restricts to the conversion of text information. For production use, the handling of tables, figures, form fields and directories must be added.

4.2   Building up the Structure

In this chapter, the structuring tool is described. It has a graphical user interface, that supports the user with regard to structuring the contents, i.e. the classification of document segments and their content into the target structure. The tool supports any target structure, that can be presented in the form of a XML DTD.

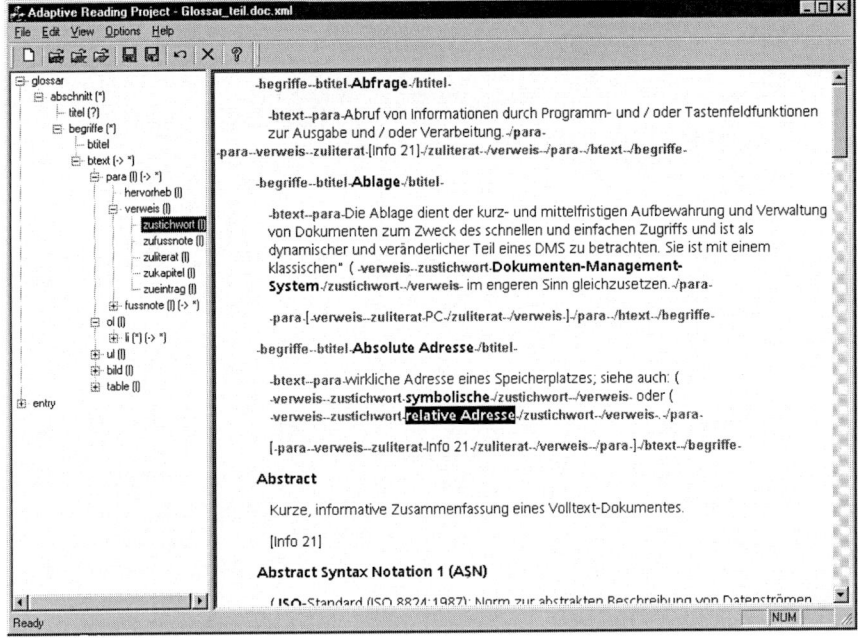

Fig. 3. User interface of the structuring tool

The prototype is implemented with C++ and uses standard components, e.g. the XML parser from Microsoft for the analysis and presentation of the target structure. In figure 3, the tree-based presentation of the target structure is shown on the left side. Beside the elements, their cardinality and sequence conditions as defined in the DTD are shown.

After the selection of the target structure, the user opens an appropriate configuration file with mapping rules, if one is available. Through this, these mapping rules can be applied to subsequently opened documents. The result is represented in a form similar to the mappings carried out by the user himself.

Now, the source document can be opened. For an appropriate presentation of the document (Fig. 3 shows an example on the right side), the layout information contained in the XML file is used.

After all, the user can structure the document through simple *drag and drop* actions. The realized associations are presented. Parallel to this, all actions are logged and later analysed in the knowledge base. The result is written into a configuration file, that can be used for the conversion of documents of the same type.

Already without knowledge of prior conversions the tool supports the user by enabling the mapping through simple drag and drop actions. However, the main benefit is the derivation of mapping rules from the processing of similar documents and the application of these rules for other documents of the same type. Through this, more and more actions are carried out automatically and conversions require less effort.

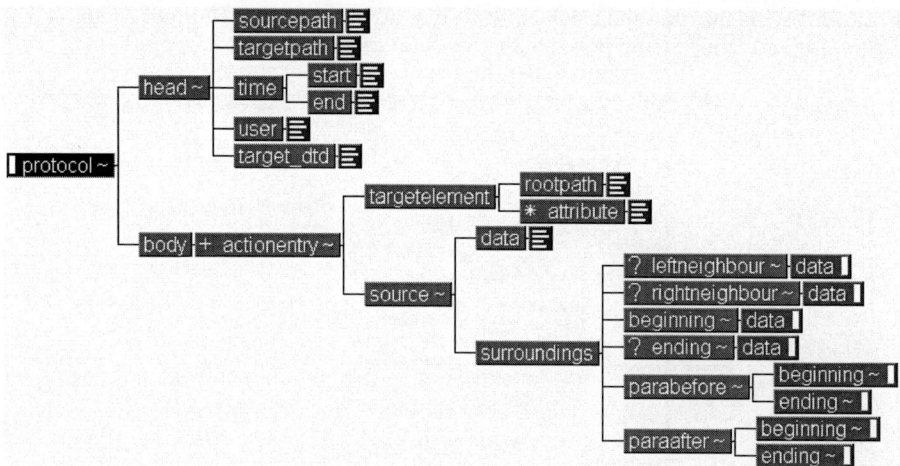

Fig. 4. The DTD of the action protocol

Thereby a combination of manual and automatic approaches appears reasonable. Thus, the result of an automatic analysis, that remains incomplete due to heterogeneously created documents, can be used as a base configuration for the manual process. Starting with this base configuration, the learning process leads to improvements with every processed document.

The user actions are logged for later analysis. With every document in the rainbow format, the tool creates – beside the document in the target structure - an action protocol for every session. The protocol entries contain information about the mapped segments, the context and their environment in the source document. The log is also written in XML. For this purpose, a DTD (see figure 4) was defined that allows the exchange of the protocol data between the structuring tool and the knowledge base.

4.3   Logging Data und Processing Knowledge

The evaluation of the protocol data takes place in the *knowledge base*, that consists of several components: a database configuration tool, an evaluation program and a completion tool. The implementation is based on the database management system Microsoft SQL Server 2000. All information, protocol and control data, is stored in the database. The learning component is also a part of the database.

The Database Configuration Tool
The import of the action protocols and the export of configuration files, particularly the mapping of the appropriate DTDs to the database, is a nontrivial task. The complexity results from structural differences between both worlds, XML and the relational model, e.g. the conversion of tree-based structures with cardinalities in DTDs.

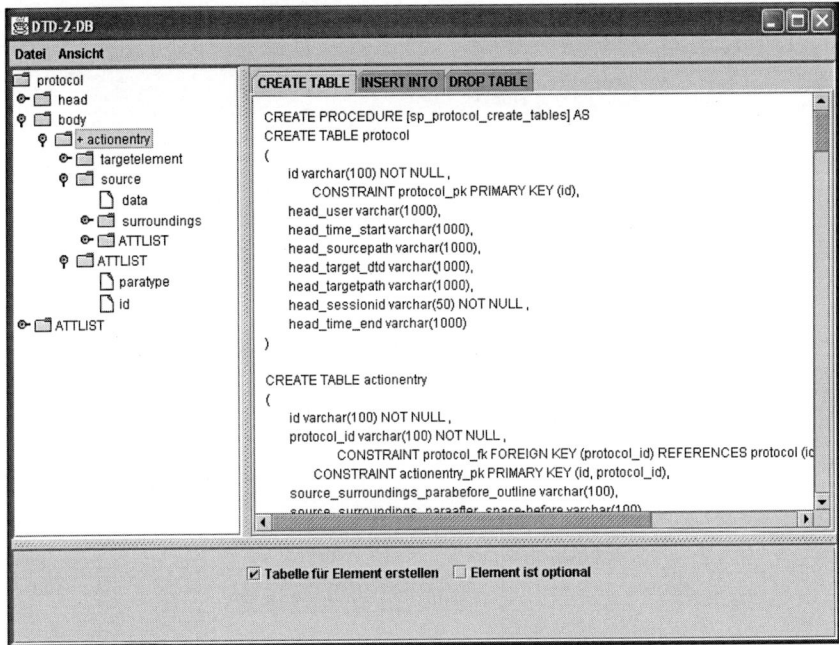

Fig. 5. Tool for mapping DTDs to relational schemes

Additionally, the structures of the action protocol and the configuration files were under development and changed frequently. Thus we decided to develop a tool that supports the mapping from DTDs to a relational scheme. Subsequently, this tool was applied within the project for all required mappings from XML structures to the database.

The tool analyses a DTD and formulates on the basis of firmly implemented heuristics, a proposal for the relational scheme. The scheme is displayed to the user, and he or she can make individual changes of the scheme. After that, the tool creates procedures that are necessary to create the database and to import and export the XML files. If there are changes made by the user, these procedures are accordingly modified. Our prototype creates stored procedures for the MS SQL Server 2000. The support of other database systems is planned, but not yet implemented.

Evaluation Program and Completion Tool

To decouple the knowledge base and the structuring tool, we defined a XML DTD for the transfer of the rule files as well. Figure 6 and 7 show a graphical representation of the DTD, cut at the element "situation".

When the user of the structuring tool chooses a target structure, he or she can then load an appropriate rule file. The rule file contains a representation of the rules from the knowledge base. They are interpreted and applied to the document that shall be processed. The user does not have to carry out all associations, he can affirm or reject the automatically executed steps. By logging these actions (affirmations and rejections), in the next iteration step the knowledge base acquires information about the correctness of the rules and can improve the rule set.

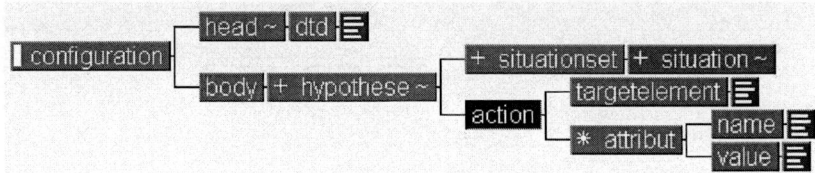

Fig. 6. DTD for rule files, Part 1

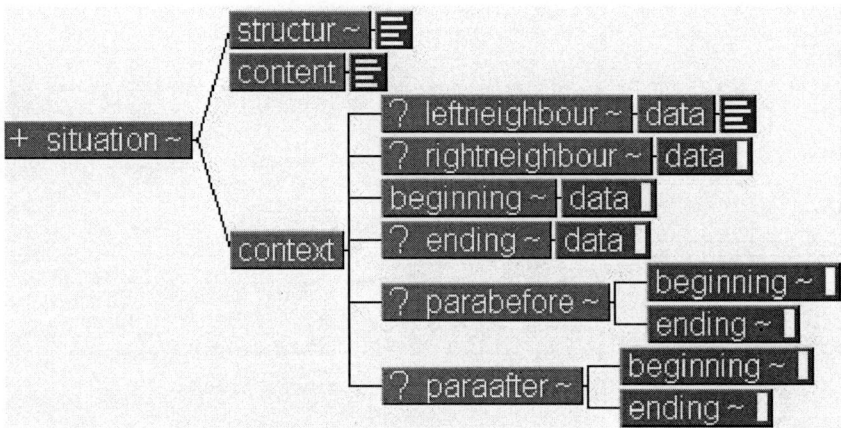

Fig. 7. DTD for rule files, Part 2

For the implementation of the knowledge base, a wide range of products can be considered. Current knowledge-based systems are normally tailored to specific fields of application. For the moment it is unclear, which complexity the rule set of a productive application will reach. In any case it should be avoided to store the rules as a hard-coded program, since permanent changes can be expected.

Thus, different products that process XML data were considered with regard to their applicability as a prototype, e.g. the XML database *Tamino* from Software AG. This product supports import and export of XML data. Especially the execution of queries that are not oriented at the XML tree structure, but lead across through the entire instance, causes problems. However, queries like 'find all terms, that occur frequently in all protocol entries' are necessary for the generation of new rules. As the result of our research it must be said, that the required set of functions is not supported by one of the evaluated products.

Relational database systems provide high flexibility with regard to the execution of queries. Thus, for our implementation we decided to use the MS SQL Server 2000. As all current relational database systems, it supports the mapping of XML data structures to relational schemas.

As an important aspect of the implementation, the rules for processing knowledge are not implemented directly in SQL, but stored in tables. Through this, the mechanism remains unchanged and the rule sets can be changed.

Possible solutions may consist of several concurrent rule sets, e.g. primarily layout-oriented and primarily content-oriented. Then an evaluation scale has to be defined to find out which result is better.

Afterwards, the result is written into the configuration file and made available to the structuring tool. This exchange is also thinkable during the processing of a document, especially when large documents frequently contain the same or similar structures, e.g. in a catalogue.

Originally we assumed that for one target structure there is exactly one configuration file, which is automatically used when the target structure is chosen. It turned out that the automatic use of a configuration file is error-prone, especially if for one target structure several clusters of documents can be found. This can happen for instance if there are several authors who use the word processor in different ways. Thus, it is reasonable to allow the creation of several configuration files for one target structure. The user can then choose the appropriate configuration file.

4.4   Experiences

The components described above have been implemented as prototypes in the project Adaptive Read. The main focus of the implementation was the evaluation of the previously designed process. The experiences from the implementation are discussed in the following section.

Experience with the Conversion Tool

The conversion tool is the first tool that is used in the process. Its objective is the transformation of the original document into the working format, that is used for further processing.

Together with the implementation of the prototype, we defined the working format as a XML DTD and developed the tool that converts word documents into this format. Due to the chosen technology VBA, the prototype is limited with regard to complexity and size of the original documents. So large documents require a long processing time. For a production environment, significant improvements should be realized through the use of another technology.

Conclusion: The chosen approach, particularly the conversion of proprietary document formats into a XML-based working format, has stand the test. To integrate other word processor formats, only the converter for this format has to be implemented. The following steps rest upon this format and are independent from the word processor.

Experience with the Structuring Tool

For the normal user, the structuring tool represents the central step within the process of structuring documents. It is the user interface of the entire system. The other components run in the background. They receive data from this tool or send data to it, in order to partly automate the process. For this reason, we attached great importance to usability aspects. Thereby, the chosen approach to display the document and the elements of the target structure side by side, could be affirmed. The document is displayed in a WYSIWYG-like style, which is created by using the layout information contained in the working format. Through this, the user obtains a sufficiently exact impression to recognize the document structure and to map it to the target structure.

Parallel to the structuring document, the elements of the target structure are displayed on the left side of the tool shown in figure 3. Thereby, the elements are arranged as a tree, showing relations, possible sequences and cardinalities. Through this, the user obtains an efficient support for carrying out the structuring. Cardinalities are presented with the characters known from XML (+, ?, *), which are initially unfamiliar for the user. However, this presentation has proven to be adequate and easy to learn.

Despite the presentation of the target structure including cardinalities and sequence conditions, the correctness of an association cannot be verified within the tool. That is, the document in process may be not valid (in the sense of XML) with regard to the target DTD. This is caused by the concept that the user does not really edit a document, he or she merely associates elements. Thus, for instance a wrong sequence of elements within the document cannot be adjusted within the structuring tool. For that, the subsequent use of another tool is necessary. We decided to separate the tasks to two tools for the following reasons:

- The implementation of the according functionality within the structuring tool would mean to build an entire XML editor, which is not the focus of our work.
- Further, this would make the processing more complex for the user, wherefore the complete functionality should not be integrated into the structuring tool

Another restriction of our prototype lies in the difficulty to process large documents. The size of the displayed elements is always the same and zooming is not supported. A zoom function could be integrated with reasonable effort, whereby readability and consequently usability would decline. The implementation of other functionality like an outline view, enabling the user to open and close parts of the document, requires considerably more effort. This is caused by a loss of information in the working format, that handles the document as a sequence of paragraphs and does not support outline functionality. Other aspects of documents, e.g. links, are not supported as well. Through an appropriate modification of the working format, i.e. the further completion of the rainbow DTD, these functionalities could be integrated in principle. However, in the current prototype they are not implemented yet.

Conclusion: In summary we may say that the procedure of structuring documents was accepted positively by the pilot users, particularly the simplicity of associations via drag and drop actions. In addition, the basic assumptions with regard to our design of the action protocol can be affirmed and the information is useful in the following steps, i.e. within the knowledge base.

Experience with the Knowledge Base
In every knowledge processing system, there are limits for the definition of rules. In our case, the information that is provided to the knowledge base can never be complete. If the set of already processed documents indicates that a rule has a certain importance, the next document to process may not correspond to this rule. For instance, when a text segment inside a paragraph is associated to a specific element of the target structure and no formatting information is available, the configuration file will come to the conclusion that the content inside or near the segment is decisive for

the association. When the terms or phrases do not reoccur in the next document in the same or in a similar way, the rule cannot be applied or improved. In other words, the available information is insufficient to create reasonable rules.

Another difficulty occurs when associations are carried out in different orders. The knowledge base tries to generate rules, that take into account the chronological order of the actions. Through this, the automatic processing of several associations, that belong together, becomes possible. This problem cannot be solved through the integration of sequence definitions in the configuration file. In fact, the sequence of the actions made by the user, affect the quality of the rule sets.

Conclusion: The mentioned points affect the quality and the complexity of the emerging rule sets, but the basic concept remains untouched. However, the observed problems reflect the restrictions of an automatic conversion particularly with heterogeneous document sets. This shows that manual activities remain necessary, which was the reason for our semi-automatic approach.

5   Application Areas

5.1   Case Study 1: Technical Documentation

Origin

The starting point of this case study is the transposition of a documentation to a media independent and/or modular format. For this, it is necessary to split the documents according to a pre-defined model into single modules. This requires logically structured documents. Often there are large sets of existing documents that have to be transferred into the new format, so that the efficient conversion gets a crucial importance. Without a conversion, it is not possible to work efficiently in the new world, because the existing documentation for the existing products must be handled further on.

An analysis of the existing documents often shows, that these documents are created with layout-oriented tools. From this the fact results, that the structure of documents with similar or equal structures differs in detail, so that a fully automatic conversion is not practicable.

Solution

The application of our tools that support the conversion of documents into a logically structured format solves the problem of converting existing documentations. The homogeneity of the documents significantly affects the extension of automation that can be realized. When the documents are very homogeneous, the rules derived by the system can be applied frequently and the user has to carry out only little manual activity. In this scenario, our tool can be applied only for the conversion of the existing documents. However, due to the large amounts of documents that can be found in practice, the application of our tool makes sense.

5.2   Case Study 2: Conversion of Catalogue Data

Origin

The starting point of this scenario is a set of unstructured catalogue data, that are made available from a business partner. The data should be imported into a business application, what requires to convert the data into a logically structured format. In other words, the logical elements of the catalogue entries, e.g. article number, unit price and unit size, must be identified. In contrast to the scenario described above, the data import is a recurring process: as long as the business partners provide the data in an unstructured format, the import must be executed repeatedly. Therefore an automation of the import implicates a high savings potential.

Solution

The conversion of the unstructured catalogue data can be done efficiently through the use of the tools developed in the project 'Adaptive Read'. Thereby, the definition of mapping and consequently the degree of automation improves with the homogeneity of the documents. The generated rules can then be applied more frequently. Thus, the process works best with automatically created documents, even though the format is unstructured. In this scenario it is supposed that due to recurring conversions with the same source format a high savings potential is practicable in the current business.

6   Conclusion

The overall idea described in this article has stand the test during the development and shows no serious weak point. Especially the separation of the processing steps, the design of different tools for these steps and the connection of the different tools through standardized interfaces defined with XML has proven helpful for the implementation. Thus, the tools could be developed independently from each other. Only the interfaces between the tools, i.e. the XML DTDs, necessary for the interchange of information, had to be coordinated. Due to the chosen format XML, components that are already present in the development tools could be used. This simplified e.g. the development of the structuring tool and the database configuration tool.

The main objective of the development of our prototype was to verify the conception. The verification succeeded. The application of the prototype in a productive environment was not intended and should be verified carefully. Further on, for productive use several functions have to be added. However, the achieved results provide a reasonable basis for the implementation of a productive system.

The response of potential users to the presentation of our concept, e.g. at the IAO panel 'content management' [28] in Stuttgart and at the tekom annual conference 2002 in Wiesbaden [29], showed that users from the field of technical documentation would appreciate such a tool.

7   References

1.   http://www.mintert.com/xml/mlweb/MarkUpLang.html, last visited 2003-08-05
2.   H. Behme, S. Minnert: *XML in der Praxis. Professionelles Web-Publishing mit der Extensible Markup Language*; Addison-Wesley Verlag, München, 2000
3.   C. Altenhofen: Document Reengineering: Der Pfad der Altbestände in eine strukturierte Zukunft, Vortrag im Rahmen der T.I.E.M. '97, 11.-13. Juni 1997, Wart
4.   H. Lobin: Informationsmodellierung in XML und SGML. Springer-Verlag, Berlin - Heidelberg - New York, 2001
5.   http://xml.coverpages.org/xmlApplications.html; last visited 2003-02-21
6.   P. Soto, Text Mining : Beyond Search Technology, DB2 magazine online; available at http://www.db2mag.com/db_area/archives/1998/q3/98fsoto.shtml; last visited 2003-01-30
7.   H. Ahonen: Automatic generation of SGML content models, Electronic Publishing -- Origination, Dissemination and Design, 8(2\&3), 195--206, Wiley Publishers, 1996; available at http://www.cs.helsinki.fi/~hahonen/helena_ep96.ps; last visited 2003-01-30
8.   H. Ahonen: Disambiguation of SGML content models, Proceedings of the Workshop on Principles of Document Processing '96, 23. September, Palo Alto, USA, 1996; available at http://www.cs.helsinki.fi/~hahonen/ahonen_podp96.ps; last visited 2003-01-30
9.   H. Ahonen: Generating Grammars for Structured Documents Using Grammatical Inference Methods, PhD-Thesis, Series of Publications A, Report A-1996-4, Department of Computer Science, University of Helsinki, November 1996; available at http://www.cs.Helsinki.FI/u/hahonen/fogram.ps.gz; last visited 2003-01-30
10. H. Ahonen, B. Heikkinen, O. Heinonen, M. Klemettinen: Improving the Accessibility of SGML-Documents - A Content-analytical Approach, SGML Europe ´97, S.321-327, CGA, Mai 1997; available at
      http://www.cs.helsinki.fi/u/oheinone/publications/Improving_the_Accessibility_of_ SGML_Documents_-_A_Content-analytical_Approach.ps.gz; last visited 2003-01-30
11. B. Klein, P. Fankhauser, Error tolerant Document Structure Analysis, GMD-IPSI Darmstadt, P-97-18, in: International Journal on Digital Libraries, 1(4):344-357, December 1997
12. H. Ahonen, O. Heinonen, M. Klemettinen, A.I. Verkamo: Applying Data Mining Techniques in Text Analysis, Report C-1997-23, Department of Computer Science, University of Helsinki, 1997; available at
      http://www.cs.helsinki.fi/u/oheinone/publications/ Applying_Data_Mining_Techniques_in_Text_Analysis.ps.gz; last visited 2003-01-30
13. B. Heikkinen, Generalization of Document Structures and Document Assembly, PhD-Thesis, Series of Publications A, Report A-2000-2, Department of Computer Science, University of Helsinki, April 2000; available at http://www.cs.Helsinki.FI/u/bheikkin/ bh_thesis.zip; last visited 2003-01-30
14. O. Zeigermann, Strukturierte Transformation, Diploma thesis at the University of Hamburg, Department of Computer Science, February 2000
15. http://www.vftis.com; last visited 2003-01-30
16. http://www.docconsult.de; last visited 2003-02-28
17. http://www.stellent.com; last visited 2003-02-07
18. Autonomy Technology White Paper, Autonomy Corporation 2000, http://www.autonomy.com/echo/userfile/germanwhitepaper.pdf, last download 2000-11-13
19. http://www-3.ibm.com/software/data/iminer/; last visited 2003-02-07
20. http://www.temis-group.com/; last visited 2003-02-07
21. http://www.inxight.com; last visited 2003-02-07

234   J. Drawehn et al.

22. P. Ludemann, Enhancing Searching and Content Management with XML Tags and Linguistic Processing, WhitePaper of Inxight Software, Inc. 2000, available at http://www.firstworld.net/~ludemann/XML.html; last visited 2003-02-07
23. http://www.inxight.com/products/oem/linguistx/index.php; last visited 2003-02-07
24. http://www.omnimark.com/home/home.html; last visited 2003-02-07
25. http://www.zeigermann.de/xtal; last visited 2003-02-07
26. http://www.antlr.org/; last visited 2003-01-30
27. ftp://ftp.ifi.uio.no/pub/SGML/Rainbow/; last visited 2003-01-31
28. Aufbereitung unstrukturierter Dokumentinhalte; in: Bullinger, H.-J. (IAO) ; Weisbecker, A.: Content Management - Digitale Inhalte als Bausteine einer vernetzten Welt; Fraunhofer IRB Verlag, Stuttgart, 2002, S.1-7
29. C. Altenhofen: Semi-automatische Informationsstrukturierung in 'Adaptive-READ'; presentation in the XML user panel of the tekom annual conference, 2002-11-20, proceedings of the conference, pg. 61-63

Inspecting Document Collections

Ulrich Bohnacker, Jürgen Franke, Heike Mogg-Schneider, Ingrid Renz

DaimlerChrysler AG, Research Center Ulm,
Institute of Information Technology,
Department of Information Mining, RIC/AM
Postfach 23 60, 89013 Ulm, Germany
{ulrich.bohnacker, juergen.franke, ingrid.renz,
heike.mogg-schneider}@daimlerchrysler.com

Abstract. The paper introduces two procedures which allow information seekers to inspect large document collections. The first method structures document collections into sensible groups. Here, three different approaches are presented: grouping based on the topology of the collection (i.e. linking and directory structure of intranet documents), grouping based on the content of the documents (i.e. similarity relation), and grouping based on the reader's behavior when using the document collection. After the formation of groups, the second method supports readers by characterizing text through extracting short and relevant information from single documents and groups. Using statistical approaches, representative keywords of each document and also of the document groups are calculated. Later, the most important sentences from single documents and document groups are extracted as summaries. Geared to the different information needs, algorithms for indicative, informative, and thematic summaries are developed. In this process, special care is taken to generate readable and sensible summaries. Finally, we present three applications which utilize these procedures to fulfill various information-seeking needs.

1 Motivation

In the past, the key problem in information acquisition was to achieve access to written documents (papers, books); yet nowadays with the access to the internet, intranet, and intra-company textual databases, this is no longer an obstacle. Today the main focus is on getting the "right" (personalized and extracted) information without undue effort. The approach described in this paper is to help the user in inspecting document collections by condensing the information contained in the collection. The initial approach is to group the collection into sensible parts from different perspectives, analyzing the topological structure of the collection, the content of the documents or how the reader uses the documents. The second step is to characterize these groups and the individual documents by means of characteristic words (keywords) and by a summary of the contents.

Algorithms of corpus-based linguistics, information retrieval, and statistical pattern recognition are employed to compute the similarity of texts in a given electronic text collection. The chief characteristic of our approach is that no external knowledge

A. Dengel et al. (Eds.): Adaptive READ Research Project, LNCS 2956, pp. 235-251, 2004.

(lexicon, terminology, concepts, etc.) is used. It's based solely on knowledge internal to the collection (i.e. statistics). The system automatically adapts to any collection (unsupervised learning). Therefore the technology can be utilized for texts in any language and on any subject.

The paper is structured as follows: first the basic technology is sketched, i.e. how documents are transformed into a mathematical representation so that various mathematical and pattern recognition-based approaches such as the calculation of similarity, clustering and categorization can be applied. Then different approaches to group documents in a collection are introduced. One concept groups documents by the topological link structure of the documents in a file system, whereas the second structures the collection using some kind of similarity measures. The third approach is to form groups on the basis of user profiles and activities. In the third part of the paper, approaches targeting characterization of documents and document groups by automatically generated keywords and summaries are introduced. Real-world applications of the approaches proposed are described at the end of the paper.

2   Basic Technology: The Vector Space Model

In information retrieval [10], the vector space model is widely used for representing textual documents and queries. Given a document collection, a set of terms or features has to be defined. Then, for each document, a (high-dimensional, sparsely filled) vector is generated from this feature set together with the associated weights. The weights are usually computed by methods such as *tfidf* weighting (i.e. raw term frequency *tf* in given document multiplied by the inverse document frequency *idf* in the overall collection).

The most common text features are (a subset of all) the words the texts at hand consist of. When these words are fractionalized into overlapping strings of a given length N (here: 4), N-grams (here: quadgrams) result as a second feature representation. For example, the word *feature* consists of 6 quadgrams: *_fea, feat, eatu, atur, ture, ure_*. As a consequence, the completely different word strings *features* and *feature* have 5 quadgrams in common (and are therefore similar in the vector space model). N-grams are tolerant of textual errors [4] but also well-suited for inflectionally rich languages such as German. Computation of N-grams is fast, robust, and completely independent of language or domain. In the following, we exclusively consider quadgrams beneath the word features as experience gained in various experiments on our document collections have shown that they by far top trigrams.

Thus, the first procedure is simply to count all the words and quadgrams which occur in each document and in the entire collection. This yields two lexica (words, quadgrams) with the frequency (text frequency *tf* and document frequency *df*) of the items we call these features *texels* (*text el*ements). Apart from these texel lexica generated for the whole collection for each document, two texel vectors are generated: they include the information about the occurrence and frequencies of words and quadgrams in the document.

As the only external knowledge base, we can define linguistically motivated stopwords such as the articles, prepositions, conjunctions (e.g. the, in, and) in addition to application-specific stopwords (e.g. car, accident, brake in the application of accident reports). The number of texels in practical applications (see section 5) is enormously high (~150,000 for full forms and more than 350,000 for quadgrams), too high for the subsequent computing step. Therefore, next, most of the texels in the lexica are eliminated using the *df* values. The criterion is to eliminate very frequent and very infrequent items from the further processing, see [6]. As a consequence of Zipf's Law, about half of the texels only occur once in the whole collection, see [12]. The typical lengths of the resulting feature lexicon and vectors range in our applications (see section 4) from 1,000 to 20,000.

After feature extraction, each document is represented through a feature vector containing real values calculated using the *tfidf* method [6].

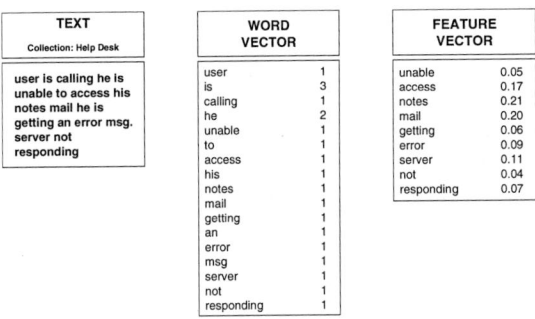

Fig. 1. Example of a text and its texel and feature vector representation

Typically the number of different words and quadgrams in a single document is small, so its representation in feature vector space is sparse (most of the vector components are zero). These so-defined feature vectors (two for each document: words and quadgrams) are the foundation for all the computations employed to define the groups of documents, keywords, and extracted summaries explained in the paper.

3   Grouping Document Collections

A basic task in searching for information in document collection is similar to that of search engines in the internet: to find relevant documents for a query. In more closed environments such as the intranet or when inspecting document collections, e.g. customer relationship management or repair orders, other interesting tasks can be solved. For a collection of documents, it may be sensible to search for the most relevant topics which occur in the collection. So the issue is not to obtain an answer to a query but instead an overview about what a relevant problem is, e.g. in customer complaints or in repair reports. For this reason, different algorithms were developed to group documents in a collection (explained in this section) and to characterize these groups by means of keywords or summaries, see section 4. First, three different approaches to group collections are discussed:

- Grouping by structure
  In this approach the topological structure of the collection is analyzed. The structure is given by the links the owners of the documents have drawn individually.
- Grouping by content
  The main idea with this grouping is to analyze the content of the documents with text mining methods in order to find textually sensible groups by measuring the similarity between the documents.
- Grouping by usage
  This grouping is done individually by the reader of documents by following the personal click path or by storing reading preferences and, therefore, adapting to a single user's behavior.

3.1   Grouping by Structure

When developing our intranet retrieval tool WIR (see section 5.1), we found two interesting results:

- Many documents were too small (length of textual information) to gain any statistical relevance within the WIR system.
- Many documents do not contain valuable information for the reader when considered alone: they are only useful when embedded in their environments (e.g. a frame set).

Hence, we developed a method which is able to detect groups of documents by analyzing the topological structure of the HTML files in the collection instead of analyzing the content with the vector space model. For details, see [2]. We call these groups of documents a logical document. The algorithms are based on the link structure between these files and the frame set definition in the files. A collection of linked HTML files can be regarded as a graph, with the files representing the nodes and the links considered directed edges. In our application, we implemented and developed the approach for HTML-linked documents. Most algorithms can be deployed for any linked document collection.

The link graph: In HTML a link is coded as hyperlink within a source file and points to a destination file. The first task is to transform a set of files into a computable representation of the link graph. Since there are different types of links, different types of edges have to be created.

From hyperlinks to typed graph edges: A node is created for every file (document) in the collection and, by parsing the files for each node, the outgoing links are determined. Each edge is assigned typed information about which link type it represents.

Adding implicit edges: A special problem with links to or inside HTML frames is that the underlying link structure has to be enhanced, since the defined link structure in the documents does not directly match what a user sees on the screen. Therefore we added implicit links as depicted in figure 2. This approach works not only for simple but also for nested frame sets.

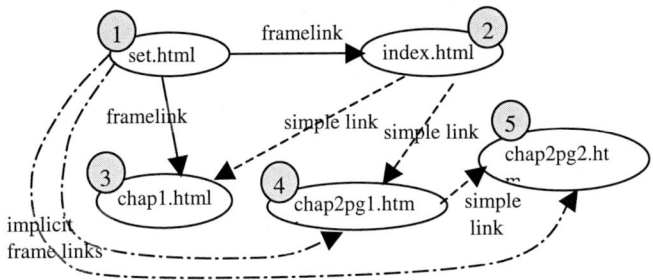

Fig. 2. A typical link structure of a frame set with added implicit edges (dotted-dashed lines).

From typed graph edges to weighted graph edges: When examining how HTML files are organized in intranets or in the internet, we found certain statements to be true in most cases, e.g:

- Files in the same frame set have a strong relationship due to the fact that the user can see them at the same time in the same browser window.
- Files with bi-directional hyperlinks - file *A* has a link to file *B* and file *B* has a link to file *A* - are more closely related than files with a simple uni-directional hyperlink, see also [2].

Thus the typed edges are transferred to edge weights using a lookup table. The table is determined manually by statements such as those above and by their importance to linking documents to a group: different types of links (hyperlinks, frame links, etc.). Additionally some heuristic rules utilize the location of the linked files in the file system.

Detecting sub-graphs: When the overall weighted graph structure has been built, the sub-graphs which are the logical documents have to be detected. A heuristic clustering algorithm defines the sub-graphs by means of the stronger links present between each other than with any neighboring nodes not in the sub-graph. When detecting sub-graphs, a number of aspects has to be taken into account:

- We have to define criteria in order to place a value on how good a hypothesis for a sub-graph is. These criteria are modeled as a combination of fuzzy valuation functions. Some of these criteria are largely dependent on the application.
- We have to come up with an algorithm that finds a division of the graph into good sub-graphs according to the valuation function. Due to the size of the graph - some 10,000 files - we use a heuristically straightforward algorithm, looking only a single step ahead to find a good solution without running into combinatorial problems.

- We prefer a bottom-up approach starting with each file being a logical document, as most of the files represent a logical unit of its own even when they contain links to other files.

Valuation functions: For the above algorithm, it is essential to calculate a value to decide whether logical sets should be merged or not, at the end of the process, all the documents of an intranet will be contained in a single logical document:

- Weights of all edges in the logical set $-f_1$
- Number of nodes in the logical set $-f_2$
- Amount of text counted in words $-f_3$
- Weights of the connecting edges between the sub-collections D_k and D_l-f_4
- Nodes with incoming edges $-f_5$

These functions are combined in a valuation function (1). The parameters of the function must be adapted to a collection and cannot be determined generally, for details see [2].

$$f_{VAL} = f_1 * \frac{f_2 + f_3}{2} * f_4 * \left(\frac{n}{x} * f_5 + \left(1 - \frac{n}{x} \right) \right). \tag{1}$$

Finding the core node: When the logical sets are defined, their core nodes (central document) have to be determined. The core node is a node that represents an entry point for the logical document. In general such an entry point should fulfill two requirements:

- It should provide a kind of introduction, overview or table of contents for the logical document.
- A user should be able to reach all parts of the logical document in the easiest possible manner.

Since we are not automatically able to check the first requirement without knowledge of the documents contents, we rely on the second. In HTML all the other nodes of the logical document must be reachable from the core node via links – a link path – inside the logical document. This allows a user to browse the whole logical document without leaving it, starting from the core node.

Again some criteria are modeled as fuzzy functions and then combined using methods of fuzzy logic. All nodes of a logical document are valued with this combination of fuzzy functions, and the best node is considered to be the core node.

Evaluation: We tested the above algorithms on an intranet with about 50,000 HTML files and evaluated the logical documents generated. In most cases, the grouped logical documents were sensible except for the documents found in archives as they were not linked by content but for archival reasons. In the WIR system, a logical document is presented to the reader by its core file with a list of all the documents included in the logical document added. As set out in section 4, the keywords and summaries are determined for the complete set of documents.

3.2   Grouping by Content

The underlying idea of this approach is to find interesting groups in a collection of documents by analyzing the content of the documents. The aim of this grouping is, for example, to detect previously unknown topics in a collection by clustering or to track relevant topics in a growing collection or in an intranet by categorization. This thus makes it possible to present an overview for a collection and to identify top-ten topics. Sometimes it is not the large groups containing "normal" information that are of interest but the more abnormal information that is of relevance: so it becomes important to detect outliers.

First we focus on clustering approaches. In all these grouping applications it is important to characterize the text groups through short informational units such as keywords and summaries for the group, see section 4, and to define a representative text as is explained in this section.

In our approach toward grouping documents by their similarity, all the calculations in clustering or categorizing the documents are performed with the feature vectors defined in section 2, i.e. feature vectors calculated using *tfidf* from the word and quadgram statistics of the single documents and the overall collection. Apart from measuring the Euclidean distance between feature vectors, we also employ the cosine similarity measure:

$$\cos(a,b) = \frac{a^T * b}{|a| * |b|} = \frac{a^T}{|a|} * \frac{b}{|b|}$$

The advantage of the cosine is that only those components of the vectors are relevant for calculation where non-zero values occur in both vectors. As mentioned earlier, the feature vectors of documents are sparse, allowing the number of calculations to be reduced dramatically by choosing the cosine measure. For the cosine similarity the vectors have to be normalized to a vector of length 1, which can be done for all feature vectors as an initial procedure. The effect of this is that the cosine similarity between two vectors remains unchanged even if one of the initial feature vectors is multiplied by a factor. Thus, this normalization equalizes the length of documents (number of word or quadgrams): given a new text with a feature vector in which each feature has twice as large values, the similarity still remains equal.

The standard representation, i.e. for each document a feature vector is stored in the file system, can be transformed to an inverted file, see [13]. The inversion of the information is done by storing, feature by feature, the documents in which they occur. This technical transformation enables the calculation of the cosine similarities to be sped up significantly.

All these preliminary steps are carried out to calculate the similarities between all pairs of documents for both representations (words, quadgrams) and to store them in a similarity matrix. Such a similarity matrix (sometimes a matrix containing the combined similarity values from the word and quadgram approach is used) is the input for the clustering process. For our system, the complete link and the group average clustering algorithms are employed [11]. At the end of the clustering process, a tree is generated, representing the cluster steps and the compactness of the clusters.

By customizing different parameters to the specific application, the cluster tree can be cut at different compactness levels, generating different sets of cluster subsets.

To find out which subset partition is most suitable for a special application and to gain a quick insight into the subsets, an overview report can be generated. Essential for these reports are the group specific keywords and summaries generated by the methods set out in section 4. As stated in the preceding section, the central document for a group is then determined. For this purpose, all the feature vectors of a group are added to the mean vector, also normalized to length 1, representing an unreal (artificial) document $\underline{f}$. Then all similarities between $\underline{f}$ and the members of its group are determined by means of the inverted file representation of the cosine similarity. The most similar one is regarded as the central document of the collection. In the presentation of the group, all its documents can be sorted by this similarity measure, enabling the reader to derive most of the information about the group by reading only the most similar ones. Moreover, if interested in outliers, the reader need only inspect the most dissimilar (documents at the end of the group list).

Should some of these automatically found cluster groups (topics) be of general interest for the users, they can be exploited to define categories. With the aid of such categories, a classifier can be trained to investigate new documents for these topics. The adaptation of such a classifier can be done with well-known approaches such as multi-reference classifiers or support vector machines.

3.3   Grouping by Usage

The above methods are static methods that neither promote nor allow any kind of interaction with the information-seeker. In this section we sketch how the user's activities can be evaluated to generate dynamic subsets in the collection in order to improve the search process for documents and to adapt the keyword and summarizing process to the user's needs. The basic idea is that the user defines groups which do not exist in the collection by their structure or contents.

We focused on two approaches toward grouping the documents according to the individual user's needs:

- Building and storing user profiles on the basis of user feedback (see section 5.2, Infobroker)
- Building ad-hoc user profiles by tracking the user's click path when browsing the intranet (see section 5.1, Weaving Intranet Relations)

In the first approach, the user helps the system by choosing different news categories of particular personal interest. Through daily usage of the Infobroker system, i.e. the reading of suggested articles and a possible response to characterizing an article as interesting, the system builds user profiles which are stored in a database for administration purposes. Even the response of the user stating that an article is not relevant can be utilized, allowing collection of negative examples of documents. With the different profiles for each category that the reader is interested in, the system can sort the daily news through the items' positive and negative similarity to the positive and negative feedback of the user. This grouping of the documents into categories and a proximity to the user's profile permits the generated keywords and summaries to be optimized by a more personalized extraction (see section 4). The benefit of this approach is that it enables the documents to be grouped and characterized differently for each user of the system.

In the second approach the system does not interact directly with the user, instead analyzing the user's activities by storing the click path. The tracking of the click path can be implemented via cookies. When the user searches for related documents, the query document (see sect. 5.1) together with each document of the list of related documents then forms individual groups of documents. When the user continues the search for information by searching again for related documents from a document on the list, the system acquires a chain of documents that the user is interested in. This chain can be interpreted as a group of related documents from the user's point of view. So the information in the documents in the chain can be taken to adapt the algorithms for determining the keywords and summaries for the documents in the list of similar documents. With this approach, readers obtain individually adapted descriptions of the documents that focus on their particular needs.

4   Characterizing Document Collections

Grouping text documents according to their structural relations, content or usage is necessary to inspect document collections. Yet these groups also have to be examined and an overview of their content has to be generated. Such an overview serves to inform the information-seeker who cannot scan any proposed document or document group.

To sum up, we need methods which characterize documents and document groups through concise and pertinent information. Since our approach must be able to analyze arbitrary document collections, techniques which do not need external information but extract information from the collections themselves instead are strongly preferred.

As result of such document condensation approaches, not only single words, i.e. keywords, but also whole extracts, i.e. summaries compiled from sentences or paragraphs, are selected and presented as the most informative text parts for the current reader or current task. In the following we outline a number of aspects of keyword and summary extraction from arbitrary document collections.

4.1   Characterization by Keywords

A major feature of many text mining systems is their ability to characterize text by keywords as the simplest kind of text condensation.

An extensive survey of summarization is set out in [5], where topic identification as a type of a summary also subsumes keyword extraction. As best-known approaches, the author lists position method, cue phrase indicator criteria, frequency criteria, and connectedness criteria. These approaches differ according to the resources they need and with respect to the universality of application. Position method is certainly restricted to specific genres. Both cue phrase indicator criteria and connectedness criteria call for language-specific resources: in the former case, simple lists may be sufficient, but in the latter, an in-depth linguistic analysis is needed. Only topic identification based on frequency criteria can be generally applied to any given document or document collection. This property is essential if keyword extraction is to be applied to an arbitrary document collection. Here, an efficient and effective keyword extraction method which is language, domain, genre, and application independent is needed.

As stated in section 2 where we introduced the vector space model, we represent a document not only through its words, but also (and this is of paramount importance here) through the quadgrams associated with their *tfidf* weights. Now, the basic idea for extracting keywords is that smaller text units indicate the importance of bigger ones, i.e. that weighted quadgrams indicate relevant words. For example, given that in a document quadgrams such as *cate, tego, izat* are highly weighted, then words such as *categorization* (3 hits), *categorize, category,* and *categories* (2 hits) which contain these quadgrams are relevant.

We pursued this approach both for single documents and for whole document groups (built by content as well as by structure or usage – see section 3). Since a document is represented by vectors of word and quadgram weights, a document group can be represented by a summarized vector which adds up the word and quadgram weights of its respective documents. For this calculation, the relations between the documents may also be incorporated by weighting their feature weights as a function of their similarity. Thus, our keyword extraction was found applicable not only for single documents but also for document groups. Furthermore, when a personalized document group is given, the extracted keywords are also adapted to this specific information requirement. This applies to documents which are grouped by usage, for example by analyzing their click path when browsing through a document collection (see section 3.3). Here, the distance of the documents in the click path together with their content-based similarity is integrated into the weights of the keywords. In any event, both document groups and single documents are represented by a quadgram feature vector.

Our algorithm for keyword extraction basically adds up the *tfidf* weights of all (n) quadgrams which the word contains in order to compute the weight of a keyword. However, this pushes the scale in favor of longer words, which consist of more quadgrams. Therefore, a normalization is needed. Yet normalization to word length strongly penalizes long words, so that normalization to the logarithm of word length adjusts this drawback. But since the number of all the quadgrams in a collection is too great to be handled in the vector space model, feature selection chooses only the most relevant ones (e.g. by *tfidf* weights) as features, see section 2. Thus, not all quadgrams are available after feature selection and can be used for keyword extraction. We exploit this fact for normalization and use, as measure for keyword selection, the sum of the weights of quadgram features contained in a word divided by the number of quadgrams features (n) in this word.

Normalization to number of quadgram features:

$$Weight_{Word} = \frac{\sum_{i=1}^{n} Weight_{Quadgram}(i)}{n} \tag{2}$$

A second modification of the basic idea is needed: the presented quadgram-based keyword extraction suffers from "word similarities". The above example illustrates that highly weighted quadgrams often appear in (inflectionally or morphologically) related words. In order to optimize the information content of the keywords presented, these related words must be identified and only a single representative should be presented to a reader.

A simple, fast, and general algorithm to identify similar word forms is the edit or Levenshtein distance [7]. Here, the number of edit operations (deleting or inserting one character) which are needed to transform one word form (W_1) into another (W_2) is counted. When computing the word distance (D_{Lev}), the lengths of the word forms have to be considered, as well.

Levensthein Distance:

$$D_{Lev}(W_1, W_2) = \frac{\sum EditOps(W_1, W_2)}{Length(W_1) + Length(W_2)} \tag{3}$$

If two keywords (W_1, W_2) have a low distance, the less frequent keyword is removed. But how do we then handle the weight of the remaining keyword? Certainly, its weight should be augmented in order to incorporate the weight of the removed keyword. Yet adding both weights may overshoot the scope of weights ($[0,1]$). Therefore, we employ a formula based on Einstein's velocity addition relationship. It has the needed properties to augment the weight without exceeding the scope:

$$Weight_{total} = \frac{Weight_1 + Weight_2}{1 + Weight_1 * Weight_2} \tag{4}$$

In order to evaluate our quadgram-based keyword extraction, we compared it to the other resource-free, language- and domain-independent extraction method: the one based on frequency criteria, i.e. we choose words with the highest *tfidf* measure as keywords, in the following called *tfidf-keywords*.

Runtime properties: On a Pentium II, 400 MHz computer used for the analysis of 45,000 intranet documents, the step of keyword extraction took 115 (under two minutes) seconds using tfidf-keywords and 848 seconds using quadgram-based keywords.

Quality of keywords: A general measure similar to recall/precision in information retrieval basically cannot be defined since the readers' evaluation of quality is extremely subjective. Inspecting keywords from concrete documents show that, among the top 10 keywords, approximately 30% are not merely tfidf-keywords, they are also quadgram-based keywords. It thus follows that roughly 70% are different.

Context sensitiveness: We investigated which keywords would be computed if the document were to be situated in different collections. In our experimental setup, we took an arbitrary 10,000 documents (set 1) and 2,000 documents (set 2) from the original exemplary collection (45,000 documents). Analyzing keywords of documents belonging to each set showed that quadgram-based keywords are quite insensitive to their collection, i.e. barely any difference was found. In contrast, tfidf-keywords change to a greater extent. This is a consequence of the used *tfidf* measure employed, where document frequency of a word directly plays a crucial role. For quadgram-based keywords, the document frequency of quadgrams is only indirectly used. For more information about the above approach, see [ficzay].

4.2 Characterization by Summary

To discover what a document or document group is about, single words may offer a first glance at the content. But for a deeper understanding, more than just the keywords are required: this necessitates some kind of summarization, i.e. a briefer text than the original document or document group.

Several approaches toward minimizing the content of documents are reported in [8]. Basically, two approaches can be distinguished: summarization consisting of parts of the original documents, i.e. extracting, and summarization creating new text, i.e. abstracting. Whereas abstracting calls for a deeper text understanding than our statistical text mining approach allows, extracting is an appropriate technique which fits in well with the general vector space model (see section 2).

As for extracting keywords, the basic idea for generating a text extract is that smaller text units indicate the importance of bigger ones. Here, we pursue the notion that highly weighted words of a document refer to relevant sentences which, together, build a good summary of the document in question.

However, in contrast to keyword generation, summary generation based on extracted sentences poses a few tricky problems. First, a document has to be separated into sentences, meaning that examining the punctuation marks is a starting point which must be complemented by heuristic rules. But not every sentence can be correctly found, and not everything that is detected is a sentence. Given more or less proper sentences, these sentences are linked to each other by text-coherent means such as anaphora. When these text-coherent means are ignored, the extracted sentences lose their readability, i.e. they cannot be understood when standing alone. The resolution of anaphora is not possible in our statistically-based text mining approach, but detecting whether a sentence contains them can be done. In the case of such an anaphora-containing sentence, either the previous, hopefully anaphora-free sentence must also be presented or the summary must do without this sentence.

Thus, instead of weighting relevant sentences based solely on the weights of their words, further heuristic parameters need to be integrated: the number and kind of anaphora and related text-coherent means; a sentence length that is not too long or too short; a preferred sentence position at the beginning or the end of a text or paragraph against positioning in the middle.

When generating an extract from a whole document group instead of just one document, these considerations regarding key parameters for a relevant summary also apply. But a further pivotal aspect has to be kept in mind: while documents of whole groups have a lot of content in common, and this should not be repeated in the summary, these documents also contain different content, thus complementing one another.

A simple approach for multi-document summarization which avoids some of the afore-mentioned difficulties is the selection of a central document of the group to be used as the summary. This central document can easily be found by employing grouping techniques, see section 3. It is the centroid of a content-based group or the main text of a structure-based group. With such a central document as summary, neither anaphora nor repeating content pose a problem. Yet it is missing the content of all other documents belonging to the same group. Therefore, even if this central document is a good starting point for summarization, it needs enhancements to be able to serve as a good summary for a document group. Thus any irrelevant sentences from this central document have to be removed and relevant sentences from the other documents inserted.

A further key aspect of summarization is the intended purpose of the summary. Three different types are distinguished with respect to their common information needs: indicative, informative, and thematic summaries. Indicative summaries succinctly present only the most relevant content and are very short. Their aim is to provide readers with sufficient information to decide whether to continue reading the documents. Informative summaries are more extensive. They contain any relevant information from the original documents, aiming to replace them. The overall objective is that the reader does not need to read them. Both kinds of summaries are general, in terms of giving the same – indicative or informative – summary of the considered documents for any application. A more adaptive kind of summary is the thematic one: the theme or subject has to be specified (like a query) and the summary focuses on it. Consequently, given different subjects for the same documents, different thematic summaries are generated.

Our summarization approach is able to account for these distinctions. When ranking all the sentences of a document or document group, those sentences which are highest-ranked contain relevant information. Presenting this information then fulfills the demand for an indicative summary. An informative summary for a single document consists of all sentences with a weight greater than a given threshold. For a document group, an informative summary consists of its (condensed) central document enhanced by relevant sentences from the other documents. Finally, the characteristic typical of thematic summaries is included by computing the similarity of the subject with the documents.

Evaluation of a summarization technology is even more difficult than assessment of a keywording method: depending on the different tasks and readers, different summaries might be more or less adequate. In order to give an initial impression of their quality, we compiled a test suite of selected documents and document groups. Then our summarization technology and commercially available summarization tools were applied. In addition, summaries generated by a person were also part of the test suite. All these summaries were made anonymously and given to 15 readers who had to judge readability and relevance. As expected, all automatically generated summaries were less readable, but with respect to relevance, summaries computed using our approach were rated equally high as those chosen by humans (and higher than those of other summarization tools).

5   Applications

Electronic document collections which have to be inspected and analyzed play a key role in many knowledge-intensive processes. Efficient handling of important business tasks is strongly related to the fast access to and immediate handling of information. More and more today, intranet and internet applications are influencing our daily work. Further innovative services are contingent on an appropriate processing of documents and document collections.

In the following, we present three applications whose success is based on proper usage of the document-grouping and document-characterizing technologies introduced in the previous sections.

5.1   Intranet Retrieval Tool: Weaving Intranet Relations

Nowadays, intranets have come to play a vital role in large companies, and their impact on efficient business communication and administration as knowledge management tools is growing steadily. Thus at an early stage in a search, the intranet collection of texts, images, videos, etc. presented to the user may easily turn into a confusing mire of information. In this case, tools for inspecting document collections available on an intranet can be a great help for the processes of finding and integrating documents. General search tools can be integrated to help in finding documents containing the words of a query, but further collection-inspecting tools are still needed. Our retrieval tool Weaving Intranet Relations (WIR) makes innovative retrieval functions available.

For the typical reader of huge electronic document collections, the greatest proportion of the work is made up of finding the relevant information. This search usually involves looking for some user-defined words as search terms. Every text which contains these words is presented to the reader as a good candidate according to the inquiry. However, the chief problem is that the reader has to know the exact words the author wrote. And in new and innovative areas, in particular, this is a difficult task.

This is the major reason why a fully text-oriented retrieval more often leads to better results and is preferable whenever the amount of the data collection is estimable and similarity computation is feasible within an acceptable time frame. Due to this, we employ the deductive method of computing text relations from a large collection of documents as the foundation for intranet retrieval. These text relations may be based on the content (see section 3.2) or on the structure (see section 3.1) of the document collection. Whereas structural relations help to define which files together belong to a text document, content-based relations define which documents are thematically related.

For the information-seeker, our retrieval tool presents, for a given text (i.e. a query consisting not only out a few words or concepts), all the thematically related documents. This query text might be in the form of single words just as in a common search engine, yet the approach is geared for entire documents or document groups. The presentation of these retrieved documents utilizes extracted keywords and summaries to give an initial impression of the content. This serves to facilitate the reader's decision as to whether a document is relevant.

The system architecture of our retrieval tool is divided into an offline computation which calculates relevant characteristics and relations of the texts and an online inspection of this information aligned with a given query (i.e. a text).

This retrieval tool was transferred to an intranet of more than 100,000 pages. A number of additional monitoring and feedback processes were implemented: the monitoring makes the system robust and practical in its everyday use, the feedback yields the only real evaluation information - the opinion of the intranet readers.

5.2   News Assistant: Infobroker

Electronic news articles are available from many internet sources. Conventional news providers such as newspapers and magazines as well as broadcasting corporations put their content into various media (text, audio, video) on internet servers where the interested public can satisfy its information needs.

For this task, we developed an electronic news assistant, the Infobroker, a tool which presents an individualized information offering based on electronically available written news articles. Basically, this tool explores the readers' interests and offers the current news re-ranked according to the readers' information needs. The ranking of the news is again a kind of grouping documents, here based on the reader's behavior.

The first step for a reader who wants to use Infobroker is to personalize a few settings: the choice of the article sources, i.e. the magazines or newspapers articles are to be taken from, and the choice of categories, for example: sports or lifestyle, politics or business news. Here, the reader defines the kind of news to be presented by Infobroker. The second step is to continuously utilize Infobroker. Initially, all the articles from the selected sources and categories are presented, together with characterizing information like keywords and summaries. Some of these articles might be of interest for the reader – and are read. Then Infobroker remembers these articles and automatically builds a user profile based on these articles (and considering their categories and sources). Whereas this profile develops passively, i.e. without any further action on the reader's part except for the reading itself, an active adaptation is possible by giving feedback about the article ("interesting", "not interesting"). This feedback is optional, but it enhances customization of Infobroker to the reader. After a few days, the user profile is elaborated enough to weight all new articles. Then, the articles which correspond to the user profile are accorded a high priority and are re-ranked as the most relevant articles for this reader. However, also low-ranked articles are presented. Thus, a reader can choose to browse articles about previously unknown topics – further developing the user profile through the individual reading activities.

Both the user profiles and the articles managed by Infobroker are represented in our common vector space model. Apart from grouping based on usage (reading behavior), document-characterizing technology, i.e. keyword and summary extraction, is essential for this task.

Infobroker is deployed as a internal prototype which demonstrates innovative services for personalized information access.

5.3   Internet Retrieval Tool: Looking for Others – loofo

General search engines are able to retrieve billions of texts by using elaborate, but still superficial, technology. Specific search engines working locally on the document server (e.g. intranet) are able to analyze their texts more deeply but are restricted to the texts which are locally available. Our tool loofo "Looking for Others" tries to bridge this gap between generally usable tools and in-depth analysis. Starting from a retrieval tool for the analysis of intranet sites [1], we slightly modified this technology for text searches on any site (outside or inside the organization) that a reader specifies.

"Looking for Others - loofo" [3] is a server application with browser interface for the information-seeking reader. This interface allows users to define the search space (the sites) and to specify the texts to be found (according to a query which may consist of single words or even whole texts). Subsequently, the reader's task is finished, and the system takes over on the loofo server. There, it starts to acquire any text on the specified sites accessible by a link, transforms it into our internal vector representation, compares the query (also internally represented), and computes a ranked list with links to related texts characterized by keywords and summaries. After completing its search tasks, loofo sends an email with a result link to the reader.

This application was transferred to a department with global information-seeking tasks. Their internet investigations could be successfully supported with our approach.

6   Conclusion

The applications discussed show that document-inspecting technology based on the vector space model and on statistical methods is useful, efficient, and effective in supporting the wide variety of needs of readers.

Nevertheless, these approaches still leave room for improvement. A statistically-based analysis of word meaning might help not only to relate documents to each other but also to connect different words and word forms. This will lead to further insight into the content of documents and documents collections. Also a careful integration of knowledge-based methods should be considered. However, here, we must act with caution: we need to take care to conserve the benefits of our general, i.e. language-, domain-, genre-, and application-independent approaches based on pattern recognition, statistics, and information retrieval.

A further step is to look for other useful applications: numerous tasks and processes, may they be personal or professional, still lack appropriate support through provision of the right information at the right time. Here, document-inspecting technology which optimizes information access is essential and will be enhanced as called for in response to topical, real needs.

References

1. Bohnacker, U., Dehning, L., Franke, J., Renz, I., Schneider, R.: Weaving Intranet Relations - Managing Web Content. In: RIAO2000: Content-Based Multimedia Information Access, Paris (France) (2000) pp. 1744-1751.
2. Bohnacker, U., Schorr, A.: Finding Logically Connected Documents in a Large Collection of Files. In: IAWTIC 2001 - International Conference on Intelligent Agents, Web Technology and Internet Commerce, Las Vegas (USA) (2001).
3. Bohnacker, U., Renz, I.: Document Retrieval from User-Selected Web Sites. In: Proceedings of SIGIR - International Symposium on Information Retrieval, Toronto (Canada) (2003).
4. Cavnar, W., Trenkle, J.: N-Gram-Based Text Categorization. In: Proceedings of Symposium on Document Retrieval and Information Retrieval, Las Vegas (1994) pp. 161-175.
5. Hovy, E.: Automated Text Summarization. In: R. Mitkov (ed.). Oxford University Handbook of Computational Linguistics. Oxford: Oxford University Press (2002).
6. Joachims, T.: A Probabilistic Analysis of the Rocchio Algorithm with TFIDF for Text Categorization. Proceedings of ICML-97, 14th International Conference on Machine Learning (1996).
7. Levenshtein, V.: On the Minimal Redundancy of Binary Error-Correcting Codes. In: Information and Control, 28 (4) (1975) pp. 268-291.
8. Mani, I.: Automatic Summarization. John Benjamins Publishing Company Amsterdam (2001).
9. Renz, I., Ficzay, A., Hitzler, H.: Keyword Extraction for Text Characterization. In: Proceedings of NLDB'03 - 8th International Conference on Applications of Natural Language to Information Systems, Burg (Deutschland (2003).
10. Salton, G., McGill, M.: Introduction to Modern Information Retrieval. McGraw Hill (1983).
11. Späth, H.: Cluster Analysis algorithms For Data Reduction and Classification of Objects. England: John Ellis Horwood Limited (1980)
12. Zipf, G. K.: Human Behaviour and the Principle of Least Effort. Cambridge, Massachusetts, Addison Wesley (1949).
13. Zobel, J., Moffat, A., Sacks-Davis, R.: An efficient indexing technique for full-text database systems: Proc. International Conference on Very Large Databases, pp. 352--362, Vancouver, Canada, (1992).

Introducing Query Expansion Methods for Collaborative Information Retrieval

Armin Hust

German Research Center for Artificial Intelligence (DFKI GmbH)
P.O. Box 2080, 67608 Kaiserslautern, Germany
armin.hust@dfki.de

Abstract. The accuracy of ad-hoc document retrieval systems has plateaued in the last few years. At DFKI, we are working on so-called collaborative information retrieval (CIR) systems which unobtrusively learn from their users' search processes. We focus on a restricted setting in CIR in which only old queries and correct answer documents to these queries are available for improving a new query. For this restricted setting we propose new approaches for query expansion procedures. This paper describes query expansion methods to be used in collaborative information retrieval. We define collaborative information retrieval as a task, where an information retrieval system uses information gathered from previous search processes from one or several users to improve retrieval performance for the current user searching for information. We show how collaboration of individual users can improve overall information retrieval performance. Performance in this case is expressed in terms of quality and utility of the retrieved information regardless of specific user groups.

1   Introduction

In this section we introduce the research area of Collaborative Information Retrieval (CIR). We motivate and characterize the primary goals of this work, query expansion procedures for CIR and outline the structure and contents of this work.

1.1   Information Retrieval

Although Information Retrieval has now been studied for decades there is no clear and comprehensive definition for Information Retrieval.

One of the older definitions, referenced by Cornelius J. van Rijsbergen [50], refers to the book of F.W. Lancaster [31], where it is stated that "Information retrieval is the term conventionally, though somewhat inaccurately, applied to the type of activity discussed in this volume. An information retrieval system does not inform (i.e. change the knowledge of) the user on the subject of his inquiry. It merely informs on the existence (or non-existence) and whereabouts of documents relating to his request."

A newer definition, according to the IR-group of the German Informatics Society [14], states that "IR considers information systems according to their role in the knowledge transfer process from a human knowledge producer to an information seeker. The problems arising from vague queries and uncertain knowledge are the main focus of the IR-group. Vague Queries are characterized by the fact that answers to these queries

A. Dengel et al. (Eds.): Adaptive READ Research Project, LNCS 2956, pp. 252–280, 2004.

are a priori not uniquely defined (...). The uncertainty and/or the incompleteness of the knowledge often results from a restricted representation of its semantics, since the representation of the knowledge is not limited to some special forms (e.g. text documents, multimedia documents, facts, rules, semantic nets). Additionally IR considers applications where the stored knowledge itself may be uncertain or incomplete (e.g. technical or scientific data sets)" and states that "From these problems the necessity for an evaluation of the quality of the answers of an information system arises, where the utility of the system according to the support for the users with respect to solving their problems has to be considered."

This definition is very general. It stresses the vagueness and uncertainty of stored knowledge and queries. It also stresses the utility of the retrieved information for the users, helping them to solve their problems.

Utility is an idea introduced by the von Neumann-Morgenstern utility theory [53] and is closely connected with their idea of preference relations, both of which come from the field of economics. A preference relation and a utility function can be seen, from a global point of view, as equivalent for an informal and a formal description of the same concept. A preference relation is a partial order on a set of elements with a binary relation between each two elements. A preference relation can describe such statements like "situation B is better than situation A". Whereas a preference relation is only a qualitative measure, the idea of the utility function introduces the quantitative measure. The utility function assigns a number to each element of the set and allows us to compare the utility of these elements, i.e. the utility function adds a cardinality aspect to the preference relation aspect, such that one can say how useful the choice is. If we can formalize the utility function an a set of elements, then it naturally induces a preference relation on that set. In this sense the quality of the answers of an IR system can be measured.

Let us state an example to show the different preference relations users may have. A physician, a chemist and a lawyer may query an IR system for information about the medicament "Lipobay" or its American name "Baycol". While the physician may be interested in medication, indication and contra-indication, the chemist may by interested in chemical structure and undergoing reactions of the active ingredient; the lawyer may be interested in legal cases, lawsuits, court decisions and compensations. It is clear that each of these users has his or her own personal preferences as to which documents an IR system presents in response to the query. These preferences may also be influenced by the context the user is working in and it is clearly possible that they may change somehow over time.

Another research area overlapping with the IR area (see figure 1) is the usage of context knowledge for a more detailed specification of the information need. Because queries can be vague, it might be possible to use knowledge about the context the user is working in to influence the query processing and achieve better retrieval results. Some of the aspects of the user's context (according to [18]) are: which tasks the user is busy with at the time of the query, which documents have been viewed within the last few minutes, which document is currently being processed by the user. Research in this area integrates modelling and representation of the context information, and integrates this information into the IR processes.

Much work has been done on improving IR systems, in particular in the Text Retrieval Conference series (TREC) [49]. In 2000, it was decided at TREC-8 that this task should no longer be pursued within TREC, in particular because the accuracy has plateaued in the last few years [55]. We are working on new approaches which learn to improve retrieval effectiveness from the interaction of different users with the retrieval engine. Such systems may have the potential to overcome the current plateau in ad-hoc retrieval.

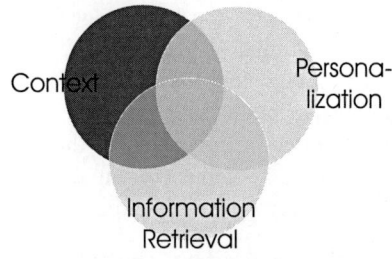

Fig. 1. Overlap of Research Areas

1.2   Collaborative Information Retrieval

The ultimate goal in IR is finding the documents that are useful to the information need expressed as a query. There is a natural preference relation, namely "document A is more useful than document B" or "documents A and B are equally useful" for the information need stated by the user. An approach for formalizing this preference relation is the concept of "relevance" introduced for quality measures of IR systems.

Here relevance has two meanings: On the one hand it means the judgements made by assessors to determine the documents which are satisfying the information need. As we will see later (in section 4.1) relevance judgements are established after experiments are carried out. Assessors review the documents that are retrieved by an experiment and judge the documents as either relevant or non-relevant to the information need expressed as a query. In doing so they neglect personal interests or context related information, thus ignoring personal preference relations a user may have (as stated in the example above) [55]. On the other hand a relevance value is computed as a numerical value and assigned to each of the documents presented by an IR system in response to a user's query. Then documents are ranked according to their relevance in the same way as currently done by web search engines. This so computed relevance value should reflect the user's preference relation.

We call our approach Collaborative Information Retrieval (CIR), learning to improve retrieval effectiveness from the interaction of different users with the retrieval engine. CIR on top of an IR system uses all the methodologies that have been developed in this research field. Moreover, CIR is a methodology where an IR system makes full use of all the additional information available in the system, especially

- the information from previous search processes, i.e. individual queries and complete search processes
- the relevance information gathered during previous search processes, independent of the method used to obtain this relevance information i.e. explicitly by user relevance feedback or implicitly by unobtrusively detected relevance information.

The collaborative aspect here differs from other collaborative processes. We don't assume that different users from a working team or a specific community collaborate loosely or tightly through some information exchange or workflow processes. Instead we assume that users can benefit from search processes carried out at former times by other users (although those users may not know about the other users and their search processes) as long as the relevance information gathered from these previous users has some significant meaning.

Figure 2 illustrates the general scenario of CIR. An information retrieval system is typically used by many users. A typical search in a retrieval system consists of several query formulations. Often, the answer documents to the first query do not directly satisfy the user so that he has to reformulate his query taking into consideration the answer documents found. Such refinement may consist of specializations as well as generalizations of previous queries. In general, satisfying an information need means going through a search process with many decisions on query reformulations. Hence gathering information for fulfilling the information need of a user is an expensive operation in terms of time required and resources used. The same expensive operation has to be carried out if another user has the same information need and thus initiates the same or a similar search process.

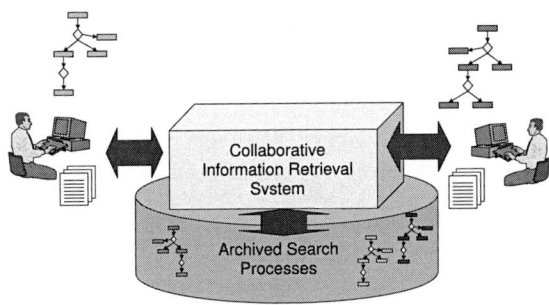

Fig. 2. Scenario of CIR

The idea of CIR is to store these search processes as well as the ratings of documents returned by the system (if available) in an archive. Subsequent users with similar interests and queries should then benefit from knowledge automatically acquired by the CIR system based on the stored search processes. This should result in shorter search processes and better retrieval quality for subsequent users if the following basic assumptions can be fulfilled by an CIR system:

- relevance judgements for retrieved documents can be derived from users' actions
- previous queries by some users will be useful to improve new queries for other users

Subject to these assumptions we expect that collaborative searches will improve overall retrieval quality for all users.

Thus we can see a CIR system as a trusted and experienced advisor where we request help for fulfilling our information need. We explain the new task to the system and hope that the advisor has gathered previous experiences with similar information needs.

Our query expansion methods for CIR realize the advisor: the users describe their information need as a query. We then find previous queries similar to the new query and the documents that have been judged as relevant to the previous queries. Instead of running the original query entered by the users we expand the query by terms gathered from relevant documents of previous queries.

1.3 Delimitation of Collaborative Information Filtering

The description here follows the papers of Alsaffar et al. [2], Olsson [34] and Tian et al. [48]. A comprehensive overview of research papers in the field of Information Filtering is available from Thornton [47]. The objective of information filtering (IF) is to classify/categorize documents as they arrive in the system. IF is the process that monitors documents as they enter the system and selects only those that match the user query (also known as a user profile). Thus, IF makes decisions about relevance or non-relevance rather than providing a ranked output list. In IF the document collection can be seen as a stream of documents trying to reach the user, and unwanted documents are removed from the stream. The collaborative approach, called Collaborative Information Filtering (CIF) takes into account user preferences of other "like-minded" users.

While in CIR as described above the user query is the central focus point, in CIF the documents are central. CIF can be described as a "push" technology, where documents are pushed against the user query (or user profile), while CIR is a "pull" technology, drawing the relevant documents from the collection.

1.4 Outline of This Work

In this work we limit ourselves to the text retrieval field, sometimes also called text mining, which is only a part of the information retrieval research area. As a first approach to CIR we also limit ourselves to developing, analyzing and evaluating algorithms which can be used for IR effectiveness improvements, based on individual queries which may be stated by different users. In this work we don't consider complete search processes of users, we especially ignore such vague queries, which can only be answered in dialogue by iterative reformulations of the queries (depending on the previous answers of the system).

This paper is organized as follows:

- section 2 describes related work in the field of query expansion.
- section 3 introduces the vector space model and query expansion procedures that have been developed for use in the vector space model.
- section 4 describes the document collections we use for evaluating our new algorithms and includes the evaluation of some basic IR procedures.
- section 5 introduces the environment of Collaborative Information Retrieval and describes the methodology used in the experiments and in the evaluation.
- section 6 shortly describes the algorithms that have been developed to be used in CIR.
- section 7 summarizes the improvements that we have achieved by our different algorithms.
- section 8 summarizes this paper, draws some conclusions, and shows the essential factors for improving retrieval performance in CIR.

2 Related Work

Research in the field of query expansion (QE) procedures has been done for several years now. Usage of short queries in IR produces a shortcoming in the number of documents ranked according to their similarity to the query. Users issuing short queries retrieve only a few relevant documents, since the number of ranked documents is related to the number of appropriate query terms. The more query terms, the more documents are retrieved and ranked according to their similarity to the query [36]. In cases where a high recall is critical, users seldom have many ways to restate their query to retrieve more relevant documents.

Thus IR systems try to reformulate the queries in a semi-automatic or automatic way. Several methods, called query expansion methods, have been proposed to cope with this problem [3], [32]. These methods fall into three categories: usage of feedback information from the user, usage of information derived locally from the set of initially retrieved documents, and usage of information derived globally from the document collection. The goal of all query expansion methods is to finally find the optimal query which selects all the relevant documents.

Research in the field of query expansion procedures has been done for several years now. Query expansion is the process of supplementing the original query with additional terms and should lead to an improvement in the performance of IR systems. This process also includes the reweighting of terms in a query after it has been enriched by additional terms. A lot of different procedures have been proposed for manual, automatic or interactive query expansion. Some of the first publications describing query expansion procedures are Sparck-Jones [46], Minker et al. [33] and Rijsbergen [50]. Some of the older procedures are described by Donna Harman in [17] and [16], experiments in the SMART systems have been described by Salton [42] and Buckley [5]. A comprehensive overview of newer procedures is available from Efthimiadis in [12]. Another newer technique, called local context analysis (LCA), was introduced by Xu and Croft in [60] and [61]. While pseudo relevance feedback assumes that all of the highly ranked documents are relevant, LCA assumes that only some of the top ranked documents initially retrieved for a query are relevant and analyzes these documents for term co-occurrences.

Newest procedures in the field of query expansion are dealing with query bases, a set of persistent past optimal queries, for investigating similarity measures between queries. The query base can be used either to answer user queries or to formulate optimal queries (refer to Raghavan, Sever and Alsaffar et al. in [37], [44] [2]). Wen et al. ([57] and [58]) are using query clustering techniques for discovering frequently asked questions or most popular topics on a search engine. This query clustering method makes use of user logs which allows to identify the documents the users have selected for a query. The similarity between two queries may be deduced from the common documents the users selected for them. Cui et al. [10] take into account the specific characteristics of web searching, where a large amount of user interaction information is recorded in the web query logs, which may be used for query expansion. Agichtein et al. [1] are learning search engine specific query transformations for question answering in the web.

Gathering relevance feedback is another field of research in this area. Automatic acquisition of relevance information is necessary for improving IR performance, since users are not willing or do not intend to give feedback about the relevance of retrieved documents. [59] compare two systems, where one is using explicit relevance feedback (where searchers explicitly have to mark documents relevant) and one is using implicit relevance feedback. They focus on the degree to which implicit evidence of document relevance can be substituted for explicit evidence. [24] acquires relevance information by merely using the clickthrough data while the documents presented to the user have been ranked by two different IR systems.

Work in the field of term weighting procedures has been done ever since IR research. The dynamics of term weights in different IR models have been discussed in [7], [8] and [6], going back to the work of [51] and [52]. The different models analyze the transfer of probabilities in the term space, mainly for, but not limited to, the probabilistic IR models.

3   Basics and Terminology

In this section we introduce the vector space model (VSM) which is employed in our work. We motivate the different techniques that have been applied to the VSM for performance improvements, since this is also the basic model for the development of our CIR methods. For further reading we recommend the books of Cornelius J. van Rijsbergen [50], Ricardo Baeza-Yates and Berthier Ribeiro-Neto [3] and Christopher D. Manning and Hinrich Schütze [32] and the new book from Reginald Ferber [13].

3.1   Vector Space Model

The vector space model, introduced by Salton [40], assigns weights to index terms in queries and in documents. These term weights are ultimately used to compute the degree of similarity between each document stored in the system and the user query. By sorting the retrieved documents in decreasing order of this degree of similarity, the vector space model takes into consideration documents which match the query terms only partially.

Definition 1 (Vector Space Model). *Documents as well as queries are represented by vectors in a vector space. The set of N documents is denoted by*

$$D = \{d_j | 1 \leq j \leq N\}, \tag{1}$$

the set of L queries is denoted by

$$Q = \{q_k | 1 \leq k \leq L\}. \tag{2}$$

Each individual document d_j is represented by its vector

$$d_j = (d_{1j}, d_{2j}, ..., d_{Mj})^T, \tag{3}$$

each individual query q_k is represented by its vector

$$q_k = (q_{1k}, q_{2k}, ..., q_{Mk})^T, \tag{4}$$

where M is the number of terms in the collection and T denotes the transpose of the vector.

Each position i in the vectors corresponds to a specific term t_i in the collection. The values d_{ij} or q_{ik} respectively indicate the weighted presence or absence of the respective term in the document d_j or query q_k. The weights d_{ij} and q_{ik} are all greater than or equal to 0.

Term weights d_{ij} and q_{ik} in equations (3) and (4) can be computed in many different ways. Different weighting schemes, so called tf-idf weighting schemes, have been developed by Salton and Buckley [41], the older work by Salton and McGill [43] reviews various term-weighting techniques. A newer work by Kolda [29], [30] evaluates different weighting schemes and compares the results achieved by each of the weighting methods. The main idea behind the most effective term weighting schemes is related to the basic principles of clustering techniques [43]. Moreover it allows the usage of different weighting schemes for the document representation and the query representation.

Despite its simplicity, the vector space model is a resilient ranking strategy with general collections. It yields ranked answer sets which are difficult to improve upon without query expansion or relevance feedback within the framework of the vector space model. A large variety of alternative ranking methods have been compared to the vector space model but the consensus seems to be that, in general, the vector space model is either superior or almost as good as the known alternatives. Furthermore, it is simple and fast. For these reasons, the vector space model is a popular retrieval model nowadays.

Definition 2 (Cosine Similarity). *The ranking function normally used in the vector space model is the so called **cosine-similarity**. The vector space model proposes to evaluate the degree of similarity of the document $d_j = (d_{1j}, d_{2j}, ..., d_{Mj})^T$ with regard to the query $q_k = (q_{1k}, q_{2k}, ..., q_{Mk})^T$ as the correlation between the vectors d_j and q_k. This correlation can be quantified, for instance, by the cosine of the angle between these two vectors. That is, the similarity* sim *between a document d_j and a given query q_k is measured by the cosine of the angle between these two M dimensional vectors:*

$$\mathrm{sim} : \mathbb{R}^M \times \mathbb{R}^M \to \mathbb{R}^+$$
$$(d_j, q_k) \mapsto \mathrm{sim}(d_j, q_k) \tag{5}$$

with

$$\mathrm{sim}(d_j, q_k) = \frac{d_j^T \cdot q_k}{\|d_j\| \cdot \|q_k\|} = \frac{\sum_{i=1}^{M} d_{ij} \cdot q_{ik}}{\|d_j\| \cdot \|q_k\|} \tag{6}$$

where $\| \cdot \|$ is the Euclidean norm of a vector. In the case that the vectors are already normalized (and hence have a unit length) the similarity is simply the scalar product between the two vectors d_j and q_k

$$\mathrm{sim}(d_j, q_k) = d_j^T \cdot q_k = \sum_{i=1}^{M} d_{ij} \cdot q_{ik} \tag{7}$$

Figure 3 illustrates (in the 2-dimensional space) the document and query vectors of unit length lying on the surface of the unit-hypersphere. The cosine of angle α measures the similarity between a document and a query.

For our purposes we also need to measure the similarity between documents (called inter-document similarity) and between queries (called inter-query similarity). The definitions are comparable to definition 2.

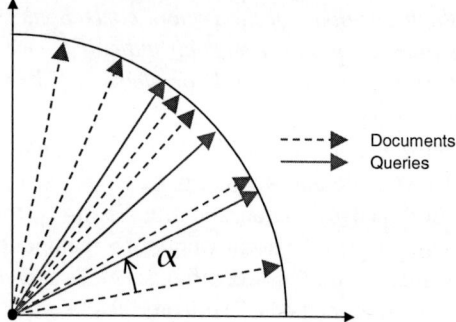

Fig. 3. Similarity and Distance of Documents and Queries

Definition 3 (Inter-Document and Inter-Query Similarity). *The similarity* sim *between two documents d_j and d_k and between two queries q_k and q_l is measured by the cosine of the angle between these two M dimensional vectors*

$$\text{sim} : \mathbb{R}^M \times \mathbb{R}^M \to \mathbb{R}^+$$
$$(d_j, d_k) \mapsto \text{sim}(d_j, d_k) \tag{8}$$

$$\text{sim} : \mathbb{R}^M \times \mathbb{R}^M \to \mathbb{R}^+$$
$$(q_k, q_l) \mapsto \text{sim}(q_k, q_l) \tag{9}$$

according to equations 5, 6 and 7.

3.2 Pseudo Relevance Feedback

Pseudo relevance feedback (PRF) avoids the interaction of the IR system with the user after the list of the retrieved documents is created in the first stage. PRF works in three stages: First documents are ranked according to their similarity to the original query. Then highly ranked documents are all assumed to be relevant (refer to [61]) and their terms (all of them or some highly weighted terms) are used for expanding the original query. Then documents are ranked again according to their similarity to the expanded query.

In this work we employ a variant of pseudo relevance feedback described by Kise et al. [25], [26]. In our comparisons with the newly developed methods, we will use the PRF method.

Let E be the set of document vectors given by

$$E = \left\{ d_j \middle| \frac{sim(d_j, q_k)}{\max_{1 \leq i \leq N}\{sim(d_i, q_k)\}} \geq \theta \right\} \tag{10}$$

where q_k is the original query and θ is a threshold parameter of the similarity. Then the sum D_k of the document vectors in E

$$D_k = \sum_{d_j \in E} d_j \tag{11}$$

is used as expansion terms for the original query. The expanded query vector q'_k is obtained by

$$q'_k = q_k + \alpha \frac{D_k}{\| D_k \|} \tag{12}$$

where α is a parameter for weighting the expansion terms. Then the documents are ranked again according to their similarity $sim(d_j, q'_k)$.

Parameters θ in equation (10) and α in equation (12) are tuning parameters. During evaluation best parameter value settings have been obtained by experiment and those which give the highest average precision were selected for comparison against other methods.

4   The Text Collections

In this section we describe the contents of the text collections used in the evaluation. We then show some properties of the collections which are limiting factors for the retrieval performance of an IR system.

4.1   Contents of the Text Collections

We use standard document collections and standard queries and questions provided by the SMART project [45] and the TREC (Text REtrieval Conferences) conferences series [49]. In addition we use some special collections that we have generated from the TREC collections to show special effects of our algorithms. Additionally we use two real world collections that have been gathered especially for these experiments by a company providing a web search engine [35].

In our experiments we used the following 16 collections:

- The SMART collections ADI (articles about information sciences), CACM (articles from 'Communications of the ACM' journal), CISI (articles about information sciences), CRAN (abstracts from aeronautics articles), MED (medical articles) and NPL (articles about electrical engineering).
- The TREC collections CR with 34 queries out of topics 251 - 300 using the "title", "description" and "narrative" topics to investigate the influence of query length, FR with 112 queries out of topics 51 - 300.
- the TREC QA (question answering) collection prepared for the Question Answering track held at the TREC-9 conference [56], the QA-AP90 collection containing only those questions having a relevant answer document in the AP90 (Associated Press articles) document collection, the QA-AP90S collection (extracted from the QA-AP90 collection) having questions with similarity of 0.65 or above to any other question, and the QA-2001 collection prepared for the Question Answering track held at the TREC-10 conference [54].
- The PHIBOT collections PHYSICS (articles about physics) and SCIENCE (articles about sciences except physics) are real world collections gathered by a web search engine [35]. Ground truth data has been gathered from documents the user has clicked on from the list which is presented to the user after the query has been executed.

On the one hand by utilizing these collections we take advantage of the ground truth data for performance evaluation. On the other hand we do not expect to have queries having highly correlated similarities as we would expect in a real world application (see section 4.3 for a description of some properties of the collections). So it is a challenging task to show performance improvements for our method.

4.2 Preparation of the Text Collections

Terms used for document and query representation were obtained by stemming and eliminating stopwords. Then document and query vectors were created according to the so called tf-idf weighting scheme (see section 3.1), where the document weights d_{ij} are computed as

$$d_{ij} = \frac{1}{n_j} \cdot tf_{ij} \cdot idf_i \tag{13}$$

where n_j is the normalization factor $n_j = \sqrt{\sum_{i=1}^{M}(tf_{ij} \cdot idf_i)^2}$ and tf_{ij} is a weight computed from the raw frequency f_{ij} of a term t_i (the number of occurrences of term t_i in document d_j)

$$tf_{ij} = \sqrt{f_{ij}} \tag{14}$$

and idf_i is the inverse document frequency of term t_i given by

$$idf_i = \log \frac{N}{n_i} \tag{15}$$

where n_i is the number of documents containing term t_i and N is the number of documents in the collection and the query weights q_{ik} are computed as

$$q_{ik} = \frac{1}{n_k} \cdot \sqrt{f_{ik}} \tag{16}$$

where n_k is the normalization factor $n_k = \sqrt{\sum_{i=1}^{M} f_{ik}}$ and f_{ik} is the raw frequency of a term t_i in a query q_k (the number of occurrences of term t_i in query q_k).

4.3 Properties of the Text Collections

Table 1 lists statistics about the collections after stemming and stopword elimination has been carried out, statistics about some of these collections before stemming and stopword elimination can be found in Baeza-Yates [3] and Kise et al. [25], [26].

Evaluation of the Basic Models. We used the vector space model (VSM) and the pseudo relevance feedback (PRF) model in our evaluation. Additionally we used the Okapi-BM25 model (OKAPI), and from the dimensionality reduction models we used the latent semantic indexing (LSI) model (refer to [15], [11], [4] and [9]) in the following evaluation (no description of these models is given here because of space shortage).

Table 1. Statistics about the test collections

	ADI	CACM	CISI	CRAN	MED	NPL	PHY-SICS	SCI-ENCE
size(MB)	0.1	1.2	1.4	1.4	1.1	3.8	4.9	20.6
number of documents	82	3204	1460	1400	1033	11429	375	2175
number of terms	340	3029	5755	2882	4315	4415	35312	104891
mean number of terms per document	17.9 (short)	18.4 (short)	38.2 (med)	49.8 (med)	46.6 (med)	17.9 (short)	308.2 (long)	322.1 (long)
number of queries	35	52	112	225	30	93	230	1108
mean number of terms per query	5.7 (med)	9.3 (med)	23.3 (long)	8.5 (med)	9.5 (med)	6.5 (med)	1.9 (short)	2.0 (short)
mean number of relev. documents per query	4.9 (low)	15.3 (med)	27.8 (high)	8.2 (med)	23.2 (high)	22.4 (high)	1.7 (low)	2.0 (low)

	CR-desc	CR-narr	CR-title	FR	QA	QA-AP90	QA-AP90S	QA-2001
size(MB)	93	93	93	69	28.2	3.7	3.7	20.1
number of documents	27922	27922	27922	19860	6025	723	723	4274
number of terms	45717	45717	45717	50866	48381	17502	17502	40626
mean number of terms per document	188.2 (long)	188.2 (long)	188.2 (long)	189.7 (long)	230.7 (long)	201.8 (long)	201.8 (long)	220.5 (long)
number of queries	34	34	34	112	693	353	161	500
mean number of terms per query	7.2 (med)	22.8 (long)	2.9 (short)	9.2 (med)	3.1 (short)	3.2 (short)	3.5 (short)	2.7 (short)
mean number of relev. documents per query	24.8 (high)	24.8 (high)	24.8 (high)	8.4 (med)	16.4 (med)	2.8 (low)	3.2 (low)	8.9 (med)

The OKAPI model is evaluated using the BM25 weighting scheme [39] and the Roberston-Sparck Jones term weights as described in [38]. For the evaluation of the LSI model we used the dimensionality $k = 300$.

First we show the average precision obtained by each of the methods in table 2. For each collection the best value of average precision is indicated by bold font, the second best value is indicated by italic font. Then a recall/precision graph is presented in figure 4.

Table 2. Average precision obtained by basic methods

	ADI	CACM	CISI	CRAN	MED	NPL	PHY-SICS	SCI-ENCE
VSM	0.375	0.130	0.120	0.384	0.525	0.185	*0.616*	*0.569*
PRF	*0.390*	*0.199*	*0.129*	**0.435**	**0.639**	**0.224**	**0.638**	**0.587**
OKAPI	**0.421**	**0.290**	0.128	0.339	0.480	*0.200*	0.535	0.489
LSI	0.376	0.122	**0.132**	*0.424*	*0.597*	0.163	0.615	0.495

	CR-desc	CR-narr	CR-title	FR	QA	QA-AP90	QA-AP90S	QA-2001
VSM	*0.175*	*0.173*	0.135	0.085	*0.645*	0.745	0.643	*0.603*
PRF	**0.204**	**0.192**	**0.169**	*0.113*	**0.685**	**0.757**	*0.661*	**0.614**
OKAPI	0.078	0.055	*0.136*	**0.236**	0.633	*0.751*	**0.666**	0.536
LSI	0.106	0.106	0.096	0.051	0.508	0.709	0.601	0.482

Statistical tests provide information about whether observed differences in different methods are really significant or just by chance. Several statistical tests have been proposed [19], [62]. We employ the "paired t-test" described in [19]. In table 3 we show the significance indicators from statistical testing of the experimental results.

- An entry of $++$ ($--$) in a table cell indicates that the null hypothesis is rejected for testing X against Y (Y against X) at significance level $\alpha = 0.01$. This means that method X (Y) is almost guaranteed to perform better than method Y (X).

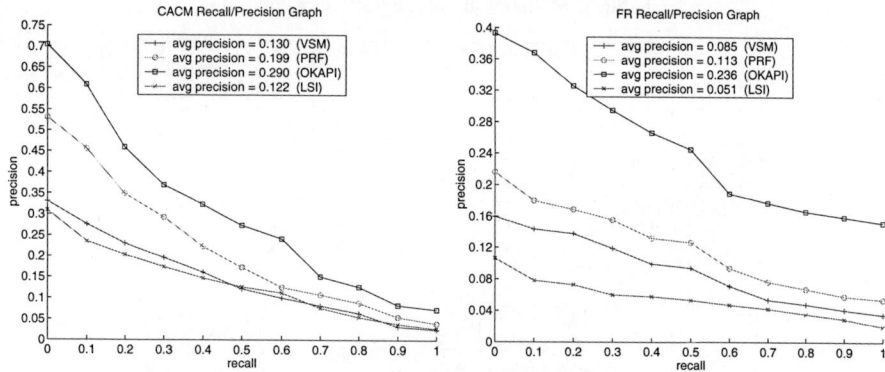

Fig. 4. CACM and FR: recall/precision graphs of basic models

- An entry of $+$ ($-$) in a table cell indicates that the null hypothesis is rejected for testing X against Y (Y against X) at significance level $\alpha = 0.05$, but can not be rejected at significance level $\alpha = 0.01$. This means that method X (Y) is likely to perform better than method Y (X).
- An entry of o in a table cell indicates that the null hypothesis can not be rejected in both tests. This means that there is low probability that one of the methods is performing better than the other method.

Table 3. Paired t-test results for basic methods for significance levels $\alpha = 0.05$ and $\alpha = 0.01$

methods		ADI	CACM	CISI	CRAN	MED	NPL	PHY-SICS	SCI-ENCE
X	Y								
PRF	VSM	+	++	++	++	++	++	+	++
OKAPI	VSM	o	++	o	−−	−−	o	−−	−−
OKAPI	PRF	o	++	o	−−	−−	o	−−	−−
LSI	VSM	++	o	++	++	++	−	o	−−
LSI	PRF	o	−−	o	o	−−	−−	−	−−
LSI	OKAPI	o	−−	o	++	++	−	++	o

methods		CR-desc	CR-narr	CR-title	FR	QA	QA-AP90	QA-AP90S	QA-2001
X	Y								
PRF	VSM	++	+	+	+	++	+	o	++
OKAPI	VSM	−−	−−	o	++	o	o	o	−−
OKAPI	PRF	−−	−−	o	++	−−	o	o	−−
LSI	VSM	−	−	o	−	−−	−−	−−	−−
LSI	PRF	−−	−−	−	−−	−−	−−	−−	−−
LSI	OKAPI	o	o	o	−−	−−	−−	−−	−−

Analysis of the Results. Results achieved by the basic models are non-uniform. From paired t-test results we can see that in most cases PRF performs significantly better than the VSM model. The OKAPI model performs better than VSM and PRF in only two cases, but performs significantly worse in 7 (8) cases than VSM (PRF). LSI performs better than VSM in only 4 cases and worse in 9 cases, and in no case does it perform better than PRF but performs worse than PRF in 13 cases. LSI performs significantly better than OKAPI in only 3 cases, but performs significantly worse in 7 cases.

From average precision analysis we can see that pseudo relevance feedback seems to be the top performer in this evaluation of the basic models. In 11 cases it has the best average precision, and in the other 5 cases it has the second best average precision.

Similarities of Queries to Documents. Some of the current limitations of IR can easily be shown. The following graph 5 shows for each query the similarity between the query and the documents. The graph on the left side shows the similarity of each query to its relevant documents. The graph on the right side shows the similarity of each query to its non-relevant documents. The dots show the similarity of an individual document to a query. The thin connecting line shows the average similarity of all relevant (or non-relevant) documents for each query. The thick line averages these similarities over all queries.

From the graph we can see that average similarity of a query to its relevant documents is higher than average similarity of a query to its non-relevant documents. But very often it occurs that there are non-relevant documents having a higher similarity to a query than relevant documents. From this observation it follows that retrieval precision is decreasing if similarity between a query and non-relevant documents is high.

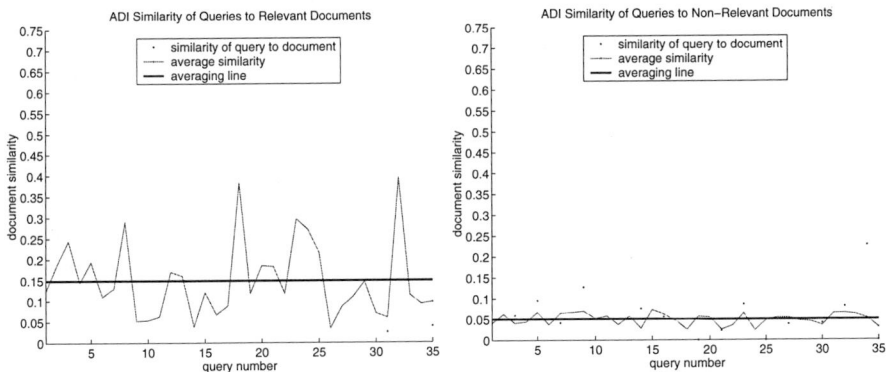

Fig. 5. ADI: similarities of relevant and non-relevant documents

5 Collaborative Information Retrieval

In this section we first explain the motivation for our new approaches to Collaborative Information Retrieval. Then we show the general methodology we are using in our algorithms and delimit the new algorithms from existing procedures. Then we show the general principle of evaluation of our new algorithms.

5.1 Motivation for Collaborative Information Retrieval

In our approach we use global relevance feedback which has been learned from previous queries instead of local relevance feedback which is produced during execution of an individual query. The motivation for our query expansion method is straightforward, especially in an environment where document collections are static, and personal preferences and context knowledge are ignored:

- If documents are relevant to a query which has been issued previously by a user, then the same documents are relevant to the same query at a later time when that query is re-issued by the same or by a different user. This is the trivial case, where similarities between the two different queries is the highest.
- In the non-trivial case a new query is similar to a previously issued query only to a certain degree. Then our assumption is that documents which are relevant to the previously issued query will be relevant to the new query only to a certain degree.

It does not necessarily follow that if a new query is dissimilar to a previously issued query, the documents which are relevant to the previously issued query are not relevant to the new query.

We will illustrate this fact in a short example with queries taken from the TREC QA text collection. Some of these queries are shown below:

1. What was the name of the first Russian astronaut to do a spacewalk?
2. How many astronauts have been on the moon?
3. What is the name of the second space shuttle?
4. Who was the first woman in space?
5. Name the first Russian astronaut to do a spacewalk.
6. Who was the first Russian astronaut to walk in space?
7. Who was the first Russian to do a spacewalk?

From these queries it is very clear that

- documents being relevant to query 1 are necessarily relevant to queries $5-7$ and vice versa
- documents being relevant to queries $2-4$ are not necessarily relevant to queries 1 and $5-7$

In the following table 4 we show the similarities between the queries (also called the inter-query similarity) with the corresponding similarities between the relevant documents (also called the inter-document similarity) in parenthesis in the second line of each row.

Note that for query 3 there are no documents marked as relevant in the text collection and thus the inter-document similarity of the documents relevant to query 3 is defined to be 0.

Our approach to CIR is to find the exact degree of similarity between queries (which of course includes finding the exact degree of dissimilarity) that maximizes the improvements in retrieval performance. We do this by expanding the newly issued query to include terms from previous issued queries and/or documents known as being relevant to the previously issued queries.

5.2   Inter-query Similarities

In our preliminary considerations for usage of similarities between different queries for retrieval performance improvements we decided to analyze the inter-query similarities.

Table 4. Similarities of sample queries and their relevant documents

query (document)	1	2	3	4	5	6	7
1	1.0 (1.0)	0.408 (0.138)	0.0 (0.0)	0.0 (0.259)	1.0 (1.0)	0.577 (1.0)	0.816 (1.0)
2	0.408 (0.138)	1.0 (1.0)	0.0 (0.0)	0.0 (0.192)	0.408 (0.183)	0.353 (0.183)	0.0 (0.183)
3	0.0 (0.0)	0.0 (0.0)	1.0 (0.0)	0.5 (0.0)	0.0 (0.0)	0.353 (0.0)	0.0 (0.0)
4	0.0 (0.259)	0.0 (0.192)	0.5 (0.0)	1.0 (1.0)	0.0 (0.259)	0.353 (0.259)	0.0 (0.259)
5	1.0 (1.0)	0.408 (0.183)	0.0 (0.0)	0.0 (0.259)	1.0 (1.0)	0.577 (1.0)	0.816 (1.0)
6	0.577 (1.0)	0.353 (0.183)	0.353 (0.0)	0.353 (0.259)	0.577 (1.0)	1.0 (1.0)	0.353 (1.0)
7	0.816 (1.0)	0.0 (0.183)	0.0 (0.0)	0.0 (0.259)	0.816 (1.0)	0.353 (1.0)	1.0 (1.0)

As we already stated at the end of the text collections description (refer to section 4.1) we did not expect to have queries having highly correlated similarities as we would expect in real world applications. In the event, however, the results were even worse than expected.

Indeed, the following histogram in figure 6 shows very low inter-query similarity (as for most of the text collections). The graph on the left side shows the distributions of the query-to-query similarity, including those similarities which are 0. Since this is the dominating factor in each of the graphs, we also produced the same histogram leaving out query-to-query similarities of 0. This is the graph on the right side in each row. For each distribution we also computed the mean and the median value as well as the variance and the standard deviation. These values are shown in the header line of each graph. The vertical lines in the graphs are: the mean similarity (solid line), and the values of the mean similarity ± the standard deviation (dotted lines).

The SMART collections do not incorporate queries having a high similarity to any other query. From the TREC collections only those especially prepared have some high inter-query similarities (refer to the description of the QA, QA-AP90 and QA-AP90S collections in section 4.1). In our real world collections obtained from PHIBOT (the PHYSICS and SCIENCE collection) we also have some high inter-query similarities.

5.3 Correlation between Query Similarities and Document Similarities

In our considerations about similarities between different queries we considered to analyze to inter-query similarities as opposed to the inter-document similarity of the relevant documents. If there were a direct correlation between inter-query similarities to inter-document similarity of the relevant documents, it would be easy to derive the relevant documents for a given new query from the documents being relevant to the existing old queries. This would directly match the expectations stated in the motivation for this chapter (see 5.1).

From these considerations we derived the creation of the following graphs (see figure 7): each graph shows the inter-query similarities for each two pairwise different queries on the x-axis and the inter-document similarity of the relevant documents

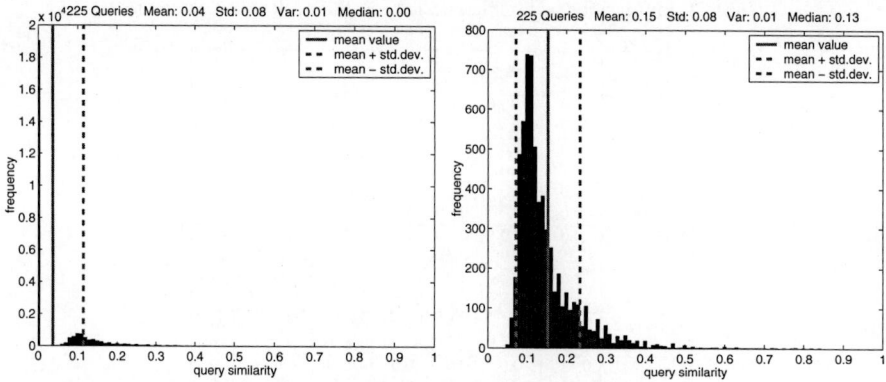

Fig. 6. CRAN: distribution of query similarities

on the y-axis as a dot. A dot at coordinates $(0.5, 0.9)$ shows that there are two queries having an inter-query similarity of 0.5 and their relevant documents have an inter-document similarity of (0.9). Another example is a dot at coordinates $(0.4, 0.0)$, which means that there are two queries having an inter-query similarity of 0.4 and their relevant documents have an inter-document similarity of (0.0). The line in each graph is the least-squares estimator for the polynomial of degree 1 fitting best to the clouds of dots.

Here we see that there is no simple correlation between inter-query similarity and inter-document similarity. There are low inter-query similarity and their relevant documents have a high inter-document similarity and vice versa. From the TREC collections only those collections especially prepared have a high correlation between inter-query and inter-document similarity. Also for the PHIBOT collections there seems to be a correlation between a few inter-query similarities to the inter-document similarity, and the least-squares estimator has a low slope.

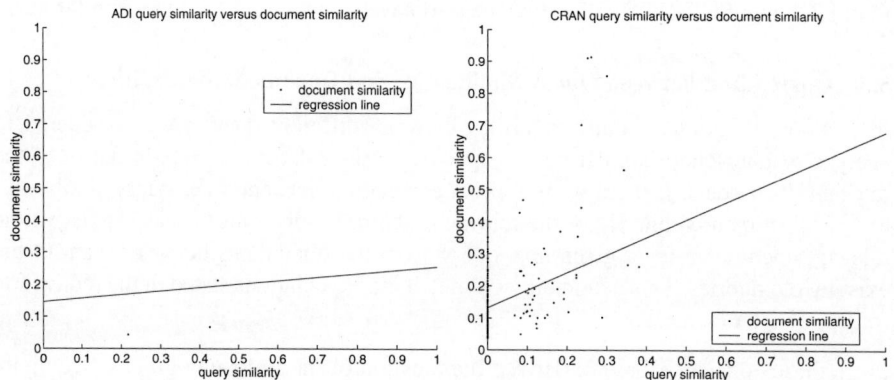

Fig. 7. ADI and CRAN: query similarity vs. document similarity

5.4   Overlap of Relevant Documents

It is essential for achieving retrieval performance improvements to have some "overlapping" relevant documents for pairs of queries. Thus we define the overlap of relevant documents as follows:

Definition 4 (Overlap of Relevant Documents). *Let $q_k, q_l \in Q$, $k \neq l$ be two different queries. Let RD_k, RD_l be the sets of documents being relevant to the queries q_k and q_l respectively. Then the overlap of relevant documents for these two queries is the number of documents in the set $O_{kl} = RD_k \cap RD_l = \{d_j \mid d_j \in RD_k \wedge d_j \in RD_l\}$.*

For all our new query expansion procedures we expect retrieval performance improvements if the overlap of relevant documents is high. The following table 5 gives some statistics about the overlap of relevant documents. Graph 8 shows the individual overlap for each pair of queries. The x-axis and y-axis show the query number and the z-axis shows the overlap for each pair of queries. Since the overlap between each pair of queries is symmetric ($|O_{kl}| = |O_{lk}|$), we left out the symmetric part for clarity.

Table 5. Statistics about overlap of relevant documents

	ADI	CACM	CISI	CRAN	MED	NPL	PHY-SICS	SCI-ENCE
pairs of queries	595	1326	6216	25200	435	4278	26335	613278
max overlap	7	17	70	18	0	36	1	4
query pairs with overlap	90	134	1154	686	0	181	25	75
percentage of query pairs with overlap	15.1%	10.1%	18.6%	2.7%	0.0%	4.2%	0.1%	0.01%

	CR-desc	CR-narr	CR-title	FR	QA	QA-AP90S	QA-AP90	QA-2001
pairs of queries	561	561	561	6216	239778	12880	62128	124750
max overlap	27	27	27	10	140	16	16	11
query pairs with overlap	35	35	35	385	760	195	237	259
percentage of query pairs with overlap	6.2%	6.2%	6.2%	6.2%	0.3%	1.5%	0.4%	0.2%

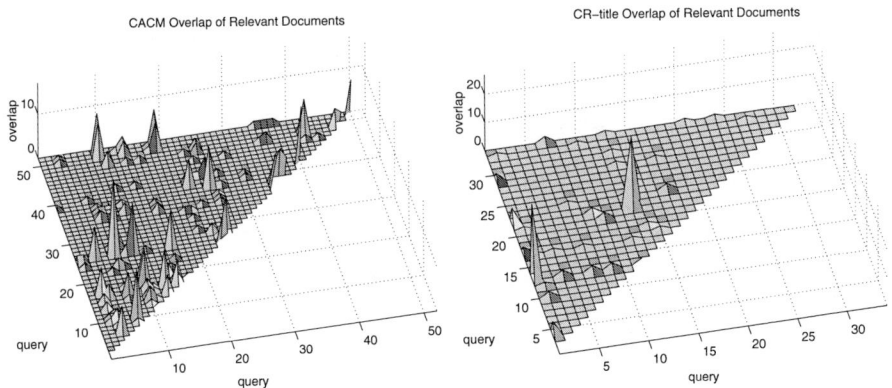

Fig. 8. CACM and CR-title: overlap of relevant documents

5.5   Methodology of Collaborative Information Retrieval Methods

As stated in the motivation for CIR we use global relevance feedback which has been learned from previous queries. Thus we here first describe the query expansion procedures based on query similarities and their relevant documents from a high level approach and will then give a more algorithmic description followed by the formal description.

All our new query expansion procedures work as follows:

- for each new query to be issued compute the similarities between the new query and each of the existing old queries
- select the old queries having a similarity to the new query which is greater than or equal to a given threshold
- from these selected old queries get the sets of relevant documents from the ground truth data
- from this set of relevant documents compute some terms for expansion of the new query
- use this terms to expand the new query and issue the new expanded query

The algorithmic description is given here:

```
for each new query q do
      compute the set  S = {q_k| sim(q_k, q) ≥ σ, 1 ≤ k ≤ L}
      compute the sets RD_k = {d_j|q_k ∈ S ∧ d_j is relevant to q_k}
      compute the expanded query q' = cirf(q, S, RD_k)
            by some function cirf
end
```

where S is the set of existing old queries q_k with a similarity of σ or higher to the new query q, RD_k are the sets of the documents being relevant to the queries q_k and f is a function for query expansion.

Our methods in Collaborative Information Retrieval are characterized by a generalized function

$$cirf : Q \times 2^{Q \times 2^D} \to Q$$
$$(q, ((q_1, RD_1), (q_2, RD_2), \cdots, (q_L, RD_L))) \mapsto q' \qquad (17)$$

where the sets RD_i are the sets of documents whi·

The goal now is to find suitable functions $cirf$ which can be efficiently computed and which maximize the effectiveness of the new query q' in terms of recall and precision. As is shown in figure 9 our approach is searching for neighbors of the new query. If suitable neighbors of a query q within a given distance are found, we try to derive information about the documents which are relevant to q from its nearest neighbors.

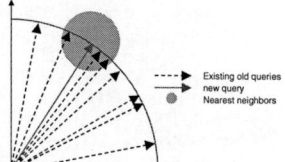

Fig. 9. Motivation for CIR methods: usage of the nearest neighbors

These functions introduce a new level of quality in the IR research area: while the term weighting functions such as tf-idf only work on documents and document collections, and relevance feedback works on a single query and uses information from their assumed relevant and non-relevant documents only, CIR now works on a single query, and uses the information of all other queries and their known relevant documents.

5.6   Methodology of Evaluation Method

The evaluation follows the "leave one out" technique used in several areas such as document classification, machine learning etc.

From the set of L queries contained in each text collection we select each query one after the other and treat it as a new query $q_l, 1 \leq l \leq L$. Then for each fixed query q_l we use the algorithm as described in section 5.5. Of course the now fixed query q_l itself does not take part in the computation of the query expansion. We vary parameters of the algorithms according to suitable values, and select those parameters where highest performance improvements (in terms of average precision over all queries) has been achieved.

6   Query Expansion Methods for CIR

In this section we shortly describe the query expansion methods which we have developed for CIR. For detailed information refer to [21], [22], [23] and [20].

6.1   Methods Description

Query Similarity and Relevant Documents. Method QSD (refer to [21] and [23]) uses the relevant documents of the most similar queries for query expansion of a new query. The new query is rewritten as a sum of selected relevant documents of existing old queries, which have a high similarity to the new query.

Query Linear Combination and Relevant Documents. Method QLD (refer to [22] and [23]) uses the relevant documents of the most similar queries, which are used in re-writing the new query as a linear combination of the most similar queries. This query expansion method reconstructs the new query as a linear combination of existing old queries. Then the terms of the relevant documents of these existing old queries are used for query expansion.

Document Term Reweighting. Method DTW [20] uses the relevant documents of the most similar queries for giving more weight to those ambiguous terms in the documents, that match the semantics of the same terms in the queries. If, for example, the queries use the term 'bank' in conjunction with other terms related to financial topics, then the term 'bank' meaning 'financial institution' will be weighted higher than the term 'bank' meaning 'dike' or 'wall'.

Query Term Reweighting. Method QTW [20] uses the relevant documents of the most similar queries for giving more weight to those ambiguous terms in the queries, that match the semantics of the same terms in the documents.

6.2   Other Collaborative Methods

Other methods, denoted as Term Concept Learning (TCL), have been developed in the field of CIR. These methods are used to learn the concept of a term in a new query from the usage of the term in documents which are relevant to existing old queries. These methods are not evaluated herein, refer to [27], [28] and [23] for further information.

6.3   Experiments Description

Methods VSM (vector space model), PRF (pseudo relevance feedback) and the newly developed methods QSD, QLD, DTW and QTW were applied. Best parameter value settings for method PRF had been obtained previously by experiment and those which give the highest average precision were selected and used.

The newly developed methods were evaluated using different settings for parameters σ (see section 5.5) and following our evaluation methodology (see section 5.6). During evaluation best parameter value settings have been obtained by experiment and those which give the highest average precision were selected for comparison against other methods.

In the next steps we combined two methods of query expansion in this ways: First, after having expanded the new query using the PRF method, we applied one of the methods QSD, QLD, DTW and QTW against the expanded query. These methods are reported as the PRFxxx methods. Second, after having expanded the new query using the QSD, QLD and QTW methods, we applied the PRF method against the expanded query. These methods are reported as the xxxPRF methods.

A recall/precision graph showing results from methods QSD and QLD is shown in figure 10.

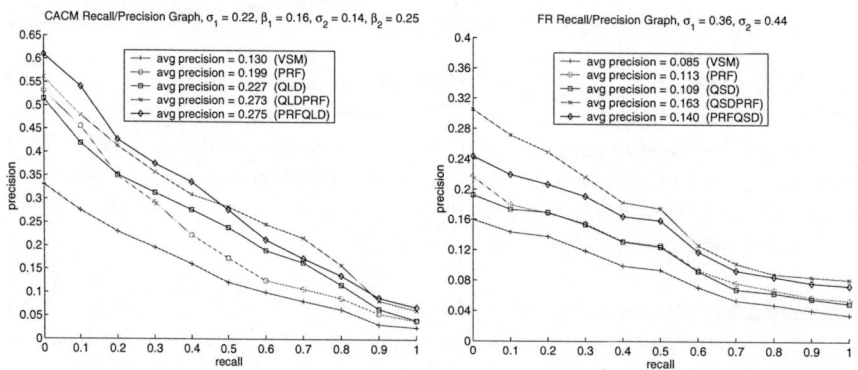

Fig. 10. CACM and FR: recall/precision graphs for QLD and QSD method

7   Improvements

In this section we summarize the results of the query expansion methods developed in this work and analyze the results.

Tables 6 and 7 summarize the results of the newly developed basic methods QSD, QLD, DTW and QTW and show the results from significance testing. For each collection the best value of average precision is indicated by bold font, the second best value is indicated by italic font.

From average precision analysis we can see that methods QSD and QLD perform better than PRF in 7 out of 16 cases, and PRF performs better than any of the newly developed methods in 9 out of 16 cases. Methods DTW and QTW never perform better than QSD or QLD, but in 4 (resp. 5) cases perform better than PRF.

From significance testing we can see that QLD outperforms QSD in 3 cases and in no case performs significantly worse than QSD. QLD performs significantly better than DTW and QTW in 6 cases and performs in no case worse than DTW or QTW.

Table 6. Average precision obtained in different methods

	ADI	CACM	CISI	CRAN	MED	NPL	PHY-SICS	SCI-ENCE
VSM	*0.375*	0.130	0.120	0.384	*0.525*	0.185	*0.616*	0.645
PRF	**0.390**	0.199	0.129	*0.435*	**0.639**	**0.224**	**0.638**	0.685
QSD	0.374	**0.237**	*0.142*	0.428	0.503	0.184	0.612	*0.727*
QLD	0.369	*0.227*	**0.171**	**0.436**	0.507	*0.185*	0.614	**0.734**
DTW	0.356	0.142	0.122	0.386	0.494	0.182	0.599	0.727
QTW	0.364	0.154	0.131	0.420	0.500	0.183	0.611	0.716

	CR-desc	CR-narr	CR-title	FR	QA	QA-AP90	QA-AP90S	QA-2001
VSM	*0.175*	0.173	0.135	0.085	0.645	0.745	0.643	0.603
PRF	**0.204**	**0.192**	**0.169**	**0.113**	0.685	0.757	0.661	**0.614**
QSD	0.172	0.173	0.152	*0.109*	*0.727*	0.810	*0.786*	0.603
QLD	0.175	*0.175*	*0.164*	0.108	**0.734**	**0.812**	**0.789**	*0.603*
DTW	0.150	0.173	0.132	0.098	0.727	0.785	0.732	0.601
QTW	0.150	0.173	0.144	0.106	0.716	0.808	0.762	0.601

Table 7. Paired t-test results for significance levels $\alpha = 0.05$ and $\alpha = 0.01$ in different methods

methods X	Y	ADI	CACM	CISI	CRAN	MED	NPL	PHY-SICS	SCI-ENCE
QLD	QSD	o	o	++	o	o	o	o	++
QLD	DTW	o	++	++	++	o	o	++	o
QLD	QTW	o	++	++	+	o	o	o	++
QSD	DTW	o	++	o	++	o	o	++	o
QSD	QTW	o	++	++	+	o	o	o	+
QTW	DTW	o	o	o	++	o	o	++	−−

methods X	Y	CR-desc	CR-narr	CR-title	FR	QA	QA-AP90	QA-AP90S	QA-2001
QLD	QSD	o	o	o	o	++	o	o	o
QLD	DTW	o	o	o	o	o	++	++	o
QLD	QTW	o	o	o	o	++	o	++	o
QSD	DTW	o	o	o	o	o	++	++	o
QSD	QTW	o	o	o	o	+	o	++	o
QTW	DTW	o	o	+	o	−−	++	+	o

Tables 8 and 9 summarize the results of the combined methods PRFQSD, PRFQLD, PRFDTW, PRFQTW, QSDPRF, QLDPRF and QTWPRF, and show the results from significance testing. In significance testing we only tested each PRFxxx method against each other PRFxxx method as well as we tested each xxxPRF method against each other xxxPRF method. We did no significance testing for testing methods PRFxxx against xxxPRF methods.

Table 8. Average precision obtained in different methods

	ADI	CACM	CISI	CRAN	MED	NPL	PHY-SICS	SCI-ENCE
VSM	0.375	0.130	0.120	0.384	0.525	0.185	0.616	0.569
PRF	0.390	0.199	0.129	0.435	**0.639**	0.224	**0.638**	**0.587**
PRFQSD	*0.391*	0.256	0.151	*0.463*	0.611	0.223	0.634	0.584
PRFQLD	**0.394**	**0.275**	*0.169*	**0.470**	*0.631*	*0.225*	*0.638*	*0.587*
PRFDTW	0.372	0.208	0.133	0.431	0.602	0.221	0.627	0.575
PRFQTW	0.388	0.231	0.133	0.453	0.606	0.222	0.635	0.583
QSDPRF	0.388	0.257	0.145	0.451	0.609	**0.225**	0.636	0.582
QLDPRF	0.385	*0.273*	**0.173**	0.453	0.613	0.207	0.611	*0.587*
QTWPRF	0.380	0.206	0.137	0.455	0.609	0.224	0.635	0.582

	CR-desc	CR-narr	CR-title	FR	QA	QA-AP90	QA-AP90S	QA-2001
VSM	0.175	0.173	0.135	0.085	0.645	0.745	0.643	0.603
PRF	0.204	0.192	0.169	0.113	0.685	0.757	0.661	*0.614*
PRFQSD	0.196	0.192	0.180	0.140	*0.754*	0.813	0.781	0.613
PRFQLD	*0.208*	**0.193**	**0.190**	0.144	**0.757**	0.814	0.782	**0.615**
PRFDTW	0.200	0.191	0.154	0.123	0.752	0.791	0.733	0.611
PRFQTW	**0.221**	0.191	0.180	0.127	0.739	0.809	0.755	0.612
QSDPRF	0.195	0.191	0.177	**0.163**	0.739	0.813	*0.786*	0.614
QLDPRF	0.204	*0.192*	0.184	*0.161*	0.747	**0.815**	**0.789**	0.613
QTWPRF	0.179	0.192	*0.189*	0.157	0.740	*0.815*	0.764	0.613

Table 9. Paired t-test results for significance levels $\alpha = 0.05$ and $\alpha = 0.01$ in different methods

methods X	Y	ADI	CACM	CISI	CRAN	MED	NPL	PHY-SICS	SCI-ENCE
PRFQLD	PRFQSD	o	o	+	o	o	o	o	o
PRFQLD	PRFDTW	+	++	++	++	o	+	+	++
PRFQLD	PRFQTW	o	o	++	+	o	o	o	+
PRFQSD	PRFDTW	o	++	o	++	o	o	+	++
PRFQSD	PRFQTW	o	+	++	++	o	o	o	o
PRFQTW	PRFDTW	+	++	o	++	o	o	+	++
QLDPRF	QSDPRF	o	o	++	o	o	−	−−	o
QLDPRF	QTWPRF	o	++	++	o	o	o	−	++
QSDPRF	QTWPRF	o	++	++	o	o	o	o	o

methods X	Y	CR-desc	CR-narr	CR-title	FR	QA	QA-AP90	QA-AP90S	QA-2001
PRFQLD	PRFQSD	o	o	o	o	o	o	o	o
PRFQLD	PRFDTW	o	o	+	+	o	++	++	+
PRFQLD	PRFQTW	o	o	+	+	++	+	++	o
PRFQSD	PRFDTW	o	o	o	+	o	++	++	o
PRFQSD	PRFQTW	o	o	o	+	++	o	++	o
PRFQTW	PRFDTW	o	o	+	o	−−	++	+	o
QLDPRF	QSDPRF	o	o	o	o	++	o	o	o
QLDPRF	QTWPRF	o	o	o	o	o	o	++	o
QSDPRF	QTWPRF	o	o	o	o	o	o	++	o

From average precision analysis we can see that QLDPRF performs best in 3 out of 16 cases, and PRFQLD performs best in 7 out of 16 cases. For the other 6 cases, PRF performs best in 3 cases, QSDPRF performs best in 2 cases, and in 1 case PRFQTW performs best. Methods PRFQTW and PRFDTW never perform best or second best, except for the 1 case mentioned above. QTWPRF performs second best in 2 cases. In those 9 cases where PRFQLD is not performing best, it is the second best method in 6 cases.

From significance testing we can see that PRFQLD performs significantly better than PRFQSD in 1 case, and in all cases where PRFQSD outperforms the PRFDTW method, PRFQLD also outperforms this method. In all but for 2 cases where PRFQSD outperforms the PRFQTW method, PRFQLD also outperforms PRFQTW.

Methods QLDPRF and QSDPRF seem to perform similar. In 12 cases there is no significant improvement or degradation, and in each 2 cases one of these methods is outperforming the other. The QLDPRF method outperforms QTWPRF in only 4 cases, and performs significantly worse then QTWPRF in 1 case. QSDPRF outperforms QTWPRF in 3 cases, and is in no case significantly worse than QTWPRF.

For a quick overview figure 11 shows the average precision achieved by each method in bar graphs.

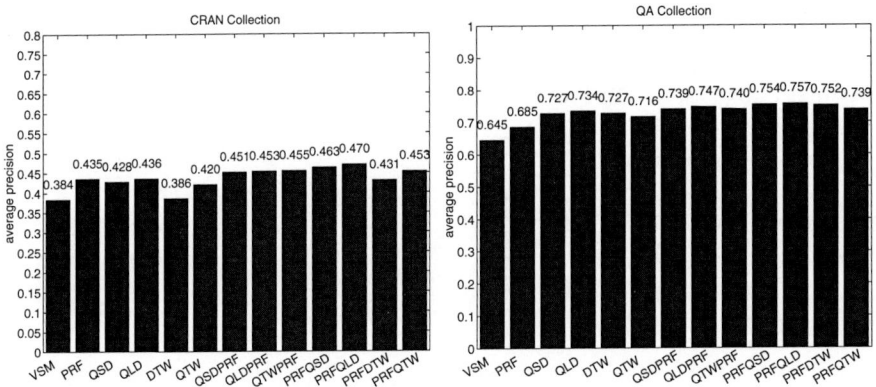

Fig. 11. CRAN and QA: average precision comparison

8   Conclusions

We have studied methods for improving retrieval performance in a restricted Collaborative Information Retrieval environment where information about relevant documents from previous search processes carried out by several users is available for the current query.

Specifically, we developed, evaluated and analyzed new algorithms for query expansion, since query expansion methods are known to be successful in improving retrieval performance.

Results of the newly developed methods are encouraging. Retrieval performance improvements were achieved in most cases. From the basic methods QSD, QLD, DTW and QTW best results were achieved in the combination with the Pseudo Relevance Feedback (PRF) method.

For some text collections no significant retrieval performance improvements could be achieved, neither in the basic methods nor in applying the methods after learning similarity functions.

In the analysis of the results we identified three essential factors for retrieval performance improvements:

1. similarity between queries, also called inter-query similarity (refer to section 5.2)
2. similarity of queries to their relevant documents and similarity of queries to their non-relevant documents (refer to section 4.3)
3. the overlap of relevant documents for pairs of queries (refer to section 5.4)

We think that the first two factors are more important for achieving improvements than the last factor. Best performance improvements have been achieved in text collections, were the inter-query similarity is high, although the overlap in relevant documents is not high.

Low or no retrieval performance improvements were achieved in those cases were the inter-query similarity in the average is low. Also for text collections were similarity of queries to their non-relevant documents is high in the average, we could not achieve high performance improvements.

Acknowledgements. This work was supported by the German Federal Ministry of Education and Research, bmb+f (Grant: 01 IN 902 B8).

References

1. Eugene Agichtein, Steve Lawrence, and Luis Gravano. Learning search engine specific query transformations for question answering. In *Proceedings of the 10th International World Wide Web Conference*, pages 169–178, Hong Kong, 2001.
2. Ali H. Alsaffar, Jitender S. Deogun, and Hayri Sever. Optimal queries in information filtering. In *Foundations of Intelligent Systems, 12th International Symposium, ISMIS 2000, Charlotte, NC, USA, October 11-14, 2000, Proceedings*, volume 1932 of *Lecture Notes in Computer Science*, pages 435–443. Springer, 2000.
3. Ricardo Baeza-Yates and Berthier Ribeiro-Neto. *Modern Information Retrieval*. Addison-Wesley Publishing Company, 1999.
4. Michael W. Berry, Zlatko Drmac, and Elizabeth R. Jessup. Matrices, vector spaces, and information retrieval. *Society for Industrial and Applied Mathematics Review*, 41(2):335–362, 1999.
5. Chris Buckley, Gerard Salton, James Allan, and Amit Singhal. Automatic query expansion using smart. In Donna Harman, editor, *Proceedings of the Third Text Retrieval Conference (TREC-3)*, pages 69–80, Gaithersburg, MD, 1995.
6. Fabio Crestani and Cornelis J. van Rijsbergen. A study of probability kinematics in information retrieval. *ACM Transactions on Information Systems (TOIS)*, 16(3):225–255, 1998.
7. Fabio Crestani and Cornelius J. van Rijsbergen. Information retrieval by imaging. *Journal of Documentation*, 51(1):1–15, 1995.

8. Fabio Crestani and Cornelius J. van Rijsbergen. Probability kinematics in information retrieval: A case study. In Edward A. Fox, Peter Ingwersen, and Raya Fidel, editors, *Proceedings of the 18th Annual International ACM SIGIR Conference on Research and Development in Information Retrieval*, pages 291–299, Seattle, Washington, USA, July 1995. ACM Press, New York, NY, USA.

9. N. Cristianini, H. Lodhi, and J. Shawe-Taylor. Latent semantic kernels for feature selection, 2000.

10. Hang Cui, Ji-Rong Wen, Jian-Yun Nieand, and Wei-Ying Ma. Probabilistic query expansion using query logs. In *Eleventh International World Wide Web Conference*, Honolulu, Hawaii, USA, May 2002.

11. S. Deerwester, S. T. Dumais, G. W. Furnas, T. K. Landauer, and R. A. Harshman. Indexing by latent semantic analysis. *Journal of the American Society for Information Science and Technology*, 41(6):391–407, 1990.

12. Efthimis N. Efthimiadis. Query expansion. *Annual Review of Information Science and Technology*, 31:121–187, 1996.

13. Reginald Ferber. *Information Retrieval - Suchmodelle und Data-Mining-Verfahren für Textsammlungen und das Web*. dpunkt.verlag, Heidelberg, 2003.

14. Norbert Fuhr. Goals and tasks of the IR-group. Homepage of the IR-group of the German Informatics Society, 1996. `http://ls6-www.cs.uni-dortmund.de/ir/fgir/mitgliedschaft/brochure2.html`.

15. G. W. Furnas, S. Deerwester, S. T. Dumais, T. K. Landauer, R. A. Harshman, L. A. Streeter, and K. E. Lochbaum. Information retrieval using a singular value decomposition model of latent semantic structure. In Yves Chiaramella, editor, *Proceedings of the 11th Annual International ACM SIGIR conference on Research and Development in Information Retrieval*, pages 465–480, Grenoble, France, May 1988. ACM Press, New York, NY, USA.

16. Donna Harman. Relevance feedback and other query modification techniques. In William B. Frakes and Ricardo Baeza-Yates, editors, *Information Retrieval - Data Structures & Algorithms*, pages 241–263, New Jersey, 1992. Prentice Hall.

17. Donna Harman. Relevance feedback revisited. In Nicholas Belkin, Peter Ingwersen, and Annelise Mark Pejtersen, editors, *Proceedings of the 15th Annual International ACM SIGIR Conference on Research and Development in Information Retrieval*, pages 1–10, Copenhagen, Denmark, June 1992. ACM Press, New York, NY, USA.

18. Andreas Henrich. IR research at university of bayreuth. Homepage of the IR-research group, 2002. `http://ai1.inf.uni-bayreuth.de/forschung/forschungsgebiete/ir_mmdb`.

19. David Hull. Using statistical testing in the evaluation of retrieval experiments. In Robert Korfhage, Edie Rasmussen, and Peter Willett, editors, *Proceedings of the 16th Annual International ACM SIGIR Conference on Research and Development in Information Retrieval*, pages 329–338, Pittsburgh, Pennsylvania, USA, June 1993. ACM Press, New York, NY, USA.

20. Armin Hust, Markus Junker, and Andreas Dengel. A mathematical model for improving retrieval performance in collaborative information retrieval. 2003. to appear.

21. Armin Hust, Stefan Klink, Markus Junker, and Andreas Dengel. Query expansion for web information retrieval. In Sigrid Schubert, Bernd Reusch, and Norbert Jesse, editors, *Proceedings of Web Information Retrieval Workshop, 32nd Annual Conference of the German Informatics Society*, volume P-19 of *Lecture Notes in Informatics*, pages 176–180, Dortmund, Germany, October 2002. German Informatics Society.

22. Armin Hust, Stefan Klink, Markus Junker, and Andreas Dengel. Query reformulation in collaborative information retrieval. In Marc Boumedine, editor, *Proceedings of the International Conference on Information and Knowledge Sharing, IKS 2002*, pages 95–100, St. Thomas, U.S. Virgin Islands, November 2002. ACTA Press.

23. Armin Hust, Stefan Klink, Markus Junker, and Andreas Dengel. Towards collaborative information retrieval: Three approaches. In Ingrid Renz Jürgen Franke, Gholamreza Nakhaeizadeh, editor, *Text Mining - Theoretical Aspects and Applications*. Physica-Verlag, 2003.
24. Thorsten Joachims. Unbiased evaluation of retrieval quality using clickthrough data. Technical report, Cornell University, Department of Computer Science, 2002.
25. Koichi Kise, Markus Junker, Andreas Dengel, and Keinosuke Matsumoto. Experimental evaluation of passage-based document retrieval. In *Proceedings of the Sixth International Conference on Document Analysis and Recognition ICDAR-01*, pages 592–596, Seattle, WA, September 2001.
26. Koichi Kise, Markus Junker, Andreas Dengel, and Keinosuke Matsumoto. Passage-based document retrieval as a tool for text mining with user's information needs. In Klaus P. Jantke and Ayumi Shinohara, editors, *Proceedings of Discovery Science, 4th International Conference DS-2001*, volume 2226 of *Lecture Notes in Computer Science*, pages 155–169, Washington, DC, USA, November 2001. Springer.
27. Stefan Klink, Armin Hust, Markus Junker, and Andreas Dengel. Collaborative learning of term-based concepts for automatic query expansion. In *Proceedings of ECML 2002, 13th European Conference on Machine Learning*, volume 2430 of *Lecture Notes in Artificial Intelligence*, pages 195–206, Helsinki, Finland, August 2002. Springer.
28. Stefan Klink, Armin Hust, Markus Junker, and Andreas Dengel. Improving document retrieval by automatic query expansion using collaborative learning of term-based concepts. In *Proceedings of DAS 2002, 5th International Workshop on Document Analysis Systems*, volume 2423 of *Lecture Notes in Computer Science*, pages 376–387, Princeton, NJ, USA, August 2002. Springer.
29. Tamara G. Kolda. Limited-memory matrix methods with applications. Technical Report CS-TR-3806, University of Maryland, 1997.
30. Tamara G. Kolda and Dianne P. O'Leary. A semidiscrete matrix decomposition for latent semantic indexing information retrieval. *ACM Transactions on Information Systems*, 16(4):322–346, 1998.
31. F. W. Lancaster. *Information Retrieval Systems: Characteristics, Testing and Evaluation*. Wiley, New York, 1968.
32. Christopher D. Manning and Hinrich Schütze. *Foundations of Natural Language Processing*. MIT Press, 1999.
33. Jack Minker, Gerald Wilson, and Barbara Zimmerman. An evaluation of query expansion by the addition of clustered terms for a document retrieval system. *Information Storage and Retrieval*, 8:329–348, 1972.
34. Tomas Olsson. Information filtering with collaborative agents. Master's thesis, Department of Computer and Systems Sciences, Royal Institute of Technology, Sweden, 1998.
35. Phibot search engine. Homepage, 2002. http://phibot.org.
36. Yonggang Qiu and Hans-Peter Frei. Concept-based query expansion. In Robert Korfhage, Edie Rasmussen, and Peter Willett, editors, *Proceedings of the 16th Annual International ACM SIGIR Conference on Research and Development in Information Retrieval*, pages 160–169, Pittsburgh, Pennsylvania, USA, June 1993. ACM Press, New York, NY, USA.
37. Vijay V. Raghavan and Hayri Sever. On the reuse of past optimal queries. In Edward A. Fox, Peter Ingwersen, and Raya Fidel, editors, *Proceedings of the 18th Annual International ACM SIGIR Conference on Research and Development in Information Retrieval*, pages 344–350, Seattle, Washington, USA, July 1995. ACM Press, New York, NY, USA.
38. Stephen E. Robertson and Karen Sparck-Jones. Relevance weighting of search terms. In *Journal of the American Society for Information Science*, volume 27, pages 129–146, 1976.
39. Stephen E. Robertson, Stephen Walker, and Micheline Hancock-Beaulieu. Okapi at TREC-7: automatic ad hoc, filtering, VLC and interactive track. In *Proceedings of the Seventh Text Retrieval Conference (TREC-7)*, 1998.

40. Gerard Salton. *The SMART retrieval system - experiments in automatic document processing.* Prentice Hall, Englewood Cliffs, New Jersey, 1971.

41. Gerard Salton and Chris Buckley. Term weighting approaches in automatic text retrieval. *Information Processing & Management,* 24(5):513–523, 1988.

42. Gerard Salton and Chris Buckley. Improving retrieval performance by relevance feedback. *Journal of the American Society for Information Science and Technology,* 41(4):288–297, 1990.

43. Gerard Salton and M. J. McGill. *Introduction to Modern Information Retrieval.* McGraw-Hill Book Co., New York, 1983.

44. Hayri Sever. *Knowledge Structuring for Database Mining and Text Retrieval Using Past Optimal Queries.* PhD thesis, University of Louisiana, Lafayette, LA, May 1995.

45. Ftp directory at cornell university. Homepage, 1968–1988. `ftp://ftp.cs.cornell.edu/pub/smart`.

46. Karen Sparck-Jones and Roger M. Needham. Automatic term classification and retrieval. *Information Storage and Retrieval,* 4:91–100, 1968.

47. James Thornton. Collaborative Filtering Research Papers. Homepage of James Thornton, 2003. `http://jamesthornton.com/cf/`.

48. Lily F. Tian and Kwok-Wai Cheung. Learning user similarity and rating style for collaborative recommendation. In Fabrizio Sebastiani, editor, *Advances in Information Retrieval, 25th European Conference on IR Research, ECIR 2003,* volume 2633 of *Lecture Notes in Computer Science,* pages 135–145, Pisa, Italy, April 2003. Springer.

49. Text REtrieval Conference (TREC). Homepage, 1992–2003. `http://trec.nist.gov`.

50. Cornelius J. van Rijsbergen. *Information Retrieval.* Butterworths, London, 1979.

51. Cornelius J. van Rijsbergen. A non classical logic for information retrieval. *The Computer Journal,* 29(6):481–485, 1986.

52. Cornelius J. van Rijsbergen. Towards an information logic. In N. J. Belkin and C. J. van Rijsbergen, editors, *Proceedings of the 12th Annual International ACM SIGIR Conference on Research and Development in Information Retrieval,* pages 77–86, Cambridge, Massachusetts, USA, June 1989. ACM Press, New York, NY, USA.

53. John von Neumann and Oskar Morgenstern. *Theory of Games and Economic Behavior.* Princeton University Press, Princeton, New Jersey, 1944.

54. Ellen M. Voorhees. Overview of the TREC 2001 question answering track. In *Proceedings of the Tenth Text Retrieval Conference (TREC-10),* 2002.

55. Ellen M. Voorhees and Donna Harman. Overview of the eighth text retrieval conference (TREC-8). In *Proceedings of the Eighth Text Retrieval Conference (TREC-8),* 2000.

56. Ellen M. Voorhees and Donna Harman. Overview of the ninth text retrieval conference (TREC-9). In *Proceedings of the Ninth Text Retrieval Conference (TREC-9),* 2001.

57. Ji-Rong Wen, Jian-Yun Nie, and Hong-Jiang Zhang. Clustering user queries of a search engine. In *Proceedings of the 10th International World Wide Web Conference,* pages 162–168, Hong Kong, May 2001.

58. Ji-Rong Wen, Jian-Yun Nie, and Hong-Jiang Zhang. Query clustering using user logs. *ACM Transactions on Information Systems,* 20(1):59–81, January 2002.

59. Ryen W. White, Ian Ruthven, and Joemon M. Jose. The use of implicit evidence for relevance feedback in web retrieval. In Fabio Crestani, M. Girolami, and Cornelis J. van Rijsbergen, editors, *Advances in Information Retrieval, 24th BCS-IRSG European Colloquium on IR Research, ECIR 2002, Proceedings,* volume 2291 of *Lecture Notes in Computer Science,* pages 93–109, Glasgow, UK, March 2002. Springer.

60. Jinxi Xu and W. Bruce Croft. Query expansion using local and global document analysis. In Hans-Peter Frei, Donna Harman, Peter Schaübie, and Ross Wilkinson, editors, *Proceedings of the 19th Annual International ACM SIGIR Conference on Research and Development in Information Retrieval*, pages 4–11, Zurich, Switzerland, August 1996. ACM Press, New York, NY, USA.
61. Jinxi Xu and W. Bruce Croft. Improving the effectiveness of information retrieval with local context analysis. *ACM Transactions on Information Systems*, 18(1):79–112, 2000.
62. Yiming Yang and Xin Liu. A re-examination of text categorization methods. In Fredric Gey, Marti Hearst, and Richard Tong, editors, *Proceedings of the 22nd Annual International ACM SIGIR Conference on Research and Development in Information Retrieval*, pages 42–49, Berkeley, California, USA, August 1999. ACM Press, New York, NY, USA.

Improving Document Transformation Techniques with Collaborative Learned Term-Based Concepts

Stefan Klink

Department of Database and Information Systems (DBIS),
University of Trier, D–54286 Trier, Germany,
klink@uni-trier.de

Abstract. Document Transformation techniques have been studied for decades. In this paper, a new approach for a significant improvement is presented based on using a new query expansion method. In contrast to other methods, the regarded query is expanded by adding those terms that are most similar to the concept of individual query terms, rather than selecting terms that are similar to the complete query or that are directly similar to the query terms. Experiments have shown that Document Transformation techniques are significantly improved in the retrieval effectiveness when measuring the recall-precision.

1 Introduction

Due to the widespread use of computers for the acquisition, production, and archiving of documents, more and more information exist in electronically form. The ease with which documents are produced and shared has lead to a potentiation of information reachable by each user.

Already 40 years ago, Maron and Kuhns predicted that indexed scientific information will double every 12 years [23] and a current study of the *International Data Corporation (IDS)* shows that the capacity of data in enterprise networks will increase from 3,200 Petabyte in the year 2002 up to 54,000 Petabyte in the year 2004. Even in the academical area, new conferences, journals, and other publications are appearing quickly and they increase the huge amount of existing data in an alarming manner. Cleverdon estimates that the number of new publications in the most important scientific journals will be 400,000 per year [6].

Storing these information masses in Document-Management-Systems is a problem but searching specific information is a challenge which has appeared recently. These tremendous masses of data make it very difficult for a user to find the "needle in a haystack" and nearly impossible to find and flip through all relevant documents. Because a human can no longer gain an overview over all information, the risk of missing important data or of getting lost in the haystack is very high.

Before the world wide web or Document-Management-Systems were established information retrieval systems were mainly handled by a professional human indexer or

A. Dengel et al. (Eds.): Adaptive READ Research Project, LNCS 2956, pp. 281–305, 2004.

specialists in libraries or archives, i.e. for searching for needed literature or for getting an overview of some topic. Commonly these specialists were working as a translator. They tried to formulate the current information need of the user – developed during a more or less detailed dialog – in a query syntax which is adapted to the retrieval system. The important difference between the professional search specialists and the unskilled amateur is that the first ones know the documents and the internal representation of the system, they have more experience with boolean operators, and know how to use and to combine the right search terms.

But modern information retrieval systems are designed directly for unskilled amateurs – without the assistance of specialists. This often leads to the situation that a user is overwhelmed from the flood of information and that they helplessly "poke in the haystack", getting lost in the retrieved (and mostly irrelevant) information. To illustrate this problem let's have a look at the following situation:

> A user currently has a certain problem and needs more information to solve it. For this, an information retrieval system should be the right thing to satisfy his information need. The difficulty here is that the user only has his problem in mind but doesn't know exactly what he is searching for to solve his problem. Furthermore, he doesn't know how to formulate any of this as a search query. In most cases he arbitrary uses a couple of terms which cross his mind concerning the current topic and the retrieved documents are more or less astonishing. These documents inspire him to reformulate the former query to get hopefully better documents next time.
>
> But a decisive problem of the (short) initial query is if the user chooses wrong terms to begin with, then they will receive a set of misleading documents. This causes the reformulations to get worse and more off track. The consequence is that the user gives up the search for the urgent needed information and is frustrated. Now, the original problem gets all the more complicated.

The following sections discuss the illustrated formulation problem and introduce some solutions. The paper is organized as follows:

- section 2 elucidates the central problem of terminology and describes the way from the user's problem to the query representation.
- section 3 explains the vector space model and how it is used for traditional document retrieval.
- section 4 introduces the idea of Collaborative Information Retrieval and illustrates the scenario used in this work.
- section 5 gives overview of relevance feedback techniques and elucidates the two approaches described in this work, namely Document Transformation and query expansion techniques.
- section 6 our new approach for query expansion based on term-based concepts is introduced.
- section 7 describes how this approach is used to improve Document Transformation techniques.
- section 8 shows experiments and results of the approaches.
- section 9 summarizes our work and gives some prospects for the future.

2   Terminology as a Central Problem

A central point in this work is the formulating problem of the user (see figure 1). The starting point of each information retrieval process is that the user has a current problem. For solving it, he needs more information, i.e. the user has an *information need*. Depending on the user he has a more or less vage understanding of the problem but a limited understanding of how to express it with a search query.

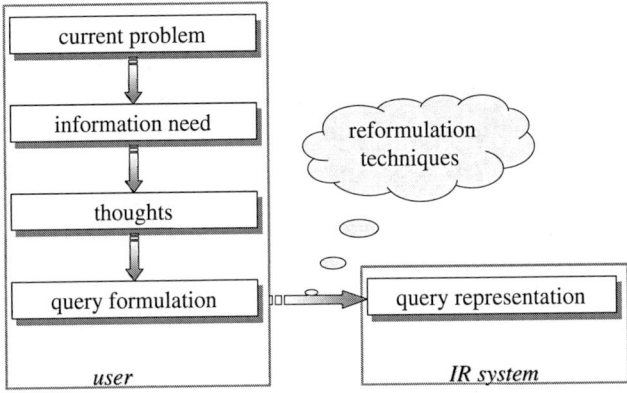

Fig. 1. The way from the user's problem to the query representation

Particularly, the formulation of an appropriate query is a serious problem for many users. In easy cases specific information of some known topic is searched. But this case is rare. In most cases the user has a vage and indistinct imagination of what he is searching for. He rummages with trivial and very short queries (1-2 terms) randomly within the document collection – always with the hope to find an interesting document which then serves as a starting point for a more focused search.

Even when the user has an exact idea of his information need and is able to formulate a query, a further hurdle exist in the construction of a precise query with a correct syntax which can be transmitted to the IR-System. In most cases only a couple of (up to 3) terms are used to form the query. To connect the terms boolean operators are rarely explicitly used. The terms are just written sequently one after another and the default operators of the IR system are used.

Now, this very short query is everything that the IR-System knows about the information need of the user and at that point the biggest problem arises. Here a considerable gap exists between the ideas the user had in mind and the query he has given to the IR-System.

The next step in the information retrieval process is to transform the given term-based query into the basic model of the IR-System. But the crux of the matter is the substantial gap between the user's mind and the formulated query which leads in mediocre or bad retrieval results. Some reasons for this are:

1. a few terms are not enough, i.e. the query is too short to fully describe the information needed. The retrieval with short queries is considerable more difficult than with long queries because short queries contain less information about the user's needs and his problem. The terms used in short queries are rarely a good description of what the user is really searching for. This is one of the main factors which contributes a negative effect on the performance of IR-Systems.

2. the term(s) are simply wrong and the user should form the query with other terms which better describe the desired topic. Thereby many irrelevant documents are retrieved because and despite they contain the (wrong) query terms. Or, the terms have spelling mistakes which the underlying IR-System is not able to handle.

3. terms of the query do not occur in the documents of the collection, i.e. the choice of terms does not fit the documents. Even when users have the same information needs, they rarely use the same terms to form their query or use the same terms which occur in the documents, because these documents were written by other authors. Most IR-Systems are still based on the fact that relevant documents must contain (exactly) the terms of the query. Thereby many relevant documents are not found.

4. terms of the query are mistakable or ambiguous, i.e.
   'bank': with the meaning of a money institution or a riverbank.
   'golf': with the meaning of a kind of sport or the name of a German car (VW).
   'lake': with the meaning of a kind of a sea or of a red color.
   In such a case, many irrelevant documents are retrieved although they contain the right term but the documents contain the wrong topic.

5. and last but not least, the user has no clear idea of what should be searched for and which information is needed to solve the current problem. In that case, he arbitrary uses a couple of terms which cross his mind concerning the topic with the hope that he will find some relevant documents which contain some useful information.

On the way from the user's problem to the representation of the query within the IR-System there exist a series of hurdles and transformations which could distort the meaning of the query. As a result, the IR-System is unable to help the user solve their problem. Up to now, no system exists which helps the user on all steps, especially no system is known which reads the user's mind and automatically generates a query appropriate to the underlying retrieval model.

To reduce the terminology problem of the items (1), (2), and (3) many approaches were developed and tested in the last decades. The approaches in the following sections try to reduce these problems with several techniques. Our approach try to reformulate the query on the way from the user's formulation (the last step on the user side) to the query representation (on the system side) (see Fig. 1). But before our new approach and the combination with Document Transformation techniques are introduced in section 6.2 and 7, respectively, common techniques in the field of information retrieval and the usage of relevance feedback are explained in the following.

3 Traditional Document Retrieval in the Vector Space Model

In this section the vector space model is explained which is the basis of our work. Essential parts of this model are the representation of documents and queries, a scheme for weighting terms, and an appropriate metric for calculating the similarity between a query and a document.

3.1 Representation of Documents and Queries

The task of traditional document retrieval is to retrieve documents which are relevant to a given query from a fixed set of documents, i.e. a document database. A common way to deal with documents, as well as queries, is to represent them using a set of index terms (simply called terms) and ignoring their positions in documents and queries. Terms are determined based on words of documents in the database.

In the following, t_i $(1 \leq i \leq m)$ and d_j $(1 \leq j \leq n)$ represent a term and a document in the database, respectively, where m is the number of terms and n is the number of documents.

The most popular retrieval model is the vector space model (VSM) introduced by Salton [29], [1], [8]. In the VSM, a document is represented as an m dimensional vector

$$\mathbf{d}_j = (w_{1j}, \ldots, w_{mj})^T \tag{1}$$

where T indicates the transpose, w_{ij} is the weight of a term t_i in a document $\mathbf{d}_j$. A query is likewise represented as

$$\mathbf{q} = (w_{1q}, \ldots, w_{mq})^T \tag{2}$$

where w_{iq} is the weight of a term t_i in a query $\mathbf{q}$.

3.2 Weighting Schemes

The weighting of these terms is the most important factor for the performance of an IR system in the vector space model. The development of a good weighting scheme is more art than science: in literature several thousand of weighting schemes are introduced and tested in the last 30 years especially in the SMART project [4]. Although Salton experiments in the 1960s with term weights [33], most of the methods are introduced in the 1970s until the late 1990.

An overview of the earlier methods are given in [2] or in [13]. Salton, Allen, and Buckley summarized in 1988 the results of 20 years development of term weighting schemes in the SMART system [31]. More than 1800 different combinations of term weighting factors were tested experimentally and 287 of them were clearly seen as different. Fuhr and Buckley [10] introduced a weighting scheme which is based on a linear combination of several weighting factors. The INQUERY system developed in the late 1980s is using a similar linear combination for calculating the term weights [38]. The start of the TREC conferences in 1992 gave a new impulse to the development of new weighting schemes.

In our work, we are using the most distributed weighting scheme: the standard normalized *tf idf* of the SMART system which is defined as follows [28]:

$$w_{ij} = tf_{ij} * idf_i \tag{3}$$

where tf_{ij} is the weight calculated using the frequency of the term t_i occuring in document d_j, and idf_i is the weight calculated using the inverse of the document frequency.

3.3 Similarity Measurements

The result of the retrieval is represented as a list of documents ranked according to their similarity to the query. The selection of a similarity function is a further central problem having decisive effects on the performance of an IR system. A detailed overview of similarity functions can be found in [39].

A common similarity function in text-based IR systems is the cosine metric which is also used in the SMART system and in our approach. For this metric, the similarity $sim(\mathbf{d}_j, \mathbf{q})$ between a document $\mathbf{d}_j$ and a query $\mathbf{q}$ is measured by the standard cosine of the angle between the document vector $\mathbf{d}_j$ and the query vector $\mathbf{q}$:

$$sim(\mathbf{d}_j, \mathbf{q}) = \frac{\mathbf{d}_j^T \cdot \mathbf{q}}{||\mathbf{d}|| \cdot ||\mathbf{q}||} \tag{4}$$

where $|| * ||$ is the Euclidean norm of a vector.

4 Collaborative Information Retrieval

In this section an encouragingly area in the field of Information Retrieval is introduced which is the motivation of our work. The general idea as well as the application to standard document collections are described.

4.1 No Memory in ad hoc Search

A shortcoming of the ad-hoc IR-Systems currently being used is their absence of any memory and their inability to learn. All information of a previous user or a previous query of the same user are gone immediately after the presentation of the list of relevant documents. Even systems with relevance feedback (see section 5) do not learn. They only integrate the last given feedback information with the current query. All information about previous feedback is not stored and is unavailable for future queries, unless the feedback is explicitly coded within the new query.

4.2   Basic Idea of Collaborative Information Retrieval

To overcome this imperfection we are using in our work an approach called *Collaborative Information Retrieval* ([20], [22], [21], or [15, section 1.2]. This approach learns with the help of feedback information of *all* previous user (and also previous queries of the current user) to improve the retrieval performance with a lasting effect.

Generally, for satisfying the user's information needs it is necessary to traverse a complex search process with many decisions and deliberations to achieve an optimal query. On the way from the initial query to a satisfying set of documents the user has invested a lot of effort and time which is lost in a common ad-hoc IR-System after the sending of the query. If another users (or the same user in the future) is searching for the same information then they must invest the same time and effort again. In the case of complex search processes it is virtually impossible to reconstruct all decisions and query reformulations in the same way. The users will not find the needed information (again) and will frustratedly give up the search.

The idea of Collaborative Information Retrieval is to store all information obtained during a search process in a repository and to use this information for future queries. A successional user with similar information needs can profit from this automatically acquired wisdom on several ways:

- the current search process will be shorten and focussed to the desired topic
- the retrieval performance of the IR-System will be improved with the help of acquired wisdom of other users.

4.3   Restricted Scenario

This work is based on standard document collections, i.e. the TREC collections [37], to ensure the comparability with standard retrieval methods described in literature. But a shortcoming of these collections is that they do not contain any search processes as described above. They only contain a set of documents, a set of queries and the appropriate and relevant documents to each query (see also equation 5). Due to this shortcoming a restricted scenario is used for this work. The scenario has the following characteristics:

No complex search processes: The standard document collections only contain a set of documents, a set of user queries and for each query a list of relevant documents.

No personalization: The scenario is using one single global user querying the IR-System. No differentiation of several users, group profiles or personalization hierarchies are taken into consideration. (See [19] for further information about this topic.)

No user judgement: The user queries are qualitatively not differentiated and there is no judgement or assessment of the user (queries).

No reflection over time: The queries are absolutely independent and no reflections or changes over time are made. An example problem which is not considered is the following: a user is initially searching for some publications to get an overview of a current problem. In the meantime he is learning more and more about the topic and the next time he looks for more 'deeper' documents and specific information, even though he is formulating the same query.

Nlobal relevance feedback: The approaches shown here are based on global relevance feedback and learn with the complete learning set of queries, in contrast to ordinary local feedback which is used in every step within the search process to generate the new query. In our approach the global feedback is used to directly form the new query in one single step.

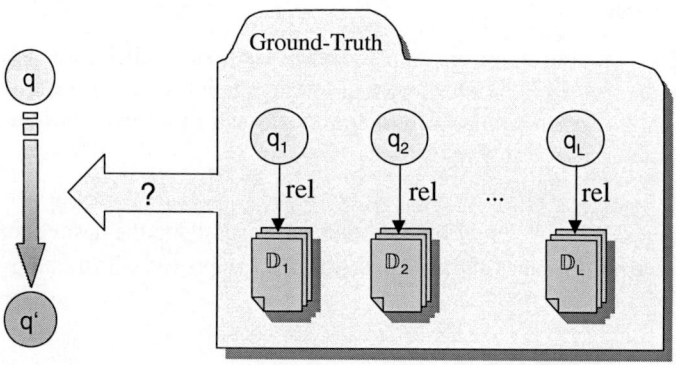

Fig. 2. Restricted scenario of the Collaborative IR with TREC collections.

Figure 2 illustrates the scenario used in this work. The user query q is transformed to the improved query q' with the help of relevance feedback information which is provided by the document collection.

A set of relevant documents is assigned to each query. Relevance information r_k for a query q_k is represented by a N-dimensional vector:

$$r_k = (r_{1k}, r_{2k}, \ldots, r_{Nk})^T, \ 1 \leq k \leq L, \tag{5}$$

whereas

$$r_{jk} = \begin{cases} 1 \text{ document } j \text{ is relevant to query } k \\ 0 \text{ document } j \text{ is } not \text{ relevant to query } k \end{cases} \tag{6}$$

N is the number of documents and L is the number of test queries in the collection. $()^T$ is the transpose of a matrix or a vector.

5   Relevance Feedback Techniques

Because both retrieval techniques discussed in this work belong to the family of relevance feedback techniques, this section gives a short overview of relevance feedback techniques before in the following section our new query expansion approach is introduced and how it is used to improve Document Transformation techniques.

5.1   Taxonomy of Relevance Feedback Techniques

As seen in the introduction a common way of searching information is to start with a short initial query and to reformulate it again and again until satisfying results are returned. To reach this, a lot of effort and time has to be invested by the user.

The main idea of relevance feedback techniques is to ask the user to provide evaluations or 'relevance feedback' on the documents retrieved from the query. This feedback then is used for subsequently improving the retrieval effectiveness in order to shorten the way to more satisfying results.

The feedback is given by marking just the relevant documents in the result list or more specifically by marking the relevant and the irrelevant documents. The marking itself can be boolean (marked or not) or within a given scale in more advanced systems.

In general relevance feedback techniques are not restricted to specific retrieval models and can be utilized without a document assessment function which is responsible for the ranking of the retrieved documents.

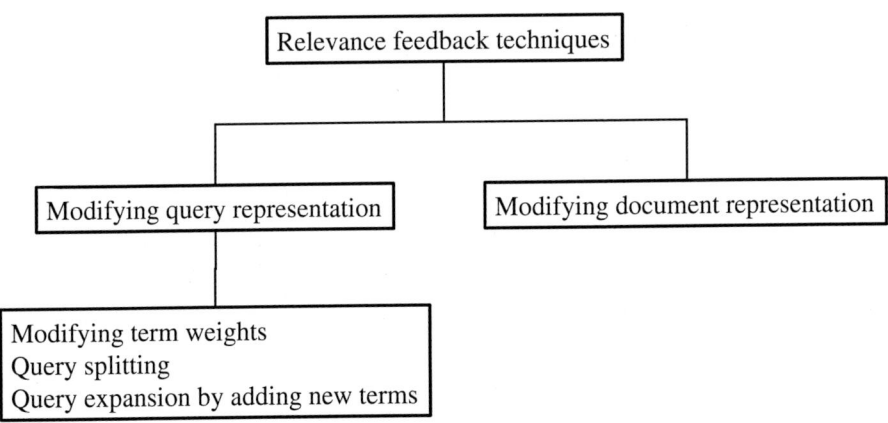

Fig. 3. A taxonomy of relevance feedback techniques

In literature a lot of different strategies are described and many implementations are tested. Figure 3 shows how the two main strategies for relevance information are utilized.

First, the user's search query is reformulated and second, documents of the collection are changed.

Both approaches have their pros and cons. Approaches which reformulate the search query only influence the current search and do not effect further queries of the same or other users. On the other side approaches which change the documents within the collection possibly do not effect the current search.

Especially of interest is the way in which the query is reformulated because the approach described in this work also try to answer this question.

In general, all introduced approaches in the following sections are reaching improvements after some iterations.

5.2   Changing the Document Collection

Information retrieval methods which change documents within the collection are also known as 'Document Transformation methods' [17] or 'user-oriented clustering' [3], [11].

The hope of information retrieval in the vector space model lays in the fact that the vector of a document relevant to the user's query is located near to the vector of the query. Document transformation approaches aim to improve those cases where this is not accomplished by moving the document vectors relevant to the query to the direction of the query. Those which are irrelevant are moved away.

When moving the document vectors (either closer to or away from the query vector) close attention must be paid so that each single movement is very small. This is because the assessment of a single user is not inevitably concurred by other users.

Document transformation methods were already described in the late 1960s by the SMART team [4], [9]. It is one of the strategies which is easy and efficient enough to be part of big search machines. Although these approaches are introduced early they achieved only little attention and were only tested in a restricted way. 20 years later Salton identifies the main reason for this negligence [30, S.326]:

> "Document-space modification methods are difficult to evaluate in the laboratory, where no users are available to dynamically control the space modifications by submitting queries."

Direct Hit for example is one of the few current search machines which claims to be adaptive to their user by relevance feedback techniques. The authors state that their system learns by observing which pages the user looks for, which links they are following, and how long they stay at a particular page [7]. So far the exact algorithms have not been published. They seem to be too new and valuable for a public submission.

In literature some algorithms for Document Transformation can be found. Some examples are given in [17]:

$$D = (1 - \alpha)D + \alpha\frac{|D|}{|Q|}Q \tag{7}$$

$$D = D + \beta Q \tag{8}$$

$$D = D_{original} + D_{learned}, \quad whereas \tag{9}$$

$$D_{learned} = \begin{cases} D_{learned} + \beta\,Q & if\ |D_{learned}| < l \\ (1 - \alpha)D_{learned} + \alpha\frac{|D_{learned}|}{|Q|}\,Q & otherwise \end{cases}$$

Here Q is the user query and D is the relevant document. $|D|$ is the norm of D, i.e. the sum of all term weights in D. l is a threshold.

The strategy in equation (7) ensures that the length of the document vector stays constant. [4] and [34] show that this strategy is able to improve the retrieval results on small and middle sized document collections.

The strategy in equation (8) is the most simple, but it performs well on a low quantity (less than 2000) of queries [17]: terms of Q are weighted with β and then added to the document vector D. It should be noted that this way of summation causes the length of the document to grow without limits.

Both strategies are sensitive to a supersaturation. If many queries are assigned to a relevant document then the effect of the initial document terms is decreased with the growing amount of queries and the effect of the query terms dominates. This document saturation is a serious problem in search machines which utilize variants of these formulae.

The strategy in equation (9) is developed to solve this problem. With a growing amount of queries (document length) the effect of queries is decreasing.

In general Document Transformation techniques have been shown to improve retrieval performance over small and medium-sized collections [4], [34]. There was no winner among the strategies that have been tried: different strategies perform best on different collections [34].

One notable and important difference between the Document Transformation methods and the methods modifying the query described next is that only the first ones leave permanent effects on a system.

5.3   Reformulation of the Query

As opposed to Document Transformation methods, which try to move relevant documents nearer to their appropriate queries, methods for reformulating the query try to solve the retrieval problem from the other side. They try to reformulate the initial user query in a way that the query moves nearer to the relevant documents.

Basically, three different approaches to improve the retrieval results are known in literature: First, methods which modify weights of the query terms, second, methods for query splitting, and most importantly, methods for query expansion by adding new terms. The approach in section 6.2 used in our work belongs to this group.

Modification of Term Weights: Methods which modify the weights of the query terms do not add any terms to the initial query but merely in-(de-)crease the available weights with the help of the feedback information. The problem of this approach is that no additional information (new terms) is placed in the query.

Query Splitting: In some cases relevance feedback techniques only supply unsatisfying results, i.e. documents marked as relevant are not homogeneous, meaning that they do not have a single topic in common and do not form a common cluster in the vector space. Another problem is irrelevant documents that lie near (or in between) relevant documents. In this case the initial query vector will be moved also to these irrelevant documents by the feedback.

To discover these cases a common method is to cluster the documents marked as relevant and therewith to analyze if the documents share a topic and if they are homogeneous in the vector space. If the relevant documents are separable into several clusters then the initial query is split appropriately into the same amount of subqueries. The term weights are adjusted according to the document clusters [11].

Query Expansion: The third and in general most distributed group of methods for modifying the user query is the expansion of the query by adding new terms. These new terms are directly choosen after the presenting of the retrieved document with the help of the user feedback. They are added to the initial query with adequate weights.

Experimental results have shown that positive feedback, i.e. marking only relevant documents, is generally better than using positive and negative feedback. The reason for this is that documents of the relevant document set are positioned more homogeneous in the vector space than the documents in the negative set, i.e. which are marked as irrelevant.

Rocchio Relevance Feedback: Rocchio [27] suggested a method for relevance feedback which uses average vectors (centroids) for each set of relevant and irrelevant documents. The new query is formed as a weighted sum of the initial query and the centroid vectors. Formally the Rocchio relevance feedback is defined as follows:

Let q be the initial query and n_1 be the amount of relevant and n_2 be the amount of irrelevant documents. Then the new query q' is formed by:

$$q' = q + \frac{1}{n_1} \sum_{relevant} \frac{D_i}{|D_i|} - \frac{1}{n_2} \sum_{non-relevant} \frac{D_i}{|D_i|}. \tag{10}$$

An important nature of this method is that new terms are added to the initial query and the former term weights are adjusted. Salton and Buckley [32] have tested a mass of variants of this linear vector modification. They asserted that this technique needs only a low calculation effort, and in general, achieves good results. But they also observed that the performance varies over different document collections. Furthermore, they stated that these techniques have bigger gains in cases with poor initial queries than in cases where the initial query provides very good results.

Pseudo Relevance Feedback: The Rocchio relevance feedback of the previous section supplies good results but is has a crucial disadvantage. It needs user feedback. However this is very hard to get in real IR-Systems because only few user are willing to do the job of assessing documents.

One idea to simulate this explicit user feedback is to rely on the performance of the IR system and to postulate: "The best n_1 of the ranked document list are relevant." These are used as positive feedback for the relevance feedback method.

In contrast to the Rocchio relevance feedback no negative feedback is considered. It may be possible to postulate: "The last n_2 documents are irrelevant" and use them as a negative feedback. But this variation is uncommon and generally leads to lower results.

Like the Rocchio relevance feedback the pseudo relevance feedback works in three steps: 1. The initial query is given to the system and the relevant documents are determined. 2. In opposite to the Rocchio relevance feedback these relevant documents are not presented to the user for marking but the most similar n documents are selected automatically to reformulate the query by adding all (or just some selected) terms of these documents to the query. 3. The reformulated query is given to the system and the relevant documents are presented to the user.

An interesting variation of the pseudo relevance feedback is described by Kise et al. [18]:

Let **E** be a set of relevant document vectors for expansion given by

$$\mathbf{E} = \left\{ \mathbf{d}_j^+ \,\middle|\, \frac{sim(\mathbf{d}_j^+, \mathbf{q})}{\max_{1 \le i \le N} \sim (\mathbf{d}_j^+, \mathbf{q})\}} \ge \theta, \ 1 \le j \le N \right\} \tag{11}$$

where **q** is the original query vector, $\mathbf{d}_j^+$ is a document vector relevant to the query and θ is a similarity threshold. The sum $\mathbf{d}_s$ of these relevant document vectors

$$\mathbf{d}_s = \sum_{\mathbf{d}_j^+ \in \mathbf{E}} \mathbf{d}_j^+ \tag{12}$$

can be considered as enriched information about the original query[1]. With this, the expanded query vector $\mathbf{q}'$ is obtained by

$$\mathbf{q}' = \frac{\mathbf{q}}{\| \mathbf{q} \|} + \beta \frac{\mathbf{d}_s}{\| \mathbf{d}_s \|} \tag{13}$$

where β is a parameter for controlling the weight of the newly incorporated terms. Finally, the documents are ranked again according to the similarity $sim(\mathbf{d}_j, \mathbf{q}')$ to the expanded query.

This variation has two parameters: first, the weighting parameter β which defines how big the influence of the relevant documents is vs. the initial query. Secondly, the similarity threshold θ which defines how many documents are used as positive feedback.

---

[1] Remark that the sum $\mathbf{d}_s$ is a single vector.

As opposed to the previously described approach, which defines a fixed amount of positive documents (n_1), the threshold θ only describes 'how relevant' the documents must be to be used as positive feedback. Thus, the amount of documents used is dynamic and individual, depending on the document collection and the current query. If many documents are similar to the initial query then the document set E used for the expansion of the query is very big. But assuming the same θ, if only one document is sufficient similar to the given query then E contains only this single document.

6   Learning Term-Based Concepts for Query Expansion

In this section some central aspects of query expansion techniques in general are discussed and our new approach for learning term-based concepts is introduced.

6.1   Central Aspects of Query Expansion Techniques

The crucial point in query expansion is the question: Which terms (or phrases) should be included in the query formulation? If the query formulation is to be expanded by additional terms there are two problems that are to be solved namely:

- how are these terms selected and
- how are the parameters estimated for these terms.

For the selection task, three different strategies have been proposed:

Dependent terms: Here terms that are dependent on the query terms are selected. For this purpose the similarity between all terms of the document collection has to be computed first [26].

Feedback terms: From the documents that have been judged by the user, the most significant terms (according to a measure that considers the distribution of a term within relevant and non-relevant documents) are added to the query formulation [28]. Clear improvements are reported in [28] and more recently in [16].

Interactive selection: By means of one of the methods mentioned before a list of candidate terms is computed and presented to the user. The user then makes the final decision over which terms are to be included in the query [1].

Many terms used in human communication are ambiguous or have several meanings [26] but most ambiguities are resolved automatically without noticing the ambiguity. The way this is done by humans is still an open problem of psychological research, but it is almost certain, that the context in which a term occurs plays a central role [35], [24].

Most attempts at automatically expanding queries failed to improve the retrieval effectiveness and it was often concluded that automatic query expansion based on statistical data was unable to bring a substantial improvement in the retrieval effectiveness [25].

But this could have several reasons. Term-based query expansion approaches are mostly using hand-made thesauri or just plain co-occurrence data [5], [12]. They do not use learning technologies for the query terms. On the other hand, those who use learning technologies (Neural Networks, Support Vector Machines, etc.) are query-based. That means these systems learn concepts (or additional terms) for the complete query.

The vital advantage of using term-based concepts and not learning the complete query is that other users can profit from the learned concepts. A statistical evaluation of log files has shown that the probability that a searcher uses exactly the same query as a previous searcher is much lower then the probability that parts of a query (phrases or terms) occur in other queries. So, even if a web searcher never used the given search term, the probability that other searcher had used it is very high and then he can profit from the learnt concept.

6.2   Learning Term-Based Concepts

A problem of the standard VSM is that a query is often too short to rank documents appropriately. To cope with this problem, an approach is to enrich the original query with terms which occur in the documents of the collection.

Our method uses feedback information and information globally available from previous queries. Feedback information in our environment is available within the ground truth data provided by the test document collections. The ground truth provides relevance information, i.e. for each query a list of relevant documents exists.

Relevance information for each query is represented by a N dimensional vector:

$$r_k = (r_{1k}, r_{2k}, \ldots, r_{Nk})^T, \quad 1 \leq k \leq L, \tag{14}$$

with

$$r_{jk} = \begin{cases} 1, & \text{if document } \mathbf{d}_j \text{ is relevant to query } \mathbf{q}_k \\ 0, & \text{if document } \mathbf{d}_j \text{ is } not \text{ relevant to query } \mathbf{q}_k \end{cases} \tag{15}$$

where N is the number of documents and L is the number of queries in the collection.

In contrast to traditional pseudo relevance feedback methods, where the top j ranked documents are assumed to be relevant and then their terms are incorporated into the expanded query, we use a different technique to compute relevant documents [20]. The approach is divided into two phases (see also Fig. 4):

- The *learning phase* for each term works as follows:
  1. Select old queries in which the specific query term occurs.
  2. From these selected old queries get the sets of relevant documents from the ground truth data.
  3. From each set of relevant documents compute a new document vector and use these document vectors to build the term concept.
- The *expansion phase* for each term is then performed as documented in literature:
  1. Select the appropriate concept of the current term.

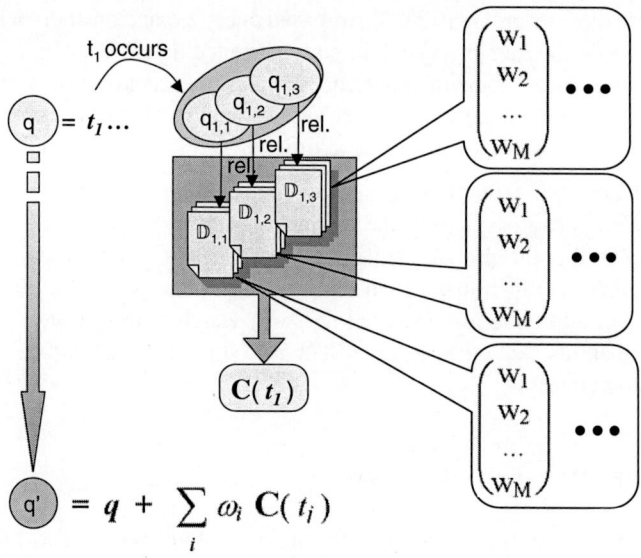

Fig. 4. Strategie of learning term-based concepts

2. Use a weighting scheme to enrich the new query with the concept.

For the formal description of the learning phase we need the following definitions:

- $\mathbf{D} = \mathbf{d}_1, \ldots, \mathbf{d}_N$: the set of all documents.
- $\mathbf{Q} = \mathbf{q}_1, \ldots, \mathbf{q}_L$: the set of all known queries.
- $\mathbf{q}_k = (w_{1k}, \ldots, w_{ik}, \ldots, w_{Mk})^T$ represented within the vector space model. For each term of the query the appropriate weight w_{ik} is between 0 an 1.
- $\mathbf{R}^+(\mathbf{q}_k) = \{\mathbf{d}_j \in D | r_{ij} = 1\}$: the set of all documents relevant to the query $\mathbf{q}_k$ (see also equation 6).

Now, the first step of the learning phase collects all queries having the i-th term in common[2]:

$$\mathbf{Q}_i = \{\mathbf{q}_k \in \mathbf{Q} \mid w_{ik} \neq 0\} \tag{16}$$

Step two collects all documents which are relevant to these collected queries:

$$\mathbf{D}_{ik} = \{\, \mathbf{d}_j \mid \mathbf{d}_j \in \mathbf{R}^+(\mathbf{q}_k) \wedge \mathbf{q}_k \in \mathbf{Q} \,\} \tag{17}$$

In the last step of the learning phase the concept of each i-th term is built as the sum of all documents (i.e. vectors of term weights) which are relevant to the known queries which have the term in common:

$$\mathbf{C}_i = \sum_{\mathbf{d}_j \in \mathbf{D}_{ik}} \mathbf{d}_j \tag{18}$$

---

[2] If the i-th term doesn't occur in any query $\mathbf{q}_k$ then the set $\mathbf{Q}_i$ is empty

As with queries and documents, a concept is represented by a vector of term weights. If no query $\mathbf{q}_k$ contains term i, then the corresponding concept $\mathbf{C}_i$ is represented as $(0,\ldots,0)^T$.

Now, that the term-based concepts have been learnt, the user query $\mathbf{q}$ can be expanded term by term. Thus, the expanded query vector $\mathbf{q}'$ is obtained by

$$\mathbf{q}' = \mathbf{q} + \sum_{i=1}^{M} \omega_i \mathbf{C}_i \tag{19}$$

where ω_i are parameters for weighting the concepts. In the experiments described below ω_i is globally set to 1.

Before applying the expanded query, it is normalized by

$$\mathbf{q}'' = \frac{\mathbf{q}'}{||\mathbf{q}'||} \tag{20}$$

For this approach, the complete documents (all term weights w_{ij} of the relevant documents) are summed up and added to the query. Although, in literature it is reported that using just the top ranked terms is sufficient or sometimes better, experiments with this approach on the TREC collections have shown that the more words are used to learn the concepts the better the results are. So, the decision was made to always use the complete documents and not only some (top ranked) terms.

If no ground truth of relevant documents is available, (pseudo) relevant feedback techniques can be used and the concepts are learnt by adding terms from the retrieved relevant documents.

The advantage of the Document Transformation approach, that it leaves permanent effects on a system, also holds for learnt concepts.

7   Improving Document Transformation

As described above, Document Transformation aims in moving the document vectors towards the query vector. But with all approaches up to now just terms of the query are added to their relevant documents. In our mind this is not enough. If the current user formulates the same information need with different query terms then potential relevant documents might be moved away from this query.

To cope with this problem, we improved the Document Transformation approach with our concepts learnt from complete documents. Thus, these concepts contain more than just a few words.

The improvement is achieved by combining both techniques:

- First, all concepts for the current user query are learned from relevant documents of selected previous queries as described in section 6.2. This is done before the Document Transformation step to prevent the concepts being learnt with already moved documents, i.e. to avoid a mixture of both approaches.

- Second, the Document Transformation approach is applied as usual (see section 5.2). This means that documents relevant to previous queries are moved to the direction of 'their' queries.
- In the last step, the current user query is expanded with the appropriate term-based concepts, i.e. the current query vector is moved to (hopefully) relevant documents.

The evaluation was done in the common way again using the expanded user query and all documents (incl. all documents moved by the Document Transformation).

8 Experiments and Results

In this section the test collection and the setup of the experiments is described. Furthermore results with document transformation and improvements with term-based concepts are presented.

8.1 Test Collections

We made comparisons using a representative selection of four standard test collections. From the SMART project [36] the collection *CACM* (collection of titles and abstracts from the journal 'Communications of the ACM') and from disks of the TREC series [37] the collections *CR* (congressional reports), *FR* (federal register), and *ZF3* (articles from the 'computer select' discs of Ziff Davis Publishing). All document collections are provided with queries and their ground truth (a list of documents relevant to each query). For these collections, terms used for document representation were obtained by stemming and eliminating stop words.

Table 1. Statistics about test collections

	CACM	CR title	FR	ZF3
number of documents	3204	27922	19860	161021
number of different terms	3029	45717	50866	67108
mean document length	18.4	188.2	189.7	85.0
	(short)	(long)	(long)	(med)
number of queries	52	34	112	50
mean query length	9.3	2.9	9.2	7,4
	(med)	(short)	(med)	(med)
mean of relevant documents per query	15.3	24.8	8.4	164.3
	(med)	(high)	(med)	(high)

Table 1 lists statistics about the collections after stemming and eliminated stop words. In addition to the number of documents, an important difference is the length of the documents: CACM and ZF3 consists of abstracts, while CR and FR contain much longer documents.

Queries in the TREC collections are mostly provided in a structured format with several fields. In this paper, the "title" (the shortest representation) is used for the CR and ZF3 collection whereas the "desc" (description; medium length) is used for the CACM and FR collection.

8.2   Evaluation

A common way to evaluate the performance of retrieval methods is to compute the (interpolated) precision at some recall levels. This results in a number of recall/precision points which are displayed in recall-precision graphs [1]. However, it is sometimes convenient to have a single value that summarizes the performance. The average precision (non-interpolated) over all relevant documents is a measure resulting in a single value [1], [36]. The definition is as follows:

As described in section 3, the result of retrieval is represented as the ranked list of documents. Let r(i) be the rank of the i-th relevant document counted from the top of the list. The precision for this document is calculated by i/r(i). The precision values for all documents relevant to a query are averaged to obtain a single value for the query. The average precision over all relevant documents is then obtained by averaging the respective values over all queries.

8.3   Results and Comparison to the Standard

Term weights in both, documents and queries, are determined according to the normalized $tf\ idf$ weighting scheme and the similarity is calculated by the VSM cosine measure, see also equation (3).

For the results of the standard vector space (VSM) model each query is used unchanged (just stemmed, stop words removed and $tf\ idf$ normalized). The recall/precision result is averaged over all queries.

For all approaches a common 'leave-one-out' strategy is used. This means that for all queries in a collection we are using one after the other each individual query as the test query and all other queries (with their relevant documents as the ground truth) as the learn set. Again, the recall/precision result is averaged over all queries. This is done to guarantee that we are not using the test query with its relevant documents for learning and that we have as much as possible to learn. Furthermore, this reflects more the real situation of a search scenario: the user formulates one individual (new) query to a system trained by all previous queries.

For the Document Transformation approach the results are gained as follows: for each query of the respective learn set all relevant document vectors are moved to the appropriate query, see also formula (8). After that, all documents are ranked against the test query with the cosine similarity and the recall/precision results are calculated. The final recall/precision results are averaged over all queries.

For the improved Document Transformation approach the results are gained similar: for each query of the respective learn set all relevant document vectors are moved to the appropriate query. After that, for all terms of the test query concepts are learnt and the initial test query is expanded with these concepts. Then, all documents are ranked against the expanded test query. Again, the final recall/precision results are averaged over all queries.

Figures 5 - 8 show the recall/precision graphs and the average-precision results of the original query (VSM), the Document Transformation (DT) and the improved Document Transformation (improved DT).

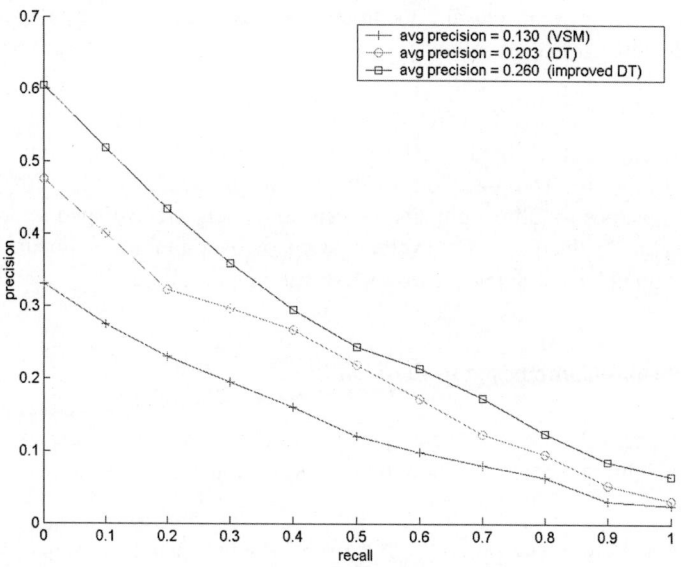

Fig. 5. Recall/precision graph of CACM

The figures indicate that the automatic query expansion method yields a considerable improvement of the Document Transformation in the retrieval effectiveness in all collections over all recall points. There is no indication that the improvement is depending on the size of the collection, the number of documents nor on the number or size of the queries.

Comparing collections, CACM and FR showing huge precision improvements on low recall levels (0.0 to 0.2). This area is important especially for web retrieval where a good precision of the top 10 documents is essential. On the ZF3 collection improvements are

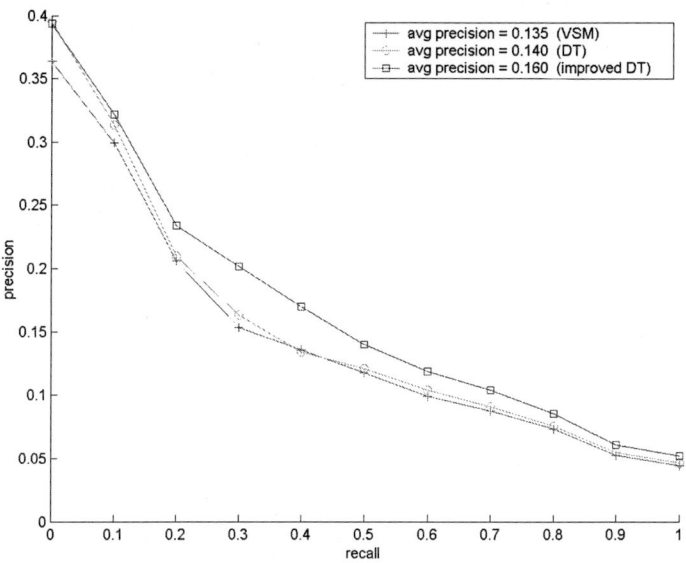

Fig. 6. Recall/precision graph of CR

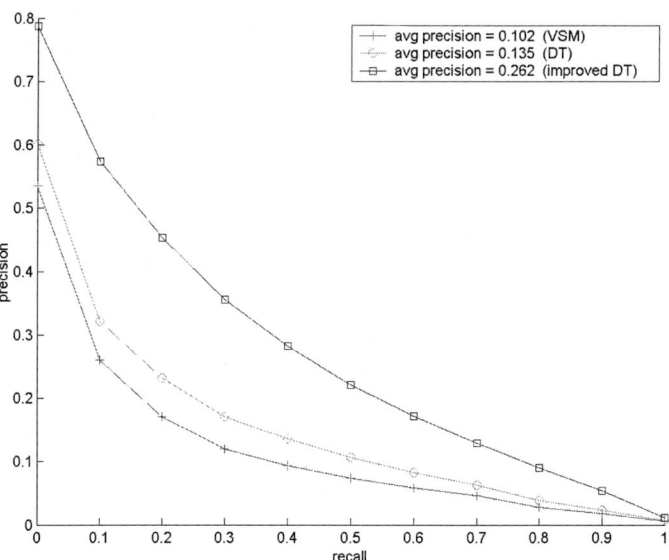

Fig. 7. Recall/precision graph of FR

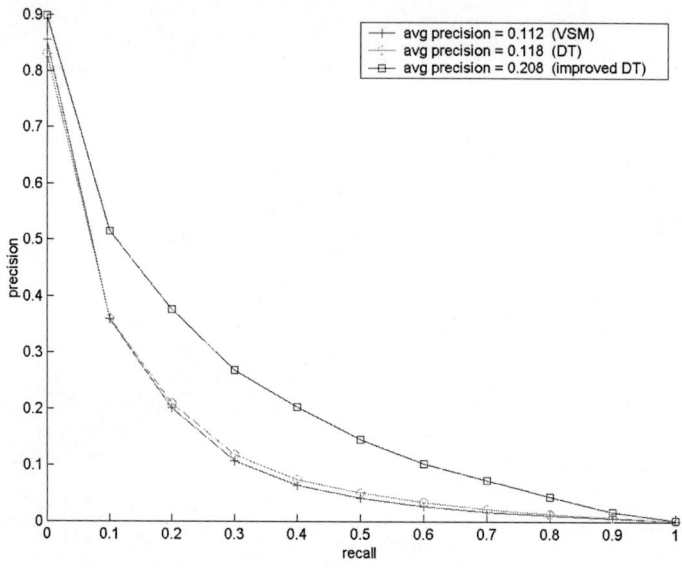

Fig. 8. Recall/precision graph of ZF3

achieved on low recall levels and especially on middle recall levels. On the CR collection improvements are not that impressive but still significant.

On the CR and on the ZF3 collection it is remarkable that although the Document Transformation gains only slight improvements over the standard VSM our method outperforms the Document Transformation method considerably.

On a closer look at the figures the impression could arise that the method performs better on longer queries. But experiments with the CR collection with different query representations have shown that 'title' queries result a better precision than 'description' or 'narrative' queries. This behavior is in contrast to the first impression of the figures.

Additionally, as described above, the more words and documents that are used to learn the concept the better the results. Experiments have shown that the precision continues to increase as more documents are used.

9   Conclusions and Prospects

In this work a new query expansion method was presented which learns term-based concepts from previous queries and their relevant documents. In contrast to other methods, the regarded query is expanded by adding those terms that are similar to the concept of individual query terms and belong to the same context, rather than selecting terms that are similar to the complete query or that are directly similar to query terms.

Besides to the improvement which is gained by this new query expansion method alone (see [20], [21], or [22] for details), we have shown that this method is capable to improve common Document Transformation techniques by combining them to an integrated approach.

The experiments made on four standard test collections of different sizes and document types have shown considerable improvements vs. the original queries in the standard vector space model and vs. the Document Transformation. The improvements do not seem to be depending on the size of the collection.

Furthermore, the results have shown that both approaches are not from the same class, i.e. it is evidently *not* the same if queries are moved to 'their' relevant documents or if relevant documents are moved 'their' queries. Otherwise the improvements of the Document Transformation would have been not that remarkable.

In contrast to Document Transformation the new query expansion method does not rely on thresholds ($\omega = 1$) which are dangerous and mostly differ from collection to collection. Of course in a next step we will do some analysis about the influence of this weighting factor to see if even better improvements are possible.

Furthermore, this approach can be perfectly used in search machines where new queries with their appropriate relevant (user-voted) documents can be easily added to the 'collection'. These can be used to build an increasing approach and can be used for a constant learning of the stored concepts. Current search machines [7] and tests with a self-made search machine integrating the new query expansion method have shown encouraging results [14].

An approach on passage-based retrieval by Kise [18] has shown good improvements vs. LSI and Density Distribution. An interesting idea for the future is to not use the complete relevant documents for expanding the query, nor using the N top ranked terms, but to use instead the terms of relevant passages within the documents. With this idea just the relevant passages can be used to learn the concepts. This surely will improve the results and we will be able to do a further evaluation of each concept in a greater detail, i.e. on the word level.

References

1. Ricardo Baeza-Yates and Berthier Ribeiro-Neto. *Modern Information Retrieval*. Addison-Wesley Publishing Company, 1999.
2. Nicholas J. Belkin and W. Bruce Croft. Retrieval techniques. *Annual Review of Information Science and Technology*, 22:109–145, 1987.
3. Jay N. Bhuyan, Jitender S. Deogun, and Vijay V. Raghavan. An Adaptive Information Retrieval System Based on User-Oriented Clustering. *submitted to ACM Transaction on Information Systemes*, January 1997.
4. T. L. Brauen. *Document vector modification*, chapter 24, pages 456–484. Prentice-Hall Inc., Englewood Cliffs, NJ, 1971.

5. Jen Nan Chen and Jason S. Chang. A Concept-based Adaptive Approach to Word Sense Disambiguation. In *Proceedings of 36th Annual Meeting of the Association for Computational Linguistics and 17th International Conference on Computational Linguistics (COLING/ACL-98)*, volume 1, pages 237–243, University of Montreal, Montreal, Quebec, Canada, August 10-14 1998. Morgan Kaufmann Publishers.

6. Cyril W. Cleverdon. Optimizing convenient online access to bibliographic databases. *Information Services and Use*, 4:37–47, 1984.

7. Direct Hit. *The Direct Hit popularity engine technology: A white paper*, 1999. www.directhit.com/about/products/technology_whitepaper.html.

8. Reginald Ferber. *Information Retrieval - Suchmodelle und Data-Mining-Verfahren für Textsammlungen und das Web*. dpunkt.verlag, Heidelberg, March 2003. 352 pages.

9. S. R. Friedman, J. A. Maceyak, and Stephen F. Weiss. *A relevance feedback system based on document transformations*, chapter 23, pages 447–455. Prentice-Hall Inc., Englewood Cliffs, NJ, 1971.

10. Norbert Fuhr and Christopher Buckley. A probabilistic learning approach for document indexing. *ACM Transactions on Information Systems*, 9:223–248, 1991.

11. Venkat N. Gudivada, Vijay V. Raghavan, William I. Grosky, and Rajesh Kasanagottu. Information Retrieval on the World Wide Web. *IEEE Internet Computing*, 1(5), September/October 1997.

12. Joe A. Guthriee, Louise Guthrie, Homa Aidinejad, and Yorick Wilks. Subject-Dependent Co-occurrence and Word Sense Disambiguation. In *Proceedings of 29th Annual Meeting of the Association for Computational Linguistics*, pages 146–152, University of California, Berkeley, California, USA, June 18-21 1991.

13. Donna K. Harman. *Ranking algorithms*, pages 363–392. Prentice Hall, 1992.

14. Thorsten Henninger. Untersuchungen zur optimierten und intelligenten Suche nach Informationen im WWW am Beispiel einer auf physikalische Inhalte ausgerichteten Suchmaschine, November 4 2002.

15. Armin Hust. Query expansion methods for collaborative information retrieval. In Andreas Dengel, Markus Junker, and Anette Weisbecker, editors, *this book*. Springer, 2004.

16. Bernard J. Jansen, Amanda Spink, and Tefko Saracevic. Real Life, Real Users, and Real Needs: A Study and Analysis of User Queries on the Web. *Information Processing and Management*, 36(2):207–227, 2000.

17. Charles Kemp and Kotagiri Ramamohanarao. Long-term learning for web search enginges. In Tapio Elomaa, Heikki Mannila, and Hannu Toivonen, editors, *Proceedings of the 6th European Conference of Principles of Data Mining and Knowledge Discovery (PKKD2002)*, Lecture Notes in Artificial Intelligence 2431, pages 263–274, Helsinki, Finland, August 19-23 2002. Springer.

18. Koichi Kise, Markus Junker, Andreas Dengel, and K. Matsumoto. Passage-Based Document Retrieval as a Tool for Text Mining with User's Information Needs. In *Proceedings of the 4th International Conference of Discovery Science*, pages 155–169, November 2001.

19. Stefan Klink. Query reformulation with collaborative concept-based expansion. In *Proceedings of the First International Workshop on Web Document Analysis (WDA 2001)*, pages 19–22, Seattle, Washington, USA, 2001.

20. Stefan Klink, Armin Hust, and Markus Junker. TCL - An Approach for Learning Meanings of Queries in Information Retrieval Systems. In *Content Management - Digitale Inhalte als Bausteine einer vernetzten Welt*, pages 15–25. June 2002.

21. Stefan Klink, Armin Hust, Markus Junker, and Andreas Dengel. Collaborative Learning of Term-Based Concepts for Automatic Query Expansion. In *Proceedings of the 13th European Conference on Machine Learning (ECML 2002)*, volume 2430 of *Lecture Notes in Artificial Intelligence*, pages 195–206, Helsinki, Finland, August 2002. Springer.

22. Stefan Klink, Armin Hust, Markus Junker, and Andreas Dengel. Improving Document Retrieval by Automatic Query Expansion Using Collaborative Learning of Term-Based Concepts. In *Proceedings of the 5th International Workshop on Document Analysis Systems (DAS 2002)*, volume 2423 of *Lecture Notes in Computer Science*, pages 376–387, Princeton, NJ, USA, August 2002. Springer.

23. M. E. Maron and J. L. Kuhns. On relevance, probabilistic indexing and information retrieval. *Journal of the Association for Computing Machinery*, 7(3):216–244, 1960.

24. Jong-Hoon Oh and Key-Sun Choi. Word Sense Disambiguation using Static and Dynamic Sense Vectors. In *Proceedings of the 19th International Conference on Computational Linguistics (COLING2002)*, number coling-252, Taipei, Taiwan, August 24 - September 1 2002.

25. Helen J. Peat and Peter Willet. The limitations of term cooccurrence data for query expansion in document retrieval systems. *Journal of the ASIS*, 42(5):378–383, 1991.

26. Ari Pirkola. *Studies on Linguistic Problems and Methods in Text Retrieval: The Effects of Anaphor and Ellipsis Resolution in Proximity Searching, and Translation and Query Structuring Methods in Cross-Language Retrieval*. Doctoral Dissertation, Department of Information Science, University of Tampere, Finland, June 1999.

27. Joseph J. Rocchio. *Document Retrieval Systems - Optimization and Evaluation*. Ph.D. Thesis, Harvard Computational Laboratory, Cambridge, MA, March 1966.

28. Joseph J. Rocchio. *Relevance feedback in information retrieval*, pages 313–323. Prentice-Hall Inc., Englewood Cliffs, NJ, 1971.

29. Gerard Salton. *The SMART Retrieval System – Experiments in Automatic Document Processing*. Prentice-Hall Inc., Englewood Cliffs, NJ, 1971.

30. Gerard Salton. Automatic Text Processing: The transformation, analysis, and retrieval of information by computer. MA, 1989. Addison-Wesley, Reading.

31. Gerard Salton, James Allen, and Christopher Buckley. Term-Weighting Approaches in Automatic Text Retrieval. *Information Processing & Management*, 24(5):513–523, 1988.

32. Gerard Salton and Christopher Buckley. Improving Retrieval Performance by Relevance Feedback. *Journal of the American Society for Information Sciences*, 41(4):288–297, 1990.

33. Gerard Salton and Michael Lesk. Computer evaluation of indexing and text processing. *Journal of the ACM*, 15(1):8–36, 1968.

34. Jacques Savoy and Dana Vrajitoru. Evaluation of learning schemes used in information retrieval. Technical Report CR-I-95-02, Faculty of Sciences, University of Neuchâtel, 1996.

35. Hinrich Schütze. Automatic word sense discrimination. *Computational Linguistics*, 24(1):97–123, 1998.

36. The SMART document collection. currently: ftp://ftp.cs.cornell.edu/pub/smart/.

37. Text REtrieval Conference (TREC). http://trec.nist.gov/, 2003.

38. Howard R. Turtle and W. Bruce Croft. Evaluation of an inference network-based retrieval model. *ACM Transactions on Information Systems*, 9(3):187–222, 1991.

39. Randall Wilson and Tony R. Martinez. Improved Heterogeneous Distance Functions. *Journal of Artificial Intelligence Research*, 6:1–34, 1997.

Passage Retrieval Based on Density Distributions of Terms and Its Applications to Document Retrieval and Question Answering

Koichi Kise[1], Markus Junker[2], Andreas Dengel[2], and Keinosuke Matsumoto[1]

[1] Dept. of Computer and Systems Sciences, Graduate School of Engineering,
Osaka Prefecture University,
1-1 Gakuencho, Sakai, Osaka 599-8531, Japan,
{kise, matsu}@cs.osakafu-u.ac.jp
[2] German Research Center for Artificial Intelligence (DFKI),
P.O.Box 2080, 67608, Kaiserslautern, Germany,
{Markus.Junker, Andreas.Dengel}@dfki.de

Abstract. A huge amount of electronic documents has created the demand of intelligent access to their information. Document retrieval has been investigated for providing a fundamental tool for the demand. However, it is not satisfactory due to (1) inaccuracies of retrieving long documents with short queries (a few terms), (2) a user's burden on finding relevant parts from retrieved long documents. In this paper, we apply a passage retrieval method called "density distributions" (DD) to tackle these problems. For the first problem, it is experimentally shown that a passage-based method outperforms conventional document retrieval methods if long documents are retrieved with short queries. For the second problem, we apply DD to the question answering task: locating short passages in response to natural language queries of seeking facts. Preliminary experiments show that correct answers can be located within a window of 50 terms for about a half of such queries.

1 Introduction

The growing number of electronic textual documents has created the demand of adaptive and intelligent access to the information implied by them. Document retrieval is one of the fundamental tools for fulfilling the demand. The task of document retrieval is to retrieve relevant documents in response to a query which describes a user's information need. Its basic operation is to measure the similarity between a document and a query. Documents with high similarity are presented to the user as the results of retrieval.

Although its research field has several decades of history, there still exist some open problems as follows:

Problem 1 Accuracy

The requirement of accuracy has not yet been fulfilled. We focus here on the following two problems.

A. Dengel et al. (Eds.): Adaptive READ Research Project, LNCS 2956, pp. 306–327, 2004.

Multi-topic documents: If a document is beyond the length of abstracts, it sometimes contains several topics. Even though one of them is relevant to the user's information need, the rest are not necessarily relevant. As a result, these irrelevant parts disturb the retrieval of documents.

Short queries: In general, the user's information need is fed to a retrieval system as a set of query terms. However, it is not an easy task for the user to transform his/her need into adequate query terms. From the analysis of Web search logs, for example, it is well-known that typical users issue quite short queries consisting of several terms. Such queries are too poor to retrieve documents appropriately.

Problem 2 Presentation

We have another problem on the user side if documents are long. Even if the relevant documents are retrieved, the demand is far from being fulfilled since the user is still burdened with the task of finding parts of documents in which the required information is written. Because it is practically unknown whether retrieved documents are relevant or not, the task is more troublesome for the user. Although it is necessary to locate the required information in documents, such a facility of presentation is beyond the scope of document retrieval.

In order to tackle the above problems, we focus in this paper on passage retrieval. The task of passage retrieval is to retrieve not documents but portions of documents or *passages* relevant to queries.

The notion of passage retrieval was first introduced to document retrieval mainly for solving the problem of "multi-topic documents". Document retrieval based on passages is sometimes called passage-based document retrieval. In this scheme, documents are retrieved based only on passages in order not to be disturbed by the irrelevant parts. It has been shown in the literature that passage-based methods outperform conventional methods in processing long documents [1,2,3,4,5,6].

In this paper, we experimentally show that a passage-based method is also superior to conventional methods for the problem of "short queries" under the condition that documents are not too short. As a method of passage-based retrieval, we utilize a method based on "density distributions" [7,8,9,10], which is capable of segmenting documents into passages adaptively in response to queries.

For the problem 2, we employ very short passages consisting of 10 or 50 terms as the output of retrieval on condition that queries are for searching facts. This task is called *question answering* (QA) in the literature [11]. As compared to state-of-the-art methods presented in, for example, the TREC conferences [12], a QA method described in this paper is simple. Our intention is to investigate to what degree the performance is achieved without any extensive efforts and tune-ups.

The rest of this paper is organized as follows. In Sect. 2, we describe the proposed method of passage retrieval. Section 3 is devoted to introduce the use of passage retrieval as a method of document retrieval, as well as some representative conventional methods. The results of experimental comparison

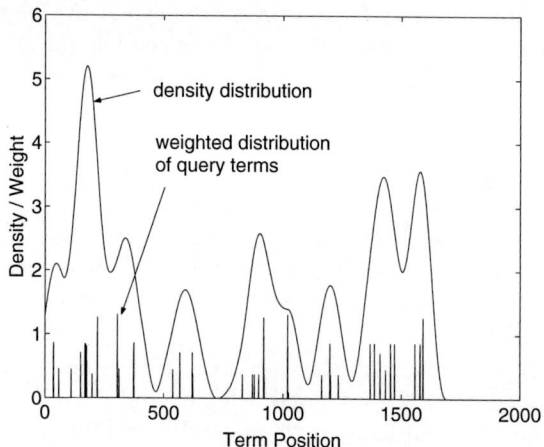

Fig. 1. Density distribution

of these methods are also reported in this section. Next, in Sect. 4, a simple question answering system based on the proposed passage retrieval method is described with some results of preliminary experiments. Section 5 presents some concluding remarks.

2   Passage Retrieval Based on Term Density Distributions

Passages used in passage retrieval can be classified into three types: discourse, semantic and window passages [1]. Discourse passages are defined based on discourse units such as sentences and paragraphs. Semantic passages are obtained by segmenting text at the points where a topic of text changes. Window passages are determined based on the number of terms.

As a method based on window passages, we have proposed the method called "density distributions"(DD) [7,8,9,10]. A notion of density distributions was first introduced to locate explanations of a word in text [13] and applied to passage retrieval by some of the authors. Comparison of various windows for document retrieval and other tasks can be found in [5,14].

An important idea of DD is the assumption that parts of documents which densely contain terms in a query are relevant to it. Figure 1 shows an example of a density distribution. The horizontal axis indicates the positions of terms in a document. A weighted distribution of query terms in the document is shown as spikes on the figure: their height indicates the weight of a term. The density distribution shown in the figure is obtained by smoothing the spikes with a window function. The details are as follows.

Let us first introduce symbols used for explanations. The task of passage retrieval is to retrieve passages from a fixed set of documents or a document database. In a common way to deal with documents as well as queries, they are represented using a set of index terms (simply called terms from now on). Terms are determined based on words of documents in the database. Let t_i $(1 \leq i \leq m)$ and d_j $(1 \leq j \leq n)$ be a term and a document in the database, respectively, where m is the number of different terms and n is the number of documents in the database. In the passage retrieval, each document is viewed as a sequence of terms. Let $a_j(l)$ $(1 \leq l \leq L_j)$ be a term at a position l in a document d_j where L_j is the document length measured in terms.

In general, some terms in a query are more important than others for locating appropriate passages. For example, a term "retrieval" in papers about information retrieval is ubiquitous and thus gives little evidence for distinguishing passages relevant to the query. In order to represent such information, we utilize the weight called "inverse document frequency" idf_i for a term t_i defined as follows:

$$\mathrm{idf}_i = \log \frac{n}{n_i} \tag{1}$$

where n is the total number of documents in the database and n_i is the number of documents which include the term t_i.

Using the weight idf_i, the weighted distribution $b_j(l)$ of query terms is defined as

$$b_j(l) = w_{iq} \cdot \mathrm{idf}_i \tag{2}$$

where $a_j(l) = t_i$ and w_{iq} is the weight of a term t_i in a query. The weight w_{iq} is defined based on the frequency f_{iq} of the term t_i in the query as

$$w_{iq} = \log(f_{iq} + 1) \ . \tag{3}$$

Smoothing of $b_j(l)$ enables us to obtain the density distribution $dd_j(l)$ for a document d_j:

$$dd_j(l) = \sum_{x=-W/2}^{W/2} f(x) b_j(l - x) \ , \tag{4}$$

where $f(x)$ is a window function with a window size W. We employ the Hanning window function defined by

$$f(x) = \begin{cases} \frac{1}{2}(1 + \cos 2\pi \frac{x}{W}) & \text{if } |x| \leq W/2 \ , \\ 0 & \text{otherwise} \ . \end{cases} \tag{5}$$

whose shape is shown in Fig. 2.

3   Document Retrieval

In this section, we describe how to use DD as a document retrieval method as well as some conventional methods. The latter are employed as methods for comparison in the experiments.

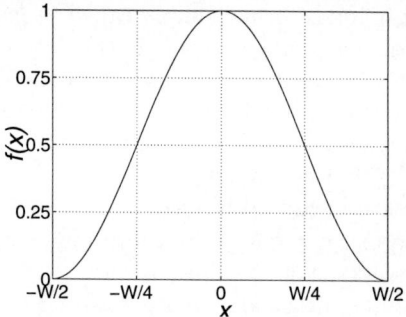

Fig. 2. Hanning window function

3.1   DD as Document Retrieval

The task of document retrieval is to retrieve documents relevant to a given query from a document database. In order to utilize DD as a document retrieval method, scores of documents should be calculated based on their density distributions. In our method, the score of d_j for a query q is simply defined as the maximum value of its density distribution as follows:

$$\text{score}(d_j, q) = \max_l dd_j(l) \ . \tag{6}$$

Note that the maximum operation prevents us from being affected by irrelevant parts. Results of retrieval are represented as a list of documents ranked according to their scores to the query.

3.2   Simple Vector Space Model

The simple vector space model (VSM) [15,16] is the simplest retrieval model. In the VSM, both a document d_j and a query q are represented as m-dimensional vectors:

$$\boldsymbol{d}_j = (w_{1j}, ..., w_{mj})^T \ , \tag{7}$$

$$\boldsymbol{q} = (w_{1q}, ..., w_{mq})^T \ , \tag{8}$$

where T indicates the transpose, w_{ij} is a weight of a term t_i in a document d_j, and w_{iq} is a weight of a term t_i in a query q.

In this paper, we employ a standard weighting scheme called "tf-idf" defined as follows:

$$w_{ij} = \text{tf}_{ij} \cdot \text{idf}_i \ , \tag{9}$$

where tf_{ij} is the weight calculated using the term frequency f_{ij} (the number of occurrences of a term t_i in a document d_j), and idf_i is the inverse document frequency defined by Eq. (1). In computing tf_{ij}, the raw frequency is usually dampened by a function. As in Eq. (3), we utilize $\text{tf}_{ij} = \log(f_{ij} + 1)$. The weight w_{iq} has been defined by Eq. (3).

Results of retrieval are likewise represented as lists of documents ranked according to their similarity to the query. The similarity $\text{sim}(d_j, q)$ between a document d_j and a query q is measured by the cosine of the angle between d_j and q:

$$\text{sim}(d_j, q) = \frac{d_j^T q}{\|d_j\| \, \|q\|} \, . \tag{10}$$

where $\| \cdot \|$ is the Euclidean norm of a vector.

3.3   Pseudo Relevance Feedback

A problem of the VSM is that a query is often too short to rank documents appropriately. To cope with this problem, a variety of query expansion techniques have been proposed [15]. A method called "pseudo relevance feedback" [16] is known as one of such techniques. In this method, first, documents are ranked with an original query. Then, high-ranking documents are assumed to be relevant and their terms are incorporated into the original query. Documents are ranked again using the expanded query.

In this paper, we employ a simple variant of pseudo relevance feedback. Let E be a set of document vectors for expansion given by

$$E = \left\{ d_j^+ \left| \frac{\text{sim}(d_j^+, q)}{\max_i \text{sim}(d_i, q)} \geq \tau \right. \right\} \, , \tag{11}$$

where q is an original query vector and τ is a threshold of the similarity. The sum d_s of document vectors in E:

$$d_s = \sum_{d_j^+ \in E} d_j^+ \tag{12}$$

can be considered as enriched information about the original query. Then, the expanded query vector q' is obtained by

$$q' = \frac{q}{\|q\|} + \lambda \frac{d_s}{\|d_s\|} \, , \tag{13}$$

where λ is a parameter for controlling the weight of the newly incorporated component. Finally, documents are ranked again according to the similarity $\text{sim}(d_j, q')$.

3.4   Latent Semantic Indexing

Latent semantic indexing (LSI) [17] is another well-known way for improving the VSM. Let D be a term-by-document matrix:

$$D = (\hat{d}_1, ..., \hat{d}_n) \, , \tag{14}$$

where $\hat{d}_j = d_j/\|d_j\|$. By applying the singular value decomposition, D is decomposed into the product of three matrices:

$$D = USV^T \ , \tag{15}$$

where U and V are matrices of size $m \times r$ and $n \times r$ ($r = \mathrm{rank}(D)$), respectively, and $S = \mathrm{diag}(\sigma_1, ..., \sigma_r)$ is a diagonal matrix with singular values σ_i ($\sigma_i \geq \sigma_j$ if $i < j$). Each row vector in U (V) is a r-dimensional vector representing a term (document).

By keeping only the $k(\ll r)$ largest singular values in S along with the corresponding columns in U and V, D is approximated by

$$D_k = U_k S_k V_k^T \ , \tag{16}$$

where U_k, S_k and V_k are matrices of size $m \times k$, $k \times k$ and $n \times k$, respectively. This approximation allows us to uncover *latent* semantic relation among terms as well as documents.

The similarity between a document and a query is measured as follows [18]. Let $v_j = (v_{j1}, ..., v_{jk})$ be a row vector in $V_k = (v_{ji})$ ($1 \leq j \leq n, 1 \leq i \leq k$). In the k-dimensional (approximated) space, a document d_j is represented as

$$d_j^* = S_k v_j^T \ . \tag{17}$$

An original query is also represented in the k-dimensional space as

$$q^* = U_k^T q \ . \tag{18}$$

Then the similarity is obtained by $\mathrm{sim}(d_j^*, q^*)$.

3.5   Experimental Comparison

In this subsection, we show the results of experimental comparison. After the description of test collections employed for the experiments, criteria for evaluating the results are described. Next, the results of experiments are presented and discussed.

Test Collections. We made a comparison using four test collections: MED (Medline; medicine), CRAN (Cranfield; aeronautics), FR (federal register), CR (congressional record). The collections MED and CRAN are available at [19], and FR and CR are contained in the TREC disks No.2 and No.4, respectively [12]. For these collections, terms used for the document representation were obtained by stemming and stopword elimination. We also applied a filer by frequency: words occurring only once in a collection were also eliminated.

In the TREC collections, each information need or *topic* is represented in several different lengths. In order to investigate the influence of query lengths, we employed three types: "title"(the shortest representation), "desc" (description; middle length) and "narr" (narrative; the longest).

Table 1. Statistics about documents in the test collections

	MED	CRAN	CR	FR
size [MB]	1.1	1.6	235	209
no. of doc.	1,033	1,398	27,922	19,789
no. of terms	4,284	2,550	37,769	43,760
doc. len. min.	20	23	22	1
max.	658	662	629,028	315,101
mean	**155**	**162**	**1,455**	**1,792**
median	139	142	324	550
mean no. of diff. terms in a doc.	47.5	50.6	187.6	190.0

Table 2. Statistics about queries in the test collections

	MED	CRAN	CR			FR		
			title	desc	narr	title	desc	narr
no. of queries	30	171		22			27	
query len. min.	2	4	2	4	12	1	5	13
max.	33	21	5	19	79	7	19	93
mean	**10.8**	**9.2**	**2.7**	**7.6**	**28.1**	**3.3**	**11.0**	**40.4**
median	9.0	9.0	2.5	6.0	22.5	3.0	11.0	36.0

Queries for FR and CR were defined as follows. From the topics 51–300 [12], we first selected topics described by at least above three types. Next, for each collection, we further selected topics which have at least *five* relevant documents. Finally, we defined queries by applying stemming and eliminating stopwords to original representations of the selected topics. Note that we utilized the original representations as queries, though in TREC it is allowed to define queries manually or automatically based on the representations.

Tables 1 and 2 show some statistics about the collections, where the length is measured in terms. In Table 1, an important difference is the length of documents: MED and CRAN consist of abstracts, while FR and CR contain much longer documents. In Table 2, a point to note is the difference of query length.

Evaluation

Mean Average Precision. A common way to evaluate the performance of retrieval methods is to compute the (interpolated) precision at 11 recall levels [15]. This results in a number of recall / precision points which are displayed in recall-precision graphs. However, it is sometimes convenient to have a single value that summarizes the performance. *Mean average precision over all relevant documents* [15,19,20] (simply called the mean average precision henceforth) is such a measure. The definition is as follows.

In general, results of retrieval are represented as ranked lists of documents. Let $r(i)$ be the rank of the i-th relevant document counted from the top of the list. The precision up to retrieving this document is calculated by $i/r(i)$. To obtain average precision p_k for a query k, precision values for all documents relevant to a query are averaged:

$$p_k = \frac{1}{N_k} \sum_{i=1}^{N_k} i/r(i) \tag{19}$$

where N_k is the number of relevant documents for a query k. The mean average precision p is obtained by averaging the respective values over all queries:

$$p = \frac{1}{N} \sum_{k=1}^{N} p_k \tag{20}$$

where N is the number of queries.

For example, consider two queries q_1 and q_2 which have two and three relevant documents, respectively. Suppose the ranks of relevant documents for q_1 are 2 and 5, and those for q_2 are 1, 3 and 10. The average precision for q_1 and q_2 is computed as $(1/2 + 2/5)/2 = 0.45$ and $(1/1 + 2/3 + 3/10)/3 = 0.66$, respectively. Then the mean average precision which takes into account both queries is $(0.45 + 0.66)/2 = 0.56$.

Statistical Test. The next step for the evaluation is to compare the values of the mean average precision obtained by different methods. An important question here is whether the difference in the mean average precision is really meaningful or just by chance. In order to make such a distinction, it is necessary to apply a statistical test.

Several statistical tests have been applied to the task of information retrieval [21,22]. In this paper, we utilize a test called "the paired t-test" [21] (called " macro t-test" in [22]) The following is the summary of the test.

Let a_k and b_k be the scores (e.g., the average precision) of retrieval methods A and B for a query k , and define $\delta_k = a_k - b_k$. The test can be applied under the assumptions that the model is additive, i.e., $\delta_k = \mu + \varepsilon_k$ where μ is the population mean and ε_k is an error, and that the errors are normally distributed. The null hypothesis here is $\mu = 0$ (A performs equivalently to B in terms of the scores), and the alternative hypothesis is $\mu > 0$ (A performs better than B).

It is known that the Student's t-statistic

$$t = \frac{\bar{\delta}}{\sqrt{s^2/N}} \tag{21}$$

follows the t-distribution with the degree of freedom of $N - 1$, where N is the number of samples (queries), $\bar{\delta}$ and s^2 are the sample mean and variance:

$$\bar{\delta} = \frac{1}{N} \sum_{k=1}^{N} \delta_i \ , \tag{22}$$

Table 3. Values of parameters

	param.	MED, CRAN	CR, FR
PRF	λ	1.0, 2.0	1.0, 2.0
	τ	0.71 ~ 0.99 step 0.02	0.71 ~ 0.99 step 0.02
LSI	k	60 ~ 500 step 20	50 ~ 500 step 50
DD	W	60 ~ 300 step 20	20 ~ 100 step 10, and 150, 200, 300

Table 4. Best parameter values

		MED	CRAN	CR title	desc	narr	FR title	desc	narr
PRF	λ	2.0	1.0	1.0	1.0	1.0	1.0	1.0	1.0
	τ	0.73	0.91	0.81	0.93	0.99	0.73	0.73	0.71
LSI	k	40	240	300	500	500	350	450	400
DD	W	80	60	40	20	30	70	30	20

$$s^2 = \frac{1}{N-1} \sum_{k=1}^{N} (\delta_i - \bar{\delta})^2 \ . \tag{23}$$

By looking up the value of t in the t-distribution, we can obtain the P-value, i.e., the probability of observing the sample results δ_k $(1 \le k \le N)$ under the assumption that the null hypothesis is true. The P-value is compared to a predetermined significance level α in order to decide whether the null hypothesis should be rejected. As significance levels, we utilize 0.05 and 0.01.

Results for the Whole Collections. The methods PRF (pseudo relevance feedback), LSI (latent semantic indexing) and DD (density distributions) were applied by ranging the values of parameters as shown in Table 3. The values which yielded the best mean average precision are listed in Table 4. The results shown in the following are based on these values.

Table 5 shows the mean average precision where the best and the second best values of mean average precision among the methods are indicated in bold and italic fonts, respectively.

The results of the paired t-test for all pairs of methods are shown in Table 6. The meaning of the symbols such as "$\gg$", "$>$" and "$\sim$" is summarized at the bottom of the table. For example, the symbol "$<$" was obtained in the case of PRF compared to LSI for the MED collection. This indicates that, at the significance level $\alpha = 0.05$, the null hypothesis "PRF performs equivalently to the LSI" is rejected and the alternative hypothesis "PRF performs worse than the LSI" is accepted. At $\alpha = 0.01$, however, the null hypothesis cannot be rejected. Roughly speaking, "$A \gg (\ll)B$", "$A > (<)B$" and "$A \sim B$" indicate that "A is

Table 5. Mean average precision

	MED	CRAN	CR			FR		
			title	desc	narr	title	desc	narr
VSM	0.526	0.371	0.124	0.149	0.156	0.058	0.076	0.167
PRF	*0.641*	**0.428**	**0.155**	**0.189**	**0.165**	*0.062*	*0.119*	*0.188*
LSI	**0.681**	*0.413*	0.106	0.133	0.133	*0.062*	0.085	0.134
DD	0.509	0.340	**0.155**	*0.150*	*0.163*	**0.135**	**0.153**	**0.228**

Table 6. Results of the paired t-test

methods A B	MED	CRAN	CR			FR		
			title	desc	narr	title	desc	narr
DD - VSM	~	≪	~	~	~	≫	≫	≫
DD - PRF	≪	≪	~	~	~	≫	≫	≫
DD - LSI	≪	≪	~	~	~	≫	≫	≫
PRF - VSM	≫	≫	>	>	~	≫	≫	≫
PRF - LSI	<	>	~	>	~	≫	≫	≫
LSI - VSM	≫	≫	~	~	~	≫	≫	≪

$$\gg, \ll : \quad \text{P-value} \leq 0.01$$
$$>, < : 0.01 < \text{P-value} \leq 0.05$$
$$\sim \quad : 0.05 < \text{P-value}$$

almost guaranteed to be better (worse) than B", "A is likely to be better (worse) than B" and "A is equivalent to B", respectively. [1].

For the collections of short documents (MED and CRAN), the methods PRF and LSI outperformed the rest. For the collection CR which includes long documents, these four methods almost performed equivalently. For the collection FR which also includes long documents, on the other hand, DD clearly outperformed the other methods. The advantage of PRF and LSI for the collections of short documents did not hold here.

From the above results, the influence of the length of documents and queries to the performance of the methods remains unclear. Although it has been shown that DD is inferior to PRF and LSI for short documents, DD outperformed the other methods only for one of the collections with long documents. This could be because of the nature of the collections CR and FR. Although these collections

---

[1] Voorhees *et al.* [20] show the empirical relation among the topic set size (the number of queries), the difference of the mean average precision between two methods, and the error rate of the statement that one method is superior to the other, based on the analysis of past TREC results. For example, the absolute difference of 0.05 (0.09) is required to obtain an error rate no larger than 5% based on the result for 50 (25) queries. However, in Table 6, the symbols >, <, ≫ and ≪ are obtained even in the cases that do not satisfy the above condition. The reason is as follows. In this paper, we apply t test with the information about "pairs", which is not used in [20]. It is known that this information makes t-test more powerful.

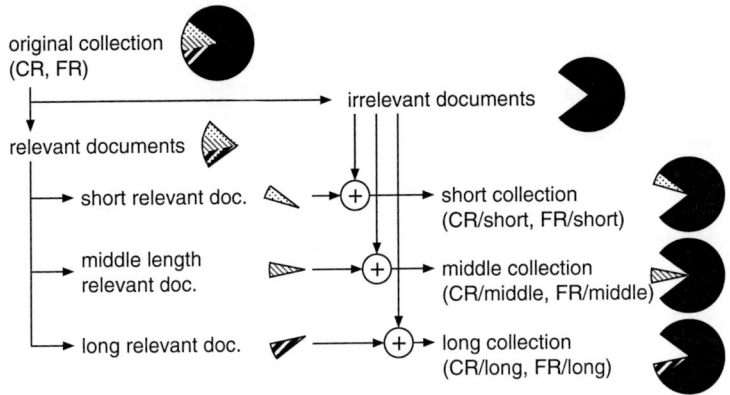

Fig. 3. Partition of the collections according to the length

Table 7. Statistics about the partitioned collections

	CR				FR			
	relevant doc.			irrel.	relevant doc.			irrel.
	short	middle	long	doc.	short	middle	long	doc.
no. of doc.	**251**	**251**	**252**	27,168	**148**	**148**	**148**	19,345
doc. len. min.	67	604	3,055	22	114	1,554	6,037	1
max.	601	3,029	629,028	385,065	1,512	5,994	315,101	124,353
mean	**334**	**1,315**	**33,550**	1,169	**859**	**3,075**	**35,982**	1,528
median	303	1,078	11,236	318	835	2,886	17,037	536
no. of queries	22	22	21	—	20	23	23	—

include much longer documents than MED and CRAN, they also include many short documents as shown by the gap between the mean and the median in Table 1.

Results for Partitioned Collections. In order to clarify the relation between the performance and the length of documents and queries, we partitioned each of the collections CR and FR into three smaller collections as shown in Fig. 3. Documents in the collections were first split into two disjoint sets: documents relevant to at least one query, and those irrelevant to all queries. The set of relevant documents was further divided into three disjoint subsets of almost equal size according to the length of documents: short relevant documents, middle length relevant documents, and long relevant documents. By combining each subset with the set of irrelevant documents, we prepared three partitioned collections called "short", "middle" and "long". As queries for each partitioned collection, we took the queries which are relevant to at least one document in the partitioned collection. The statistics about the partitioned collections are shown in Table 7.

Table 8. Results of the paired t-test for the partitioned collections

doc.	methods	CR			FR		
length	A B	title	desc	narr	title	desc	narr
short	DD - VSM	$<$	$\ll$	$\ll$	$\sim$	$\sim$	$\ll$
	DD - PRF	$\ll$	$\ll$	$<$	$\sim$	$\sim$	$<$
	DD - LSI	$\sim$	$<$	$\sim$	$\sim$	$\sim$	$\sim$
middle	DD - VSM	$>$	$\sim$	$\sim$	$>$	$\sim$	$\sim$
	DD - PRF	$\sim$	$\sim$	$\sim$	$>$	$\sim$	$\sim$
	DD - LSI	$\sim$	$\sim$	$<$	$\sim$	$\sim$	$\sim$
long	DD - VSM	$\gg$	$\gg$	$\gg$	$\gg$	$\gg$	$\gg$
	DD - PRF	$>$	$\sim$	$\sim$	$\gg$	$\sim$	$>$
	DD - LSI	$\gg$	$\gg$	$\gg$	$\gg$	$\gg$	$\gg$

For the methods PRF, LSI and DD, values of parameters were set again to the best for each of the partitioned collections. The following results are based on these best values.

Table 8 shows the results of the statistical test for the partitioned collections. DD yielded significantly better results in most of the cases for the "long" partitions. These results confirm that passage-based document retrieval is better for longer documents, which has already been reported in the literature [5,6].

Next, let us focus on the results for the shortest queries (title). It is shown that DD was superior or equivalent to all of the others except for short documents. The advantage disappears as the queries become longer.

Figure 4 illustrates the mean average precision for the partitioned collections. Each graph in the figure represents the results for a partitioned collection. The horizontal axes of the graphs indicate the query length.

For the "short" partitioned collections, no clear relation between the effectiveness of the methods and the query length could be found. On the other hand, for the "middle" and "long" partitioned collections with the shortest queries (title), DD was always the best among the methods. In these graphs, it can also be seen that the advantage of DD shrinks as the query length becomes longer.

In order to clarify the reason why DD worked better, we analyzed documents that were ranked highly only by DD. As a result, the documents were classified into two categories: (1) documents including *compound terms* such as "genetic engineering" that are provided as a query, (2) documents including a representative term quite frequently within a *narrow* range of text. Some examples of a representative term are as follows: "carcinogens" in the query "research into & control of carcinogens", "submarine" in "world submarine force" and "solar" in "solar power".

In such cases it is essential to take into account the *proximity* of query terms, as done only by DD among the methods.

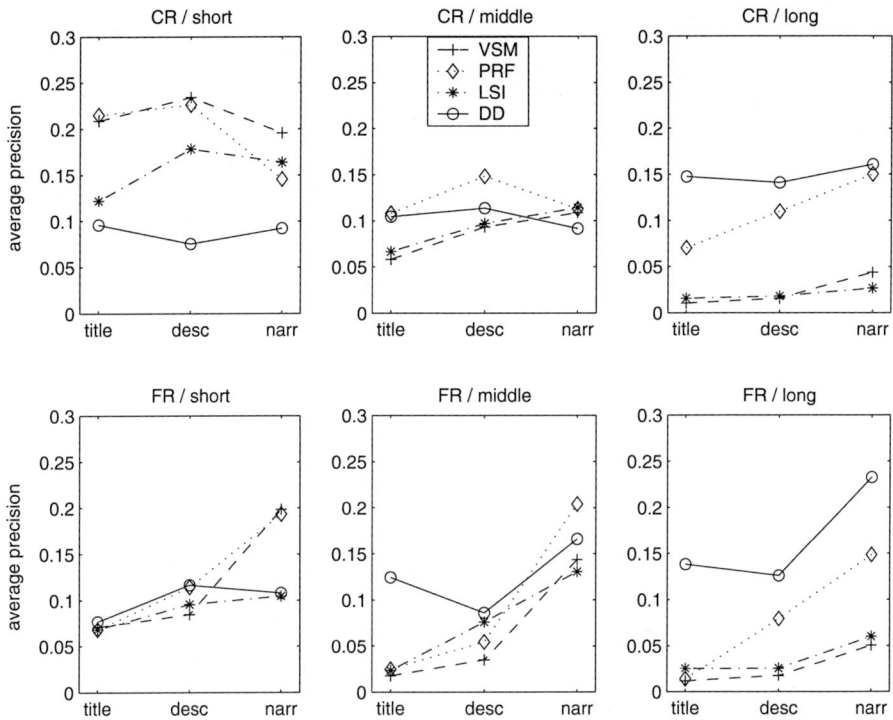

Fig. 4. Mean average precision for the partitioned collections (horizontal axes : query length)

4 Question Answering

Let us now turn to the next application, question answering. The task of question-answering (QA) is to find a text portion which contains an answer to a given query from documents. For example, a typical interaction between a user and a QA system is as follows:

User What is the population of Japan?
System ... Ministry said last month Japan's population was 122.74 million at
...

In the scenario of the QA task in the TREC conference [12], it is not required to return only an answer ("122.74 million" for the above example), but allowed to return short snippets which may contain an answer. The task of locating the answer in the snippets is open for the user. Since snippets are considered as short window passages, the task is suitable for evaluating passage retrieval methods.

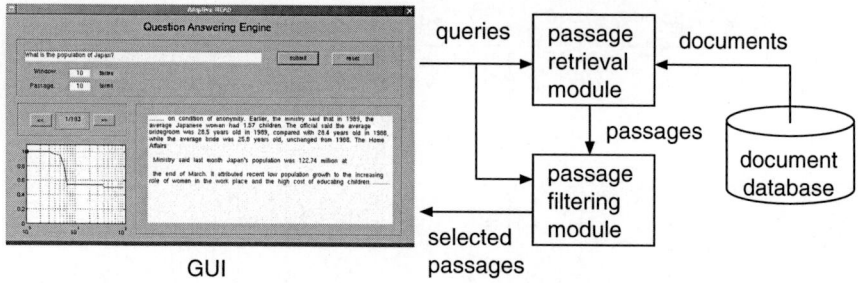

Fig. 5. Question answering system

4.1   Overview of the System

A standard structure of QA systems is

1. to apply a passage retrieval method to obtain passages,
2. to filter out some passages which contain no information required by a query.

The system proposed in this paper follows this structure.

Figure 5 illustrates an overview of the proposed QA system. The system consists of the following four modules: a graphical user interface (GUI), a passage retrieval module, a passage filtering module, and a document database. An outline of processing is as follows. First, the system takes as input a natural language query from a user through the GUI. Next, the query is sent to the passage retrieval module for extracting passages from documents in the database. Passages at this point are likely to include correct answers from the viewpoint of passage retrieval. Extracted passages are then transfered to the filtering module for examining whether or not they include entities required by the query. Lastly filtered passages are sorted according to their scores and the top ranking passage is displayed on the GUI.

4.2   Types of Queries and Terms

An important point specific to the QA task is in the filtering module: some "types" are assigned to terms as well as queries for the purpose of filtering. These types are employed for clarifying the following points:

- What does a query ask about? (types of queries),
- Which terms can be a part of an answer to the query? (types of terms).

We currently use the same types shown in Table 9 for queries and terms. Note that more than one type can be assigned to a term as well as a query, while a lot of terms and queries have no type. In the case that a query has a type, passages which contain the terms of the same type can be possible answers.

Table 9. Types of queries and terms

type	examples of queries	examples of terms
Money	How much money ... ?	$10
Time	How long ... ?	10:00, a.m., P.M.
Month	What time of year ... ?	Jan., December
Number	How far ... ?	10,000, 0.5
Name	Who ... ?	Bush

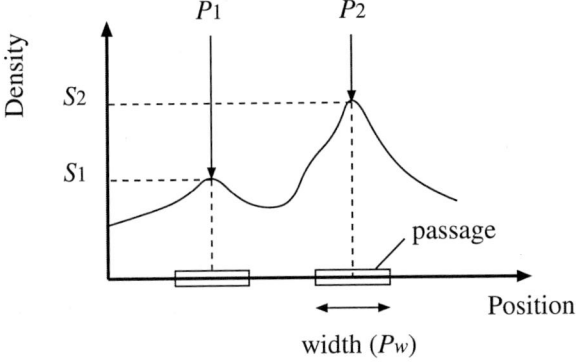

Fig. 6. Passages extracted from a density distribution

4.3   Processing Steps

As described in Sect. 4.1, the processing of the system is twofold: (1) passage retrieval and (2) passage filtering.

Passage Retrieval. We employ the passage retrieval method "density distributions" described in Sect. 2. The outline of processing in the system is as follows. First, stemming and stopword elimination are applied to the query. Next, density distributions such as in Fig. 1 are calculated for all documents. Passages are then extracted based on every peak in the density distributions. For an example of a density distribution shown in Fig. 6, there are two peaks P_1 and P_2. For each peak, a passage with the fixed width (P_w) is extracted by taking the position of a peak as a center of the passage. Each passage has its score defined as the density of its peak. In Fig. 6, S_1 and S_2 are the scores. Finally, passages extracted from all density distributions are ranked according to their scores.

Note that we do not take account of "types" of queries and terms in extracting passages. At this step, passages are obtained based only on the density of terms in the query.

Table 10. Statistics about the small test collection

no. of documents	no. of queries	document length				no. of rel. doc. / query			
		mean	median	min.	max.	mean	median	min.	max.
723	344	590	570	115	1,672	2.83	2	1	18

Table 11. The number of queries for each type

type	no. of queries
Money	2
Time	2
Month	35
Number	58
Name	68
others	213
overall	344

Passage Filtering. This step is to filter out inappropriate passages using the types. The filtering strategy is simple. If types are assigned to a query, passages which include at least a term of one of the types are retained; passages without such terms are removed from the ranked list of passages.

In the current implementation, filters were realized as a collection of manually prepared regular expressions.

4.4   Preliminary Experiments

In order to measure the performance of the QA system, some preliminary experiments were conducted with a small test collection.

Test collection. The documents contained in the collection are a subset of the AP newswire articles published in 1990 (AP90). The subset were determined as follows. First, we selected all relevant entries concerning AP90 from the relevance judgment file for the TREC9 QA track [23]. Each entry of the relevance judgment file consists of a query ID number, a document ID number, a relevance judgment (relevant or not), and the passage on which the judgment was made. In other words, we selected documents from AP90 on condition that they were relevant to at least one query. Note that this defined the subset of documents as well as queries. The queries listed in the selected relevant entries were employed for the experiments. Original queries from which the queries were selected can also be found at [23].

The statistics of the collection are shown in Table 10. Table 11 shows the number of queries for each type. In the table, "others" indicates the queries with no type. Since more than one type can be assigned to a query, the total number of queries is different from the sum of the numbers for all types.

Table 12. Parameter values

passage size (P_w) [terms]	50, 10
window size(W) [terms]	2, 6, 8, 10, 20, 30, 40, 50, 60, 70, 80, 90, 100, 150, 200, 300

Table 13. Mean reciprocal rank ($W = 10$) with the filter

passage size	50 terms		10 terms	
type	MRR	STD	MRR	STD
others	0.675	0.372	0.438	0.422
Money	0.500	0	0.500	0
Time	0.078	0.066	0.005	0.007
Month	0.551	0.422	0.444	0.481
Number	0.510	0.401	0.479	0.450
Name	0.710	0.369	0.544	0.451
overall	0.652	0.383	0.464	0.434

Evaluation. For the task of information retrieval, recall and precision are the standard criteria of evaluating results. However, recall is useless for the QA task since receiving a correct answer more than once seems meaningless.

A widely accepted criteria for evaluating QA systems is called "mean reciprocal rank" defined as follows [11]. Let r_i be the *highest* rank of a passage which contains a correct answer for a query q_i [2]. The reciprocal rank RR_i for the query is defined by:

$$RR_i = \begin{cases} 1/r_i & \text{if there is a passage containing the answer,} \\ 0 & \text{otherwise.} \end{cases} \tag{24}$$

The mean reciprocal rank (MRR) is the mean of reciprocal ranks over all queries:

$$MRR = \frac{1}{N_q} \sum_i RR_i \tag{25}$$

where N_q is the number of queries.

Results. The system was evaluated by applying the values of parameters shown in Table 12. As a result, it was turned out that the maximum MRR was obtained using the window size (W) of 10 terms for both passage sizes. The results are shown in Table 13 where "STD" indicates the standard deviation of reciprocal ranks (RR's).

Next, in order to test effectiveness of the filtering, MRR was calculated without the filtering. Table 14 shows the results. By comparing Tables 13 and 14,

---

[2] Although up to top five passages are considered for r_i in the TREC QA task, we do not apply this limit to the evaluation in this paper. This yields slightly larger values of MRR.

Table 14. Mean reciprocal rank ($W = 10$) without the filtering

passage size	50 terms		10 terms	
type	MRR	STD	MRR	STD
others	0.675	0.372	0.438	0.422
Money	0.500	0	0.321	0.253
Time	0.059	0.057	0.001	0.001
Month	0.556	0.416	0.298	0.385
Number	0.453	0.390	0.279	0.350
Name	0.706	0.374	0.514	0.438
overall	0.647	0.384	0.427	0.419

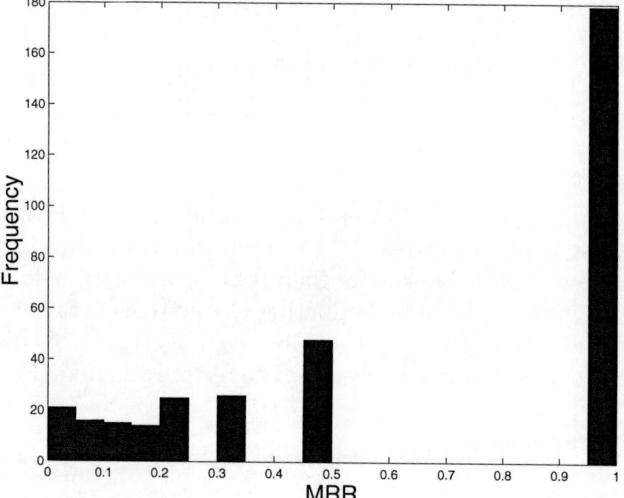

Fig. 7. RR by $W = 10$ and $P_w = 50$ with filtering

it can be said that the results with the filtering are slightly better than those without the filtering. This was mainly because the types assigned to terms and queries were not so accurate. In order to make filtering more effective, it is necessary to introduce some statistical learning techniques [24,25] for defining more accurate expressions of types.

Figures 7 and 8 illustrate the histograms of reciprocal rank (RR) for individual queries obtained by using $P_w = 50$ and $P_w = 10$, respectively. The summary of individual RR's are listed in Table 15. In this table, "= 1.0" indicates that correct answers were obtained at the top of the lists of passages. The row "≥ 0.2" shows the case that correct answers were in fifth position or higher. The row "= 0.0" shows that no correct answer was obtained.

The experimental results show that, with $P_w = 50$ ($P_w = 10$), about a half (1/3) of correct answers were at the top of the rank. This was beyond

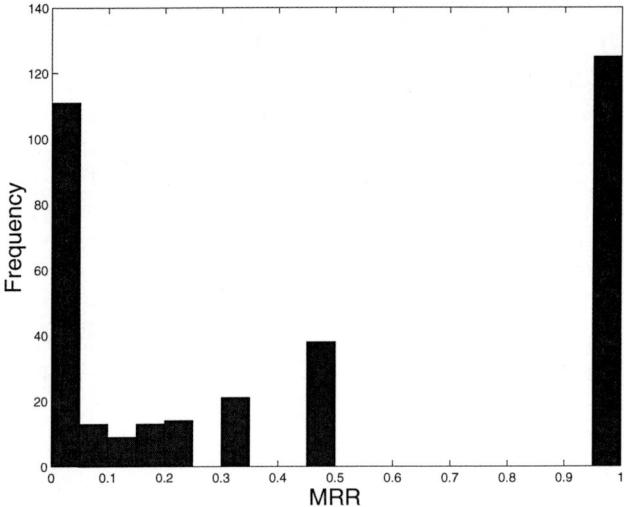

Fig. 8. RR by $W = 10$ and $P_w = 10$ with filtering

Table 15. Summary of individual RR's.

RR	no. of queries (% to total)	
	$P_w = 50$	$P_w = 10$
$= 1.0$	179 (52.0%)	125 (36.3%)
≥ 0.2	290 (84.3%)	203 (59.0%)
$= 0.0$	3 (0.9%)	86 (25.0%)

our expectation for the proposed method which is a simplest form of question answering. It is also shown in the table that the results for $P_w = 50$ were better than those for $P_w = 10$. This indicates that, for some queries, passages were not so accurate to include right answers in their middle.

5   Conclusion

In this paper, we have presented a method of window-based passage retrieval called density distributions and its applications to document retrieval as well as question answering. The passage retrieval method is based on the assumption that passages are relevant to a query if they densely contain terms in the query. From the experimental results on document retrieval, it has been shown that the proposed method outperforms conventional methods on condition that long documents are retrieved with short queries. For the question answering, the passage retrieval method is simply applied for finding very short snippets of documents. Preliminary experiments show that it is capable of locating correct answers in first ranked passages for about a half of queries.

In order to use the passage retrieval method as a tool of intelligent assess to documents, however, the following points should be further considered. First, the window size appropriate for analyzing documents should be determined automatically. Second, sophisticated learning techniques must be incorporated in order to avoid manual adjustment of processing parameters including expressions for the type identification in the QA task. These issues will be a subject of our future research.

Acknowledgment. This work was supported in part by the German Ministry for Education and Research, bmb+f (Grant: 01 IN 902 B8), the Grant-in-Aid for Scientific Research (C) from Japan Society for the Promotion of Science (No.14580453).

References

1. Callan, J. P.: Passage-level evidence in document retrieval. in Proc. SIGIR '94, pp.302-310, 1994.
2. Salton, G., Allan, J., Buckley, C.: Approaches to passage retrieval in full text information systems. in Proc. SIGIR '93, pp.49-58, 1993.
3. Salton, G., Singhal, A., Mitra, M.: Automatic text decomposition using text segments and text themes. in Proc. Hypertext '96, pp.53-65, 1996.
4. Kaszkiel, M., Zobel, J.: Passage retrieval revisited. in Proc. SIGIR '97, pp.178–185, 1997.
5. de Kretser, O., Moffat, A. Effective document presentation with a locality-based similarity heuristic. in Proc. SIGIR '99, pp.113–120, 1999.
6. Mochizuki, H., Iwayama, M., Okumura, M.: Passage-level document retrieval using lexical chains. RIAO 2000, pp.491-506, 2000.
7. Kise, K., Mizuno, H., Yamaguchi M., Matsumoto, K.: On the use of density distribution of keywords for automated generation of hypertext links from arbitrary parts of documents. in Proc. ICDAR'99, pp.301–304, 1999.
8. Kise, K., Junker, M., Dengel, A., Matsumoto, K.: Experimental evaluation of passage-based document retrieval. in Proc. ICDAR'01, pp.592–596, 2001.
9. Kise, K., Junker, M., Dengel, A., Matsumoto, K.: Passage-based document retrieval as a tool for text mining with user's information needs. in *Proc. Discovery Science 2001*, pp.155–169, 2001.
10. Kise, K., Junker, M., Dengel, A., Matsumoto, K.: Effectiveness of passage-based document retrieval for short queries. Trans. IEICE Japan, 2003 (to appear).
11. Voorhees, E. M., Tice, D. M.: The TREC-8 question answering track evaluation. in *Proc. TREC-8*, 1999., available at
    http://trec.nist.gov/pubs/trec8/t8_proceedings.html.
12. http://trec.nist.gov/ .
13. Kurohashi, S., Shiraki, N., Nagao, M.: A Method for detecting important descriptions of a word based on its density distribution in text. Trans. Information Processing Society of Japan, Vol.38, No.4, pp.845–853, 1997 [In Japanese].
14. Kozima, H., Furugori, T.: Segmenting narrative text into coherent scenes. *Literary and Linguistic Computing*, Vol.9, No.1, pp.13–19, 1994.

15. Baeza-Yates, R., Ribeiro-Neto, B.: Modern Information Retrieval. Addison-Wesley Pub. Co., 1999.
16. Manning, C.D., Schütze, H.: Foundations of Statistical Natural Language Processing. MIT Press, 1999.
17. Deerwester, S., Dumais, S., Landauer, T., Furnas, G., Harshman, R.: Indexing by latent semantic analysis. Journal of the American Society of Information Science. Vol.41, No.6, 391-407, 1990.
18. Berry, B., Drmac, Z., Jessup, E.: Matrices, vector spaces, and information retrieval. SIAM Review, Vol.41, No.2, pp.335-362, 1999.
19. `ftp://ftp.cs.cornell.edu/pub/smart/`.
20. Voorhees, E. M, Buckley, C.: The effect of topic set size on retrieval experiment error. in Proc. SIGIR '02, pp.316–323, 2002.
21. Hull, D.: Using statistical testing in the evaluation of retrieval experiments. in Proc. SIGIR '93, pp.329–338, 1993.
22. Yang Y., Liu, X.: A re-examination of text categorization methods. in Proc. SIGIR '99, pp.42–49, 1999.
23. `http://trec.nist.gov/data/qa/t9_qadata.html`.
24. Bikel, D. M., Schwartz, R. L., Weischedel, R. M: An algorithm that learns what's in a name, Machine Learning, Vol.34, No.1-3, pp.211–231, 1999.
25. Kudo, T., Matsumoto, Y.: Chunking with support vector machines, in Proc. NAACL 2001, pp.192–199, 2001.

Results of a Survey about the Use of Tools in the Area of Document Management

Christoph Altenhofen[1], Haigo R. Hofmann[2], Thomas Kieninger[3], and
Mirjana Stanišić-Petrović[1]

[1] University of Stuttgart, Institute for Human Factors and Technology Management,
Nobelstraße 12, 70569 Stuttgart, Germany
{Christoph.Altenhofen, Mirjana.Stanisic}@iao.fraunhofer.de
[2] Océ Document Technologies GmbH, Max-Stromeyer-Straße 116,
78467 Konstanz, Germany
Haigo.Hofmann@oce-odt.com
[3] German Research Center for Artificial Intelligence (DFKI) GmbH,
Erwin-Schrödinger-Straße 57, 67608 Kaiserslautern, Germany
Thomas.Kieninger@dfki.de

Abstract. Two market surveys are part of the achievements in the project Adaptive READ and they will both be discussed in this paper. Their evaluation indicates that paper, as a medium, plays a leading role as information carrier in today's organisations. Furthermore it was ascertained that there is a growing demand for tools to support information retrieval and that the goals of Adaptive READ fit to actual customers needs. The focus of this paper shows only a small extract of the results and concentrates on the use of tools in document management as well as the users acceptance of new technologies in information retrieval.

1   Introduction

In Adaptive READ we conducted two successive market surveys in 2001 and 2002. Both surveys dealt with the use of tools in the area of document and information management and focussed on tools as well as on problems and success factors of system installation processes. The methods applied to the surveys and the topics we dealt with in the questionnaires are discussed consecutively. Furthermore statistical details of the various different samples are presented. Both surveys took place to support the project by elaborating some information about actual problems, possible customers of the technology developed within the project are dealing with, and how these possible customers think about the project approaches. Additionally a short market survey should be worked out.

So in the next chapter, the process of both surveys is shown. Furthermore basic statistical details as for example the pattern of participants in relation to their business value is given.

After this introduction, in the chapter "The Actual Use of Different Tool-Categories" we take a deeper look at the actual use of tools in the area of document and information management. So it was elaborated how many organisations actually

A. Dengel et al. (Eds.): Adaptive READ Research Project, LNCS 2956, pp. 328–354, 2004.

use a document-management-system or scanning technology. Additionally in some cases a comparison of the answers to both surveys is shown.

In the next chapter "Information Retrieval" we first take a look at different aspects of the state of the art in searching for documents in today organisations, before in the chapter "A Glance at Research" various questions concerning actual research topics are given. This chapter especially addresses the question, how the technologies developed within Adaptive READ to enhance the retrieval for documents are accepted by real customers.

After these project-oriented chapters, in "The Market Perspective" different statements about the market perspective, given by experts from all over the world, are presented. These statements deal with looking at the past as well as trying to look in future evolution of the market of electronic document tools. This chapter couldn't be worked out of the surveys but by evaluating other public available sources and has to be seen as a completion of the surveys.

Finally in the last chapter "Summary" a short summary of this paper is given.

As a matter of course in this article only a few details of the results of both surveys can be presented. Additional information and more documentation can be requested from the authors of this paper.

2   Outline over Both Surveys

In this chapter a short outline over both surveys and some basic statistical background of the participants at the surveys will be shown.

2.1   The Process of the First Survey

The first survey took place in Spring 2001. We divided the questionnaire into two parts, a general part with four pages, dealing with currently used tools, communication structure, information retrieval and media in everyday business, and a two page supplement of, addressing the field of capturing paper-based documents.

We sent the questionnaire to over 15 000 people in Germany, addressing different industrial sectors and different company sizes, ranging from 5 to over 100 000 employees.

2.2   The Process of the Second Survey

The second survey was carried out in Summer 2002. That questionnaire reflected the experiences that we had made during the first survey. Consequently, it was much more detailed concerning the actual use of different tool categories and contained, besides a general part of more than five pages, special modules for the tool categories shown in the following table, each about three pages long.

Table 1. Tool-Categories handled in Detail in the Second Questionnaire

Category	Short description
Electronic Document Management System (DMS)[1]	System to manage "classical" electronic documents. Deals for example with creation, storage, archiving and retrieval of documents
Workflow Management System (WfMS)	System to build, control and maintain workflows
Content Management System (CMS)	System to manage modular electronic documents mostly in web-environments
Knowledge Management System (KMS)	System that deals with different aspects of inter-organisational knowledge, e.g. storing success-factors or expert-knowledge
Electronic Data- & Document-Capturing System (EDDCS)	System to capture paper-based documents and to extract information out of these captured documents
Customer Relationship Management System (CRMS)	System to manage customer data

In contrast to the first questionnaire, which had been sent out on paper, the second questionnaire was put online. Additionally, only participants of the first survey and people who had shown interest in the results of the market survey previously were in formed and received a letter of invitation to take part in the second survey. Furthermore we also wrote to about 4 000 people by email. Whereas the response rate of the addressees contacted by letter was very satisfying, the response rate of those contacted by email was insignificant.

2.3   Statistical Background

The statistical details of the response for both surveys are shown in the following table.

Table 2. Statistical Details of Both Surveys

	First Survey	Second Survey
Time-frame of the survey	February - June 2001	July - October 2002
Questionnaires sent out	15 000	750
Feedback	719	101
Response rate	4.8%	13.8%

Underlying the analysis of both surveys is the fact that the participants' pattern of distribution in both surveys is comparable to one another, as shown in the following two tables.

---

[1]   In Germany the acronym DMS is used, while in the Anglo-American language area the acronym EDMS is used. In this article we use the German version.

Table 3. Pattern of Distribution in Relation to the Business Value

Business Value (First / Second Survey)	First Survey	Second Survey
< 5 m DM / < 3 m Euro	2%	12%
5 m – 50 m DM / 3 m – 25 m Euro	54%	33%
50 m – 100 m DM / 25 m – 50 m Euro	14%	21%
100 m – 500 m DM / 50 m – 250 m Euro	19%	21%
> 500 m DM / > 250 m Euro	11%	12%

As shown in the pattern regarding the business values, the same impression arises when looking at the patterns of both surveys in relation to the participants' number of employees.

Table 4. Pattern of Distribution in Reference to the Number of Employees

Number of Employees	First Survey	Second Survey
< 50 employees	7%	12%
51 – 500 employeeso	73%	63%
501 – 1 000 employees	8%	13%
> 1 000 employees	12%	12%

Despite the fact that both surveys were based on different samples of different size, the results of both surveys can be compared to each other because of the similarity of their patterns.

3   The Actual Use of Different Tool-Categories

In this chapter some statistical information about the use of different tool-categories in the area of electronic document management is given. Furthermore the results of the topics system integration and document capture are presented.

3.1   The Use of Document-Related Tools

Both surveys focus on different tool categories and on how often these different categories are used in organisations today. Whereas in the first questionnaire we had only asked about the use of those tools, in the second questionnaire we asked for additional information about the quality in everyday use. However in this chapter the discussion about the comparison is restricted to those results which occur in both surveys.

As already mentioned, we examined the tool category of electronic document management systems. Comparing their use rate in the first and the second survey, it can easily be stated that these rates are comparable as shown in the following table:

Table 5. Use Rate of DMS in Relation to the Number of Employees

Number of Employees	First Survey	Second Survey
< 50 employees	19.2%	50.0%
51 – 500 employees	21.4%	37.1%
501 – 1000 employees	53.6%	61.5%
> 1000 employees	65.9%	75.0%
Total	29.2%	46.5%

Despite the fact that the second survey is based on less questionnaires than the first, the results concerning the actual use of DMS are comparable. Even the eye-catching increase of system use in small enterprises can be explained by the smaller sample, because in smaller samples tinier variations in detail lead to higher variations in the overall result. This phenomenon in reverse is called "The Law of large Numbers".

A similar statement is applicable to the area of workflow management systems as shown in the following table:

Table 6. Use Rate of WFMS in Relation to the Number of Employees

Number of Employees	First Survey	Second Survey
< 50 employees	9.6%	33.3%
51 – 500 employees	9.0%	21.0%
501 – 1000 employees	23.2%	23.1%
> 1000 employees	34.1%	41.7%
Total	13.2%	25.3%

The results for those tool categories which were treated in both surveys explicitly are shown in the following table:

Table 7. Use Rate of DMS, WFMS and Intranet in Comparison

Tool Category	Quantity in First Survey	Rate in First Survey	Quantity in Second Survey	Rate in Second Survey
DMS	205	29.2%	46	46.5%
WfMS	93	13.2%	25	25.3%
Intranet	429	61.1%	78	78.8%

Looking at this table it can easily be determined that in all three tool categories examined in both surveys, the relative number of users has increased. This may be the result of either a greater willingness to participate in such a survey of those people who already use these tools or an increased use of new tool categories.

In contrast to the first survey, we accounted for further tool categories and their use in the second questionnaire. The use rates of all tool categories, as observed in the second survey, are shown in the following table

Table 8. Use Rate of All Accounted Tool Categories in the second Survey

Tool Category	Use Rate
Electronic Document Management System (DMS)	46.5%
Workflow Management System (WfMS)	25.3%
Content Management System (CMS)	11.1%
Knowledge-Management-System (KMS)	5.1%
Electronic Data- & Document-Capturing System (EDDCS)	8.1%
Customer Relationship Management System (CRMS)	17.2%
Intranet	78.8%

Only those tool categories which have use rates of more than 25% can be regarded as technologies that are established in the market.

In many organisations, more than one tool category is used in parallel but data exchange between those different tools or integration in user-interfaces is often needed to enable their efficient use. That is why in the second questionnaire we asked for the integration of tools in case of parallel use. Due to the complex topic of system integration, we only asked, how far the systems are integrated but not about the quality of the integration. The results are as follows:

Table 9. System Integration

Answer	Rate
Systems are more or less integrated	32.0%
Systems are partially integrated	29.3%
Integration needed but actually no integration	22.7%
No integration needed	16.0%

Nearly half of all organisations which use more than one tool category either do not integrate these different systems or they show only a minor degree of integration. If only those organisations which think that integrating the systems is useful for their everyday business are considered, more than 60% currently do not integrate their systems in a satisfying way. This usually leads to time-consuming media conversion, which has to be done by an often complex and error-prone manual interface. Using what is called "Enterprise Application Integration (EAI)" will in this case help to overcome these problems.

3.2   Document Capturing

In both surveys we asked for the media used in the most important business processes. The following table shows the results of both surveys:[2]

---

[2]   Only in the 2nd questionnaire we inquired about the three tool categories CMS, KMS and CRMS , that is why no comparison is possible.

Table 10. Use Rate of Media in the Most Important Business Processes

Media	First Survey	Second Survey
Loose-leaf-collection	13%	9%
Paper-based record	15%	12%
Paper-based folder	16%	20%
Electronic file system	20%	19%
Electronic database system	21%	19%
DMS	8%	10%
CMS		1%
KMS		1%
CRMS		2%
Intranet	7%	8%

The answers and their distribution show that the importance of paper in everyday processes in organisations is still high. Clearly there is a need for the development of new technologies to facilitate the migration of paper-based information into electronic media, to enable further document retrieval or working with the documents. This statement is also true, if both surveys are compared with each other, because the use of paper had not been reduced in the time span between the surveys.

The results for the use rate of scanners confirm this statement, as shown in the following table.

Table 11. Use Rate of Scanners

	First Survey	Second Survey
No use of scanners	44.1%	36.1%
Use of scanners in offices	25.4%	27.8%
Use of scanners in central departments	30.5%	36.1%

Comparing the results of both surveys it becomes obvious, that the use of scanners in organisations has increased. Although many organisations use scanners or scanning technology, the economic potential of electronic data- and document-capturing technologies, that are built on top of scanning technology, has not been realised yet. The figures in the following table, which represent the use of OCR-Technology, emphasize this result.

Table 12. Use Rate of OCR-Technology

	First Survey	Second Survey
No use of OCR-Technology	78.7%	69.1%
Use of OCR-Technology	21.3%	30.9%

Only 30% of the participants in the second survey use OCR-Technology to make paper-based information accessible for information technology tools. The use rate of those technologies is not a sign of broad use of this modern technique, even if there was an increase from the first to the second survey.

4   Information Retrieval

Besides the two aspects of general tool usage in the area of document related technologies and the media used in most important business processes, the surveys focussed on the topic of information retrieval as well. This approach was influenced last but not least by the fact that the improvement of current information retrieval technology was one of the goals of Adaptive READ.

The need for efficient support of document retrieval increased from the first to the second survey. When we asked about the importance of document retrieval in the second survey, nearly 71% of all participants responded that retrieval is of great importance for their everyday work, showing an increase of about 10% in comparison to the first survey.

Another interesting point is which information retrieval tools are currently in use. The resulting overview, based on both questionnaires, is shown in the following two tables.

The first table reveals the ratio of each statement to the total number of completed questionnaires. Because the participants had the possibility to nominate up to three tools, the overall total is more than 100%.[3]

Table 13. Use Rate of Information Retrieval-Tools

Information Retrieval Tool	First Survey	Second Survey
Colleague	28.2%	23.2%
Telephone	30.5%	20.0%
Paper-based file	11.8%	10.5%
Electronic file system	55.9%	67.4%
Information retrieval system / DMS	30.7%	32.6%
Inter-/Intranet	41.6%	35.8%
CMS		1.1%
KMS		1.1%
EDDCS		2.1%
CRMS		5.3%

The second table shows the relative amount of nominations of each statement, so the ratio of the different categories among each other is calculated.

The results show that there is a slight increase in the area of electronic information retrieval tools. But the tool predominantly used in retrieval, the electronic file system, often leads to problems, which we will discuss below. Specialised information retrieval tools are only used by one-third of all participants.

The increasing use of information retrieval tools is confirmed by the answers to the question on general use of an electronic tool for information retrieval. The results are shown in the following table 15.

---

[3] We only inquired about the four tool categories CMS, KMS, EDDCS in the 2nd questionnaire which is why no comparison is possible.

Table 14. Use Rate of Information Retrieval Tools, Compared to Each Other

Information Retrieval Tool	First Survey	Second Survey
Colleague	14.2%	11.6%
Telephone	15.3%	10.1%
Paper-based file	5.9%	5.3%
Electronic file system	28.1%	33.9%
Information retrieval system / DMS	15.5%	16.4%
Inter-/Intranet	20.9%	18.0%
CMS		0.5%
KMS		0.5%
EDDCS		1.1%
CRMS		2.6%

Table 15. Use Rate of Electronic Information Retrieval Tools (IR-tool)

Tool Category	Quantity in First Survey	Rate in First Survey	Quantity in Second Survey	Rate in Second Survey
Use of an IR-tool	451	62.7%	61	64.2%
No use	268	37.3%	34	35.8%

But we must emphasise that the use of an electronic IR-tool by itself is no guarantee that the search for information always leads to a satisfying result. This fact is confirmed by the two aspects that will be discussed in the next paragraph. In large organisations the use of a filing system, where electronic documents can be stored manually, leads, for example, to large efforts in retrieval. These problems mostly depend on the strict hierarchical structure of file systems. If different users work with different storage strategies, which happens in most organisations, retrieval in colleagues' structures is very often a time-consuming matter (if it indeed leads to a result at all).

In addition, the results of the question about problems with the correct formulation, which was asked in both surveys and is shown in the following table, displays an alarming development.

Table 16. Rate of Problems in Formulation of Queries

	First Survey	Second Survey
Problems in formulating queries exist	26.1%	51.5%
No problems exist	73.9%	48.5%

As can easily be seen, more and more people have problems getting the correct information they need for their everyday business, only because they are not able to formulate their queries correctly. This leads to the conclusion that the need for technologies to support the process of information retrieval is still on the increase.

Another problem in the area of information management in today's organisations is the repetition of information retrieval processes, i.e. to find a document which had already been handled. The following table presents the relevant figures:

Table 17. The Need for Repeated Retrieval for known documents

	First Survey	Second Survey
No repetition	0.6%	3.1%
Sometimes	64.5%	43.9%
Often	33.5%	52.0%
Ever	1.4%	1.0%

In the second survey a significant number of participants stated they had to re-search for information more often than was the case in the first survey. This is due to the fact that the need for further development of retrieval technologies is becoming more and more important and on the other hand the need to use such tools in today's organisations is continually increasing.

5   A Glance at Research

When designing the second survey, we added a new section of questions as compared to the first survey and gave it the title "A Glance at Research". Two main goals were pursued in this context.

For one thing, we wanted to know the market relevance of the new technologies developed in Adaptive READ. Due to the selection of people, or the companies they work for, as well as the power of judgement proved by their participation on the survey, the received feedback was especially highly rated. For the project consortium this is a direct indicator of the importance of the project and its closeness to the market.

The second intention was to give users an impression of the Adaptive READ research topics, as they do not usually realise improvements until they are integrated into products. Thus feedback from users to developers is only possible at a late stage. Using this type of clarification the new possibilities are shown to the potential buyer, which has a direct effect on the demand for corresponding technologies. The transfer of research results into practical applications is thereby continually supported.

When we chose the technological topics to be incorporated in the survey, we also had to take into consideration that the questionnaire should contain a clear description of improvements and practical consequences. That again presupposes that the work processes affected by the new developments are apparent to the user. New scanner technology for example, which enables a constant true colour for a unit's total lifespan brings vital advantages to image analysis but is hidden from the user and hence can only be limitedly assessed by him.

Thus, we only could primarily consider developments for the discussion, which are directly linked to the handling of information. The lists of questions, for example, correspond to the learning ability of systems, proactive information supply, assistance with the formulation of queries or with the search for experts. New technologies were developed in Adaptive READ for all these areas.

5.1   Learning Ability of Information Systems

The ability to adapt to the habits of the user illustrates the exceptional possibilities of the technologies which were developed in Adaptive READ. Regarding the way a user deals with information, one aspect is to learn about his interests and preferences through observation. A user does not have to define a profile explicitly, but rather the system deduces it automatically from observation.

Learning processes can thereby not only extrapolate the necessary information from positive but also from negative training instances. The system therefore, not only recognizes preferences, but also topics which do not interest the user.

Equipped with these learning capabilities, the next step is defined by the development of active components which monitor certain knowledge sources and point out documents, that might interest the user.

Whether such assistant systems are wanted, or whether potential users feel as if they are being patronized by this type of support, was asked in the survey. The results can be seen in the following table.

Table 18. Welcome Adaptive Characteristics

	Answer Rate
Learning with negative documents	21.5%
Learning user-profiles	69.9%
Proactive information-delivery	55.9%

The positive response to the learning of an interest-profile is remarkable (nearly 70%). The linked proactive information support (nearly 56%) also finds the approval of the majority of people. However it is surprising that there is so little interest in techniques which identify unwanted documents. One possible explanation could be the users' experience with email filters. Users do not have enough confidence in today's systems that unwanted messages will be recognized with 100% precision and therefore want to decide for themselves how to categorize a text.

5.2   Query Formulation

We already noticed in the first survey that query formulation within retrieval systems causes problems to many users. This is especially true when a search query does not provide satisfactory results in the first attempt and the user has to refine the query.

Through the various approaches towards cooperative information retrieval that were pursued in Adaptive READ, it is possible to learn about user intentions behind query patterns and hence we can potentially offer support to inexperienced users. But for this type of learning it is necessary to record search queries anonymously. That is why the users were asked what they thought about this.

78.9% of the participants were in favour of active support, 76.6% also approved the necessary logging of the search processes. The willingness of such a large percentage of people - 97% of those, who are interested in a support accepted to have their processes logged and evaluated - is an indication of the cultural maturity towards the establishment of such technologies.

5.3   Granularity of Search Queries

The answer documents received from queries are sometimes quite large. In this case, the search for the specific piece of information is not yet finished and demands more of the user's time. It was also examined, whether intelligent procedures are welcome, which refer to the relevant points in the text. 96% of the people asked answered with »yes«.

An example of a tool which supplies appropriate support is the »NarrowBot«-System developed in Adaptive READ. In response to a query, formulated in natural language, this system presents those parts of the text from large documents which answer the question.

5.4   Capturing Competence

In everyday working life there are often situations in which fellow workers face problems and need advice from competent colleagues. In such situations it is often difficult to find the right person. Systematic support is also conceivable here, because when users deal with documents, a system cannot only learn their preferences but also their competencies.

Whether such support is wanted and in return, whether there is a willingness to let the system record the user's competence, is important when making statements about whether such technologies are practicable.

The results of the survey were all positive without exception: 70.5% of the respondents would like the assistance offered; 64.2% would also let the system manage their competence.

Table 19. Attitude of the Survey Participants Towards Competence Management in Electronic Systems

	Competence approval accepted	No approval of competence
Competence search welcome	60.0%	10.5%
Search unwelcome	4.2%	25.3%

In this context the correlation between the answers to the two questions – as seen in the table above - is also interesting: Only 10.5% would welcome this kind of technology but do not want their own competence to be registered. Another 25.3% do not want to disclose their competence but on the other hand they are also not interested in expert search either.

Summing up we can say that the vast majority of potential users sees an advantage in the new technology and is also willing to take part in it actively.

5.5   Integration of Heterogeneous Document Sources

The potential applications of an information system become more diverse the more data sources are integrated. For example, whether only electronic documents of common office applications are included, or whether all incoming paper documents are included as well? Are web documents also searchable or even existing paper archives? The more diverse the integrated sources in the system are, the more concentrated and faster the search is for the user. However all named advantages do in contrast imply additional effort and costs, which have to be invested for the integration and acquisition of data.

Which capability characteristics can ultimately be put into effect or are worth having is judged differently from case to case. As new approaches were developed in Adaptive READ for information extraction and retrieval, which directly affect the costs for data acquisition, it was also of interest which degree of importance the users assign to the individual sources of information.

In the survey we deliberately separated this aspect from concrete plans and therefore took it up in the „Glance at Research" questionnaire. The answers can be seen in the following table.

Table 20. Documents to be Recorded

	Answer Rate
Standard office tools	97.7%
Daily paper-based documents	87.1%
Web-documents	74.7%
Existing paper-based archives	74.2%

The most importance by far with almost 98% was given to the documents of standard office tools, followed by daily paper-based documents (87%). This emphasises the importance of document capturing technologies which are also topics of Adaptive READ research. Web-Documents (75%) and existing paper archives (74%) with nearly the same results came third and fourth in the ranking.

5.6 Conclusion

To sum up the survey results of the section „A Glance at Research" we can conclude that the research topics dealt with by the consortium are very close to market needs. The answers given also showed that the general attitude of potential users towards our technology is very positive. This is also true for methods which monitor or record in some way personal ways of interaction with information. Each of these findings are in their own right an indication that the techniques developed in Adaptive READ have ideal qualifications to be incorporated quickly into new products. You can find more specific observations on market potential in the following section.

6   The Market Perspective

Information processing has become a vital productivity factor as well as part of our daily life. The complexity and rapid pace of development of information technology make its integration into existing organizations and systems a matter that requires thought, planning, and experience. This is particularly the case for document related processing such as data and document capture, electronic archiving, document management, workflow, content management, knowledge management, customer relationship management, multimedia and office communication systems.

Only about 10% of all data is available in structured databases and operative systems. The other 90% is unstructured information in documents and therefore not easily accessible (hardcopy, microfiche, proprietary electronic systems, …). But this is the knowledge of an enterprise - and this is the resource that must be tapped. In the manufacturing industry, outstanding productivity enhancements have been achieved in recent decades. In the office environment, technologies and working methods have also changed. These changes mostly have not resulted in comparable gains in productivity or cost savings in our daily office work. DMS technology is an approach to optimise business processes in the office environment and generate respective cost savings for the customer. The basic technology exists, in a host of variations. The challenge lies in the development of intelligent adaptive products and solutions for document content analysis and in the right organizational preparation and implementation, in the proper use of the technology and in the right choice of tools.

Documents and information play an important role in almost any business process. Furthermore, the explosion of new technologies (above all the Internet) leads to a dramatic increase of transactions based on documents and information. This situation creates a strong need for meta-concepts called **"Electronic Document Management Systems" (DMS)** which administrate, transport, store, etc. the documents and help to streamline the processes. Documents consist of content (information, meta-data) and of a defined layout. In recent years this concept has been expanded far beyond paper documents only. Documents can be represented in various formats and media (as paper, electronic, microfiche, etc.), but business processes based on documents and information do have a great potential for rationalization and automation, thus increasing the efficiency of the work process. This results in save-money and make-money benefits to the user, e.g. superior customer relationship. Manual data entry, for example, is the most boring thing for a technology driven company -- but making this most effective by automatic data capturing systems can be the key in many ways if you can locate and fix errors quickly and adapt the recognition system automatically for different kind of documents. The key to increase productivity dramatically is to reduce expensive staff operations. Software auto classification can be the answer.

Auto classification eliminates the time taken to sort by type and insert and remove separator pages. Automatic indexing can then use the classification which also finds and extracts the index fields. It starts with pattern recognition combined with the latest voting OCR/ICR, auto classification to mimic the manual operator's decision making – the need to look at the image, decide what it is, where the fields to enter are located – and then it can use its OCR/ICR software to capture the data. But, being an automated adaptive process, it can do it much quicker. Such an Intelligent Document Recognition (IDR) System uses classification, business rules and other approaches to automatically recognize, classify and extract data from mixed groups of semi- or un-structured documents such as invoices, claims, orders, explanations of benefits, correspondence and any other incoming documents etc., using the context of the document, and the application that it supports.

So for example in a medical claims & invoices environment, entering the data is a low cost job. But applying rules to cross check medical procedures and measure the billing vs. the procedure is a much bigger deal. In many EU-countries they employ para medicals in health insurance to check query bills at maybe €25-30 p hour. As the procedures become more complex the expertise increases, ending up with specialist Doctors at several hundred euros an hour. Starting to cut into this successfully using new adaptive technologies, not only limited to OCR/ICR, will be a compelling story to tell.

"Where expensive people have to stop and THINK is where the money is. So if there are intelligent ways to reduce their thinking, time represents REAL MONEY." [3]

6.1   General Current Market Trends and Statements

"Form me there is a clear major trend: The DMS market keeps on moving! DMS never has been so important than today.", Lee Roberts tells us.

A first glance at the current situation on the various DMS markets ostensibly presents a quite different view. The complete industrial sector in all its different attributes seems to be in an actual crisis, last but not least in Germany. An end of this crisis is not in sight. Many, even leading renowned players, if not the majority, are complaining that sales plunged about 20-30% in the current business year. Diverse, also once leading suppliers meanwhile have gone bankrupt or they are dealt as took-over candidates. The market on the supplier's side is definitely in a phase of change and consolidation. This is due not only in conjunction with the general crisis on the IT-markets and the "New Economy" but also caused by blatant individual or even criminal management failures. For this reason the question came up if these fundamental structural changes in the market will completely alter or erase the big demand we assumed for the products and technologies focused in the project and which we also assumed in our surveys. Is there really such a big need for those kind of new adaptive technologies as recently predicted? On the one hand our study could not give a distinct answer to that question because it was not the main target of our surveys to quantify and predict the market development. On the other hand we could identify and measure a stable substantial demand backed up and proven by an established and growing installation base in all categories we asked about in our interviews.

The European Information Technology Observatory Institute (EITO) came in the Update (October 2002) to its 2002 Report[1] to the following re-evaluation of the total IT-market development in Europe: "The economic uncertainty has encouraged a very cautious attitude towards investments in general and ICT investments in particular [...] As a result; EITO has downgraded its ICT growth estimates for both 2002 and 2003. The IT market in Western Europe is now expected to grow by 0.1% in 2002 compared with 5.1% forecast in the EITO edition in March 2002." There is reason to doubt at least the (from various renowned market research institutes e.g. IDC) recently predicted 20-30% growth rate p. a. for the DMS-technologies in the years from 2000-2005. This is especially true for the German end-user markets well investigated in our study. According to EITO: "Overall the German IT market is expected to decline by 3.4% in 2002 and 1.7% in 2003."

What in fact is happening is a current process of restructuring especially of the German DMS markets including mergers and acquisitions and shake-outs. The German market had been extremely competitive with a couple of strong international suppliers (of national origin). On their way to the international premium league some of the former prominent suppliers actually failed. So the situation on the supplier's side today is characterised by a national fragmentation without a clear market leader[4]. This finding is explicitly underlined by the statements of the users in our surveys. It might also be an indicator that explains the current unreadiness of the users to invest massively in such technologies. On the other hand there are also cautious optimistic experts: "We can't state that DMS has lost confidence in per se. Some single vendors definitely yes, not the total market as such." [7]

For there are also signs on the wall, which point to profound reasons to still believe in the future of DMS as you can see from the above cited EITO study: "While IT growth is experiencing a pause, there is demand for projects to simplify and optimise existing IT infrastructure. The focus is on fast ROI, making existing IT solutions more effective, and reducing costs. [...] Integration of applications that automate back-end/front-end functionality along the organisation's value chain is still seen as a hot area." There is hardly any doubt about the ongoing basic demand for advanced technologies and solutions to cope with the ever rising pile of documents. This is underpinned by a recent market study carried out by the international market research institute MORI Telephone Surveys on behalf of XEROX Ltd. "The Xerox study has been accomplished in six European countries. The results show that almost every fifth of the interviewees (19%) spends more than 60% of his working hours in document related operations." [6] This was confirmed by our 1st survey, where the average amount of working time to search for documents was asked. In this survey about 5% of all participants stated that they spent more than 30% of their average working time searching for documents.

Most of the technologies under investigation in the DMS environment are entitled to meet the expectations of the end users exactly. The technologies developed in the course of the project are also designed to deploy their potential here most effectively. Now, more and more small and middle sized enterprises open up as a new market potential, underlined by the answers of our surveys. Hence: The middle market is raring to go! For the suppliers of DMS solutions which have in the past focussed almost only on the TOP-1000-enterprises, the middle market is meanwhile becoming the most important segment for expansion. Here the DMS market is definitely in its infancy (see table 20 below). The market potential for document related technologies and solutions are substantial, but the window of real business opportunities hasn't completely been opened yet.

One reason might be that, as already mentioned earlier, the total DMS market is still in an ongoing phase of uncertainty and consolidation. Following the majority of experts and underlined by the impressions of an Adaptive READ customer workshop, the DMS market is currently in a phase of transition, moving from the status of "wild growth" into a matured phase of the life cycle. Here are just a few of the "excitements" that the industry and its customers are actually experiencing and will have to cope with in the foreseeable future: A significant re-segmentation of the market has taken place. It tends to move away from the traditional, pure technology-oriented and supplier driven:

Imaging -> workflow -> repository -> COLD-> information retrieval model

---

[4]   This statement could be approved by out first survey, because 179 users of an electronic document management system named 69 different vendors.

towards a more market-driven i.e. user-driven segmentation based around document & data capture, business process management, repository application management including content management and customer relationship management, document generation, integration of web technologies such as portals, infrastructure, groupware and infrastructure library services:

- Products are updated and expanded at short intervals
- Rapid, chaotic development is at odds with long-term information availability
- Technologies that were formerly distinct are growing together
- Large companies are buying out small ones that have innovative products
- Alliances are bringing new market concentrations
- Operating systems and standard suites are incorporating core document management functions
- The market is splitting into high-end and low-end products
- Follow-on costs are often higher than the initial investment
- A welter of mergers and acquisitions
- Fierce competition worldwide will further fuel the need for business process reengineering (BPR) and the use of new intelligent technologies for information capturing, retrieval and processing.
- The integration aspects are becoming more and more important.

6.2   The Customer's Perspective

Investment decisions for DMS applications are very often not triggered by the immediate wish to implement a DMS system. In many cases, implementation of the DMS starts with the optimisation of a business process. The ramifications caused by this "local" change lead to further requirements which are very often coped with by introducing a DMS. The core element of any DMS is the electronic repository of all documents, i.e. the archive. Therefore, many considerations on investing into a DMS system start from the archive. This was explicitly confirmed by both surveys.

The reason for investing in an archiving system is the requirement for "managing the paper". In a fair amount of applications, the mere cost of storing paper physically justifies the investment in an archiving system. Also the archiving of electronic information such as e-mail is becoming more important. Fast access to information, centralized databases, ease of version control and access from remote locations are further strong arguments. The investment decisions for archiving systems are long term decisions. The lifetime of installations ranges from 5 to 10 years. The customer is very much dependent on the supplier of the archiving system for data security and migration to new technology. Hence a typical Electronic Document Management System (DMS) seems to show a concentric structure focused round the archive system as an integral part (see figure 1). Starting from that the successful marketing of a DMS system is closely related to a high performance archive system and its seamless integration into the business processes of the customer.

From an end-users perspective, the seamless dovetail connection together with the optimisation of all DMS related business processes is becoming more and more important, as the next figure 2 points out. Intelligent Document Input Management is been looked at as an integral part of it.

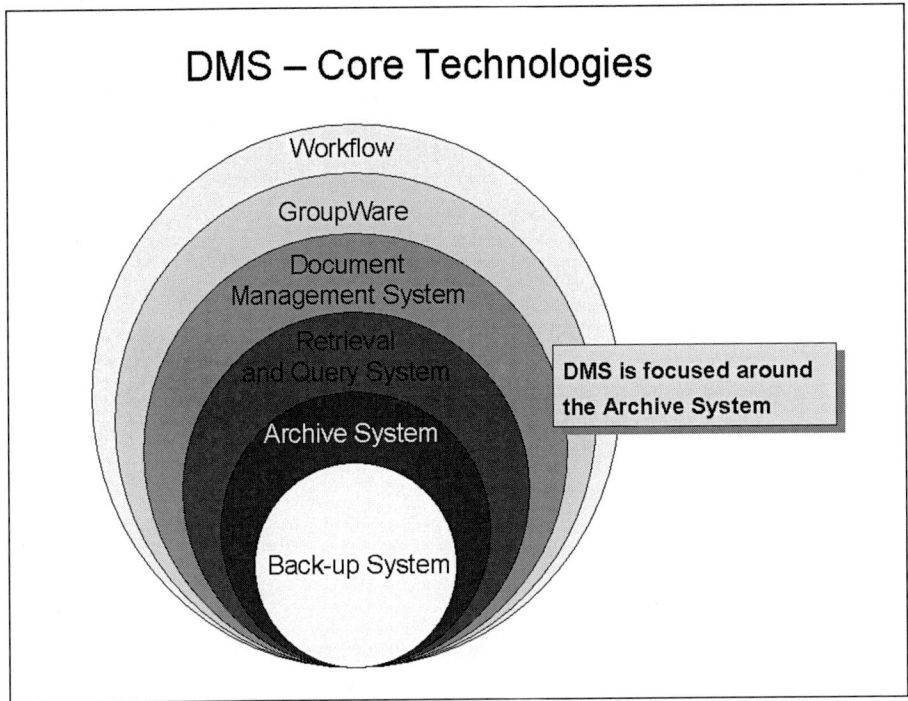

Fig. 1. Nape model of DMS-functionalities

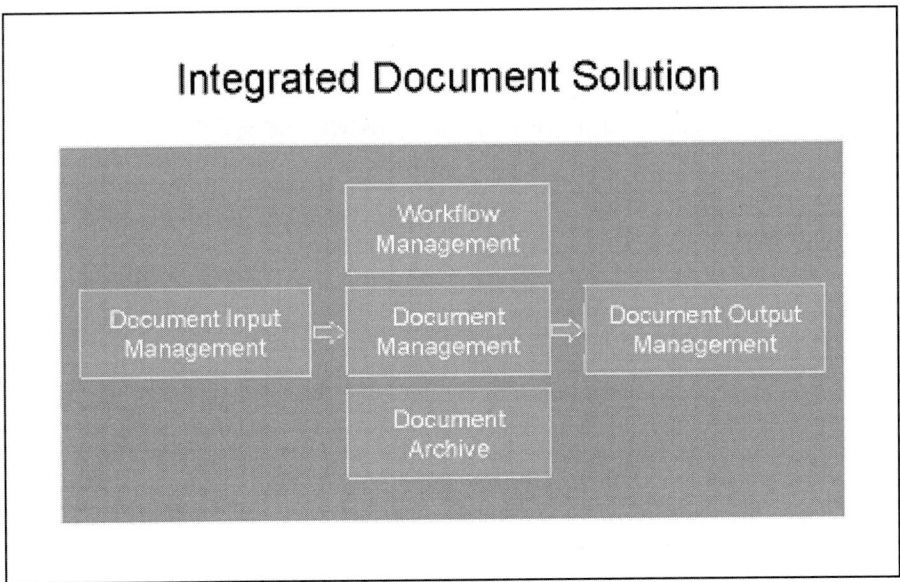

Fig. 2. Dovetail connection in the DMS-environment

6.3   Selected Examples and Conclusions from the Two Surveys

Both surveys have produced a lot of relevant and generative consolidated findings especially in relation to the user's perspective. Many of the findings from the first survey seemed representative because of the high number of respondents (719). Both surveys by comparison gave a good and very detailed impression of the current situation on the market from a customer's perspective.

Derived from our surveys the major key success factors for players in the DMS market today are:

- Solid standing, name reputation & market acceptance as reliable player
- DMS focused organization & resources (beyond the critical mass) with clear business mission & responsibilities
- Clear and convincing value proposition for the customers, underlined by a clear cost effective analysis
- Solid & successful track record and references
- Competitive product portfolio covering DMS core market segments (archive) including all kind of professional services
- Services orientated culture & skills
- Managed strategic alliances & partnerships
- Clearly defined (regional & vertical) target market segments
- Intensive interaction with customers – based on working customer relationship management
- Fast response to changing market/customer requirements (only the fast survive)

Each sample is assumed to be representative. Therefore it is possible to draw some valuable conclusions with regard to the current situation on the market. Some seem to be a little surprising e.g. we can assume a certain saturation of the market in a few selected vertical segments, especially within the fortune 500 segment, where archive- and WfMS (Workflow Management System)-solutions are already widespread: 75% DMS and 42% WfMS market penetration in companies with more than 1000 employees. Whereas in SME's (up to 500 employees) DMS doesn't even reach the 40% mark, WfMS are just over 20% (see table below). In doing so for all company sizes, small to middle document volumes are clearly dominant. Whereby the enterprise-wide usage is prevalent but not so much the department wide. Astoundingly occasional and daily usage keeps the balance, which is mirrored also when comparing the two studies. Overall only slight increases could be noted in comparison to the market penetration of all kinds of DMS technologies. This is a clear sign for a decrease in dynamics of the market. At least no growth tendencies can be found as against the very cautious main market trend. What is becoming vaguely visible is a certain renaissance of WfMS and it's more and more perfect correlation with the parallel usage of an archive/ DMS. This becomes evident in the fact that all WfMS users also have an archive/ DMS.

Our surveys indicate that new market potentials and new market segments for DMS technologies are in fact located in the so called "SME segment". Here there is room for a further significant increase in market penetration.

Table 21. Usage of an Archive/DMS or WfMS depending on the number of employees

Number of employees	Use of DMS	Use of WFMS
Up to 50	50,0%	33,3%
51 – 500	37,1%	21,0%
501 – 1000	61,5%	23,1%
More than 1000	75,0%	41,7%
Usage in total	46,5%	25,3%

Looking at the table below, it can be seen that there is no market saturation in customer segments in relation to our second survey.

Table 22. Market penetration of different systems categories

System category	Use Rate
Electronic-Document-Management-System (DMS)	46,5%
Workflow-Management-System (WfMS)	25,3%
Content-Management-System (CMS)	11,1%
Knowledge-Management-System (KMS)	5,1%
Electronic-Data- & Document-Capturing-System (EDDCS)	8,1%
Customer-Relationship-Management-System (CRMS)	17,2%
Intranet	78,8%

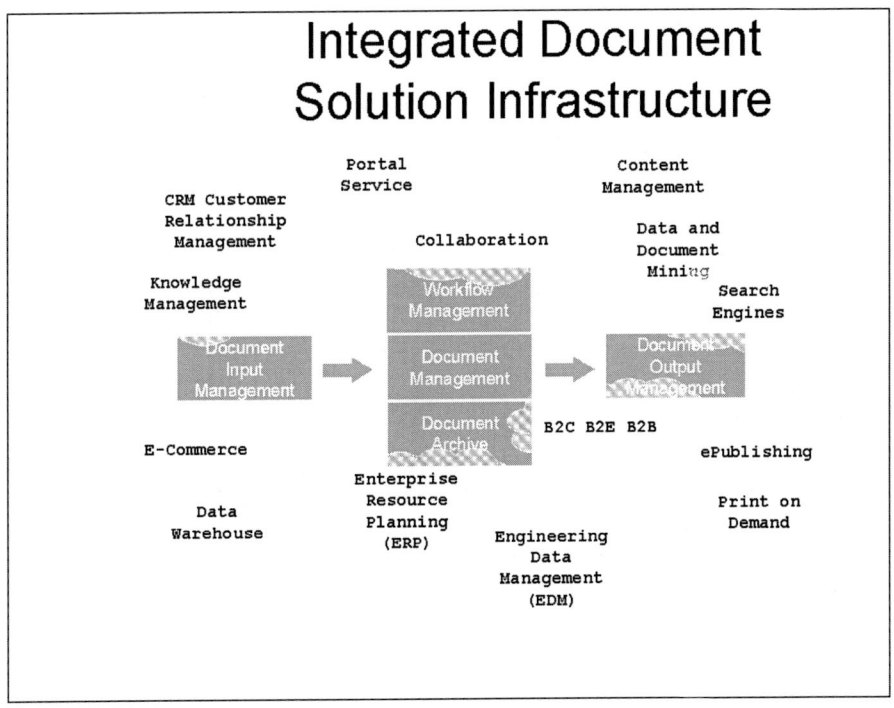

Fig. 3. DMS core Market Segments and the relevant Market Environment

In any case one can deduce from the different nominations that there is no faking for the other system categories. They also have already a certain substantial demand. After the waning of the "Buzz-Word-Hype" within the last few years one can state a new, by far more down-to earth oriented interaction with formerly exotic system categories like KMS or CRMS. Along with that is a systematic expansion of the definition of the relevant markets for DMS technologies (See Figure 3). Whereas the core segments archive/DMS und WfMS basically remained the same in both surveys, it isn't exaggerated to refer to archive/DMS and WfMS as leading applications. CMS/KMS/CRM/EDDCS as applications are seldom stand-alone systems but often integrated into or in combination with other leading applications such as Archive/DMS, WfMS or ERP systems. "The DMS market typically is not a homogenous one with easily comparable products and solutions (like e.g. CAD software) but rather it comprises of a variety of fairly different segments with a multitude of different offers." [8]

Therefore it's getting more and more complicated and problematic to define generic selection criteria for the different system categories and market segments. The interfaces are manifold and the transitions are becoming more and more blurred between the different system categories – especially from a technological standpoint. From a users perspective however this picture is quite different. The users are primarily focused on the clear benefits of a distinct system category – beyond all technological considerations. It was a little surprising that the big majority of customers across all system categories are quite content with the benefits of their system. In most cases even the projected costs were not exceeded. In the majority of the successful projects clear targets have been defined; especially in relation to archive/DMS and WfMS as well as EDDC projects. This is an indication for a majoritarian? good planning procedure and fairly good customer know-how. In a nutshell an increasing awareness and competence of the customer could be asserted, which is linked to the possibilities and the limitations of the different systems. This is confirmed by the fact that 60% of all system categories have an in-house solution is in use, whereby it's interesting to note that this percentage of 48% is by far the lowest in the most commonly installed archive/DMS category. This could be considered as an additional subtle hint for the growing maturity of this system category.

According to Dr. Kampffmeyer's line of the argument: "the SME's will have to cope with DMS-technologies. The increasing distribution of electronic signatures, the second wave of e-business, legal aspects on safe keeping of relevant digital documents and data, the growing need for combination and consolidation of information from all different kind of not only electronic sources and the ongoing accelerating of all processes only keep space for the question »on how?«" [5]

There is no doubt about the fact that there is currently not only one answer for all technology or solution. However a big variety of mainly national but also some international players could be found on the market. No supplier really dominates either the markets or the technology in one of the systems' categories. This picture doesn't significantly change in the course of the two surveys. So the question in dispute remains if this is going to change in the not too distant future and one player will become widely accepted. But according to our surveys not much speaks for that. This is where the loop is closing on the not or the inadequately made available market opportunities for the new adaptive technologies focussed on in the Adaptive READ project. They are definitely not yet standard elements of conventional archive/DMS and Workflow-Systems; whereas in KMS und EDDCS-systems their usage is by far more frequent, based on an already distinct demand from the customer. Nevertheless, in the other major system categories archive/DMS and WFMS the customers make demands on essential adaptive technological elements focused in the project namely: Automatic classification, indexing and extraction. But these functionalities are only partially integrated in a few DMS/WFMS systems today .

So this is a convincing positive signal from the market. His is because one main focus and challenge of the consortium has been the analysis of documents in form and contents with adaptive technologies for recognition, indexing, classification and extraction of data and information.

Table 23. Usage of Scanner

	1st survey	2nd survey
No Scanner in Usage	44,1%	36,1%
Scanner in Decentralised Usage	25,4%	27,8%
Scanner in Central Usage	30,5%	36,1%

It could be stated that the necessary technologies in document management today are only sporadically established. E.g. automatic document classification using the already available high performance OCR/ICR-technology bears a big rationalisation potential in combination with early scanning. This might be partially caused by the limited maturity of such technologies. Scanner and scanning technology on the contrary is widely-used, which is actually "state of the art" as our survey shows (see table 22). In fact, the huge full potential of electronic data- and document capturing systems (EDDC) may not be understood and tapped yet (see table 23).

Table 24. Usage of OCR-technology

	1st survey	2nd survey
No OCR in Usage	78,7%	69,1%
OCR in Usage	21,3%	30,9%

It could be stated that there are a lot of unsaturated market segments in almost every DMS market category for the technologies focused and developed in the course of the Adaptive READ project. However no quantification of the prospective market volumes can be derived from the surveys. Admittedly, the market development is noticeably slower than expected at the beginning of the project. This is due to market related cyclical reasons as well as for technological reasons. Technology doesn't sell by itself. DMS technologies are typically embedded in business processes. Hence the cost-benefit calculation must be convincing and this is not always an easy task in complex business environments. Many of the emerging applications are horizontal in nature, with applications such as invoice processing and mailroom automation being applicable across multiple market sectors. The market is now expanding to include medical claims management, remittance processing and mailroom applications, delivering benefits in terms of customer service as well as in internal cost-cutting metrics?. This is driving growth in the financial and utilities sectors in particular.

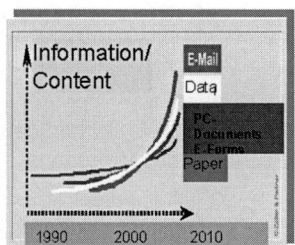

Trends

Documents are and will remain crucial "Content Containers" in business processes.

Coexistence of paper
and digital documents:

1) Linear growth for **paper documents** (doubled by year 2005), mainly as "hard copy" of digital sources

   ➡ **Stagnating need for Data Capture from paper documents**

2) Exponential growth for **digital documents**, importance of content

   ➡ **Growing need for Document and Content Management**

Fig. 4. Trends

6.4   Future Outlook, Trends and Tendencies

As already mentioned and stressed at the beginning of this chapter there are several substantial reasons to further believe in the future of progressive DMS technologies and solutions. One simple but often overlooked reason is the ongoing nearly explosive growth rate of all kind of documents. Even the traditional document medium paper is still just about to grow (Figure 4). It is only possible to meet this challenge with more and better DMS products and solutions.

Another important actual trend, which will influence DMS technologies as typical cross section technologies enormously, is a clear movement to convergence, a shown in figure 5.

But if – as some people have been predicting for a while – this will mean that DMS-technologies will become an integral part of the operating system within a short time or at least in the medium term. This is because even the results of our second survey confirmed the usefulness of dedicated disjunctive system categories in the eyes of the respondents. This is not a contradiction because the respondents are also looking more and more for seamless integrated systems on the applications- process- or enterprise level respectively. There is a clear trend to EAI (Enterprise Application Integration), but this does not necessarily mean that there must be a seamless integration on a technological level and this is in fact not a major claim of the customers – if at all. It's quite interesting to state that beyond all the overwhelming

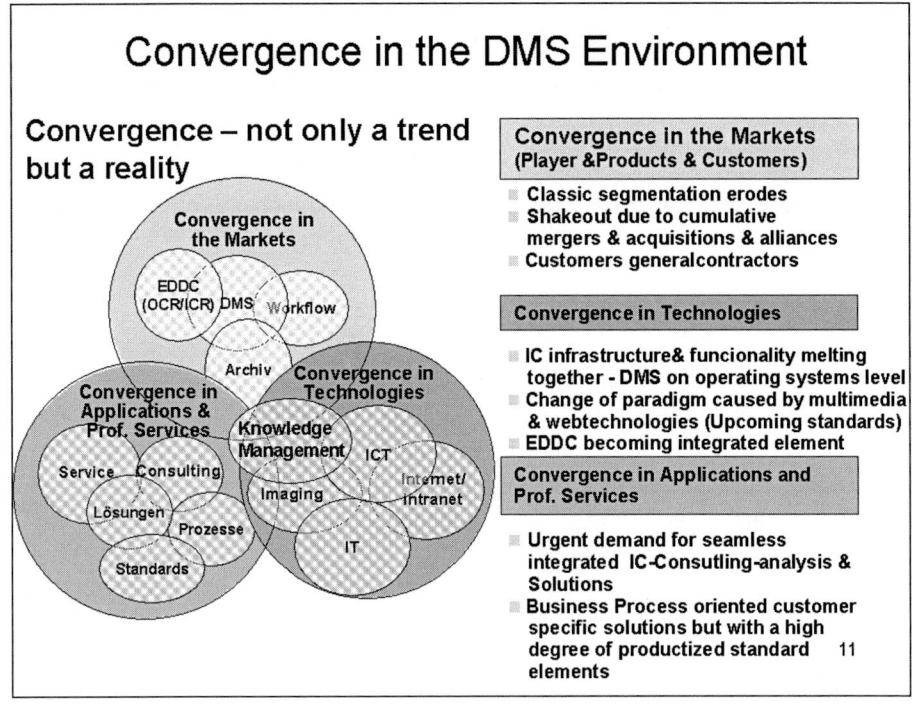

Fig. 5. Convergence in the DMS Environment

»Marketing-Hype« of many suppliers, most of the respondents seem to have a very down-to-earth estimation with relation to the possibilities and limitations of such technologies. This is indeed contrary to the opinion of some "market gurus" who have a lot of experience in the business like those from Project Consult GmbH who conceded in one of their latest "Newsletter": "Often people in call for tenders are searching for and selecting the all-in one suitable for every purpose solutions, but the realisation ends up in a pilot for ten users caused by the lack of money for the rollout." [2] Could it be that the common user is simply wiser than supposed?

6.5   Actual Applications – Invoice Processing

A really topical and very impressive example in bringing adaptive technologies to bear is automated solutions for invoice processing. An ever increasing number of companies that see medium or large quantities of invoices coming in have decided to introduce digital workflow-solutions in order to process them. These solutions lower the high cost of invoice processing which has been calculated to be 15 to 30 cents per invoice. The investment pays itself quickly, as bills are paid faster, reminder charges are avoided and cash discounts optimised. Normally invoices are scanned when they come in to the general accounting department. Instead of circulating the bills, claims and/or invoices e.g. physically within the company, only the digital image of the invoice is forwarded. The acceleration of the procedure is felt immediately, but just as important - though less obvious - is the improved control over the processing:

The controller has full information at any time on the processing status of the bill. Inputting the invoice data and the assignment to open orders in the ERP system is an important step in the electronic invoice workflow. This step can be automated to a great extent by deploying the new adaptive character recognition systems. These systems are called either Document Interpretation systems or Document Analysis Systems, their performance is considerably higher than those of the conventional OCR/ICR- or Forms Capture Software, as they do not only change electronic images to data but specifically search for the relevant information in a document.

Weaknesses of Manual Invoice Processing:

− Distribution problems: Mail is slow and expensive
− Cycle of approval is time-consuming especially:
  − Absence due to illness, vacation and business trips
  − Different locations / subsidiaries
− High personnel expenditure
− Overdue fines, unrealized cash-discounts
− Research problems through physical storage
− Financial accounting has difficulties overlooking and controlling work processes

Benefits of Digital Invoice Processing:

− Data transfer over continuous medium
− No physical transport
− Automatic capture of invoice data
− Reduction of cycle times / turnaround times
− Utilize cash discounts and elimination of overdue fines
− Financial accounting has control over invoice workflow process
− Reduction of research and retrieval times (digital archive)
− Audit security
− Cost reduction through optimized invoice processing workflow

Invoice processing as an application is a pretty good and typical example as such because users are buying Electronic Data and Document Capture Systems for pragmatic operational reasons to save money, to improve real customer service, measured in terms of fulfilment, and to comply with increasing rigorous compliance requirements. This makes this market segment more resistant to bear market pressures than others. This is unlike other "eVision" markets, such as Web Content Management and CRM, which have suffered disproportionately in the recent market downturn.

Hence this is a promising forward-looking example for productive solutions based on the new adaptive technologies explored and developed in the Adaptive READ project consortium.

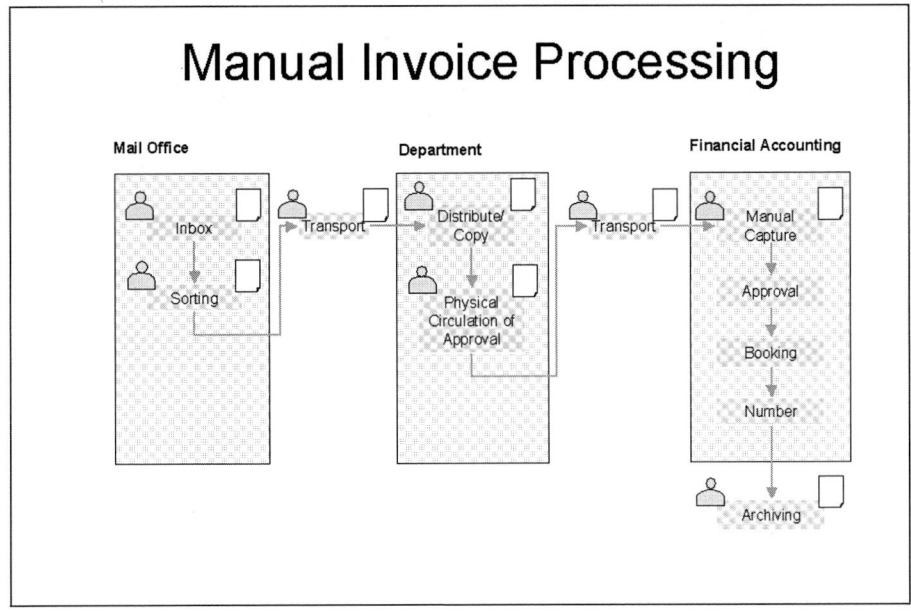

Fig. 6. Conventional Invoice Processing

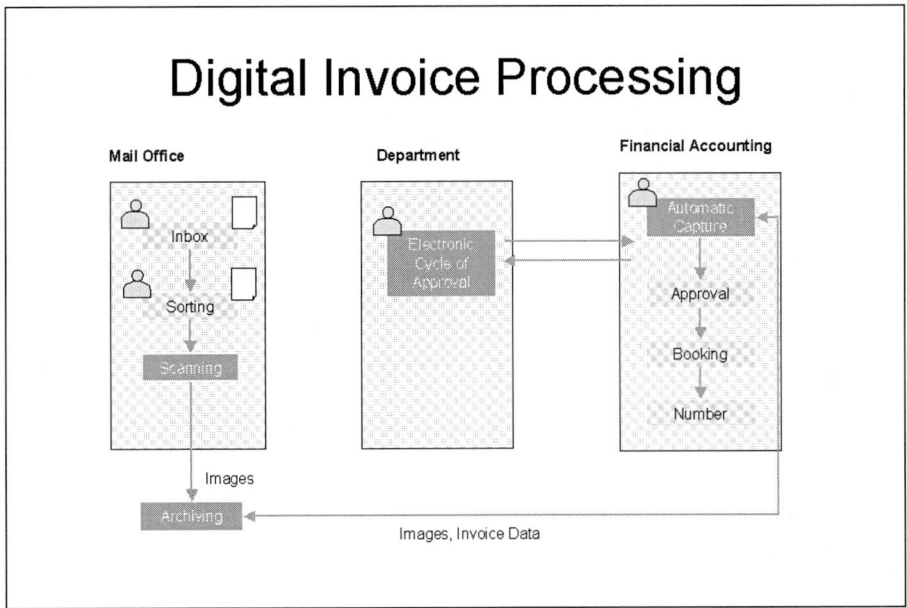

Fig. 7. Digital Invoice Processing

7   Summary

The results of both surveys show that techniques for computer-supported document capturing, as developed in Adaptive READ, can fill the gap between users' needs and the market availability of appropriate tools. Hence the full value potential of these technologies could be tapped .

Furthermore, the evaluation of the surveys indicated that paper as a medium for storing and distributing information still plays an important role in today's organisations, and that there is an increasing need for tools to help employees find and manage information.

Additionally we elaborated users' acceptance of new technologies for self-adapting assistant-tools. The tools and concepts that have been developed in Adaptive READ represent a solid basis for further evaluation and may also support existing tools to find their place in the market.

References

[1]   European Information Technology Observatory 2002, Update Oktober 2002
[2]   Project Consult Newsletter 20030122 S. 5
[3]   White Paper - Automatic Classification Improves Processes and Yields Major Reductions in Scanning Costs, By Harvey Spencer
[4]   C. Altenhofen, H. Hofmann, M. Junker, T. Kieninger, M. Stanišic-Petrovic: Adaptive READ - Lesen und Lernen - Vom Dokument zum Wissen; Empirische Studie zum Werkzeugeinsatz im Umfeld der Dokumentenverwaltung; Fraunhofer IRB-Verlag, Stuttgart; ISBN: 3-8167-6274-3
[5]   Wissensmanagement Ausgabe Oktober/November 2002
[6]   Xerox-Studie von MORI Telephone Surveys, zitiert nach »Doculine News« vom 13.12.2002, URL: http://www.doculine.com/news/2002/1202/ dokumente.shtml
[7]   Bernhard Zöller, Zöller & Partner DMS-Technologie- und Organisationsberatung zitiert in Bit 4 August 2002
[8]   Bernhard Zöller, Zöller & Partner DMS-Technologie- und Organisationsberatung zitiert in VOI Schriftenreihe »Dokumenten-Management-System: Marktübersicht, Hersteller und Produkte«, Herbst 2002

Author Index